NATIONAL GEOGRAPHIC

SCIENCE ENCYCLOPEDIA

ATOM SMASHING, FOOD CHEMISTRY, ANIMALS, SPACE, AND MORE!

NATIONAL GEOGRAPHIC
WASHINGTON, D.C.

CONTENTS

PART 1: PHYSICAL SCIENCE

MATTER

ENERGY

ELECTRONICS

FORCES AND MACHINES

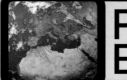
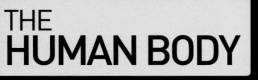

WATER CURRENT

AUTO TECHNOLOGY

LIGHT AND COLOR

LIGHTNING

ROCKET POWER

FORCE OF FRICTION

THE ATOM
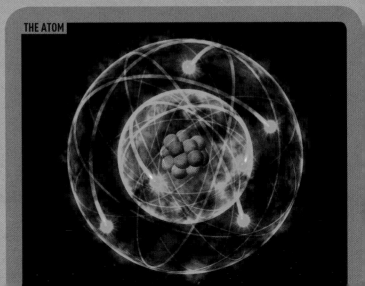

WAVE MOTION

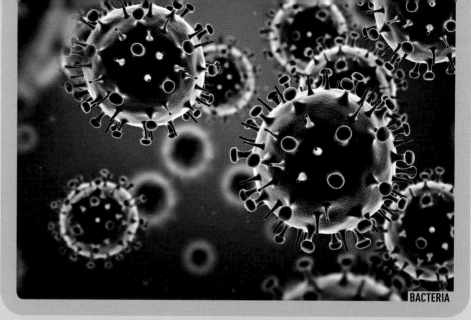
BACTERIA

LADYBUG BEETLE

METEOR SHOWER

LAVA FLOW

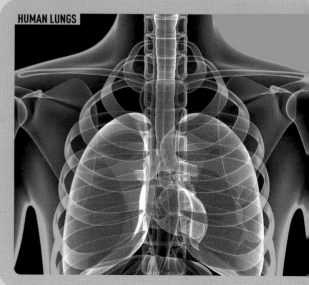
HUMAN LUNGS

WHAT IS SCIENCE?

The minute you hop out of bed in the morning, you land in the world of science.

You look at a clock, phone, or computer to check the time—these devices exist because of science. You open a refrigerator to get something to eat, and the food is fresh and tasty because the refrigerator kept it cold. The refrigerator works due to science.

Your food is based in science, too. The wheat in bread was grown using science. The baking that turns raw ingredients into bread is science in action.

Science is the way humans figure out how everything in the world works. Ever since early humans lit the first campfire, chipped the first stone tools, and created the first cave paintings, we have been scientists. Our ancestors used their powers of observation to find the best way of doing these things—and then experimented to find out what kinds of materials burned—and which ones burned best. They tested rocks to find the ones that could be carved, and they looked for substances that would stick to cave walls. These are all examples of science in action.

People study science so they can work as scientists. Many scientists find ways to make new medicines, discover cures for diseases, or invent new materials.

You've probably seen scientists in movies—they usually show up in white lab coats and work in labs filled with bubbling test tubes. Many scientists really do work in laboratories, but many also work outside them—and they don't wear lab coats! Scientists can be found digging up fossils in deserts, climbing trees in rain forests, scuba diving on coral reefs, and even floating in space, tethered to a space station.

The two main branches of science are physical science and life science. You'll learn all about both as you journey through these pages.

STAYING FRESH

Without refrigerators food wouldn't stay fresh for long. Think about a sandwich. At room temperature the bread and filling will decompose at their natural rate. But cold slows down the natural processes that make food go bad. That's why a sandwich left in the fridge overnight will taste a lot better than one left on a plate on the kitchen counter (ugh!).

FIRST SCIENTISTS

When early humans first made fire, they also became the first scientists. They were causing a chemical reaction that released energy in the form of heat and light. Ash found in a cave in L'Escale, in south-eastern France, dates from 700,000 to 400,000 B.C. and may be the earliest remains of man-made fire.

CAVE PAINTERS

Some 17,000 years ago painters of the Lascaux Caves in France ground together minerals from the earth, like iron oxide, to create colors of red, yellow, and brown. They were using the scientific process of physical change.

This ornithologist, a scientist who studies birds, climbs the rain forest trees of Costa Rica to work with parrotlike birds called macaws.

Many scientists work in laboratories, using high-powered microscopes and other equipment to understand the human body and help cure disease.

HOW SCIENTISTS WORK

Scientists focus their research on the natural world. That means they don't look for answers to questions like "Why does the world exist?" or "What is love?" They study things that can be observed and measured—everything from tiny atoms to the vast universe. A scientist's research may spring out of curiosity. Maybe she notices something interesting and wants to find out more. Or maybe he's given a problem to solve, such as finding a way to make a medicine work better. The scientist starts out by posing a question. Then he or she follows a series of steps to answer it. This is called the scientific method.

STEP ONE: The first step is to read and learn all about the topic. The scientist also talks to other scientists. They may work in teams, so the research is a group effort.

STEP TWO: All this knowledge goes into making a hypothesis. A hypothesis is a statement that provides a possible answer to a scientific question. It is the scientist's explanation for something that he or she has observed. It isn't just a "guess," because the scientist has already done lots of research to prepare for finding out more.

STEP THREE: Next, the scientist designs an experiment that tests the hypothesis. The experiment involves careful, precise observation and measurement. This process could go on for several years as the scientist records information, called "data." The scientist comes to a conclusion based on the data.

STEP FOUR: Finally, the results and conclusion are shared with other scientists. These scientists share their thoughts, and some may also test the hypothesis again to see if they get the same results.

SCIENTIFIC THEORY

Have you ever heard someone say "Oh, that's just a theory"? In everyday conversation, a theory is simply an idea that pops into somebody's head. In science, however, a theory is an explanation based on facts. A hypothesis becomes a theory only after it's been tested again and again and found to be true. A theory can change when new facts are revealed, but that doesn't mean the theory is completely wrong and tossed aside. The theory of evolution, for example, explains how living things changed over time to produce new species. Scientists may discover new information that changes the details of how evolution works, but they don't throw away the whole theory. Sometimes theories do get discarded because new information shows that they're wrong. For example, one theory said that newly evolved mammals ate dinosaur eggs, which caused the dinosaurs' extinction. This theory fell apart as scientists discovered that dinosaurs and mammals lived at the same time for some 150 million years.

MORE TO DISCOVER!

Science Encyclopedia is packed with information about science. In its pages, you'll find out about the forces and materials that shape Earth and everything in, on, and around it. You'll learn about the tools scientists use to explore and experiment. You'll meet scientists who've made fascinating discoveries.

You'll also notice that we haven't run out of things to discover. Scientists pose new questions and make new discoveries all the time. Here are just a few amazing new finds in recent years. Maybe someday you'll make discoveries that are big news, too!

In 2013, scientists discovered fossils of a new species of human relative in a cave in Africa.

In February 2015, two scientists saw warthogs in South Africa allowing turtles to eat bugs off their bodies—a behavior no one had ever noticed before.

Also in 2015, scientists revealed the discovery of land snails in China that are so small, 10 of them can line up in the eye of a needle.

In 2015, liquid water was discovered on the surface of Mars.

THE PHYSICAL SCIENCES

The physical sciences are the basis for all life. They deal with materials that are not alive and the ways in which nonliving things in the universe work. That includes matter, energy, motion, light, and sound.

In this book you will discover everything you need to know about the physical sciences, starting with the tiny but mighty atom. Atoms are the building blocks of you and everything around you—your house, your pet, the trees, the stars, and the entire universe.

Atoms are so small that we cannot see them without a high-powered microscope. Atoms combine with other atoms to create matter. Once matter exists, atoms help make that matter move, change shape, and grow. Understanding how atoms work is crucial to knowing how the sun shines, how balls bounce, and more.

The physical sciences have two main branches: chemistry and physics.

Chemistry, studied by scientists called chemists, looks at how different materials are formed. It also tells us why two materials are different, like water and wood. And it tells us how a chemical reaction can change a material from one type into another, such as water into ice. You'll find out chemistry basics in the chapter on matter. You'll also discover cool chemical processes like carbon dating, which tells us the age of ancient Egyptian mummies and other organic materials.

Scientists who study physics are called physicists. They investigate the forces that make matter move and change. For instance, a force called lift helps airplanes fly. Pressure helps water move through the pipes under your kitchen sink. You'll find out more about physics in the chapter on forces and the chapter on machines and energy. You'll also meet engineers who work with physicists to translate physics into inventions, from hi-tech cranes to the world's tiniest computer.

Without the physical sciences, the second major area of science, the life sciences, would not exist.

Life sciences deal with living things and the processes that connect them, from stars and earthquakes to giant sloths and tiny cells inside our brains that help us talk, run, and remember.

Life sciences are only possible because the physical sciences came first. Turn the page to read more about the life sciences.

THE LIFE SCIENCES

Of all the scientific topics that interest us, the most popular is probably ourselves. What makes us human? Where do we come from? How do our bodies work, and how can we avoid getting sick or even dying?

We're curious about how we connect to the life around us. How are we different from other animals? How are we the same?

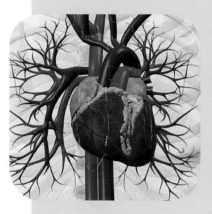

We wonder about the planet we all live on. Did the Earth always exist? What made its mountains and seas? Are there other suns, other Earths, or other people in the universe?

The life sciences tackle questions about living creatures, how they work, and how they are linked within the living world. Earth and space sciences are related to life sciences. They ask how the planet that keeps us alive is made. What powers its movements? How does it fit into the universe?

These types of questions go way back in history. As long ago as the fourth century B.C., Greek scientist and philosopher Aristotle noted that dolphins were mammals, not fish, because they breathed air and gave birth to live babies. William Harvey, a 17th-century doctor, studied animal bodies to understand how the heart pumped blood through veins and arteries. After long years of watching animals in their environments, 19th-century naturalist Charles Darwin came up with the idea of evolution through natural selection. He showed how every form of life, from dandelions to humans, has been shaped by the struggle for survival over many, many generations.

Again and again, life scientists have found that we humans are connected to other living things on Earth. It turns out that we are related to all other animals and even to plants. We all share one environment, and what we do affects the natural world.

When 16th-century astronomer Copernicus showed that the sun, not the Earth, was the center of the solar system, we realized that our planet did not hold as big a spot as we once thought. Then when 20th-century astronomers pointed out that even our galaxy is just one among billions, we realized just how small we really are.

On the other hand, we have also learned that as human beings we are part of a truly amazing web of life. The life science pages in this book will illustrate how everything is connected. You'll discover mouthless worms and walking ferns. You'll be filled in on the biggest dinosaurs and the loudest sound ever heard. And you'll learn how our bodies function from our brains to our muscles.

RECORD BREAKERS

ver since scientists in ancient Greece conducted their first experiments, we've explored the physical and life sciences, been excited about our discoveries, and welcomed them as part of our daily lives. Along the way scientists have discovered or invented the biggest, tallest, smallest, and most amazing things on our planet. Check out a few of these record breakers below. They'll whet your appetite for all the amazing discoveries you'll find throughout this book.

OLDEST FLUSH TOILET

Nearly 4,000 years ago, the Minoans built a sewer system in the Palace of Knossos, on the island of Crete. This sophisticated system used gravity to run water through three systems of pipes: one for clean water, one for dirty, and one to handle storm water. The palace housed the queen's beautiful bath and possibly the world's first flush toilet, complete with an overhead water tank and wooden seat.

WORLD'S LARGEST ICEBERG

Iceberg B-15 was 170 miles (295 km) long and 25 miles (37 km) wide. That's bigger than the U.S. state of Connecticut. The world's biggest mass of frozen water molecules calved from the Ross Ice Shelf in March 2000. Parts of it are still floating in the ocean around Antarctica.

LARGEST SELF-POWERED LAND VEHICLES EVER MADE

"Hans" and "Frans" are crawler-transporters used by NASA to transport rockets to the launchpad at Cape Canaveral in Florida, U.S.A. Each is about the size of a baseball diamond and weighs 6.3 million pounds (2.9 million kg). With their complex combination of generators and engines, laser guidance and leveling systems, hydraulics and computer systems, Hans and Frans require 30 scientists to operate. They have a top speed of one mile an hour (1.6 km/h) and can carry up to 18 million pounds (8.2 million kg).

WORLD'S SMALLEST FLYING SUBMARINE

The RoboBee is a tiny, insect-size robot that can flap its wings and fly. It can also swim. It's made from carbon fiber and weighs less than a gram (.035 oz).

THE HOTTEST PLACE ON EARTH

Satellites scanning the whole Earth's surface found a winner for hottest spot: Iran's Lut Desert. In 2005, temperatures there reached 159.3°F (70.7°C). This area is called abiotic, which means "without life." Not even bacteria have been found.

FASTEST AND SLOWEST SPINNING PLANETS

The fastest spinning planet in our solar system is also the biggest. Giant Jupiter rotates once every 9.9 hours, more than twice as fast as Earth. As for slowpoke Venus, it takes longer for it to rotate on its axis (243 days) than for it to revolve around the sun (224.7 days). So a day on Venus lasts longer than a year!

THE HARDEST PART OF YOUR BODY

It's not your bones. It's the enamel on your teeth. Enamel covers the part of your teeth you can see and is 96 percent hard minerals like hydroxyapatite. How tough is enamel? It's harder than steel and can withstand temperatures up to 1600°F (871°C). But acidic drinks like soda pop and fruit juice can dissolve it. Since there are no living cells in enamel, once it's damaged or worn away, the body can't make more of it. You can keep your enamel strong by drinking lots of water and brushing your teeth.

THE STINKIEST PLANT ON EARTH

The corpse flower's odor has been compared to the smell of a stinky diaper, decaying fish, and a garbage dump. This rare plant is enormous—it can grow to be 10 feet (3 m) tall—and blooms only once every 8 to 10 years. Its deep red color, nose-clenching odor, and warm temperature are meant to make flesh-eating insects like dung beetles and flesh flies think it's a rotting piece of meat. Why? So they'll fly into the flower, get dusted with pollen, and carry the pollen to another corpse flower and keep the species growing.

Let's celebrate! Fireworks are scientific wonders. They generate three forms of energy: sound, bright light, and heat. The tremendous booms you hear come from the rapid release of energy into the air, producing shock waves. The colors come from heating metal salts, such as calcium chloride or sodium nitrate. The atoms in each salt absorb energy and release it as breathtaking colored lights.

PHYSICAL SCIENCE

READY, TEST, GO!

Physical science plus **life science** make up **all science.** Physical science is about conducting tests to understand how things in the universe work—from atoms to light. It's also about using that knowledge to make simple machines and more!

MATTER

IT MAKES UP EVERYTHING

You, your family, your clothes, this book—all the living things and all the things you can see—are made from matter. But what is matter?

In this chapter, you'll discover, like ancient scientists did, that matter is made of little building blocks called atoms, which are in everything—you, the sun, and the rest of the universe. And most of these tiny atoms are made of even tinier particles called protons, neutrons, and electrons.

You'll learn that the science of chemistry studies the way atoms connect, interact, and change to make all kinds of matter. Scientists also study different types of atoms. Elements, such as carbon, gold, oxygen, and hydrogen, are each made of one type of atom. They cannot be divided into anything smaller. But they can combine to make more complicated forms of matter. So when the elements hydrogen and oxygen combine, they form the compound water.

Did you know that 71 percent of Earth's surface is covered in water? And about 60 percent of the human body is water. Water is the elixir of life. We can go for a long while without food, but not without water. You'll soon see how temperature and pressure can turn water, and any element, into a liquid, a gas, or a solid. Water is liquid at room temperature, but if you put it on a very hot stove, it will soon start to bubble and become a gas called water vapor. If you put that same water in your freezer, the cold temperature would turn that liquid into a solid. Scientists also study water and how light bends when it shines through it.

In this chapter, you'll also find out about chemical reactions. This is what happens when one atom breaks with another atom and makes a new connection with a different atom. When you light a campfire, the fire is a chemical reaction between oxygen in the air and the wood. This chemical reaction releases heat. The fizzy bubbles in your soda pop are caused by a chemical reaction between the compound carbon dioxide and the sugary water in your drink. A chemical reaction even causes the metal on your bike to get rusty or a bronze statue in the park to turn green.

Welders use chemical reactions to join metals together to build frames for cars. Scientists make completely new materials like glass, plastic, and medicines. Chemical reactions also make electricity. The battery in a cell phone is powered by a chemical reaction.

Chemistry is at the heart of all matter—and almost everything we understand about our world. Read on to discover more!

Did you know? Nature's 94 kinds of atoms combine in many ways to form many different kinds of matter. Scientists have identified 10 million combinations and think there are billions more.

Atoms are the building blocks for every kind of material and living thing—including you! When an atom is especially energized, like this one, scientists call it a "hot atom."

MATTER AND ATOMS

Matter is the name that scientists use for anything that has mass and takes up space.

Matter comes in all forms: solids, liquids, and gases. The axe (right) is matter that is a solid. So is the chopping block. A puddle of water is matter that is a liquid. The air we breathe is matter that is a gas. We can measure the size and shape of every piece of matter, and we can also weigh it.

Mass is how much there is of a certain kind of matter. So mass is how much wood there is in the chopping block or how much water there is in the puddle or how much air is surrounding us. The mass of each type of matter always stays the same. Mass is different from weight. The weight of matter can change if it's on Earth or on the moon, because of gravity. (More about that later!)

Regular everyday matter like the sun, or even wood, is made up of small building blocks called atoms. So what are atoms? The idea for atoms came from Greek philosophers 2,500 years ago. They said it was impossible to keep cutting matter into smaller lumps forever. At some point you would reach a small particle that could not be cut up anymore. They said this particle was *atomos*, which means "uncuttable" in Greek.

LOOKING AT ATOMS

Looking at an atom's makeup is challenging. To determine the makeup of different atoms in matter like water or wood, scientists use a procedure called an x-ray fluorescence (XRF) spectrometry. When an atom is stimulated by an energy source, it sends out particles of light. Different kinds of atoms send out light at different energy levels and in different wavelengths. XRF measures the number of light particles and their energy level and wavelength. With these, scientists determine the kind of atom they're working with.

MATTER'S BUILDING BLOCKS

Atoms are far too small to see unless you use a very high-powered microscope. They are so small that to make a line of atoms three feet (0.9 m) long, we would need as many atoms as there are people on Earth. A single atom makes up an element, which is the simplest possible substance on Earth. For instance, one kind of atom makes up the element hydrogen; another kind makes up the element oxygen. Two or more atoms make up a molecule. The atoms of elements and molecules make up all the matter on Earth.

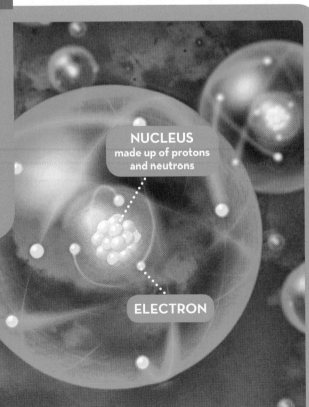

NUCLEUS
made up of protons and neutrons

ELECTRON

WORD CHECK

MASS: How much there is of an object. This is measured by how many atoms are in it.

GEEK STREAK

When one or more atoms bond together, they're called molecules. Simple molecules have only a few atoms, but they soon start to add up. It would take more than a lifetime to count up all the atoms in a tiny molecule called a bacterium, let alone in a human body. Check out these molecule counts—from mini to mega!

- Water molecule: 3 atoms
- Sugar molecule (sucrose): 48 atoms
- Bacterium: 100 trillion atoms
- Apple: 13 septillion atoms
- Human: 7 octillion atoms
- Earth: 100 quindecillion atoms
- Star: 2 octodecillion atoms
- Universe: 10 million trillion vigintillion atoms

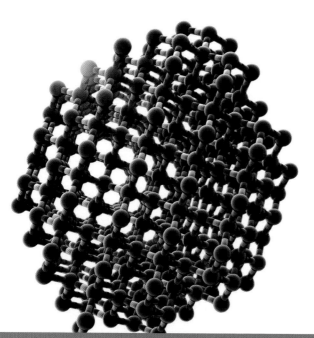

ATOM CLUSTERS

The first scientific proof that matter was made of atoms came from the English scientist John Dalton. In 1801, he explained that different gases in air move around because they are made up of little units, which he officially named atoms. Dalton also showed that different types of atoms could cluster together in groups. When two or more atoms cling together, they are known as molecules. The great variety of natural substances, from air to wood to rocks, comes from the ways their molecules cluster together.

ENERGY MAKES MATTER WORK

What gives matter the ability to move, change shape, or be warm? Energy. Scientists define energy as "the ability to do work." There are all kinds of energy including radiant, electrical, thermal, chemical, nuclear, and more. Light is radiant energy, and Earth gets a lot of it from the sun. Electrical energy is what powers our TVs and charges our electric cars. Heat, or thermal energy, is what we feel when we gather around a campfire. We use chemical energy to clean our floors and counters. Energy cannot be created or destroyed, only converted from one form to another, such as electrical to radiant heat, when we turn on an electric heater.

DARK MATTER

In the 1930s, two astronomers made a startling discovery: Most of the matter in the universe is invisible! Fritz Zwicky and Jan Oort were studying distant galaxies, which are huge clusters of stars, to see how fast they spun around. They discovered that heavy galaxies spun faster than lightweight galaxies. But they couldn't actually see the extra matter that was making one galaxy heavier than the other. They determined that nonluminous material, or "dark matter," must be present. Today, scientists still don't know exactly what dark matter is, they just know it's there.

PERSONALITY PLUS

Democritus was an ancient Greek philosopher who, with his teacher, came up with the first atomic theory: Everything in the universe is made of atoms, they are always in motion, they cannot be destroyed, and they come in different shapes and sizes. He also said that atoms in water were very slippery, which made the liquid flow easily, while the atoms in salt were covered in spikes. These stuck into your tongue when you ate them, creating the sharp, salty taste.

ATOM SMASHING

Almost everything we know about the structure of atoms comes from huge machines called particle accelerators. They re-create the kind of superfast collisions that occurred when the universe was very young and that still happen now when stars explode. They do this by accelerating atoms to almost the speed of light, which is the top speed of the universe. Then they smash the atoms together to see what happens. These collisions give scientists clues to how particles inside an atom work and help them to understand how matter was formed in the first place. This timeline highlights the scientists and their important discoveries that led to the development of the particle accelerator.

1897

Englishman J. J. Thomson discovers the first subatomic particle, the electron, using a gas-filled tube that creates a glowing beam.

1901

Guglielmo Marconi uses his wireless telegraph system, now known as a radio, to send a message from England to Newfoundland, Canada. No one knows how a beam of radio waves could go so far—more than 2,100 miles (3,380 km). It will be 12 more years before they discover that radio waves can be bounced off the upper atmosphere, which is called the ionosphere.

1907

New Zealander Ernest Rutherford and his team start firing a beam of positively charged "alpha particles" (produced by a radioactive gas) through a sheet of gold foil. Most of the particles go straight through, but a few bounce back. After several years of work, the team discovers this is because the gold's atoms have a small central core, or nucleus. This nucleus contains protons, which push back any alpha particles that come close.

1909

American Robert Millikan builds a machine for measuring the charge of electrons. He finds that every electron has the same amount of charge. Later it is found that an electron's negative charge is exactly the same size as a proton's positive charge.

1928

Hans Geiger, a German scientist who helped discover the atomic nucleus, invents a machine for detecting subatomic particles. This machine is called the Geiger counter.

1911

Scottish scientist Charles Wilson gets an idea for a particle-detecting machine while hiking in the foggy mountains. He builds a device that uses artificial fog to show the path of subatomic particles passing through it. This machine, known as a cloud chamber, can be used to measure the weight, charge, and speed of different particles.

1913

German Victor Hess flies three miles (4.8 km) into the sky in a hot-air balloon and finds that the air up there is electrified. This is due to high-speed particles from deep space smashing into Earth's atmosphere. Hess calls them "cosmic rays." The electrified layer—known as the ionosphere—is what reflects radio signals around the globe. The cosmic rays smash into the air's atoms faster than anything ever known before. They create strange particles in the high atmosphere, just like a natural particle accelerator.

1929

The first particle accelerator is built. It uses magnets and electric fields to speed up a beam of subatomic particles. Then it fires them at a target substance. Cloud chambers and Geiger counters are used to detect what particles are produced by the collisions.

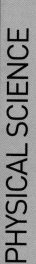

1931

American Ernest Lawrence builds a new kind of particle accelerator called a cyclotron, which works by making the beam of particles whiz around in a circle, going faster than ever before.

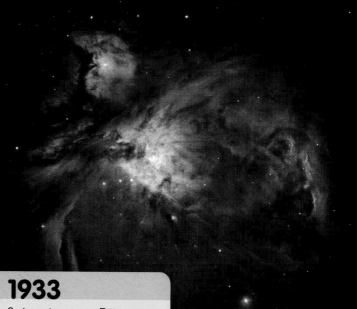

1934

Pavel Cherenkov, a Russian scientist, finds that radioactive materials create a blue glow when under water. This glow, known as Cherenkov radiation, becomes another way of showing that high-speed particles are present.

1932

For the first time, a positron, produced by a cosmic ray smash in the atmosphere, is seen passing through a cloud chamber. Positrons are a kind of antimatter. They are the same size as electrons but have a positive electric charge, not a negative one.

1933

Swiss astronomer Fritz Zwicky comes up with the name "dark matter" for the mysterious material that is invisible in the universe.

1936

Japanese scientist Hideki Yukawa had already predicted in 1935 that cosmic rays contained strange particles called mesons. But Carl Anderson, the discoverer of positrons, is the first to spot a meson with his cloud chamber.

1959

The first neutrinos are discovered. These are the smallest known particles of matter. They have a weight, but they are so tiny physicists are still trying to measure them accurately.

1974

Bubble chambers pick up the first views of quarks.

1952

American Donald Glaser invents a bubble chamber, which is a new particle detector that uses bubbles, not clouds, to track the movements of tiny particles.

1998

Construction of the Large Hadron Collider (LHC), the world's biggest particle accelerator, is begun. The underground machine will take 10 years to build and will cost nine billion dollars.

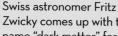

2012–2015

The Large Hadron Collider accelerates protons to just below the speed of light and smashes them together. The collision creates a new kind of particle called the Higgs boson, which scientists believe is what gives mass to particles. After a period of being turned off and upgraded, the LHC is turned back on in 2015 and is more powerful than ever.

PARTS OF AN ATOM

We used to think that atoms were the smallest things in the universe. Now we know that atoms are made up of several types of tiny particles.

In the 19th century, scientists discovered that the atom wasn't as uncuttable as the Greeks had said. It could actually be split into smaller parts. They called these small parts subatomic particles, which mean they are smaller than an atom. These three tiny particles are protons, neutrons, and electrons. At the center of the atom is the nucleus, which holds the protons and neutrons. The electrons float in a shell around the outside of the nucleus.

ELECTRONS

In 1897, J. J. Thomson discovered the first subatomic particle—the electron. Electrons have a negative electric charge and when they are made to move from atom to atom, they create electricity. The current that powers your TV is just a stream of electrons moving through a wire. When an atom loses an electron, what's left behind becomes positively charged. That means the rest of the atom contains some positively charged particles. An electric spark occurs when one object has too many electrons and another has too few. When these objects come close together, the electrons jump from one object to the other to even out the numbers, creating a spark.

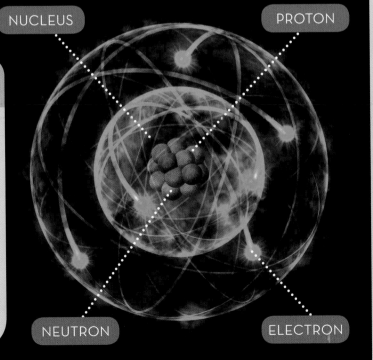

ATOMIC NUCLEUS

After electrons were discovered, scientists thought that atoms were like a fruitcake—a solid lump of positively charged matter, with raisins of electrons all mixed up inside. In 1911, scientists found that the atom is not like that at all. Instead, the negative electrons surround the outside of the atom, while the positively charged protons are packed inside a tiny core at the center, called the nucleus.

PROTONS AND NEUTRONS

A nucleus is made up of particles called protons and neutrons. A neutron has no charge at all, but a proton has a positive charge equal and opposite to the charge of the electron. Particles with opposite charges attract each other. This pull keeps the negative electrons in place in their shells around the positive protons of the nucleus. The number of protons and electrons varies between atoms, but they are always equal within the same atom, except when they are ions. Ions (see page 28) are atoms with either extra or missing electrons.

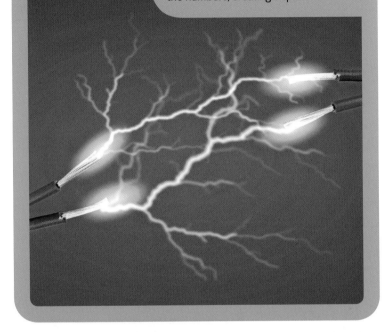

NUCLEUS   PROTON

NEUTRON   ELECTRON

QUARKS AND GLUONS

In the 1960s, researchers found protons and neutrons could each be divided into smaller particles called quarks. Quarks are held tightly together, like glue, by particles called gluons. Gluons only get stronger as quarks are pulled farther apart. The force of the gluons is so strong that they can be broken apart only if their protons or neutrons are smashed together at almost the speed of light.

This proton has three quarks.

GEEK STREAK

When scientists discovered that there are six different types of quarks, they had a lot of fun naming them. They called the types of quarks "flavors." The six flavors of quarks are up, down, charm, strange, top, and bottom.

WORD CHECK

ELECTRON: The word "electron" comes from the Greek word for amber, which is fossilized tree resin. Ancient Greeks used the honey-colored drops of resin to create static electricity. Rubbing amber with a piece of fur makes it electrically charged so that hair, dust, and even feathers cling to it—just like rubbing a balloon makes it cling to a sweater.

ROOM TO MOVE

Atoms are mostly empty space. If an atom were the size of a football field, the outermost electrons (blue dots) would be at the goal lines. The nucleus, which holds the protons and neutrons, would be the size of a flea on the 50-yard line.

PERSONALITY PLUS

In the early 20th century, scientist Ernest Rutherford of New Zealand was a leader in the discovery of subatomic particles. A man with big ideas about little things, he and his team discovered the atomic nucleus, the proton, and the neutron.

ELEMENTS

An element is a substance made entirely of one kind of atom. It is the simplest possible material found on Earth and cannot be broken down into anything else.

There are 94 elements found in nature, and many more elements have been made by humans. Some elements are familiar, like gold, carbon, oxygen, and hydrogen. Other elements are less well known: Have you ever heard of bismuth, yttrium, or osmium? Every element has a unique set of properties: Hydrogen is a gas that burns easily, while mercury is a metal that is liquid at room temperature. Sulfur is a smelly yellow powder, and copper is a reddish metal that conducts electricity very well. All of these differences come from the unique way the electrons are arranged around the nucleus of the atom of each element.

LITHIUM

CARBON-12

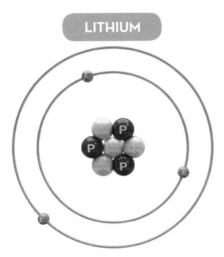
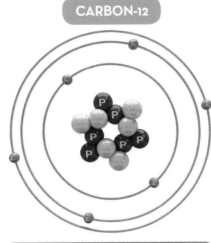

ATOMIC NUMBERS

Every element is an atom with a unique atomic number. The number represents the number of protons in the element's atom, and the number of protons in an atom is always equal to the number of electrons. Lithium (above left) is an element that has an atomic number of 3, because it has three protons and three electrons. Carbon-12 (above right) has an atomic number of 6, because it has six protons and six electrons.

WORD CHECK

PERIODIC: Occurring repeatedly from time to time

ELECTRON SHELLS

Electrons move around the outside of the atoms of an element and are arranged in layers, or shells. An element can have one electron shell or many electron shells, and each shell has a fixed maximum number of electrons. Once a shell reaches its maximum number, another shell is started. The total number of electrons in all the shells of a neutrally charged element is what makes each element unique (as do the number of protons in the nucleus). The electrons in the outermost shell allow it to connect to other elements to make a molecule of a new substance.

GROUP

Each group, or column, contains elements that have the same number of electrons in their outer shells. The members of "group one" have one electron in their outer shell. As you read from left to right, the number of electrons in each element's outer shell changes.

ATOMIC NUMBER

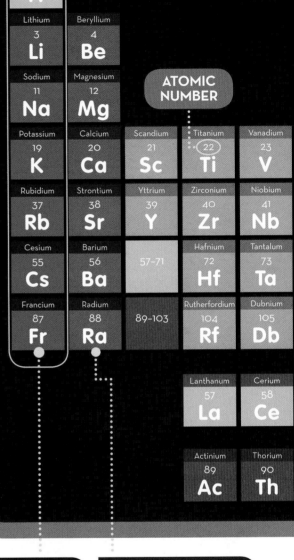

ALKALI METALS

The alkali metals are shiny, light, and bendable and are the most reactive elements. They include sodium (which is in table salt) and potassium.

ALKALINE EARTH METALS

The alkaline earth metals are the second most reactive elements. These include calcium and magnesium, which are very important to building strong bones. Radium, on the other hand, is extremely radioactive and dangerous.

PERSONALITY PLUS

To organize the elements, Russian scientist Dmitri Mendeleev created the periodic table in 1869. Mendeleev liked playing cards. He had the idea of writing the details of every element on a card. He then figured out a way to put the element cards in rows and columns according to their atomic number, and physical and chemical properties.

PERIODIC TABLE OF ELEMENTS

The elements are arranged in a chart called the periodic table. This table lists the elements according to their atomic number. It organizes them into columns known as groups, and rows called periods. Elements are also grouped into several different categories: alkali metals, alkaline earth metals, rare metals, transition metals, poor metals, metalloids, nonmetals, halogens, and noble gases.

NONMETALS

Nonmetals are mostly gases, such as hydrogen, oxygen, and nitrogen. But they also include solids like carbon and sulfur. They are not good conductors of heat or electricity and are very brittle.

ATOMIC SYMBOL

Every element has an atomic symbol. Most are based on the element's English name. For example C is for carbon and S is for sulfur. However, others are based on other languages. Lead's symbol is Pb, which stands for *plumbum*, the Latin word for "lead."

PERIOD

Each period, or row, contains elements that have the same number of shells. So "period one" has elements with one shell. "Period two" has elements with two shells, and so on up to seven shells.

			Helium 2 He

Boron 5 B	Carbon 6 C	Nitrogen 7 N	Oxygen 8 O	Fluorine 9 F	Neon 10 Ne
Aluminum 13 Al	Silicon 14 Si	Phosphorous 15 P	Sulfur 16 S	Chlorine 17 Cl	Argon 18 Ar

Chromium 24 Cr	Manganese 25 Mn	Iron 26 Fe	Cobalt 27 Co	Nickel 28 Ni	Copper 29 Cu	Zinc 30 Zn	Gallium 31 Ga	Germanium 32 Ge	Arsenic 33 As	Selenium 34 Se	Bromine 35 Br	Krypton 36 Kr
Molybdenum 42 Mo	Technetium 43 Tc	Ruthenium 44 Ru	Rhodium 45 Rh	Palladium 46 Pd	Silver 47 Ag	Cadmium 48 Cd	Indium 49 In	Tin 50 Sn	Antimony 51 Sb	Tellurium 52 Te	Iodine 53 I	Xenon 54 Xe
Tunsten 74 W	Rhenium 75 Re	Osmium 76 Os	Iridium 77 Ir	Platinum 78 Pt	Gold 79 Au	Mercury 80 Hg	Thallium 81 Tl	Lead 82 Pb	Bismuth 83 Bi	Polonium 84 Po	Astatine 85 At	Radon 86 Rn
Seaborgium 106 Sg	Bohrium 107 Bh	Hassium 108 Hs	Meitnerium 109 Mt	Darmstadtium 110 Ds	Roentgenium 111 Rg	Copernicium 112 Cn	Ununtrium 113 Uut	Flerovium 114 Fl	Ununpentium 115 Uup	Livermorium 116 Lv	Ununseptium 117 Uus	Ununoctium 118 Uuo

Praseodymium 59 Pr	Neodymium 60 Nd	Promethium 61 Pm	Samarium 62 Sm	Europium 63 Eu	Gadolinium 64 Gd	Terbium 65 Tb	Dysprosium 66 Dy	Holmium 67 Ho	Erbium 68 Er	Thulium 69 Tm	Ytterbium 70 Yb	Lutetium 71 Lu
Protactinium 91 Pa	Uranium 92 U	Neptunium 93 Np	Plutonium 94 Pu	Americium 95 Am	Curium 96 Cm	Berkelium 97 Bk	Californium 98 Cf	Einsteinium 99 Es	Fermium 100 Fm	Mendelevium 101 Md	Nobelium 102 No	Lawrencium 103 Lr

RARE METALS

Rare metals are in two rows of elements. The first row (lanthanides) are very reactive; they are used in products like permanent magnets and hybrid cars. The second row (actinides) are radioactive and mostly man-made, like uranium and plutonium, and are used in nuclear reactors and nuclear bombs. A man-made element is not found on Earth. It has to be artificially created.

POOR METALS

The poor metals include tin, lead, and aluminum, the most abundant metal in Earth's crust. They are softer than transition metals and have a lower boiling point.

TRANSITION METALS

Transition metals can bond with many elements in different shapes and are good conductors of electricity. Silver, gold, copper, and platinum are all shiny transition metals.

METALLOIDS

Metalloids, such as silicon and arsenic, are a combination of metals and nonmetals. They partially conduct electricity, which makes them invaluable in the semiconductor and computer chip industry.

HALOGENS

This is the only group that includes elements that are solids, gases, and liquids at room temperature. Halogens, such as chlorine and iodine, have low boiling and melting points.

NOBLE GASES

Almost all of the noble gases are not reactive, which makes them very stable. They are odorless and colorless. Of these elements, neon is used in advertising signs, argon in lightbulbs, and helium in balloons.

COMPOUNDS AND BONDS

WORD CHECK
PROPERTIES: The characteristics that belong to a substance, such as its color and hardness, how heavy it is, or whether it forms compounds easily

When the atoms of two different elements join together, or bond, they form a compound.

Most materials found on Earth are made from the atoms of one element connecting to the atoms of another element. When atoms of different elements bond, they form a new kind of substance called a compound. Once they've formed a compound, the structures of the elements change slightly. That means a compound's properties are different from the properties of each element and its individual atom, which make up the compound. Compounds form during chemical reactions. This is when bonds form between the atoms. Chemists have figured out that there are two main types of bonds: covalent bonds and ionic bonds. Both types basically do the same thing—they fill in the gaps in each atom's collection of electrons in its outer shell.

MOLECULES

While the smallest unit of an element is its atom, the smallest unit of a compound is its molecule. A molecule is a cluster of two or more atoms bonded together in a particular shape. Chemists use the symbols of elements to describe a compound's molecule as a chemical formula. For example, hydrogen (symbol H) and oxygen (symbol O) form the compound water. This has the formula H_2O. This tells us that one molecule of water is made up of two hydrogen atoms and one oxygen atom. Take a look at the periodic table on pages 26–27 to find the elements that make up these well-known compounds: Carbon dioxide, or CO_2, consists of one carbon atom and two oxygen atoms. Methane is the gas made by animals (including you). It is formed from one atom of carbon and four atoms of hydrogen: CH_4.

HYDROGEN

CARBON

This is what one molecule of methane (CH_4) looks like.

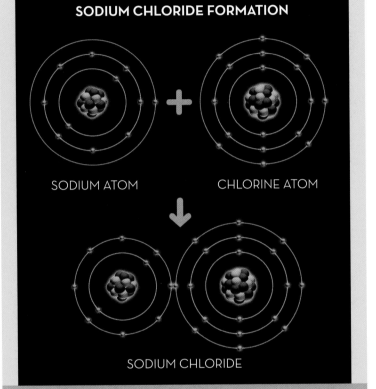

SODIUM CHLORIDE FORMATION

SODIUM ATOM   CHLORINE ATOM

SODIUM CHLORIDE

IONIC BONDS

An ion is an element that is either missing electrons or has extra electrons in its outer shell. Elements that are missing electrons are positively charged. Elements with extra electrons are negatively charged. Elements form bonds by giving and taking electrons. Since opposites attract each other, a negatively charged ion and a positively charged ion can stick together. This bonding makes a compound. So when a positively charged sodium ion meets a negatively charged chlorine ion, they form the compound sodium chloride, better known as salt. This kind of bonding is called ionic bonding. Most compounds with ionic bonds are formed by metal and nonmetal elements coming together. For example, salt (NaCl) is a compound of the metal sodium (Na) and the nonmetal chlorine (Cl).

GEEK STREAK

The single element that creates the largest number of compounds is carbon. There are 10 million carbon compounds already studied, and there are many more we don't yet know about. The ones we do know include the gas carbon monoxide (CO), the solid calcium carbonate, commonly known as chalk ($CaCO_3$), and the liquid benzene (C_6H_6). Carbon compounds can range from two atoms to many millions of atoms.

COVALENT BONDS

In some compounds, atoms share their electrons. This is how water forms. An oxygen atom has space for two more electrons in its outer shell. A hydrogen atom has room for just one. Therefore, the outer shells of two hydrogen atoms can connect to the outer shell of one oxygen atom. Then they share a full set of electrons. This kind of bonding is called covalent. Covalent bonding is normally between two nonmetals, like hydrogen and oxygen, which have just a few spaces to fill in their outer electron shells.

OUTER ELECTRON SHELL

OUTER ELECTRON SHELL

A molecule of water (H_2O)

COMPOUND RECIPES

Take a look at these common compounds. Think of them as a cake you're about to bake. Then look at the elements, which are like ingredients. There's a big difference between the final compound and the elements that bond together to make it.

WATER

Compound: Water (a clear liquid)
Elements: Hydrogen (a gas) plus oxygen (a gas)

TABLE SALT

Compound: Halite (a salty white solid)
Elements: Sodium (a soft metal) and chlorine (a smelly, poisonous gas)

SUGAR

Compound: Sucrose (a sweet white solid)
Elements: Hydrogen and oxygen (gases) plus carbon (a black solid)

CHALK

Compound: Gypsum (a soft powder)
Elements: Calcium (a silver metal), sulfur (a yellow powder), and oxygen (a gas)

SAND

Compound: Silica (a hard, clear crystal)
Elements: Silicon (a shiny solid) and oxygen (a gas)

METALS AND NONMETALS

All elements in nature occur as a gas, a liquid, or a solid. However, all elements can also be organized as metals, nonmetals, or metalloids.

Every category on the periodic table falls into one of three groups: metals, nonmetals, and metalloids. The largest group is the metals. Of the 94 elements that occur in nature, 68 are metals. Most metals are solids in normal conditions with a few exceptions like mercury and gallium. The next largest group of elements is the nonmetals. There are 17 nonmetals, including hydrogen, carbon, and sulfur. The nonmetals are mostly gases or solids. Only bromine is a liquid. Finally, there are seven metalloids: they include silicon, arsenic, and tellurium. Metalloids are all solid materials. How solid metals, nonmetals, and metalloids are is different for each group. A solid metal, such as iron, is very different from a solid nonmetal, like a lump of sulfur or iodine. A solid metalloid shares some properties with both metals and nonmetals.

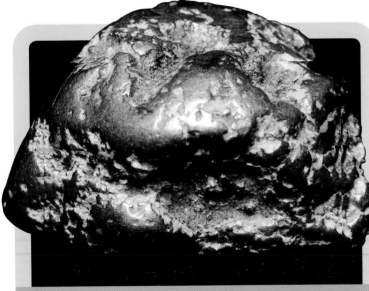

METALLIC BONDING

The reason all metals are shiny, tough, bendable, and conduct electricity is because of the way their atoms connect to each other. This process is called metallic bonding. Metal atoms have only a few electrons in their outer shells (see pages 26–27). When a piece of metal is shaped into an object like an iron bar or a gold ring, these outer electrons break free of the atoms and form an ocean of shared electrons around the atoms. This "ocean" glues all the atoms together into the new metal shape. The gluelike bonds also allow the atoms to move around a lot without breaking apart. This makes it possible for metals to bend and be hammered into all kinds of shapes. In addition, with a battery or generator, the electrons can be made to flow through the metal. This creates an electric current, so the metal is said to "conduct" electricity.

CHARACTERISTICS OF METALS

All the metal elements share a set of characteristics. Check them out here:

All metals are shiny, although you often have to polish off a dull layer of other compounds that cover the surface to see this.

Metals are tough. That means they don't crumble or crack easily.

Metals are able to bend and have their shape changed (some more easily than others), especially when they are heated and become softer. They are ductile, which means they can be stretched and drawn into long wires. They are also malleable, meaning they can be hammered flat without breaking apart.

Metals all conduct electricity.

NONMETAL SOLIDS

Nonmetals are a much more varied group than metals. They are either a gas or a solid at room temperature. Nonmetal gases are hydrogen, oxygen, and nitrogen. The solids include carbon and sulfur (below), phosphorous, and selenium. The atoms of nonmetals have more electrons in their outer shells than metals. When the atoms bond together in a particular repeating pattern, they form nonmetal solids called crystals. This makes them very brittle and not good conductors of electricity or heat. Instead, this brittleness makes nonmetal solids good insulators because they will block the flow of electricity.

Sulfur crystals are nonmetal solids.

METALLOIDS

The metalloids are sometimes called semimetals. They have some qualities of metals and some of nonmetals. The most familiar metalloid is silicon, the element used in microchips and other electronics. Metalloids are often shiny solids like metals, but they are also brittle like a nonmetal. The most important thing about metalloids is that they can be both a conductor of electricity or an insulator, which blocks electric currents. Scientists have figured out how to make a metalloid switch between conducting and insulating. That is why silicon and other metalloids are used in electronics. A microchip is made of thousands of tiny silicon switches that can turn currents on and off according to the instructions set out in a computer program.

STRETCHING AND BREAKING

A solid can alter its shape in three ways: by breaking, by stretching, or by changing its shape completely. Scientists have come up with the following terms for how solids change shape.

Brittle solids do not stretch or bend much at all—they just break in two.

Elastic solids stretch out of shape but, once the stretching force is removed, they return to their original length.

Plastic solids can change shape, or "deform," when pulled on. They stay like that when the force is removed—like play dough or putty. A plastic solid can be deformed over and over again without breaking.

BRITTLE

ELASTIC

PLASTIC

WORD CHECK

DEFORM: To change form or shape

GEEK STREAK

Gold is the most malleable of all metals. That means it is the easiest to shape, whether it be into a gold ring, a gold statue, or a gold chain. One ounce (28 g) of gold can be made into a single thin sheet that covers 96 square feet (9 sq m)— which is about the size of a parking space.

PERSONALITY PLUS

Thomas Young, a 19th-century British scientist, set up the system for measuring how stiff or stretchable a solid could be. In this system, every solid has a number known as its "Young's modulus." A low Young's modulus means the solid is stretchable or elastic, like a rubber band. A high number means the substance is stiff and strong. Young is remembered for other discoveries, too. He showed that light beams are actually waves flying through space. He figured out how to read Egyptian hieroglyphics. And he described how our eye's lens could see things at different distances.

CHEMISTRY BASICS

When we think of chemistry, we think of men and women in white coats and goggles. They're mixing liquids and powders in a laboratory filled with glass beakers, microscopes, and gas burners.

What do chemists actually do? They're trying to understand what the universe and everything in it is made of. Most early chemists, called alchemists, were looking for a way to turn metals like copper and lead into gold or silver so they'd become rich. As science progressed, modern chemists began using the "scientific method" (see page 9) to discover the simple substances, or elements, that make up the world. They asked questions, did experiments, and studied ways that substances would interact, combine, and change to form new substances. Today, chemists use lasers, high-powered microscopes, and other tools to examine these changes. Their discoveries help them create new materials and technology.

(see page 9)

WORD CHECK

DENSITY: A measure of how much matter is packed inside a substance. It is calculated by dividing the weight by the volume.

ALCHEMY

Medieval alchemists discovered many important chemical processes. In the eighth century, an Islamic alchemist known as Geber discovered hydrochloric acid, which was used in dyes. In the ninth century, alchemists in China mixed charcoal and sulfur to make what they hoped was life-extending medicine. Instead, they invented gunpowder.

A NEW SCIENCE IS BORN

By the 17th century, many alchemists stopped trying to turn metal into gold. They became chemists intent on discovering just what substances made up the physical world. Irish chemist Robert Boyle (left) said the old theory of the entire world being made of just four elements—earth, fire, water, and air—was too simple. There had to be what he called "true elements" out there, and he was going to use carefully documented experiments to discover them. Boyle defined a true element as "a substance that could not be simplified or broken down." And so, with that definition, Boyle advanced the new science of chemistry and gave it a goal—to find the elements that make up the physical world.

REAL-LIFE WIZARDS

The first chemists were alchemists who were more like wizards than scientists. Alchemy is an Arabic term meaning "black magic." It began in Egypt more than 3,000 years ago and was practiced as far away as China. Alchemists thought that chemical reactions used a force powered by ghostly spirits, so they'd often mutter spells to make them work better. They heated and mixed chemicals as they searched for a substance called the "philosopher's stone," which they believed could turn base metal into gold.

COOKING WITH COMPOUNDS

Modern chemists study chemical elements and compounds to discover how they work together in our bodies and in the world. They not only take substances apart to examine them, but they also combine them with other substances to make entirely new compounds. In this way, chemists are a little like chefs in a kitchen, creating a new dish. They take new compounds, measure their density and weight, and carefully document their melting, boiling, and freezing points. They measure the effects of these chemical compounds in various situations and their ability to connect or form a chemical bond with other atoms in a molecule.

LOL! 😄

Q: What is a wizard's favorite subject in school?

A: Spelling.

TRY THIS!

WHAT YOU NEED: A large plastic bottle half-filled with vinegar, a large balloon, a funnel, half a cup of baking soda

HOW LONG IT TAKES: 30 minutes

Become a chemist and make a balloon inflate all by itself! Using the funnel, carefully pour the baking soda into the balloon. Next, attach the end of the balloon to the top of the bottle. Be careful not to spill any of the baking soda into the bottle—not yet, anyway. When the balloon is firmly attached, hold the balloon above the bottle, so the powder inside falls into the vinegar. The baking soda and vinegar will fizz and the balloon will inflate as if by magic. (The powder and liquid are reacting to produce carbon dioxide gas, which bubbles out of the bottle and fills up the balloon.)

TESTING! TESTING!

Chemists traditionally use a series of tests to figure out what a substance is made from. First they weigh it and calculate its density to discover how much matter is packed inside it. They smell the substance and check if it dissolves in water or changes color in the air. Then they set fire to it. Different elements give out specific colored flames when they get hot: Sodium is yellow, copper is blue, and barium is green.

PERSONALITY PLUS

In 1669, the German scientist Hennig Brand made pure phosphorus by accident after boiling urine! He thought that the gold-colored liquid had real gold in it. Instead he found a hot liquid that glowed in the dark. He named it phosphorus, which means "morning star" in Greek.

AMAZING DISCOVERIES

The people who discovered how to refine copper metal from rocks, and how to mix it with tin to make bronze for pots, swords, and helmets, were chemists. Later, chemists discovered how many elements make up nature, and they went on to use them to make all kinds of new materials—from medicines and plastics to microchips and laundry powder. Thanks to chemistry, we have batteries in our phones, tablets, and touch screens. Chemists are still looking for new discoveries that might be used in the future, for everything from cleaner fuels to power systems. Check out this timeline of amazing discoveries in chemistry.

5000 B.C.

Pure copper and tin are made by heating rocks with charcoal. The carbon in the charcoal reacts with oxygen to heat the rock, which releases hot, liquid metal.

1200 B.C.

Hotter furnaces make it possible to refine iron from natural ores. Iron is much stronger than copper and tin.

A.D. 800

Gunpowder, the first explosive, is invented in China. It is made of sulfur, charcoal, and saltpeter (potassium nitrate).

1550

Georgius Agricola, a German scientist, writes a book about how to extract many kinds of metals from the ground and purify them.

1620

Francis Bacon describes a system for testing ideas about nature, which becomes known as the scientific method. It is still used by chemists today to figure out how natural substances work.

1660

Robert Boyle writes a book called *The Sceptical Chymist*. He shows how the magical ideas of alchemists are, for the most part, nonsense. Boyle is said to be the founding father of chemistry.

15	30.973762
P	
[Ne]3s²3p³	
Phosphorus	

1669

Hennig Brand discovers phosphorus. He is the first known person in history to discover a new element.

1750

Joseph Black discovers carbon dioxide gas. This discovery shows that air is not a single substance but a mixture of gases—and there are many kinds of gas compounds.

1772

Carl Scheele discovers oxygen gas but is not sure what it is. In 1774, Joseph Priestley determines it is a new kind of gas—and without it animals die.

1789

Antoine Lavoisier makes a list of "Simple Substances," or elements. His list has just 33 items, and he gets a few things wrong: The list includes heat and light, which are not made of matter.

1776

Henry Cavendish discovers hydrogen gas. He calls it "flammable air" because it burns so easily.

Antoine Lavoisier (1743–1794) discovered that water was not an element like ancient people believed. Instead it was made by combining hydrogen and oxygen in a chemical reaction. Lavoisier gave these two new gases their names and was the first person to explain that burning was a chemical reaction.

Robert Boyle (1627–1691) was the first true chemist—although he called himself a chymist. He used pumps to figure out how air behaved and asked questions about what air was made of.

1803

John Dalton shows that matter is made from atoms and that the atoms of each element have a particular weight.

1807

Humphry Davy begins to use electricity to discover new elements.

Humphry Davy (1778–1829) used a new invention—electric batteries—to investigate compounds. He found that he could break compounds up into their elements using electric currents. He discovered more elements than anyone else in history. These include sodium, potassium, calcium, magnesium, boron, barium, and chlorine.

1813

Joseph Louis Gay-Lussac figures out that water has the formula H_2O.

1813

Swedish scientist Jöns Jacob Berzelius proposes that chemical symbols be based on the Latin names of the elements. By mid-century his system is adopted by the scientific community.

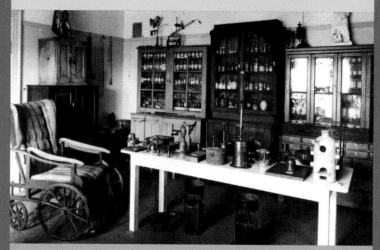

The "father of Swedish chemistry," **Jöns Jacob Berzelius** (1779–1848) developed the system of symbols and formulas that chemists still use today. He also made the first discoveries about how charged ions bond together inside compounds.

1852

Robert Bunsen builds a gas burner with a hot, clean flame designed to perform flame tests on substances. It is standard equipment in chemistry laboratories today.

1868

Helium gas is discovered on the surface of the sun using the same system chemists used to identify chemicals by the colors they produce when heated.

1869

Dmitri Mendeleev invents the periodic table of elements.

1896

Henri Becquerel discovers radioactivity.

1913

Niels Bohr discovers the way electrons and protons are arranged around the nucleus inside an atom. He creates the "Bohr Model" to illustrate this arrangement.

1930

Linus Pauling explains how chemical bonds are formed by sharing or exchanging electrons.

1985

A new ball-shaped form of pure carbon is discovered and named buckminsterfullerene.

1953

Francis Crick and James Watson figure out the structure of DNA (deoxyribonucleic acid), one of the largest molecules in the natural world and found in almost every living cell.

2012

Flerovium and livermorium are the latest elements to be discovered. Both are made inside particle accelerators and exist only for a fraction of a second.

CHEMICAL REACTIONS

Chemical reactions are happening all around us. One type of reaction provides the power that drives a car. Another allows trees to make sugars in their leaves. Yet another makes your soda fizz.

A chemical reaction is what happens when atoms are rearranged. That means the atoms are breaking the bonds that link them together and are making new connections with different atoms. The process starts with reactants. These are the substances that will change when combined with other substances in a chemical reaction. When the reaction is finished, the reactants have been transformed into a completely new set of substances called products. Reactants can be solids, liquids, or gases, and so can their products. Chemical reactions do not create or destroy atoms, they just reorganize them. The number of atoms at the start of the reaction is equal to the number at the end.

BASIC TYPES OF CHEMICAL REACTIONS

There are three basic types of chemical reactions. The first kind takes two reactants and combines them together into one product. For instance, when coal burns in air, carbon reacts with oxygen, and they combine to make carbon dioxide gas. The second kind of reaction is the opposite—a single reactant breaks apart to form two new products, like water breaking down into hydrogen and oxygen gas. The third kind is when a more reactive element replaces a less reactive one in a compound. We use this type of reaction to extract useful things like iron and copper from the Earth.

WHY DO ELEMENTS REACT?

Elements react so they can form bonds with each other. The reaction causes substances to break apart and recombine to form a new substance. The atoms are now sharing electrons, which makes them more stable. Some elements are better at forming bonds than others because they are more reactive than others. Cesium (below) is the most reactive metal element on Earth. It is used in the drilling industry, and also in atomic clocks. Cesium must be stored in oil because it explodes on contact with any moisture in the air.

ENERGY'S ROLE IN A CHEMICAL REACTION

Every chemical reaction needs a certain amount of energy to start. Very reactive elements only need a little energy and then they react almost instantly—by exploding or catching fire. Most reactions get going with a bigger boost of extra heat or energy. The extra energy breaks the bonds in a substance and allows new bonds to form to make new substances. As these new bonds form, they release more energy. So if you touch a spark to a piece of wood, the spark's energy sets off a reaction that breaks the wood's bonds as it burns. The reaction also forms new bonds that create heat and flames by again releasing energy.

COMBUSTION

The most familiar chemical reaction is called combustion. We know it better as burning. Combustion occurs when oxygen reacts with another substance and gives out flames and heat. This reaction is very useful: It keeps us warm and provides the heat for cooking and powering other chemical reactions. Even cars use it. The hot gas produced by burning fuel inside the engine is used to push the wheels around. Our bodies use combustion for power, too. Food is our fuel and we breathe in oxygen to burn it. When we exercise, we actually breathe out the weight we lose in the form of carbon dioxide.

CORROSION

Some chemical reactions happen very slowly. Corrosion, for example, is a reaction that affects metals and can take place over centuries. Corrosion makes copper objects turn green. When the Statue of Liberty was new, it was a shiny red-brown color. Soon the chemicals in the salty sea air reacted with it to create a thin layer of green corrosion called verdigris. Corrosion causes iron objects to turn into rust. Pure iron is hard and tough, but rust is very crumbly. Over time, corrosion can turn even the strongest iron beams into fine dust.

BREAKING BONDS

This building is being knocked down using a chemical reaction. An electric pulse is used to get the chemical explosives to react. The bonds in the explosives, which are unstable compounds, break down, and new bonds form to make more stable compounds. This reaction gives out a huge amount of energy very quickly in the form of an explosion that makes the building collapse.

TOOLS OF THE TRADE

Fire is a chemical reaction between oxygen in the air and a fuel like wood or gasoline. The reaction releases heat, and this energy makes the reaction run faster. When dealing with a dangerous fire, firefighters must stop the reaction to put it out. Here are three ways they do that:

■ Remove heat: Spraying water onto the fire will take away its heat. Eventually it will be cold enough to stop burning.

■ Remove oxygen: Smothering flames with sand or foam will stop the oxygen in the air from getting to the fuel.

■ Remove fuel: Cutting down trees during a wildfire creates a "fire break," or a space where there is no fuel, and so the fire does not spread.

TRY THIS!

WHAT YOU NEED: Four iron nails, four glass jars with lids, water, salt, cooking oil

HOW LONG IT TAKES: A week

This is an easy way to see chemical reactions between iron, oxygen, and water. Set four jars in a row. In jar 1: Place a nail. In jar 2: Place a nail and add water. In jar 3: Place a nail and add water and salt. In jar 4: Add boiled water that has been cooled and add the nail. Next pour a little oil on top of the water in that jar. It should float. Put the lids on the jars and leave them somewhere safe for a week. What happens in each jar?

The results tell us that rust is produced by a reaction between iron (in the nail), oxygen in the air, and water. In jar 1 there is just oxygen, so the nail is a little rusty. In jar 2 there is water and air, so the nail is rusty. In jar 3, the salt makes the reaction run very fast, so the nail is very rusty. In jar 4, there is water but no oxygen—the oil stops any from getting in. So there is no rust.

37

NOBLE GASES

Noble gases are elements that do not get involved in chemical reactions. They stay inert, or motionless.

These gases are said to be "noble" because they stay separate from the more common elements—just like kings and queens from long ago did not mix with the common people. They are also all invisible. The most familiar noble gases are helium and neon, but there are six in total, including argon, krypton, xenon, and radon. The noble gases are listed on the right side of the periodic table. That is because the outer electron shells of their atoms are completely full. A full outer shell has no way of sharing electrons with another atom, so the noble gases very rarely form chemical bonds. They stay as single atoms. Most of the noble gases are very safe and do not harm people. However, radon, the heaviest noble gas, is radioactive.

RADIOACTIVE RADON

You can't see, smell, or taste radon. It comes from different rocks, soils, and sources of underground water. If you cool radon below its freezing point of minus 96°F (-71°C), it gives off a yellow to orange-red color. Radon can cause serious health problems if you breathe it in.

HELIUM: SUN GAS

All noble gases are invisible. Because they do not get involved in chemical reactions, for a long time no one knew they were there. The first one to be discovered was helium, and it was found not on Earth, but in the sun. Scientists knew that when they heated elements, the elements would glow certain colors. They found many of these colors in sunlight. During a solar eclipse in 1868, French astronomer Pierre Jules Janssen looked at the glowing gases surrounding the sun and saw a new, unknown color: pink-orange. It was obviously a new element! He called it helium, after *helios*, the Greek word for "sun."

TOOLS OF THE TRADE

Helium is the second lightest element after hydrogen. Both of these gases float in the air and can be used in balloons. However, hydrogen explodes easily, so helium balloons are much safer. Scientists use high-altitude weather balloons to get a snapshot of the conditions at the edge of space. In fact, twice a day, every day of the year, more than 800 weather balloons are released into the upper atmosphere where they measure pressure, temperature, and relative humidity.

BREATHE DEEP!

Deep-sea divers don't breathe air. They use a mixture of helium and oxygen. At great depths, the weight of the water above pushes down hard on a scuba diver, pressing the gases in a diver's breath into his bloodstream. Human breath contains nitrogen. If this gas is pushed into the blood, it can really hurt the diver. So divers use helium instead of nitrogen in their tanks. Helium is much safer than nitrogen, but it still must be used with care. One side effect: The lightweight gas can make a diver's voice very squeaky!

WORD CHECK

INERT: Something that is motionless and does not chemically react with anything else

GEEK STREAK

When helium is cooled into a liquid it becomes a substance called a superfluid. That means it has superpowers. A superfluid might look like any other liquid: It drips, splashes, and can be poured. But if you leave it in a cup, a superfluid acts like a big wave and flows up the sides and escapes!

NEON GLOW

Just like the pinkish orange of helium, all noble gases glow with a telltale color. Chemists showed this off by putting a tiny amount of each gas inside electrified glass tubes. The tubes were then bent into different shapes to make colorful lights called neon lights. The word "neon" comes from the Greek word *neos*, which means "the new gas." Today neon lights are rare, but they were once a good way of making bright signs that lit up at night.

KRYPTON

Most moviegoers and comic book readers think of krypton as the name of the distant planet where Superman was born. But krypton is actually a noble gas named for the Greek word *kryptos*, which means "hidden." It is a colorless, odorless gas that rarely reacts with other elements. A jar of krypton would look like a jar of air. When electricity passes through krypton it gives off a very bright light, which is why it is used in airport runway lights, fluorescent lights, and flash photography. Many laser light shows also use krypton.

COOL CHEMICAL ANALYSIS

Chemists have two big jobs: synthesis and analysis. "Synthesis" means "to combine." "Analysis" means "to break down." Chemists combine elements to make a new substance. They also break down, or analyze, a substance to find out more about it.

Chemists analyze food to discover how much sugar, fats, and other ingredients are in it. This helps you decide if it is good for you to eat. Crime scene investigators use chemical analysis to examine evidence like hair, clothing fibers, and footprints. The results can link suspects to a specific crime and location. Doctors analyze the chemicals in a patient's blood to find out if the person is healthy. Here are more tools and techniques that use chemical analysis.

SOLVING PUZZLES

Chemists use an instrument called a mass spectrometer for identifying what kinds of particles are present in a substance. The particles are given an electric charge (ionized) and then shot at an electromagnetic field. The way the particles move through the field tells us their mass, or shape, and what kinds of atoms and molecules are there. Chemists can then figure out how all the molecules fit together—like a chemical jigsaw puzzle. Mass spectrometers can look like big cameras. They are connected to space probes so they can analyze the rocks on other planets.

DISCOVERING DATE AND TIME

Ever wonder how we know the age of dinosaur bones? Chemists use the natural radioactivity in animals and plants to figure out their age. It's called carbon dating. Humans and other living things contain carbon. A tiny proportion of this is a radioactive form called carbon-14. When a plant or animal is alive, the amount of carbon-14 in it stays the same. Once it dies, the amount decreases as the carbon-14 naturally breaks down. How much carbon-14 is left tells chemists the age of any object that was once part of a living thing—a piece of wood, a strand of hair, or a dinosaur bone.

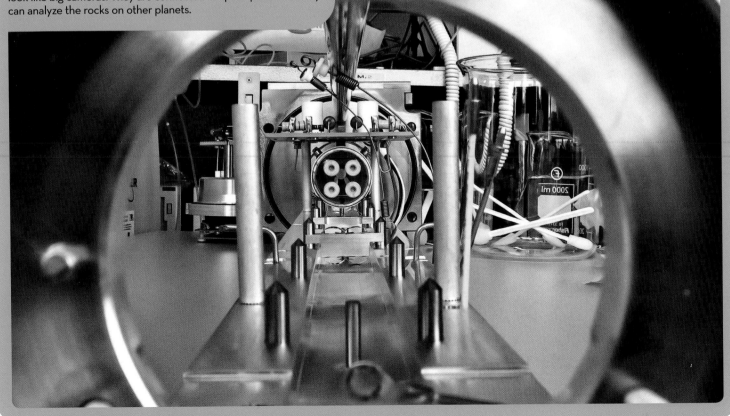

TOOLS OF THE TRADE

Diamonds make the toughest drill bits. They can cut through just about anything—concrete, bricks, and even solid rock. The diamond drill bit spins around and grinds away whatever solid it touches. That makes the drill bit get very hot—sometimes hot enough to melt the diamonds and metal parts of the bit. Diamond melts at a sizzling 6422°F (3550°C).

SPARKLING JEWEL

What makes diamond jewels glitter and gleam? As with any other transparent material, light shines through diamond. However, the surface of a diamond bends the light beams coming inside it more than most other crystals. Jewelers also cut diamonds into special shapes. This makes the light beams bounce around inside the crystal and shine back out the way they came in. The Queen of England's Imperial State Crown contains 2,868 sparkling diamonds!

TRY THIS!

WHAT YOU NEED: A spoon, a lighted candle

HOW LONG IT TAKES: 10 minutes

You can collect your own supply of pure carbon using a candle and a large metal spoon. It won't be a diamond, however—just a bit of soot! Both the candle and spoon will get hot, so you need to be careful, and ask an adult to help light the flame. Once the candle is lit, hold the spoon in the top of the flame for a few seconds. Take it out and you'll see a dark layer of carbon soot has formed. Candle wax is a carbon compound. When it burns, a little of it becomes pure carbon.

CARBON CYCLE

All living things use carbon in their bodies. Where do they get it? The answer can be found in the carbon cycle. It shows how carbon compounds move between the air, the oceans, and the soil, and in and out of living bodies.

1 Carbon dioxide gas is mixed into the air and oceans.

4 Dead plants and animals are broken down by bacteria and other organisms in the soil, which convert them to carbon dioxide.

2 Plants turn carbon dioxide into sugars using photosynthesis.

3 Animals eat the plants. The sugars fuel their bodies and return to the atmosphere as carbon dioxide.

WATER

Water covers nearly three-quarters of our planet. Without it, the life we know today would be impossible.

Water is a very simple compound of oxygen and hydrogen. Each molecule has two hydrogen atoms and one oxygen atom. This gives it the formula H_2O. It is such a common and familiar compound that we are often surprised to hear that it is actually a very unusual substance. Water occurs as a liquid, as a solid (ice), and as a gas called water vapor.

Earth and Mars are the only places we know that have liquid water on their surfaces. All other space objects we have studied, including moons, are dry. Any water on a moon's surface is frozen solid into ice, or floating in the atmosphere as vapor. Besides water there are very few other naturally occurring liquids on Earth, and most do not stay liquid for long. Lava is hot liquid rock, and it cools down very quickly into a solid. Pure liquid mercury is a metal that sometimes forms around hot volcanoes, but it always reacts rapidly with the rocks and turns back into a solid compound. Petroleum oil stays in its liquid state for a long time, but it is usually found only deep underground.

HYDROGEN BOND

Why is there so much liquid water on Earth? There is a force holding the water molecules together that stops the water from changing into ice or vapor easily. This force is a special chemical bond called a hydrogen bond. The atoms in a water molecule share some electrons, which is what bonds them together. However, the oxygen atom pulls on the electrons more than the hydrogen atoms do. That means the oxygen part of the molecule is partially negatively charged, and the hydrogen atoms are partially positively charged. The negative part of one molecule is attracted to a positive part of one of its neighbor molecules. These links are the hydrogen bonds, and they create a kind of glue that holds liquid water together.

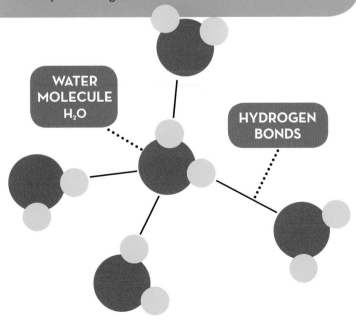

WATER MOLECULE H_2O

HYDROGEN BONDS

TOUGH LIQUID

Like all liquids, water has no fixed shape. It will fill any container and flow from one to the other. But water is still tough stuff. You may have seen a water strider skating over the surface of a pond. This little bug is able to stand on water thanks to the liquid's surface tension. The water molecules are clinging together so tightly that something as lightweight as the insect does not fall through the surface layer and get wet. The force holding water together is much stronger than that in other liquids. It is enough to keep together a spout of water 30 feet (10 m) high. If the spout goes any higher, the weight of all the water makes the spout collapse, and splash down to Earth again.

FLOATING ICE

Ice cubes in a cold drink float at the top of the glass. Pretty normal, right? Wrong. If water were like most other substances, its solid form would sink. That's because most other substances contract, or shrink, as they freeze. Water expands. That means ice takes up more room than the water it was made from. It is also less dense, so it floats. The expansion happens when hydrogen bonds push the water molecules apart as the molecules form a solid ice crystal. Because ice floats, water always freezes on the surface first. That's important if you're a fish because it leaves warmer liquid water underneath where you can swim. If icebergs sank, the world's oceans would gradually fill up with ice, and most of the planet would be frozen over.

WATER, WATER ALMOST EVERYWHERE

When Earth was very young, its surface was too hot for liquid water to exist. Today, the ocean contains 326 million cubic miles (1,358 million cu km) of water. Where did it all come from? The latest research shows that most of Earth's water was trapped in the rocks that formed deep underground, and "sweated" out over millions of years. The water leaked out through the surface, mostly as steam coming out of volcanoes. This steam filled the atmosphere and then formed into huge clouds that poured down rain. The rainstorms lasted thousands of years and filled the oceans.

GEEK STREAK

All of Earth's liquid water is salty except for one percent. This little bit of freshwater is enough to run through all the world's rivers. A fifth of all our freshwater is in one place—Lake Baikal in eastern Russia. This enormous lake is one mile (1.6 km) deep and contains more water than all the North American Great Lakes combined.

EUROPA

All life on Earth needs liquid water. Most living things are made up of at least 50 percent water. Humans are about 60 percent water. This precious liquid contains all the chemicals that make life possible, such as hydrogen and oxygen. So if life were to exist somewhere other than Earth, it would need liquid water. Space scientists think they may have found such a place. Europa is a moon of Jupiter, covered in thick ice. Scientists think a vast ocean, with more water than on Earth, might be under that ice. Scientists are planning to send a space probe to look at that ocean and see if anything lives down there.

TRY THIS!

WHAT YOU NEED: Water, vegetable oil, honey or molasses, six paper cups, a stopwatch

HOW LONG IT TAKES: 10 minutes

All liquids can flow, but some are better at it than others. A liquid with a high viscosity (stickiness) flows more slowly than one with a low viscosity. Check it out with this simple test. First, put equal amounts of the three liquids into three separate cups. Take each one in turn and pour the liquid into one of the empty cups. Have a friend time how long it takes for all the liquid to flow out of the cup. You should find that the water flows the fastest. Jot down the times. Which one takes the longest?

PERSONALITY PLUS

Until the end of the 1700s, scientists believed that water was an element. Nobody thought that it could be broken down into simpler substances. However, the French chemist Antoine Lavoisier (1743-1794) saw that he could create little droplets of water when he burned hydrogen. So he figured out that water was actually a compound made of oxygen and hydrogen atoms. Lavoisier gave hydrogen its name, which means "water maker."

AIR

The gas all around us is called air. You can't see it, but you can feel it rushing by you on a windy day.

Air exists as a layer around the Earth called the atmosphere. The atmosphere is about 50 miles (80 km) thick. Most of the air is in the first 5 miles (8 km) above the Earth. Air is actually a mixture of several gases. The most common gas is nitrogen, which makes up 78 percent of the air. Oxygen is the next most common gas, at 21 percent. The final one percent contains small amounts of several other gases. The gases in air very rarely react with each other. They are spread out evenly across the Earth. All animals extract the oxygen from air to breathe. Oxygen is also part of many other processes, like combustion in a car engine. As for nitrogen and the other gases in air, chemists have learned how to purify them and put them to good use. For instance, nitrogen is one of the essential parts of fertilizer.

OXYGEN

Most of the other planets in our solar system have atmospheres, but there is a big difference between their air and the air on Earth. The other planets have very little oxygen. Most of Earth's oxygen has been released into the atmosphere by plants and plant-like microorganisms. They produce the oxygen during photosynthesis (see pages 196–197). Oxygen is a very reactive element, which means it is quick to combine with other substances. However, plants keep on producing oxygen, so our air always has a steady amount of it. An oxygen-rich atmosphere means that objects on Earth's surface can do something that can't happen anywhere else: They can catch fire! Once a fire starts, the air supplies the blaze with oxygen. The fire will keep burning until it runs out of wood or other fuel, or until rain puts it out. But it will never run out of oxygen as long as it's exposed to the air.

AN UNCHANGING GAS

Pure nitrogen (N_2), like pure oxygen (O_2), exists as a molecule of two atoms bonded together. However, the two gases are very different. While oxygen reacts with almost any other element, nitrogen hardly reacts at all. The only time nitrogen reacts is when the air is heated to very high temperatures, such as during a lightning strike. The extreme heat breaks nitrogen's molecules apart. We use nitrogen's lack of reactivity to keep food, like salad, from going bad. Germs and mold need oxygen to live, but if salad is stored in nitrogen instead of oxygen, the germs can't react and grow on it, so the salad stays fresh.

GEEK STREAK

All the air around Earth weighs 5.5 quadrillion tons (5 quadrillion t). However, Earth itself weighs a million times more.

WORD CHECK

VACUUM: A space where there is no air—and nothing else—at all

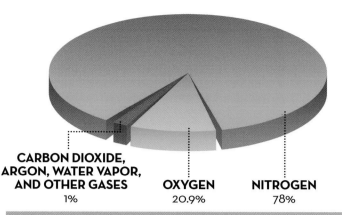

CARBON DIOXIDE,
ARGON, WATER VAPOR,
AND OTHER GASES
1%

OXYGEN
20.9%

NITROGEN
78%

OTHER GASES IN THE AIR

The third most common gas in air is argon, at just under one percent. All the other noble gases, such as krypton and xenon, are found in even smaller amounts (see page 39). The gas we breathe out is carbon dioxide. It makes up only .03 percent of the atmosphere. Carbon dioxide is also produced by burning fuel, such as gasoline and coal. The amount of water vapor in air goes up and down depending on the weather. Before a big storm, the air might be almost 2 percent water vapor. After the storm, the proportion of water vapor in the air is much lower.

TRY THIS!

WHAT YOU NEED: A candle (on a wide plate or other flat heatproof surface), a jar or glass taller than the candle, glue

HOW LONG IT TAKES: 15 to 30 minutes

Regular air contains oxygen. This is the element that makes things burn, or combust. Without oxygen in the air, nothing can burn, and you can prove it. First, squeeze a ring of glue around the rim of the jar. This will create an airtight seal when you turn the jar upside down. Next, light the candle and then cover it with the jar. Push it down enough to make a seal. The flame will burn for a while, and then it will just go out. Why? The air inside the jar ran out of oxygen, so the burning reaction stopped. The jar still contains nitrogen, but the oxygen has been replaced with carbon dioxide gas produced by burning the candle wax.

PURIFYING GASES

Purification is a way chemists remove pure gases from the air. The easiest gas to purify is nitrogen. To do this, air is mixed with hydrogen and then set on fire. The hydrogen reacts with the oxygen in the air to make water. When the water evaporates, it leaves behind a form of pure nitrogen gas that is used to make drugs, fertilizers, explosives, and much more. Purifying oxygen is more difficult. The air must be cooled down to minus 297°F (-183°C). That's where oxygen becomes a liquid that can be separated from the other gases in air. Pure oxygen is used to burn away impurities in iron to make steel. It also helps sick people with lung problems breathe easier.

TOOLS OF THE TRADE

A vacuum cleaner uses an air pump—something similar to a powerful fan—to push air out of the back of the machine. As a result an empty space, or vacuum, is formed inside the vacuum cleaner. Air rushes in to fill it through the cleaning head. We often say that air is being sucked in by the machine, but really it is being pushed. The air outside the vacuum cleaner pushes into the empty space created inside and brings all the dust and dirt along with it.

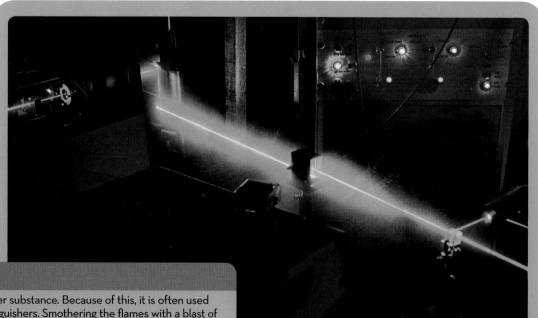

SAFETY GAS

Argon gas does not react with any other substance. Because of this, it is often used in safety applications such as fire extinguishers. Smothering the flames with a blast of argon stops oxygen from reaching the fire, so the fire goes out. Argon extinguishers are used in data centers where water or other gases would damage the computers. Argon is also used inside all kinds of lightbulbs to make the filaments last longer. Argon-ion lasers, with their distinctive green-blue light, are specialty lasers used mainly in medicine. Surgeons use them to precisely cut away damaged parts of an eye.

MIXTURES

The natural world is a mixed-up place, where all kinds of materials are jumbled together. Mud, most rocks, clouds, the ocean's water, and even milk are all different kinds of mixtures.

The first thing to know about a mixture is that it is different from a compound. In a compound, two or more elements are joined together by a chemical bond. In a mixture, the elements are mixed together, but not connected by chemical bonds. So, the ocean's water is a mixture of two compounds, salt (NaCl) and water (H_2O). Different mixtures blend together in different ways. Chemists analyze these ways to learn how to extract a pure substance, like salt, from the mixture seawater. A pure substance, which can be an element or a compound, contains nothing else but that substance. If the sample contains even small amounts of other substances, called impurities, the behavior of a substance could be very different.

EVEN AND UNEVEN

Every mixture has to have at least two separate substances in it. Scientists usually describe how one of those substances is mixed into the other as "even" (homogenous) or "uneven" (heterogeneous). Seawater is an example of an even mixture, because the salt has spread evenly throughout the water. If you could see the molecules that make up seawater, you'd always see the same number of water and salt molecules wherever you looked. The mixture of sand and pebbles on a beach is not so evenly spread out. If you stood on the beach, you'd see some patches of mostly sand and other areas of mainly pebbles. You'd also see that the ingredients of the mixture look very different and are of uneven sizes.

SOLUTIONS

An even mixture is most often called a solution. Seawater is a solution of salts evenly mixed into water. The salt is mixed in so thoroughly that it disappears in the water. This mixing process is called dissolving. Water is very good at dissolving other substances. A soda (above) is a solution of water, sugar, and carbonic acid. The sugar makes the water sweet, and the acid makes it fizz. Solutions are not always liquids. Steel is a solution of iron with carbon and a few other elements dissolved in it. A gel is a solution of a liquid dissolved in a solid. For example, a wobbly gelatin dessert is a solution made of sweet, flavored water dissolved in a solid protein called collagen (the same kind of stuff that makes our skin flexible).

LOL!

Q: What is the most important rule in chemistry?

A: Never lick the spoon!

SUSPENSION MIXTURES

In an uneven mixture, substances cling together in lumps rather than spread out, as in a solution. However, these lumps can be so small that it's impossible to see them. Mixtures like that are called suspension mixtures because the lumps of stuff are suspended—or hanging—in water or a gas. A muddy river is a suspension mixture ("suspension" for short) of specks of grit and silt that are washed along in the water. Milk is a suspension of tiny blobs of fat hanging around in water. The blobs are so small they change the way light shines through the water—and that is why milk looks cloudy white. Clouds are also suspensions, only they are made of tiny water droplets suspended in the air. They appear white for the same reason milk does.

TRY THIS!

WHAT YOU NEED: Filter paper (or blotting paper), a shallow dish, water, dark felt-tip pens of two different colors

HOW LONG IT TAKES: 2 to 3 hours

When a mixture contains many very similar ingredients, it can be hard to separate them using regular methods. Instead, a system called chromatography is used.

First, fill the shallow dish with a little water. Cut the filter paper into a strip. About half an inch (1.3 cm) from one end, draw a line across the strip with one colored pen. A little higher up the strip, mark it with the other pen. Now dip the half-inch below your first mark into the water and lay the strip of paper over the rim of the dish. The very tip of the paper needs to be wet, but the rest of the paper, including the two colored lines, must be dry to start with. The water will gradually travel up the thick paper.

Wait several hours and take a look. As the water moves up the paper, it carries with it the different colored chemicals that make up the ink in each pen. Each color moves a certain distance and then stops. How many different colors do you see? Try this with pen inks, food dyes, or other colored liquids.

SEPARATING MIXTURES

You can separate a mixture into its pure ingredients in several ways. These methods are always physical processes, never chemical ones. That means the ingredients in the mixture are not reacting or changing from one compound to another. They're simply being pulled apart. For example they might be forced to move in a certain direction or they might be boiled or frozen. Mixtures are often separated by a process called distillation. The liquid parts are boiled until they turn into gas and drift out of the mixture, leaving behind solids that have dissolved. The gases are collected and later cooled down so they become liquids again. By carefully controlling the temperature of the mixture, chemists can collect pure samples of each liquid as each one boils away at a different temperature.

TOOLS OF THE TRADE

A centrifuge is a machine that separates out the ingredients in a suspension mixture. A tube filled with the mixture is spun around at very high speeds, pushing the parts of the mixture toward the end of the tube at different speeds. If the solid material is denser than the liquid, it's pushed to the bottom, leaving the liquid behind.

FILTERS

Uneven mixtures, such as suspensions, contain ingredients of different sizes but can easily be separated with filters. A filter is any barrier with holes in it. Objects smaller than the holes drop through the filter but bigger ones get stuck. A sewage treatment plant, like this one, uses a series of filters, each with smaller holes than the last, to take out the goop that goes down our bathroom and kitchen drains from the water used to flush it. Sewage can also be filtered through thick layers of sand. The water goes through the sand, but everything solid stays behind.

GEEK STREAK

An aerogel is a solid with gas dissolved in it. SEAgel is an aerogel filled with a light gas, like helium, so it floats in the air! SEAgel is made from seaweed—so you can eat it, too!

ORGANIC CHEMISTRY

The word "organic" means "from life." Organic chemistry looks at two things: the chemicals found in living bodies, and the chemicals produced from the remains of living things by other natural processes.

All natural organic chemicals are based on a single element: carbon. Carbon atoms can make a variety of bonds with different elements. That makes it possible for nature to construct hugely complicated molecules made up of chains and rings of atoms. These in turn make up thousands of kinds of natural materials. That makes carbon very special—and why an entire area of science, organic chemistry, is devoted to it. Chemists have learned to copy and alter carbon to make all sorts of artificial organic chemicals, such as plastics, nylon, medicines such as aspirin, and most of the fuels we use.

PETROLEUM

"Petroleum" means "rock oil," and it's our main natural source of organic chemicals. Petroleum is a mixture of thousands of different kinds of hydrocarbons. It is made from the remains of ocean microorganisms buried under rocks millions of years ago. The heat and pressure deep underground converted their chemicals into petroleum. Petroleum is full of useful substances, such as petroleum jelly, which are separated at oil refineries by a process called fractional distillation. The petroleum is heated so most of it boils and rises up as gases inside a tall tower. As the gases rise, they cool, and one by one turn into liquid again. Different groups, or fractions, of organic chemicals are collected at different heights up the tower.

WORD CHECK

MICROORGANISM: A living thing with just one cell in its body. It is way too small to see without a microscope.

HYDROCARBONS

Hydrocarbons are made up entirely of hydrogen and carbon. That makes hydrocarbons the simplest family of organic chemicals. A typical molecule of hydrocarbon has a backbone chain of carbon atoms with hydrogen atoms attached all the way along. The simplest hydrocarbon is methane, or natural gas, with the formula CH_4—one carbon atom bonded to four hydrogen atoms. The next simplest is ethane (C_2H_6), then propane (C_3H_8), butane (C_4H_{10}), and pentane (C_5H_{12}). The list goes on forever, each time with one more carbon atom, and two more hydrogen atoms being added to each molecule.

ALCOHOL AND VINEGAR

Most organic chemicals have more than just hydrogen and carbon in them. For example, two very familiar organic chemicals are vinegar and alcohol. The scientific name for alcohol is ethanol. Like ethane it has two carbon atoms, but in place of one of the hydrogen atoms it has an oxygen atom connected to a hydrogen atom (an OH group), making the molecule (C_2H_6O). Ethanol is a natural substance, but chemists can make many other types of alcohol. The main molecule varies a lot, but all alcohol molecules have an OH group of atoms (and they can be very poisonous). Vinegar's chemical name is ethanoic acid. It too has two carbon atoms and an OH group of atoms, but there is also an extra oxygen atom (O) on the molecule ($C_2H_4O_2$). This structure gives vinegar its sharp taste and makes it a carboxylic acid. Other carboxylic acids include citric acid in lemon juice and formic acid, which is in some ant stings.

Vaseline
TRADEMARK®
100% PURE
MOISTURIZES!
Great for Hands & Body
PETROLEUM JELLY
NET WT. 13 OZ. (368g)
SKIN PROTECTANT

SMELLY CHEMICALS

Many of the smells we pick up are from our nose detecting certain kinds of organic chemicals. Some of the strongest smells are produced by three chemical groups: the thiols, amines, and esters.

GEEK STREAK
Flames of burning methane coming from swamps were called will-o'-the-wisps. People thought they were ghosts!

AMINES

Fishy and rotten smells come from another group of chemicals called the amines, which contain nitrogen.

THIOLS

Thiols contain sulfur, and these chemicals produce the odor of garlic and onions—and the stink from a skunk.

ESTERS

Fruity smells come from chemicals called esters. These are complicated molecules with a lone oxygen atom somewhere on them. The smell of apples, pears, bananas, and even wood and cinnamon comes from esters.

PLASTICS AND POLYMERS

Organic chemicals can have thousands of atoms in their molecules. The gooey tar used to cover roads is the biggest naturally occurring chemical in petroleum. But chemists can connect millions—even billions—of atoms to make truly enormous molecules called polymers. A polymer is a chain or network of smaller units called monomers. Most polymers are used to make plastics. A common plastic is polyethylene, which is made up of monomers called ethylene (C_2H_4). Ethylene is a reactive hydrocarbon with double carbon bonds. Plastics are very useful because they can be made into thin sheets or any other shape—and then melted down and made into something else.

PERSONALITY PLUS

Until the early 19th century, it was thought that organic chemicals, such as those found in living things, were made by a different process than regular chemicals. Chemists could not produce them artificially, people said, because they needed to be made with a special natural force. In 1828, Friedrich Wöhler proved them all wrong by producing urea (a chemical in urine) in his lab. He did it by accident, but his work proved that the rules that governed organic chemicals were the same as the ones in regular chemistry.

CATALYSTS

A catalyst is a substance that changes the rate of a chemical reaction, but the catalyst isn't used up in the process. It speeds up a chemical reaction by changing its "activation energy"—the amount of energy needed to get the reaction going.

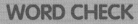
WORD CHECK
OZONE: A layer of the upper atmosphere that stops radiation from reaching Earth

A catalyst speeds up a reaction by "introducing" molecules to each other. Without the catalyst, the molecules bounce around at random. The reaction can't start until they bump into each other by chance. That's where the catalyst steps in: It attaches itself weakly to the molecules and brings them together. The catalyst breaks away again once the molecules have combined.

A catalyst also speeds things up by providing an easier path through a chemical reaction. This "shortcut" is a reaction that needs less energy to get going. Using catalysts helps industries save on energy costs.

Catalysts also function in the human body. Enzymes, for example, speed up chemical reactions in digestion. Separate chemical reactions break down food in the mouth, the stomach, and the intestines.

Only a small amount of a catalyst is needed because it assists the reaction without becoming part of the substance that's produced. So it can be used over and over again to speed up new reactions.

CATALYTIC CARS

Cars that run on lead-free gasoline often have a device called a catalytic converter in their exhaust systems. A catalytic converter turns harmful substances produced by burning fuel into less harmful ones. The converter is lined with metals that serve as catalysts that form short-lived bonds with the gases passing through. Bringing the gas molecules together changes their energy so they can combine into less harmful substances. For example, with the help of catalysts, poisonous carbon monoxide becomes carbon dioxide and water.

FACTORY USES

Zeolite is a mineral filled with microscopic spaces. When atoms and molecules are trapped in those tiny holes, they can cause chemical reactions to occur. Many industries use zeolite as a catalyst to make reactions happen at lower temperatures. The oil industry uses zeolite to break down large molecules into smaller ones. This process, called "cracking," helps turn oil into gasoline and other products. Other catalysts, like organic peroxides, make it possible to turn oil into plastic products. They speed up the combining of small molecules into long chains, a process called polymerization.

EVERYDAY ENZYMES

Enzyme catalysts are also found all around you. Enzymes in laundry detergent help get your clothes clean. Protease is an enzyme that breaks down protein-based stains, such as blood, grass, and sweat. The dairy industry uses enzymes to turn milk into yogurt and cheese. They are made by bacteria as they digest sugars in the milk. This process is called fermentation. Enzymes are used in papermaking to bleach paper and turn it white. Paper recyclers use different enzymes to remove ink and glue from old paper. Enzymes in apples and other fruits react with oxygen and turn fruit brown. Chilling in a refrigerator slows enzyme activity. So will a dab of lemon juice. A fungus rots logs by making enzymes that break down wood. Finding out how these enzymes work could someday help us make new biofuels.

OZONE

The atmosphere's "ozone layer" shields Earth from much of the sun's harmful radiation. In the 1970s, however, scientists discovered the ozone layer was thinning due to chemicals called chlorofluorocarbons (CFCs for short). CFCs were useful—they shot ingredients out of spray cans and kept refrigerators cold. But they also released chemicals into the air that worked as catalysts to break down the ozone. So most nations around the world have agreed to get rid of CFCs.

ENZYMES INSIDE YOU

Living things produce catalysts called enzymes. Most enzymes are made of protein, and they speed up reactions necessary for life. The enzymes in your body digest food by breaking it down into simple substances your cells can use. Other enzymes help produce energy, fight disease, move muscles, and build body parts. Enzymes in your eyes help cells process light. Billions of enzyme-powered processes take place in your body every second.

TRY THIS!

WHAT YOU NEED: A glass, one saltine cracker

HOW LONG IT TAKES: A minute

Your saliva contains an enzyme that starts digesting food right in your mouth. Check it out by collecting some of your spit in a glass and dropping a bit of cracker into it. The enzyme, called amylase, goes right to work breaking down starch molecules and turning them into simple sugars.

LOL!
Q: What is the most tired part of your car?
A: The exhaust pipe!

ACIDS, BASES, AND ALKALIS

Acids, bases, and alkalis are in foods, the environment, chemicals—and in our bodies.

Lemonade and grapefruit juice both taste sour for the same reason: They contain lots of acid. An acid is a substance that releases protons (positively charged hydrogen ions) when it's dissolved in water. A base is like an acid in reverse—it picks up protons. As a result, a base can cancel out an acid—a process called neutralization. A base that can dissolve in water is called an alkali. Acids, bases, and alkalis are in foods, the environment, chemicals—and in our bodies. They range from substances strong enough to eat through metal to ones that help create a lemon's taste. Your stomach has superstrong acid. An acid's strength is measured using a system of numbers called the pH scale. It's the measure of the amount of protons in a water solution. This scale ranges from a pH of 1, for very strong acids, to a pH of 14, for very strong alkalis. The middle of the scale, pH 7, is neutral. Litmus paper is specially treated with substances for detecting acids and bases. It turns red in an acidic solution and blue in an alkaline one.

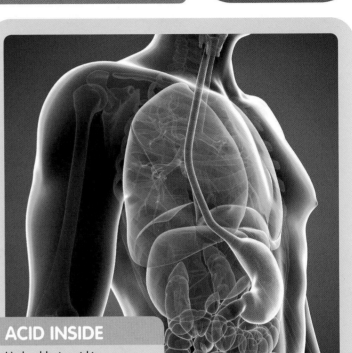

ACID INSIDE

Hydrochloric acid is a very strong acid that can burn human skin. Yet your stomach produces this acid every day. Hydrochloric acid helps break down food during digestion. The stomach is protected from the acid by a layer of mucus. It also produces a base to control, or buffer, the acid. In addition, the cells that line the stomach are replaced as often as every three to five days.

TESTING GROUND

Gardeners and farmers test soil to find out its pH. The pH shows what crops will grow best in that soil. Soil that is too acid or too alkaline may keep plants from absorbing the nutrients they need to thrive. Substances can also be added to soil to make it a better fit for plants. Acidic soil, for example, can be made more alkaline by adding a base like lime. But some plants, such as blueberry bushes, grow best in acidic soil.

NO LYE!

Lye is an extremely strong alkali. Like a strong acid, it can burn skin. Lye is used to make oven cleaners and drain cleaners because it reacts with fats and oils, scouring them off dirty oven walls and breaking up clogs in pipes. It's also used in small amounts in the preparation of foods like corn tortillas, bottled olives, pretzels, bagels, and the traditional Chinese delicacy known as "100-year-old eggs."

WORD CHECK

ALKALINE: Describes a substance that contains an alkali or a solution having a pH greater than 7

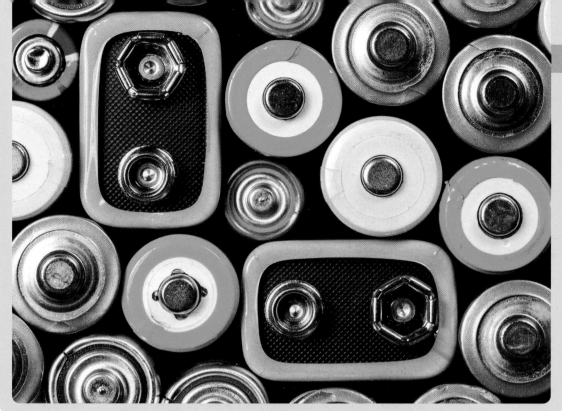

BASE OF POWER

A battery turns the energy in chemicals into electrical energy. Alkaline batteries—the kind used for flashlights and other household items—use an alkali called potassium hydroxide to conduct electricity. A lead-acid car battery, on the other hand, contains sulfuric acid. This acid is very strong, which means it produces a large quantity of hydrogen ions in water. It can burn skin, but it is an excellent conductor of electricity.

PLANT BASICS

Some plants produce chemicals known as alkaloids. People have long used alkaloids as medicines. The thick liquid inside the unopened seed capsules of opium poppies contains the alkaloids morphine and codeine. Both alkaloids are strong pain relievers. Codeine also controls coughing. Today, medicines usually contain manufactured, or synthetic, versions of these alkaloids.

WATER WATCH

Rain is naturally slightly acidic. The acid etches statues and buildings made of marble and limestone. Air pollution makes rain even more acidic. Some hot springs, like those in Yellowstone National Park in the northwestern United States, are strongly acidic (as well as boiling hot), yet one-celled organisms have adapted to live in them.

ACID STING!

The stinging nettle plant protects itself with hairlike spines that inject formic acid. Many ants spray formic acid from their hind ends when attacked. Fire ants, however, use stingers to jab a strong alkaloid called solenopsin into their victims.

TRY THIS!

WHAT YOU NEED: An egg, a cup of vinegar

HOW LONG IT TAKES: 24 hours

An eggshell is made mainly of calcium carbonate, the same material in limestone. Put an egg in a cup filled with vinegar, which has a pH of about 3. Bubbles of carbon dioxide will form as the acid and calcium carbonate react. Leave it for a day, and the entire shell will dissolve.

57

FOOD CHEMISTRY

Food, like other substances, is made up of molecules. The food molecules, known as nutrients, include proteins, carbohydrates, fats, vitamins, and minerals.

Living things need nutrients to survive, but first they must turn complex nutrient molecules into simpler molecules. A complex molecule of protein, for example, is broken down into smaller units called amino acids. This breakdown is carried out by chemical reactions that take place inside an organism. The amino acids become the building blocks the organism uses to create new molecules, which are then used for growth and repair.

Energy is released during the process of breaking down the complex chemicals. The organism uses this energy to carry out its life functions. When you run, jump, read a book, or sing, you're using energy from food to power your activities.

PROTEINS

Proteins are molecules made up of carbon, oxygen, hydrogen, and nitrogen. Some also contain sulfur phosphorus and other metals, such as calcium. Proteins form the bulk of your body's tissues as well as substances that fight diseases, carry out chemical reactions, and transport oxygen in your blood. Your body can make about half of the important amino acids it needs. The rest you get from foods such as meat, eggs, nuts, and beans.

CARBOHYDRATES

Carbohydrates, or "carbs" for short, provide much of the energy your body needs. A carbohydrate consists of sugars, which are substances made out of carbon, hydrogen, and oxygen. A simple carbohydrate is made of just one or two sugar molecules and is quickly absorbed by the body. A complex carbohydrate, or starch, is made of three or more sugar molecules. A cookie has lots of simple carbs, while whole wheat bread contains more complex carbs. Complex carbs take longer for your body to break down, giving your body longer-lasting energy.

GEEK STREAK

If you heat ice, it will melt. If you heat the puddle to boiling, it will turn into a gas. Solid, liquid, gas—water is a substance that we can see changing from phase to phase. Molecules of other nutrients, however, don't easily change phase. They're more likely to form new substances, as when heated sugar grains turn into caramel.

CARBS AND SUGARS

A starch molecule is a complex sugar. It's made of hundreds of simple sugars linked together. Glucose is a simple sugar that's easily absorbed by your body.

STARCH MOLECULE

FATS

Fats are large molecules made of carbon, hydrogen, and oxygen—the same elements carbs contain but connected in different ways. Unlike sugars, fats don't dissolve in water. Like sugars, they provide energy—twice as much as carbs and proteins. A cow's stomach is packed with bacteria and other microbes that digest plant food. They turn it into fats, proteins, and vitamins that the cow's body can absorb and use. Fat stored in your body helps keep you warm and pads your organs in a protective layer. Fat also helps your body absorb certain vitamins. Scientists refer to fats as lipids.

MINERALS

A mineral is a natural substance that doesn't come from a plant or animal. Your body needs minerals including salt, iron, and copper to work properly.

FEEL THE BURN

Food contains chemicals besides nutrients. A chili pepper, for example, contains compounds called capsaicinoids that cause a burning feeling in your mouth when you bite one.

VITAMINS

Vitamins are substances used for different chemical reactions in living things. Vitamin C, for example, is needed for tissue growth and repair. Plants can make all the vitamins they need, but animals vary in their vitamin-making abilities. Many animals can make vitamin C in their bodies. The ones who can't include guinea pigs, many fish, some bats and birds, and all primates—including humans.

Humans can make only vitamins D and K, so we must get the rest of our vitamins from food. Fortunately, we need only small amounts of them for our bodies to work well.

WATER

Water is a molecule made of two hydrogen atoms and one oxygen atom. It doesn't contain any vitamins (unless we add some to it!). But all life, as we know it, depends on water. The chemical reactions that make living things function take place in water. Plants use water to make food. Your body uses water to carry out digestion and other processes. This single nutrient forms about 60 percent of the human body.

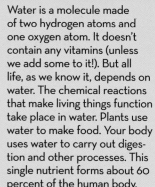

TRY THIS!

WHAT YOU NEED: A brown paper bag, a selection of foods

HOW LONG IT TAKES: 30 minutes

Test foods for fat content with a brown paper lunch bag. Rub a small amount of a food on a section of the bag, or use a spoon to dab it on if it's a liquid food. Let the spot dry. Then hold it up to the light. If light shows through the spot, the food contains fat.

SYNTHETIC MATERIALS

Synthetic materials are made of natural substances that have been changed or blended by people.

What do steel, concrete, glass, and plastic have in common? They are all man-made, or synthetic, materials. A synthetic material combines properties of the materials that formed it. It also has special properties of its own. Humans have transformed natural substances into new materials since ancient times. For thousands of years people have baked clay to make pots and heated and hammered metals to make tools. They've spun fibers into cloth and chipped stones to make weapons. About 6,000 years ago, people in Egypt and neighboring areas mixed the elements copper and tin to make a new substance, bronze. Bronze made stronger, sharper tools than copper alone. In the centuries since then, people have invented many more synthetic materials. These materials range from medicines and fabrics to the plastics used to make everything from toys to car parts.

FABRICS
Check your clothing labels to see if you're wearing man-made materials. Nylon, polyester, acrylic, spandex, and rayon are all examples of synthetic fibers.

METALS AND ALLOYS

Metals such as gold, lead, and iron are natural elements. They can be blended with other metals or with nonmetals to make new materials, called alloys. Steel, for example, is an alloy of iron and carbon. People began making steel about 4,000 years ago after figuring out that adding carbon to iron made iron stronger. By adding other materials, different kinds of steel can be produced for a variety of purposes. Today, steel is used to make everything from spoons to bridges.

PLASTICS

A plastic substance is something that can be molded, stretched, or otherwise formed into a new shape. Modern plastics are made mainly from chemicals found in oil. Plastics can be made so that they're soft and rubbery, or hard and sturdy. Plastics are great for making useful objects that are waterproof and resistant to rotting. But these qualities also make it difficult to get rid of used plastic items. Some kinds of plastic, such as water bottles, can be recycled to make new items. Scientists are working to develop plastic-making plants like switchgrass. Since "bioplastic" would break down easily in soil, it would be less harmful to the environment than oil-based plastics.

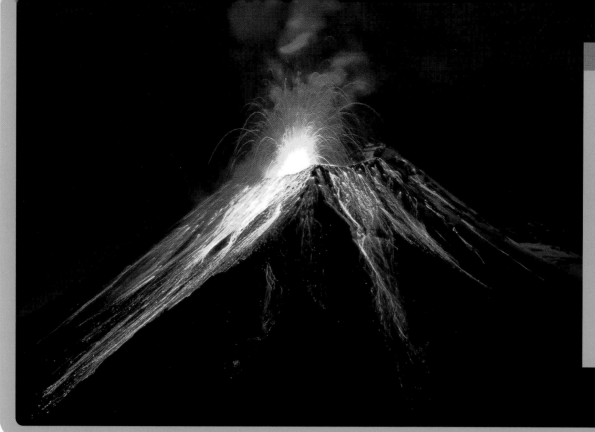

GLASS

Glass forms naturally when certain minerals are heated to very high temperatures and then cooled off quickly. If sand is struck by lightning, it forms a glassy substance. A volcanic eruption spews out hot magma that cools to form volcanic glass. Man-made glass copies this process by melting silica sand. Other substances are added to make glass for specific purposes, such as car windows. Glass reacts with few chemicals, doesn't rot, and is transparent unless it's specially treated to block light. People have made glass for more than 4,000 years.

CERAMICS

Ceramics aren't just bowls made in art class. To a materials scientist, ceramics are hard, brittle substances made by mixing materials and "firing" them under very high temperatures. Ceramics don't conduct heat, so they're very useful as insulators. The tiles on the space shuttle, for example, were ceramics made out of silica strands mixed with other chemicals. They protected the shuttle from the high temperatures of 3000°F (1648°C) created as it raced back into Earth's atmosphere.

COMPOSITES

A composite is a material made up of two or more substances. Concrete is a composite of sand and gravel mixed with water and cement. Cement is a powdery mixture made of lime and other substances. Fiberglass is plastic with glass fibers running through it. The glass adds strength and firmness to the flexible plastic. Fiberglass is so sturdy that it's used to make boat hulls, surfboards, and sports-car bodies. Light but strong bike frames are made from a composite of carbon fibers set in plastic. Some new airplanes have skins made partly from a composite that includes aluminum and glass fibers.

PAPER

Recognize this composite? The Chinese invented it about 2,000 years ago. Paper is made by mixing wood fibers with water. This mushy mixture is then pressed flat and dried on screens.

PERSONALITY PLUS

Stephanie Kwolek (1923–2014) was an American chemist who invented a synthetic fiber called Kevlar. Kevlar is lightweight but five times stronger than steel. It also resists fire. It's used to make bulletproof vests, tires, airplane parts, firefighters' boots, and sports gear such as skis and hockey sticks.

MATERIALS OF THE FUTURE

Materials scientists study the properties and structures of materials. They use this knowledge to create new materials that are designed to fix particular problems or perform certain tasks.

Plastic made from silk and shrimp shells. Ink that conducts electricity. Synthetic fibers that can sense light and sound. Concrete pavement that repairs its own potholes! These amazing inventions are among the new materials developed in recent years by materials scientists. The new materials may do a job better, faster, more cheaply, or more safely than older materials. They may help save energy or use an easy-to-find ingredient instead of one that's rare. An exciting new field for many materials scientists is nanotechnology. "Nano" means "very small." Scientists usually mix substances to make new materials. Nanotechnology lets them invent new materials by rearranging the very atoms and molecules in substances. This tinkering has led to the invention of nanotubes—tiny tubes made of carbon atoms, which can be used to make lightweight fibers that are stronger than steel.

METAL FOAM

Foam is soft and fluffy, right? Not if it's metal foam! Metal foams are metal materials that are jam-packed with air spaces. The air spaces make them lightweight, yet strong enough to absorb a tremendous shock. Metal foams may someday be used to make cars with stronger bumpers that absorb more energy in a crash. Other possible uses include artificial joints, structures to protect buildings during earthquakes, and body armor for soldiers.

SELF-CLEANING CLOTHES

Oops, you spilled juice on your favorite shirt. Someday this slip-up won't leave a stain—if your shirt contains SLIPS. SLIPS is a super-slippery coating that repels water, oil, and other substances. Researchers have used it to coat windows and metals. In experiments with clothing, they found SLIPS worked even if the fabric was twisted and rubbed. Liquid stains just formed tiny balls and rolled off the clothes! This property makes SLIPS useful for medical workers' clothes, tents, and other fabrics that need to repel liquids.

GEEK STREAK

Imagine being able to print bone, cartilage, and muscle on a 3-D printer. Biomedical researchers have designed a printer that can mold tissue into shapes like a tiny baby's ear or a piece of jaw bone—and keep the tissue alive until it is implanted. The bioprinter uses biodegradable plastic and human stem cells to create this amazing tissue.

THE "WONDER MATERIAL"

What's flexible, transparent, 200 times stronger than steel, and a million times thinner than a human hair? It's graphene—a netlike form of carbon that's just one atom thick. That makes graphene the world's first two-dimensional substance. It was discovered in 2004. Graphene conducts electricity better than any other known material. In the future, it may be used to make computer chips, better batteries, and flexible cell phones and touch screens.

SUPER ARMOR

A century ago, soldiers wore metal helmets and body armor made of alloys and strong fabrics. This armor was heavy and made it difficult to move freely. Today, body armor is made of the bulletproof fabric Kevlar and ceramic plates. This armor is stronger, but still heavy. Future soldiers may benefit from a new substance called "liquid armor." Liquid armor hardens to form a strong shell when hit. It can be added to Kevlar to make lighter, more flexible, but super-protective armor. Scientists have also developed material that can change color and texture in response to electrical signals. Soldiers may use it one day to camouflage themselves and their vehicles.

GERM POWER

Wouldn't it be great if viruses produced energy instead of disease? Scientists recently created such a virus. These special viruses are programmed so that they form into a thin film. When a force is applied to the film, proteins in the viruses twist and generate a small electrical charge called piezoelectricity. Someday, this technology could produce electricity using the pushes, pulls, and other motions of everyday life. Shoes, for example, could be fitted with tiny generators to charge a person's phone while walking.

WHAT'S NEW?

NEW SKIN

A synthetic "skin" has been invented in the United Kingdom to help researchers test better ways of decontaminating skin that has been exposed to dangerous chemicals at work or in war.

SOLAR ENERGY

Solar energy is quickly becoming cheaper thanks to a new material that contains the mineral perovskite. It is more efficient than older materials at turning sunlight into electricity.

SEEING SPACE

The new material Vantablack absorbs nearly all light that hits it. Telescopes containing it might "mop up" surplus light, giving scientists a clearer view of space.

MUSHROOM MIRACLE

Researchers are experimenting with making packing supplies, car parts, furniture, and even clothes out of mushroom fibers and plant waste from farms.

PERSONALITY PLUS

On July 13, 2012, chemist Jeannette M. Garcia was mixing chemicals. She wanted to make a strong plastic but she forgot to add one ingredient. Her "mistake" produced a very strong, light plastic that was also easy to recycle. It led to the invention of a new family of polymer materials.

FROM CAVEMEN TO CHEMISTS

Prehistoric people had no idea what a chemical substance was but they used chemistry all the time. The first person to cook over a fire, for example, caused chemical changes to occur inside a piece of food even though he or she didn't know why the food changed. Their discoveries opened the door to a time when humans would not only use chemistry to make things but also try to figure out how and why materials work the way they do.

Fire Starter

Heat can cause chemical reactions. Prehistoric people discovered this when they began using fire. When did this big leap forward first happen? Researchers hoping to answer this question look for clues like patches of reddish dirt or dark marks on rocks that might have been caused by fire in caves and ancient campsites. Evidence found in Israel shows that people used fire at least 400,000 years ago. In 2004, archaeologists also found areas of tightly packed dirt deep in a cave in South Africa. Lab tests showed the dirt contained burned animal bones and ash from leaves and twigs. Other tests showed the materials had been heated to the temperature of a small campfire. The dirt samples dated back about one million years.

Hooray for Clay!

Once prehistoric people had fire, they could bake clay to make pottery. Clay is a kind of soil made up of very tiny particles. It can be molded and left to dry, but a pot made this way isn't waterproof. Baking clay at high temperatures, however, causes chemical changes that harden it. Then it can be used to make bricks, pots, bowls, and other objects. Archaeologists have found pieces of pottery in a cave in China dating back about 20,000 years. In Japan, they've found pottery fragments that are from 13,000 to 18,000 years old.

Ancient Paint

Paint is a mixture of different materials. It's made of a color, or pigment, contained in a liquid substance that helps it spread across a surface, stick to it, and dry in place. Prehistoric people made paints from ground-up dirt, charcoal, and other materials mixed with fatty marrow dug out of mammal bones. One important pigment was red ocher, which was made by crushing rocks of iron oxide into powder. (Rust is a form of iron oxide.) In 2008, researchers found a 100,000-year-old paintmaking "factory" in a cave in South Africa. It was filled with grinding stones and big shells dusted with traces of ocher. This paint may have been used to adorn objects and people's bodies. About 40,000 years ago, people began painting cave walls, too, filling them with thundering herds of horses and bison, waving hands, and mysterious people.

Bubble, Bubble

Have you ever tasted sauerkraut, sourdough bread, or kimchi? These foods get their flavor thanks to a chemical process called fermentation. Fermentation happens when microbes break down sugar molecules in an environment that is free—or nearly free—of oxygen. The end products are chemicals called alcohols. Stone Age people living about 10,000 years ago discovered this process. They fermented grapes to make wine and barley to make beer. Archaeologists have found traces of these liquids on ancient pottery fragments.

Glass in the Past

Silica sand can melt into glass naturally: A bolt of lightning can zap sand into glass, and a volcano will make glassy rocks such as obsidian. Stone Age people used obsidian to make arrows and spear points. In Egypt, archaeologists have found stone beads with glassy coverings that are about 6,000 years old. By 2000 B.C., people in the ancient land of Mesopotamia were making glass objects.

Many Metals

About 9,000 to 11,000 years ago, people in the Stone Age experimented with gold and copper that they found in rocks. They discovered that these soft metals could be heated, hammered, and shaped to make jewelry. By 3000 B.C., people had figured out how to make copper into a stronger material by adding tin. This new alloy was bronze, and its discovery marked the beginning of the Bronze Age in human history. Bronze was used to make everything from pins and coins to swords and axes—and shields like this one.

Iron Power

About 3,200 years ago, people began to replace bronze with iron. Iron is one of the most common metals in Earth's crust—much more common than copper. But early metalworkers had to find a way to separate iron from "iron ore"—the rock containing the iron. Separating metal from ore is called smelting. People learned they could smelt iron by heating the ore in very hot furnaces fueled by charcoal. They pounded the hot lumps of iron to get rid of unwanted materials and then turned them into useful tools and weapons.

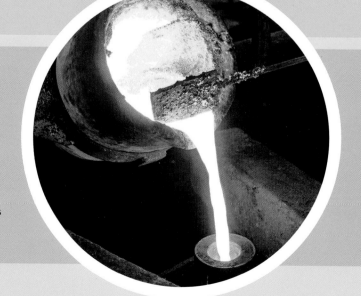

FORCES AND MACHINES

WHAT IS A FORCE? A PUSH OR PULL THAT MAKES SOMETHING HAPPEN.

Everything in our universe moves. It may move fast or slow, or barely at all, but it moves. What makes it all move? An ancient Greek philosopher named Thales asked this very question over 2,000 years ago. And this question was the start of the science called physics. Physics looks for the rules that control the way the universe works. Thales thought that the constant movement in nature was caused by water transforming into different substances and then changing back again. Two thousand years later, British physicist Isaac Newton thought that everything was either at rest or moving until it was pushed, which was mostly right. Today, with added help from scientists like Michael Faraday and Albert Einstein, we have a better understanding of what makes things move: It's called force.

Force can get an object moving, or slow it down, or make it change its movement. These scientists discovered the universe is powered by just four forces: gravity, electromagnetism, the weak force, and the strong force. Electromagnetism is the force that pushes electric currents through wires and makes magnets attract and repel each other.

Gravity is a long-distance force that pulls everything together—keeping you on the ground and holding the moon in orbit around Earth. The strong force is what keeps the nucleus of an atom together. It is very hard to break this force—it happens deep inside the sun and stars, which is what creates their heat and light. While the strong force holds things together, the weak force plays a greater role in things falling apart, or decaying. The weak force is responsible for most of the natural radiation in the universe.

Machines use force to lift, cut, or move objects around. The very first machines were sharp rocks and axes used as cutters by our ancestors two million years ago. Today, of course, our machines are a lot more complicated. There are robot rovers on Mars, solar-powered aircraft that fly for days without fuel, imaging machines that can look inside the human body—and the computers that control them all.

Did you know? Albert Einstein discovered that the force called gravity is caused by big, heavy things bending space. And these big, heavy things can change time. So huge stars and black holes actually make time slow down.

Machines use force to do everything from launching rockets into space to turning the tiny gears of a watch.

MOVEMENT AND MOTION

Every movement of every object in the universe is caused by a force. The way a force makes an object move is governed by a set of rules called the laws of motion.

English scientist Isaac Newton first formulated the laws of motion in 1687. The laws explain how the force from one object will change the way another object is moving. Newton did not fully understand it at the time, but his laws worked only for objects that have mass, the amount of matter in an object. We now understand that beams of light or heat do not have mass, so they do not entirely obey the laws of motion. However, Newton's three simple laws are all that we need to understand the way objects move—from tiny gas atoms bouncing around in a glass jar to giant ships steaming through the ocean. When astronauts started flying into space in the 1960s, Newton's three laws of motion were used to calculate exactly where their high-powered rockets would take them.

FIRST LAW OF MOTION

The first law of motion states that any object at rest will stay at rest, and any object in motion will continue in motion in the same direction and at the same speed until a force pushes it to change the way that it is moving. So, a soccer ball, placed on the field in a game, will stay at rest until it's kicked. Once the soccer ball is kicked, it will move in the same direction and at the same speed until it is kicked by another player. Then it will go in another direction. The first law is talking about a property of matter called inertia. Inertia is the resistance of any object to a change in its motion. You have to apply the second law to change its motion.

SECOND LAW OF MOTION

If you've ever thrown pebbles into a lake, you've practiced the second law of motion. This law tells us that any object, such as a pebble, overcomes its inertia and moves when a force acts on it. How fast it moves depends on its mass and the force. When you throw a small stone, the stone travels farther from shore than when you throw a big rock. The force of both throws is the same, but the little rock has less mass than the big one. As a result, the force makes the small rock speed up, or accelerate, to a higher speed than the bigger one, and so the small rock moves faster and travels farther. To make the big rock travel as far as the small one, you will need a bigger force—a much stronger throw!

TRY THIS!

WHAT YOU NEED: A quarter, a playing card, a glass or heavy cup

HOW LONG IT TAKES: 5 minutes

Remember that inertia is an object's resistance to move. Want to see inertia? Put the playing card on top of the glass, and rest the coin on top of that. Line the coin up so it is in the middle. Now take careful aim, and flick the card with your thumb and finger (the middle one is the strongest). The card will fly away, but the coin, which has inertia, will stay still and then fall into the glass.

LOL!

Teacher: What is Newton's first law of motion?

Student: Bodies in motion stay in motion; bodies at rest stay in bed till their mom gets them up!

THIRD LAW OF MOTION

The third and final law of motion says that every action has an equal and opposite reaction. Putting that another way, an action is the force produced when one object pushes against a second one. According to the third law, the second object will push back on the first with a force that is equal to the action, and the reaction will be in the opposite direction. The third law is what gets everything moving. Imagine two football players about the same weight, doing a chest bump after a goal. When their chests meet, that action will cause an equal reaction that pushes both of them backward.

SPEED OR VELOCITY?

Yes, there is a difference between speed and velocity. Speed is the distance you travel in a particular amount of time: for instance, 55 miles an hour (88 km/h). Velocity is the distance you travel in a certain direction over a certain amount of time: for instance, 55 miles an hour east (88 km/h east). So a turning vehicle may be moving at a constant speed, but not at a constant velocity, because it is no longer going in one direction.

WORD CHECK

ACCELERATION: An increase in velocity. A high acceleration quickly increases the velocity, which is the speed an object is moving in one direction.

ACCELERATION AND DECELERATION

According to the laws of motion every force makes an object accelerate or decelerate. An acceleration is a change of velocity. The engine of a race car produces a huge force that creates a large acceleration—so the car speeds up very fast. The force of the brakes creates a powerful deceleration—so the car slows down again. There are many forces that can make a car accelerate or decelerate. Wind is a force that can push or pull the car, making it go faster or slower. Friction from the resistance of the road is a force that will cause a car to slow down. If you are riding a bike down a steep hill, gravity can cause you to accelerate, or speed up.

PERSONALITY PLUS

Isaac Newton (1642–1727) was an English scientist and mathematician who figured out the laws of motion and discovered how the force of gravity works. Newton experimented with the way light moves, and he invented the kind of telescope that we use to study stars. He was also one of the first to invent and use the math we call calculus. Calculus is the study of how things change. Calculus looks at the rates of change in forces in the physical world to predict the way things can work. For example, the wind does not blow in a straight line; instead, it swirls around us, so it's impossible to measure its motion exactly. Newton's calculus solves this problem by converting the measurements into the tiniest numbers imaginable and putting them all together to create an answer. This works so well that scientists use it every day for many different calculations. Without calculus we wouldn't have computers or spaceships.

GRAVITY

Every piece of matter in the universe produces a force of gravity that pulls on every other piece of matter. That includes a planet, a star, your body, and even a single atom.

Gravity is an attractive force, which means it is always pulling things together. All objects have gravity, but larger objects, such as Earth and the sun, have a lot more gravity than others. It's the sun's gravity that keeps the Earth in orbit around the sun and at just the right distance away to keep our planet warm, but not too warm. Earth's gravity is what keeps us from floating off into space.

There is a popular story that English scientist Isaac Newton was sitting under an apple tree when an apple fell on his head. He realized that a large force from Earth must have been pulling on the apple. Whether Newton was hit by an apple or just struck by an amazing thought, he formulated his universal law of gravity, which explains how the force of gravity works on all objects and over great distances throughout the universe.

WEIGHT

Gravity is what makes things heavy. On the surface of Earth, an object with a large mass also weighs a lot. However, if we went into deep space where there's no gravity, the same object would not weigh anything at all. Weight is the force of gravity pulling an object to the ground. An object with a large mass is pulled down more strongly than an object with a small mass. The gravity on the moon is one-sixth of Earth's gravity. An object weighing 60 pounds (27 kg) on Earth would weigh 10 pounds (4.5 kg) on the moon.

ORBITS

An orbit is a path of one object circling around the other, like the moon orbiting Earth. Why does this happen? Gravity. Sir Isaac Newton saw the moon as an object similar to a ball being thrown on the surface of Earth. When thrown, the ball will curve down because of the pull of Earth's gravity. The moon would do the same except for the fact that it is traveling so fast that the curve of the moon's path matches the curve of the surface of the Earth. The moon's speed is enough to stop it from being pulled down to Earth. And the pull of Earth's gravity keeps the moon from flying off into space. So the moon continues to orbit the Earth, and this Earth-moon system orbits the sun.

UNIVERSAL LAW OF GRAVITY

The universal law of gravity depends on two things: mass and distance. Mass is a measure of how much matter is in an object. More mass equals more gravity. The sun has more mass than the Earth so its gravity is stronger than Earth's. All objects with mass have a gravitational pull. The sun pulls on the Earth, and the Earth pulls on the sun. However, the force of gravity gets weaker the farther away two objects are from each other. Since the distance between the sun and Earth is so great, the strength of the sun's pull on the Earth is just enough to keep the Earth in its orbit. Because we are standing directly on Earth, its gravitational pull is greater on us than the sun's. When we jump into a pool, for example, we are pulled toward Earth instead of out toward the sun.

PERSONALITY PLUS

In 1798, English scientist Henry Cavendish decided to weigh the Earth. Using Newton's law of gravity, which explained that there is a force of gravity that acts between all objects with mass, Cavendish built a machine. It looked like a large set of scales with a light metal ball at each end. Next to each lightweight ball hung a heavier ball. Cavendish measured the gravity of the heavy ball pulling on the lighter one. This measurement told him how gravity was related to mass. He could then calculate how much mass Earth needed in order to produce the gravity that holds us to it. The answer: 13 million billion trillion pounds (5.9 million billion trillion kg) of mass.

TRY THIS!

WHAT YOU NEED: A scale, a pencil, paper, a calculator

HOW LONG IT TAKES: 30 minutes

The sun's gravity is 28 times stronger than Earth's. So, calculate your weight on the sun by multiplying it by 28. Now figure out your weight on other planets by multiplying your weight by these numbers:

Mercury: x 0.38	Mars: x 0.38	Uranus: x 0.89
Venus: x 0.9	Jupiter: x 2.5	Neptune: x 1.1
Moon: x 0.17	Saturn: x 1.1	Pluto: x 0.07

WHY ARE ASTRONAUTS WEIGHTLESS IN SPACE?

When astronauts go into space, we see pictures of them looking like they're floating inside their spacecraft. But they aren't actually floating. The astronauts, their spaceship, and everything else inside the spaceship are all falling. Gravity is pulling them toward Earth. So why don't they hit the ground? Because the Earth is curved and the astronauts and their spaceship are moving so fast that as they fall toward Earth, Earth's surface curves away from them. They orbit the planet in an amazing 90 minutes, always falling toward Earth, but never getting there.

TOOLS OF THE TRADE

Earth is not a smooth globe, and there are large lumps of metals and heavy rocks inside that produce variations in the strength of Earth's gravity. Scientists use a machine called a gravimeter to measure the differences. Gravimeters are used by companies mining for oil and minerals. They are also used to measure the amount of water in cavities under fast-moving glaciers, helping scientists know how quickly a glacier is melting.

TERMINAL VELOCITY

When a skydiver jumps from an airplane, the force of gravity pulls on him and he starts to accelerate toward the ground. As the gravity continues to pull, the skydiver goes faster and faster until he reaches top speed, or terminal velocity. Gravity is not the only force acting on the skydiver. The air is pushing up on him as he falls. It pushes harder as he falls faster, and eventually the pull of gravity is balanced by the push of the air. At that point, the speed of the fall becomes constant depending on how much air there is. The higher you are, the faster you will fall. Below 10,000 feet (3,048 m) that speed is about 120 miles an hour (193 km/h). By opening the parachute, the skydiver helps increase the push of the air even more, so he'll slow down to a safe speed for landing.

When Albert Einstein was born in Germany in 1879, no one knew that he would grow up to be possibly the greatest scientist who ever lived. So what did Einstein do exactly? A lot! He provided the first visual evidence that atoms and molecules exist. He explained how light could work like a stream of particles and also a wave of energy. And he came up with the most well-known scientific equation ever: $E = mc^2$. In addition, he showed how gravity was produced by objects warping, or bending, space. These discoveries are combined in Einstein's general theory of relativity.

Slow Start, Big Finish!

Albert Einstein was always different. He didn't speak until he was four years old, and when he did talk, he repeated phrases over and over again. When he was five, his father gave him a compass to play with while he was sick. Einstein was amazed. No matter how he turned the compass, the needle always pointed north. Thus began his lifelong interest in science and what made things work. Einstein loved learning and reading, but he couldn't stand being forced to sit and study in school. He went to the Polytechnic Institute in Zurich, Switzerland, and got his diploma in 1900, but he always preferred to study the natural laws of physics and mathematics on his own. In 1905, when he was just 26, Einstein made four discoveries, which are listed below. Each one by itself changed the way scientists understood the universe.

Photoelectric Effect

Discovery 1: Einstein proposed that light contains packets of energy that he dubbed light quanta. We now call these photons. Then Einstein used this quantum theory of light to explain the photoelectric effect. When a beam of light is shone on sensitive metals it causes them to give off electrically charged particles called electrons. Einstein showed that the photons in the light beam knock the electrons out of the metal. This discovery was one of the first steps in an area of science called quantum physics.

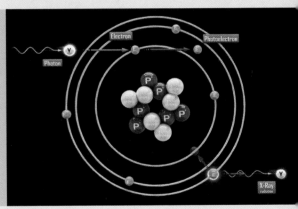

Brownian Motion

Discovery 2: In 1827, a plant expert named Robert Brown reported seeing tiny grains of pollen jiggling around in water under a microscope (left), but he didn't know what was making them move. In 1905, Einstein was able to show that this jiggling motion was caused by the grains of pollen being hit by atoms and molecules in the water. Einstein's explanation of this "Brownian motion" was used to prove atoms and molecules really exist.

Special Theory of Relativity

Discovery 3: In this discovery, called the special theory of relativity, Einstein showed that in order for the speed of light to always stay the same, space and time must change. He knew that when objects move at everyday speeds they obey Newton's laws of motion, which say that an object will keep moving in a certain direction at the same speed until something interferes with it to change its motion. However, when it travels at almost the speed of light, those laws do not work well. Einstein showed why: As the object moves faster, the space around it shrinks, its mass increases, and time even slows down. Nothing made of matter can ever travel as fast as light. If it could, it would weigh more than the whole universe put together and time would stop completely.

Mass Energy

Discovery 4: Einstein explained that matter was a kind of "frozen energy" and you could calculate how much energy it contained using the formula $E = mc^2$. This says that energy (E) is equal to mass (m) multiplied by the speed of light (c) squared (^{2}). The speed of light, at about 186,000 miles (300,000 km) per second, is a very big number. That means even a tiny amount of mass contains a huge amount of energy.

Time Travel

Einstein came up with a theory of what might happen if we could travel at the speed of light (at the moment, our fastest spacecraft goes only one-sixtieth of the speed of light). He called it the "twin paradox." One twin flies off in a superfast rocket; his brother stays on Earth. The space twin flies for a year and then returns to Earth only to discover that his twin has aged more than he has aged. The space twin has traveled into the future. This is because speed affects how time passes. So, if a spaceship flies near the speed of light, time will pass more slowly on the ship relative to the time on Earth.

Space-time Warps

When Einstein added gravity to his special theory of relativity, he explained how it works: A large mass makes space and time (space-time) bend, or warp, the way a trampoline would bend when a heavy mass, such as a large person, bounces on it. Now imagine two masses. A large mass makes space-time warp more than a small mass. The pull of gravity from the large mass creates a space-time warp that the small mass is "falling" into. In 1916, this became his general theory of relativity.

Theory of Everything

Albert Einstein died in 1955. Until the end of his life he tried to find a way of linking his general theory of relativity, which explains how big things in the universe work (such as stars and galaxies) to the theory of quantum physics, which looks at the tiniest of all atomic and subatomic materials (electrons, quarks, and bosons). He failed to find this "theory of everything," and scientists are still searching for it today.

Einstein Wisdoms

"A person who never made a mistake never tried anything new."

"I AM LIKE A CHILD. I ALWAYS ASK THE SIMPLEST QUESTIONS."

"IMAGINATION IS MORE IMPORTANT THAN KNOWLEDGE."

"Learn from yesterday, live for today, hope for tomorrow. The important thing is not to stop questioning."

FRICTION

In nature nothing is completely smooth, and every substance puts up some resistance, or drag, as it gets in the way of another material. This resistance is called friction.

Friction is caused when the rough bumps and dips on the surface of an object catch on the bumps and dips of another object rubbing past it. This slows the motion of both objects and also generates heat. Rub the palms of your hands together as hard as you can. What happens? Do you feel them getting warmer? The friction between your palms has converted the motion of your hands into heat. Friction is used to make fire. It also makes the wheels of a car or truck work. Friction can even wear away a solid surface. The friction of wind and water rubbing over solid rocks gradually erodes them into beautiful shapes. Inside a machine, friction will wear away the moving parts until they eventually break and need to be replaced.

GETTING A GRIP

There are several ways we use friction. It is used to speed up objects and to slow them down. The treads on a car's tire increase the friction between it and the road, which is also made of a rough surface to help the tires get a grip. When it is time for the car to slow down, friction is needed again. The brake on a car grabs the tire, using friction to slow its spin. The grips on the soles of sneakers stop you from slipping when you run. Human feet and hands also create friction because they are hairless. This allows us to hold on to any kind of object.

IT'S A DRAG

Solids with bumpy surfaces aren't the only objects that create friction. Liquids and gases do it as well. Their surfaces may be smooth, but they produce friction in a different way, through an effect called drag. For example, to move through water, a boat's hull has to push the water out of the way. The resistance of the water against the hull causes drag. The size and shape of the hull can help reduce drag. A long, narrow boat with a pointed bow will cut through the water more easily. One of the fastest vessels is the catamaran (above), which floats on two slender hulls with a tunnel-shaped gap in between. The same is true for pushing through air. If you run or bike fast, you are pushing through air and can feel the air's drag against you.

PERSONALITY PLUS

Benjamin Thompson (1753–1814) was an American scientist who developed weapons for the King of Bavaria, in what is now Germany. In return, the king made him a count. He chose the name Count Rumford, for his hometown in New Hampshire. In the 1790s, Count Rumford was the first person to show how friction converts motion into heat. He put a cannonball in a barrel of water and started to grind a hole in the ball with a blunt drill. The friction of the metal drill against the ball made the water heat up, and eventually boil away!

MAKING FIRE

Friction has been keeping us warm since the Stone Age. Early man first converted the energy of motion into the energy of heat. The traditional way of lighting fire was to rub two pieces of hard wood together. People still do this today. It's hard work, but the heat from the friction is enough to set dry grass, bark shavings, and other dry materials on fire.

KEEP IT SMOOTH

To reduce friction, we use lubricants. A lubricant can be made of several different substances, but it is often a gooey liquid that sticks to the surface of a solid and makes it slippery. The thick oil used to grease an engine is a good example. The lubricant forms a barrier between the hard surfaces so they do not rub together. The molecules in the lubricant move around very easily and put up less resistance to any movements. Some solids can be lubricants, too. A nonstick pan (above) is coated in a plastic called polytetrafluoroethylene, which is commonly known as Teflon. This solid is one of the most slippery substances known, and it stops food from sticking to the pan's metal surface.

SPACE FRICTION

Even astronauts have to deal with friction. When it's time to come home to Earth, a spacecraft must fly back into the atmosphere. It is traveling at 25 times the speed of sound. At that speed, the friction of the air against the spacecraft makes the vehicle glow red-hot. A heat shield covering the craft protects the astronauts inside. A similar thing happens when a meteor enters the atmosphere. The friction of the air against the space rock makes it so hot that nearly all of it will burn away into dust. You can see this happening when you spot a shooting star.

TOOLS OF THE TRADE

A lubricant called ferrofluid is a liquid filled with tiny specks of magnetic iron. Ferrofluid is used to lubricate the spinning hard disk inside a computer. The hard disk is where the software is installed, where documents are stored, and it is also used for long-term storage.

PRESSURE

When you push or press on something, the force you apply is called pressure.

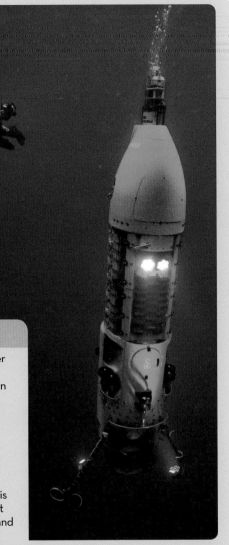

Using a bigger force or applying the same force to a smaller area increases the pressure. For example, when you hammer a sharp nail, it goes into the wood better than a blunt one would because the force of the hammer is being focused into the nail's small, pointed tip. This creates a very high pressure. Liquids, such as water, and gases in our air can produce pressure, too. The way we measure pressure is by dividing the strength of the force by the area it pushes against.

AIR PRESSURE

Air pushes down on us, and on the surface of Earth, all the time. The pressure of air pushing on every square inch of our skin is about the same as the weight of two bricks per square inch (6.5 sq cm). Air pressure is greatest at ground level where there are more air molecules being pulled down by gravity. The higher up you go in Earth's atmosphere, the lighter the pressure is, because the air has fewer molecules.

Air pressure is measured with an instrument called a barometer. It shows us when the air pressure goes up or down and lets us know that the weather is changing. Warmer air has a higher pressure than colder air. When air rushes out from a high-pressure area into low-pressure areas around it, the difference makes winds blow. Weather forecasters measure air pressure to help understand what is happening in the atmosphere and to predict storms.

WATER PRESSURE

Water is heavier than air, so it produces higher pressure. The deeper we dive in a lake or the ocean, the more water we have pressing down on us. If you swam down to 330 feet (100 m) below the surface of the ocean, your body would be squashed by a force 10 times stronger than the air pressure on the beach. The Challenger Deep, which is the deepest point in the ocean floor, is at the bottom of a trench in the Pacific Ocean that is 6.8 miles (11 km) underwater. Down there the pressure is a thousand times higher than at the surface. It would feel like having a different elephant stand on each square inch of your body!

TOOLS OF THE TRADE

In 1656, Otto von Guericke, the mayor of Magdeburg, Germany, showed just how strong air pressure could be. He built two iron half globes, or hemispheres, that fit tightly together into a globe. Then he used a pump to suck out all the air inside the globe. The Magdeburg hemispheres, as they were called, were not locked together, but the pressure of the air on the outside was strong enough to make it impossible to pull them apart. (Remember, there was no pressure inside at all, just a vacuum, or complete absence of air.) To prove this, von Guericke had two teams of eight horses pull on each hemisphere. Even they could not pull them apart. It would have taken more than 4,000 pounds (1,814 kg) of force to break apart the globe.

WORD CHECK

VACUUM: A space where there is no matter at all, including air or other invisible gases

BALANCING PRESSURE

Have your ears ever popped when you were flying in an airplane or driving through mountains? The popping is caused by your ears making sure that the air pressure inside them is the same as the air pressure outside. When mountaineers climb tall mountains, like Mount Everest, the air pressure goes way down because there are less air molecules above them pushing down. With less air, there is less oxygen. In fact, the air is so thin the climbers need to wear oxygen tanks to breathe.

PERSONALITY PLUS

Pressure is sometimes measured in pounds per square inch, but scientists often use a unit of pressure called a pascal (Pa). This unit is named for the French scientist Blaise Pascal, who proved in 1648 that the air around us produces pressure. Pascal made many other contributions to science: He built the first mathematical calculator when he was only 19, and later in life he developed the ideas around probability, or the mathematics of chance.

MAKING DIAMONDS

The highest pressures on Earth are found under its rocky surface, called the crust. Earth's crust can be more than 10 miles (16 km) thick in places. The heavy rock creates a huge pressure. This pressure forms many kinds of rocks, such as slate and sandstone, within the crust. Natural diamonds are formed even deeper down in the Earth's mantle, at about 90 miles (150 km) below the surface, where temperatures are blazing hot, at least 2000°F (1050°C). When the hot rocks that contain carbon and other minerals are squeezed by the Earth's pressure—which is around six million times more than air pressure—beautiful, superhard diamonds can form.

HYDRAULICS

How are a squirt gun and a construction crane alike? They both use hydraulics to work. Hydraulics use pressure to push liquids through pipes. In the squirt gun, squeezing the trigger pushes an air pump that presses the water through the nozzle. In the construction crane, a metal piece called a piston is pushed into one end of a tube filled with liquid. The liquid moves through the tube and pushes on another piston at the other end, making the crane's equipment part move. Hydraulics are used in many things including robot arms, car brakes, faucets, the wheels on planes, and dump trucks.

FORCE AND BALANCE

Objects in nature are rarely pushed or pulled by just one force. It is more common for them to have a lot of forces acting on them all at once—and the size and direction of those forces can change.

Sometimes the different forces pushing and pulling on an object will balance out. Scientists call this equilibrium. No changes occur because the opposing forces are equal and they cancel each other. This doesn't mean an object is staying still. It might be moving up and down like a seesaw or swinging back and forth, like a pendulum on a clock, which is in a constant, balanced rhythm.

MOMENTUM

Momentum is how force is transferred from one mass to another. Something with lots of momentum has the ability to transfer lots of force, such as when a kid on a seesaw makes a big push off the ground. A good example of momentum can be observed in a device called Newton's cradle (above). When a metal ball on one end of the device swings in and strikes the stationary balls, the force is transferred to the ball on the other end. That ball then swings out with equal force and rhythm, then comes back and hits the ball next to it. This momentum continues to transfer back and forth between the balls like a pendulum (below).

BALANCE

A seesaw is a good example of force and balance. It rocks back and forth on a center support. When two children sit on the seesaw and push off from the ground, they exert a force that moves the seesaw up and down. If the children weigh the same, the seesaw will be balanced and rock back and forth in rhythmic motion. If one child weighs more than the other, the heavier child will exert more force, throwing off the balance. The heavier child's end of the seesaw will hit the ground and the lighter child will move upward fast.

PENDULUMS

Pendulums are weights swinging on a string. They all work according to a simple law. If you apply force—by a push or by battery power—to set one swinging, it will oscillate, or move back and forth, in a balanced rhythm. The time it takes to swing back and forth is called the period. The period of a pendulum is set by the length of its string. If no force is keeping it moving, it will eventually slow down. But its balanced rhythm will always be the same.

GEEK STREAK

Zhang Heng was a scientist who lived in China 2,000 years ago. He built a machine that used a pendulum to show when an earthquake was coming (right). Tiny movements of the ground made the pendulum inside the machine swing, and that released a ball from one of several dragonheads around the machine. The ball fell into a frog's mouth beneath, showing which direction the earthquake came from.

SIMPLE HARMONIC MOTION

When one force plucks a guitar string, it swings back and forth in a balanced motion. A guitar string oscillates in the same way, but much, much faster. When you apply force by strumming a guitar string, you pull it away from its center. Then it acts like a pendulum, quickly swinging back and forth in equal distance from its center, until it loses momentum and stops.

WORD CHECK
MOMENTUM: The force or strength an object has when it is moving

TRY THIS!

WHAT YOU NEED: A string, scissors, a small weight (such as a padlock or a key), a bar that is sturdy, a watch

HOW LONG IT TAKES: 15 minutes

Want to make a pendulum? Cut a piece of string that is exactly 10 inches (25 cm) long. You will need a small weight—something easy to tie to a string. Tie the other end of the string to a sturdy object or bar so it dangles at least two feet (60 cm) off the ground with plenty of room for it to swing. Because of the length of the string, each back and forth swing of this pendulum takes one second. Set it swinging (gently) and check it with a watch.

FORCES AND DIRECTION

When one force plucked a guitar string, it swung back and forth in a balanced motion. But what happens to the balance when more than one force pushes on an object? To figure it out, you have to add and subtract forces. Imagine a boat on a river. Its motor is the force pushing it forward. The river's force is a stronger current. When the boat is traveling in the same direction as the current, you add the force of the water pushing the boat to the force of the motor. The boat goes forward at a fast rate. When the boat moves against the stronger current, you subtract the motor's force from the current's force. That current slows the boat and pushes it backward. If the current's force is the same as the motor's force, the boat will stand still, in a balanced state that equals zero, until you rev up the motor to overcome the current and move it forward. Then you subtract the current's force from the motor's force.

PERSONALITY PLUS

The Italian scientist Galileo Galilei was the first person to notice that pendulums always swing with a fixed rhythm. In 1602, while attending a church service in Italy's Pisa Cathedral, Galileo watched a large lamp covered in candles swinging on a rope from the ceiling. Galileo timed each swing with the beat of his pulse and found that the time was always the same. This led Galileo to determine that the time it took for the lamp to swing back and forth was directly related to the length of the rope that held it to the ceiling. The Italian cathedral still has that lamp inside, and today it is named for Galileo.

MOVING IN CIRCLES

It is possible to move without going anywhere. How? By spinning around on the spot. The way objects, such as a top or a carousel, spin or move in circles is called rotational motion.

Rotational motion is different than motion that makes an object move from one place to another. With rotational motion, many objects spin in a circular motion. Our planet is spinning right now. All rotating objects move around an axis—an imaginary straight line that runs through the center of the object. If you are standing on the North or South Pole, you are standing at either end of Earth's axis. This invisible line runs between the poles through the center of Earth. If you are standing on the Equator you are rotating around the Earth's axis at more than 1,000 miles an hour (1,600 km/h). That's as fast as a fighter jet. You don't feel like you are moving because the ground and air are all moving at the same speed.

CENTRIPETAL FORCE

The force that makes things move in circles is called centripetal, or center-seeking, force. This pull toward the center keeps an object on its circular path. For example, when you are spinning on a swing carousel, centripetal force, produced by the strong chains holding your seat to the ride, pulls you toward the center of the carousel. The carousel goes faster and your seat swings out to the side. Why? Newton's first law of motion, inertia, is at work. This law says a moving object will keep moving in a straight line and at the same velocity unless something interferes with it. So as the carousel spins, it feels like you are being pushed outward by inertia, but centripetal force is actually pulling you inward. This combination makes your seat swing up and out from the center, creating a thrilling ride!

TALKING TORQUE

A force that causes rotational motion has a special name: torque. Torque works in exactly the same way as the force that makes a seesaw rock up and down. A force that is applied farther from the axis, or central turning point, creates a bigger torque than the same force being applied nearer to the axis. Think about a pair of wrenches, one with a long handle, the other short. You need to loosen a tight bolt by rotating it. The bolt is on the turning point, or axis. The long wrench creates a bigger torque than the short one because it allows you to apply force farther from the bolt, or axis. That is why it is easier to loosen a tight bolt with a long wrench.

GEEK STREAK

Earth is not a perfect sphere, or globe. The inertia of air and the high-speed spin of the Earth push some of the surface out in a bulge. Scientists figured this out in the 17th century, but they could not agree where the bulge would be. The Frenchman René Descartes said Earth was shaped like a lemon with the bulge pushing out at both poles. Englishman Isaac Newton said the planet was like an orange: flat at the top and bulging around the Equator. The only way to check was to measure the shape of Earth. Some scientists went to Lapland to measure Earth's curve near the North Pole. Others went to Ecuador to measure the curve at the Equator. They found that Newton was right: Earth bulges in the middle.

KEEPING LEVEL

Have you ever wondered why a top falls over when it is not moving but stays upright when it is spinning? This is because of momentum. A spinning object has momentum just like any other moving object. But it has to keep up that rotational momentum, spinning around its axis in order to stay in a certain position. If another force makes it slow down, its position may change. In the case of the spinning top, friction from the ground it's spinning on and the air around it causes it to slow down. It loses momentum, and falls over.

TRY THIS!

WHAT YOU NEED: A bucket with a strong handle, water, an open area outside

HOW LONG IT TAKES: 10 minutes

You might think if you spin a bucket of water around in a circle that you'll get wet. Try this to find out. Fill the bucket halfway with water and take it outside away from people. Hold the bucket by the handle out to your side and spin your arm in a circle, up to the sky and back toward the ground. Spin it fast. You might feel like the bucket of water wants to fly in a straight line away from you. That's inertia, which is Newton's first law of motion. Luckily, centripetal force is pulling the bucket toward the center and keeping it spinning. This push and pull is what keeps the water in the bucket.

IN A SPIN

Figure skaters use momentum to create fast spins. Imagine an axis running through the center of the skater's body, from the top of her head to her toes. To go into a spin, she turns slowly with her arms stretched out, building momentum. Then she pulls her arms in tight, and the spin gets faster, which keeps up momentum. This is because the skater's mass is now closer to the axis.

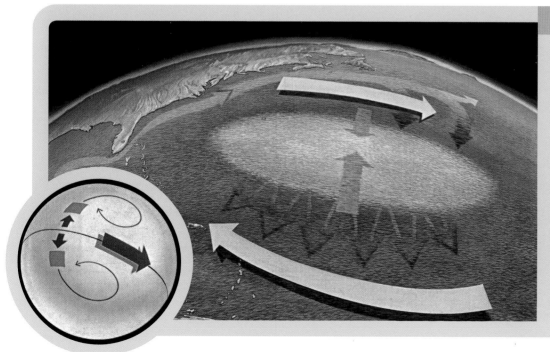

CORIOLIS EFFECT

Living on a planet that spins causes a unique effect when you move from one place on Earth to another: Your straight path becomes curved. It is called the Coriolis effect and can be seen in the flow of the wind or the flight path of an aircraft. Imagine a plane takes off in Florida, U.S.A., and is supposed to fly in a straight line north to Georgia, U.S.A. If the plane has no navigational equipment, the Coriolis effect will cause its path to curve and swing east over the Atlantic Ocean. This is because the planet is spinning. When the plane takes off, it is moving north in a straight line, but it is also moving east along with the whole planet. The Coriolis effect also causes all of those swirling masses of clouds and storms that you see in satellite photos of the Earth. It makes hurricanes and other wind systems spin around as they move over the surface of our spinning planet.

WIND AND WATER POWER

The two main natural sources of motion come from the flow of water through Earth's ocean and rivers, and the rush of winds that blow across the planet. Scientists are using these sources to make electricity.

Gravity, coming from the moon and the sun, lifts the ocean's water over coastlines twice a day and then pulls it back again. Earth's gravity is also pulling the water in rivers and streams down through valleys and over waterfalls until it reaches the sea.

Winds are caused by the air being spread unevenly over the planet. The sun heats some of the air, making it bunch together in areas of high pressure. The air then spreads out into areas with lower pressure. That spreading out is what creates the flow of wind. Finally, wind blowing over the ocean causes ripples on the surface of the water. These build into the mighty waves that crash against the shore. We've been harnessing these natural motions for centuries, and today we rely on them more and more as a source of clean, pollution-free energy.

SAILING AWAY

The first wind-powered machines were sailboats. The earliest sails date from more than 8,000 years ago, and we still use them today. A sail moves a ship by catching the wind. Wind pushes on the back of the sail, transferring some of the wind's momentum to the sail and the boat, moving the craft forward. Expert sailors learn to position sails at different angles to capture the right amount of wind for speed and direction. The fastest sail-powered boats can travel more than 60 miles an hour (100 km/h), which is faster than most engine-powered vessels.

WINDMILLS

Sails are not just used at sea. Simple windmills use sails arranged around a wheel to catch the wind. The force of the wind makes the wheel spin. This spinning motion was originally used to turn heavy stone wheels inside windmills that ground grain into flour. A modern windmill, or wind turbine, uses the spinning motion to generate electricity. The turbine's blades are not cloth sails but solid, wing-shaped fins, often made of aluminum. They convert the smooth motion of the wind flowing over them into a sideways spinning motion that produces electricity.

LOL!

Q: What did the wind turbine say to the solar panel?

A: I'm a big fan.

BLOCKING A RIVER

Rivers have long been used as a source of power. Ancient Greeks invented waterwheels to use in rivers 2,200 years ago. Large wheels with blades or scoops all around them were pushed by the flow of the river water, making the wheel spin. Modern waterwheels are inside hydroelectric dams. The term "hydroelectric" means converting water power into electricity. The dam is a sturdy concrete barrier that blocks the normal flow of a river. A deep lake builds up behind the dam, and its water is then channeled through fanlike waterwheels built deep inside the dam. These waterwheels help to power 10 percent of the world's electricity.

WAVE ENERGY

Ocean waves can be huge. Some are 60 feet (18 m) tall, about the height of a six-story building. These waves roll up and down across the surface of the deep ocean. Wave power plants float on the surface and rise up and down as the waves roll by. The energy of this up-and-down motion is then harnessed to drive electrical generators. Wave power plants need to be in deep water because the breaking waves in shallow water are not good for generating power. Making power from waves is a challenge. The waves often change direction or can become so large they wash away the whole power plant.

WORD CHECK

TURBINE: A fanlike machine that is built to turn a forward flow of air, steam, or water into a spinning motion. The spinning motion generates electricity.

TIDAL ENERGY

Tides are the rise and fall of sea levels caused by the combined gravitational forces from the moon, the sun, and the rotation of the Earth. Wind and waves come and go, but the tides rise and fall every day, making them a more reliable source of power. There are only a few tidal power plants that exist right now. They are testing out different ways to harness the inward and outward flow of water. One approach is a dam across the mouth of a river. As the tide comes in, the water rushes through windmill-like electricity turbines (above) in the dam. As the tide goes out, the same thing happens, but in the other direction. A second approach is the tidal lagoon, in which a big tank on the seafloor fills up when the tide comes in, and empties as it goes out, generating electricity.

GEEK STREAK

THE LARGEST WIND AND WATER SOURCES IN THE WORLD:
The largest wind farm: Roscoe, Texas. It has 634 wind turbines.
The largest dam: Three Gorges Dam, Yangtze River, China. Produces 10 times the electricity of the Hoover Dam.
The largest tidal power station: Sihwa Lake, South Korea
The largest wave farm: Aguçadoura, Portugal

FLOATING, SINKING, FLYING

Have you ever wondered how a steel ship the size of a stadium can float, or how 500 people can sit inside a superjumbo jet and fly in the air? Science can explain it all.

Both the ship and the airplane have weight. In other words, they are being pulled on by Earth's gravity. However, there is another force pushing on the vessels in the opposite direction. In the case of the ship, it is called the buoyant force. When the buoyant force equals the force of gravity, an object floats. When it doesn't, the object sinks. In the case of the airplane, an upward force called lift opposes the downward gravity. Buoyancy and lift are produced in different ways, but these are the forces that allow us to travel to the edge of the atmosphere and to the depths of the ocean and make it back home again.

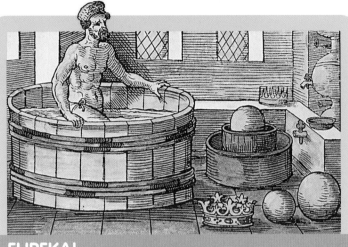

EUREKA!

An object's ability to float, or to be buoyant, depends on how dense it is. Dense objects sink; less dense objects float. Archimedes, a Greek mathematician, discovered density about 2,200 years ago. One day he sat down in his bathtub, and water was pushed out to make room for his body. Archimedes realized that the volume of the spilled water was equal to the volume of his body. He used this process, now called the "Archimedes' principle," to calculate the density of an object. Density is a measure of how much mass is packed inside a certain volume. Archimedes realized he could use his spilled water trick to measure the volume of objects of any shape and so calculate their densities. He was so excited that he jumped out of the bath and shouted "Eureka!" meaning "I've found it!"

FLOATING

The Archimedes' principle helps us determine if an object will float or sink. If the weight of the water that is pushed aside, or displaced, is less than the weight of the object, then that object will sink. However, if the object weighs less than the water it displaces, it will float. This is because the water and the object are battling for space, trying to push each other out of the way. The push of the water is the buoyant force, and if it is stronger than the gravitational force, the water wins the fight and pushes the object up to the surface. This explains how a giant ship can float. The ship pushes away a vast amount of water, but the weight of the ship—which includes its steel hull with air trapped inside—is still less than the weight of the displaced water.

GO DEEP!

A submarine is a boat that can change its buoyancy, making it capable of floating and sinking. It does this by changing its weight. At the surface, the submarine's weight is less than the weight of the water it displaces, so it floats. When it's time to dive, tanks inside the sub are flooded with seawater. That makes the boat slightly heavier than the water, so it sinks slowly down. When the sub is deep enough, the crew pumps some of the water out until the weight of the sub matches the weight of the water it displaces. The sub stops sinking and floats under the water. To get back to the surface, the tanks are pumped dry, so the sub's weight goes back to being less than the water, and it rises back to the surface.

FULL OF HOT AIR

Archimedes' principle doesn't work just for floating and sinking; it also works for flying. In 1783, the French Montgolfier brothers made a hot-air balloon of paper and silk, and it rose into the air, powered by heat from a roaring fire. Today's hot-air balloons use propane gas burners, but they work in the same way because of Archimedes' principle. Heating the air inside the balloon makes the air expand, so the balloon is filled with fewer molecules of gas and the air is less dense. The weight of the cold air displaced by the balloon on the outside is greater than the weight of the heated air inside the balloon, and so the balloon rises. A balloon or airship filled with a lightweight gas, such as helium, will do the same thing.

LIFT!

Airplanes fly in a different way than hot-air balloons do. They are heavier than the air, but their wings make a lift force that pushes them into the sky. The lift is produced thanks to the angle and shape of the wing, which is curved on top but flat underneath. At takeoff, thrust from the plane's engine powers it down the runway, going faster and faster. The air passing under the wing is pushed down and slowed by the angle of the wing. In response, the air pushes the wing up, creating lift—and also making drag. The engines overpower this drag force to keep the plane going forward, and the relative density of the air on top of the wing produces even more lift. This upper stream of air is pulled up and over the curved wing, and that makes the air flow up and spread out. The result is the air above the wing has a lower pressure and pushes down less strongly than the air below pushes up. Takeoff!

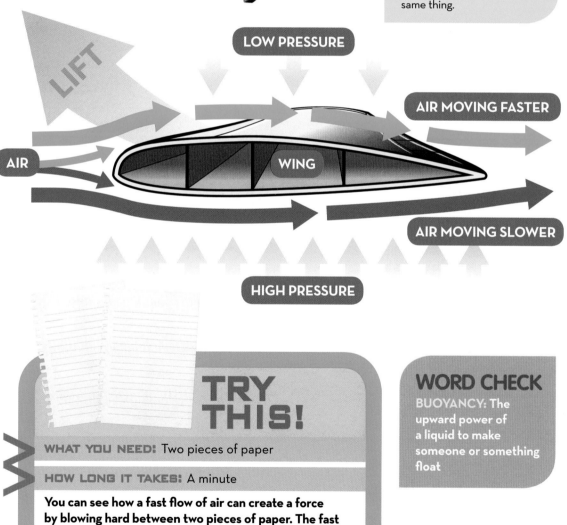

LIFT

LOW PRESSURE

AIR MOVING FASTER

AIR

WING

AIR MOVING SLOWER

HIGH PRESSURE

TRY THIS!

WHAT YOU NEED: Two pieces of paper

HOW LONG IT TAKES: A minute

You can see how a fast flow of air can create a force by blowing hard between two pieces of paper. The fast air between the papers has a lower pressure than the air above and below them, and so the paper sheets are squeezed together. (Be sure to hold the papers between your palms on the sides, and make a gap to blow through.)

WORD CHECK

BUOYANCY: The upward power of a liquid to make someone or something float

AMAZING SCIENCE! MILESTONES

SUPERSONIC!

Aircraft fly because of the way air rushes around the wings. The air has to be moving fast over the wings to make the lift force that pushes the aircraft up. The first fixed-wing airplane, created by the Wright brothers, had a top speed of just 30 miles an hour (48 km/h). That was enough for a short, low flight. To go higher and farther, airplanes needed to fly much faster. We measure the speed of fast aircraft compared to the speed of sound, which is a wave traveling through the air. Depending on the altitude and density of the air, sound waves travel at a speed of about 786 miles an hour (1,236 km/h). For an aircraft to be supersonic, it has to fly faster than the speed of sound, breaking the sound barrier.

THE SOUND BARRIER

All objects moving through air make sound. The sound is made of ripples of pressure that spread out from the object in all directions, traveling at the speed of sound. The ripples moving in front of this supersonic jet are bunched more tightly together because the jet keeps catching up with them. When the jet's speed matches the speed of the sound waves, the ripples pile up together into a shock wave. This shock wave is called the sound barrier. To go faster than sound, the jet must punch through this barrier. This makes the shock wave form into a cone that surrounds the jet. When the supersonic jet flies overhead, the shock wave cone reaches down to the ground, and we hear all of that compressed sound as a loud, cracking explosion, known as a sonic boom. Check out some of the other ways we have broken the sound barrier over time.

Prehistory

We have been listening to sonic booms throughout our history. A clap of thunder is a sonic boom created by a bolt of lightning. The flash of electricity is so hot that it makes the air swell up faster than the speed of sound—and that creates the booming sound of thunder.

1600s

The first human-made objects to break the sound barrier are bullets fired from rifles. Rifles are muskets that have had their barrels "rifled." Rifling is the process of cutting spiral grooves inside the barrel, causing the ball or bullet to spin as it flies out. That makes it travel straight and fast—so fast that it breaks the sound barrier. This is what causes the loud crack of gunfire.

1887

Ernst Mach takes a photograph of a rifle bullet breaking the sound barrier. In the picture you can see the shock wave of air around the bullet. The speed of sound is called Mach 1, in the German scientist's honor.

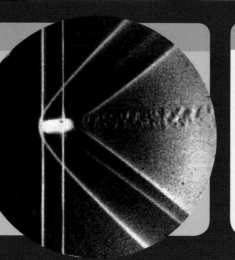

1944

The first flying machine to break the sound barrier is the V-2 rocket. This is a flying bomb built by Nazi Germany. It carries no crew but is capable of reaching Mach 3, or three times the speed of sound, as it flies to its target. The V-2 rocket is also the first human-made object to reach space.

1947

U.S. Air Force test pilot Chuck Yeager is the first person to fly faster than sound. He makes his history-making flight in a Bell X-1 aircraft that he names *Glamorous Glennis*, after his wife. It's built in the shape of a bullet to help it punch through the sound barrier and is powered by rocket engines. Yeager's flight is very dangerous—no one knows if he'll be able to control his plane after it goes supersonic. Thanks to this flying ace we know controlled speeds above Mach 1 are possible.

1961

The X-15 rocket plane reaches a speed of Mach 6, which is six times the speed of sound! It zooms to the edge of space, 50 miles (80 km) above the ground. X-15 pilots have to wear space suits and are known as astronauts. One of the fastest pilots is Neil Armstrong, who will go on to be the first man to walk on the moon.

1976

Concorde, the first supersonic passenger jet co-created by Britain and France, begins flying customers across the Atlantic. It can fly faster than Mach 2 and makes the journey from London to New York in three hours. With the five-hour time difference, passengers leave London at 12 noon and arrive in New York at 10 a.m., two hours earlier! (Concorde goes out of service in 2003.)

1997

English fighter pilot Andy Green takes the controls of Thrust SSC, the world's only supersonic car. The car is powered by two jet engines. It breaks the sound barrier on a high-speed drive across the Black Rock Desert in Nevada, U.S.A.

2001

The X-43A Hyper-X plane becomes the fastest aircraft ever as it reaches 7,000 miles an hour (11,000 km/h), which is higher than Mach 9.

2012

Austrian skydiver Felix Baumgartner jumps from a balloon that is 24 miles (39 km) above the ground. As he dives toward the ground, he reaches a speed of 843 miles an hour (1,358 km/h), or Mach 1.25. This daredevil is the only person to break the sound barrier without using an engine.

SIMPLE MACHINES

A machine is a device that can change the position or shape of an object. A machine might lift an object, move it, or cut it—or it might do all of these things.

A machine can be simple like a crowbar, or complex like a crop harvester or a car engine. Even the most complicated machines are really a number of simple machines that have been assembled to work together. Scientists have found that any type of machine can be built from just a handful of simple devices. Some are so simple you may not realize that they are even machines. For example, scissors, wheelbarrows, and hammers are all simple machines. So is a ramp.

A machine works by receiving a force that comes from outside the machine. The machine then alters the force in some way, either changing the direction in which the force is acting, or changing the size of the force. This altered force is then applied to the object by the machine.

THE LEVER

Perhaps the simplest machine is the lever. All it takes to make a lever is a strong stick and a fulcrum to rest it on. The fulcrum is the point where the lever goes up and down. The most basic lever will magnify a small force applied at one end into a bigger force at the other. For instance, applying force to the grip of a hammer allows a bigger force at the hammer's claw to remove the nail. A seesaw is a lever, too. The fulcrum is the middle block it rests upon. The riders take turns applying force to one end and sending the rider at the other end into the air with a bigger force.

THE RAMP

A skateboarder uses a ramp to catch some air. This ramp, or inclined plane, is another simple machine. It takes less effort to move a heavy object up a ramp over a longer distance than to lift it straight up. You simply use a series of small forces to move the object, or load, up the ramp by giving it several pushes instead of using one big force to lift the load to the same height at once. A staircase is a special kind of inclined plane that allows you to climb up in small, easy steps.

GEEK STREAK

Some 2,200 years ago in Italy, Archimedes invented many different simple machines. To help during wartime, he created a crane with an iron claw that could lift attacking enemy ships partially out of the water and then drop or capsize them. About the lifting power of levers he said: "Give me a place to stand, and a lever long enough, and I will move the world."

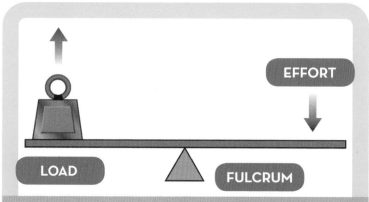

EFFORT AND LOAD

All simple machines, such as this lever, change one force, known as the effort, into another one called the load. The effort end is the end you use to operate the lever. The load end does the actual work. Effort is just a specific type of pressure and load is just a type of weight. A lever transforms a small effort into a bigger load to lift heavy objects.

TRY THIS!

WHAT YOU NEED: A book, a ruler, a block of wood

HOW LONG IT TAKES: 5 minutes

You can investigate the power of levers yourself with a long wooden or plastic ruler. You will also need something for the fulcrum—a small block of wood is good. Rest the ruler on the block and put a heavy book (the load) on one end. Can you lift the book with the effort end of the lever? Try moving the fulcrum to a different position. Does that make the lever easier or harder to use?

TOOLS OF THE TRADE

The stone blocks used to build the ancient Egyptian pyramids were cut using wedges made of wood. The ancient stone workers would chisel a hole in the rock and bang in a dry wooden wedge. They then poured water onto the wedge, which made it swell up. The swollen wedge got too big for its hole and pushed on the stone for more space—and cracked it in two.

THE SCREW

Even a screw is a simple machine. The spiral thread running around it is really an inclined plane, or ramp, twisting around the screw. When it is turned, the screw's thread converts that twisting force into a straight-line force. That straight-line force is what pulls a wood screw into a plank. A screw also allows a drill to cut a hole, and can hold a screw bottle cap in place.

THE WEDGE

A wedge is a simple machine used for cutting. Chisels, knives, and axes are all wedges. The wedge has a thick end and a thin end, which is used for cutting. A force that is applied to the thick end is transferred to the thin end and then focused into the sharp edge. All that focused force is enough to cut through materials. Hand axes were the first machines fashioned by our ancestors more than two million years ago. They were simple stone wedges used for cutting.

COMPLEX MACHINES

What's the most important complex machine in history? There are lots to choose from: cars, jet engines, electrical generators, or perhaps the computer. These are all machines that have changed the way we live. But they all make use of the earliest complex machine: the wheel.

No one really knows when the wheel was invented. But 5,000 years ago, people in the Middle East were using potters' wheels to make clay bowls and cups. They were also building the first wheeled wooden carts. Wheels were soon being used in other ways, such as making a winch to haul water up from deep wells. A winch is a wheel-like instrument with a rope tied to it. Turning the winch allows the rope to coil or uncoil. The winch led to the invention of the pulley, one of the most amazing machines ever made because it can multiply the strength of one person into the strength of many.

GETTING AN ADVANTAGE

The pulley is a complex machine that uses a stationary wheel (one that stays in place), with a rope looped around it. A pulley like this does only one thing: It changes the direction of a force. When you pull the rope down, the rope loops around the wheel and pulls the load up the same distance. A pulley will take the same force exerted to lift the weight as the weight exerts on the rope. Add more wheels to the pulley, and you multiply the effort into a bigger load force, but you cannot lift it as high. This is called mechanical advantage.

HOW A WHEEL WORKS

For a wheel to work properly it must be connected to an axle. This is a rod connected to the wheel's center. The wheel spins around this axle. On a car, the two front wheels are connected through their centers by an axle. So are the back two wheels. The engine turns the axles, which spins the wheels. The tires grip the road as they spin, moving the car forward. Larger wheels take more energy from the engine to move, but they exert a larger force on the ground moving the car forward.

TOOLS OF THE TRADE

Instead of wings, a helicopter is a complex machine that has a series of rotors arranged in a wheel to produce its lift. Each rotor is shaped like an airplane wing. While an airplane must race down a runway to make the air rush over the wings to produce lift, a helicopter achieves the same result by spinning its rotors. So it has lift without moving forward. That's why it can go straight up on takeoff—and hover in the air!

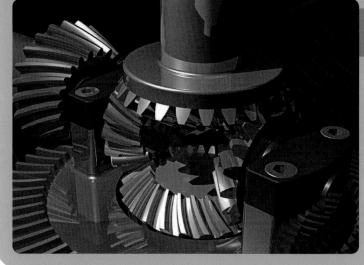

PUTTING IT ALL TOGETHER

Many complex machines, such as clocks (top right), robot arms, and computer disk drives use some combination of wheels, pulleys, and gears (left). But the construction crane (top left) uses them all. It has a complex pulley and a winch that can lift huge weights. The pulley rolls backward and forward along the crane's arm, using wheels on rails. And gears allow the whole crane to rotate on a turntable, which is another wheel, moving the load wherever it's needed.

LOL! 😄

Q: What's big and scary and has three wheels?

A: A monster riding a tricycle.

GEARS

A gear is a complex machine that is a wheel with gaps, or teeth, that interlock with the teeth of another gear. Gears are used to transfer torque (see page 80) from one part of a machine to another. As you peddle a bike, that peddling power is transferred to the back wheel of the bike with the help of the toothed chain (a type of gear), and the bike rolls forward. You can use gears to do two things: increase speed (helping you go faster) or increase force (helping you bike up a hill). When you change gears on your bike to go uphill you are using mechanical advantage.

ENGINES

LOL! 😄

Q: How did the rocket lose its job?

A: It was fired.

A complex machine that changes energy, such as heat from burning gasoline, into mechanical motion is called an engine.

For many years, what we could lift or move, and how fast we could go, was limited by muscle power and the use of simple machines. Engines changed that. An engine is a complex machine with wheels, levers, and gears, but it also has its own source of power. The power comes from a fuel, usually a substance that burns easily, like gasoline or coal. The engine takes the heat from this burning fuel and converts it into a source of motion. All types of engines do this, but in different ways.

CAR ENGINE

A car engine is a type of internal combustion engine. The heat source is inside a set of cylinders. Gasoline is mixed with air and then made to explode with a spark of electricity from the spark plug. The little explosion produces a mixture of hot gases, which expand inside the cylinder, forcing the piston down. As the pistons fire in sequence, they turn the crankshaft, which carries the power to the wheels.

STEAM ENGINE

Over a century ago the engines that powered railroad trains and boats were steam engines. Heat from a furnace boiled water in a tank, making very hot, high-pressure steam. The steam pushed into a chamber called a cylinder and forced a piston inside the cylinder to slide backward. Then the steam was redirected to the other end of the cylinder, pushing the piston back the other way. This back-and-forth motion made the engine's wheels rotate, using a lever system called a crank. Locomotives powered by steam were the fastest vehicles in the world until the early 1900s.

JET ENGINE

A jet engine is an internal combustion engine like a car engine, but it has no pistons or cylinders. Air sucked into the front of the engine is compressed, sprayed with fuel, and then set alight with an electric spark. The resulting explosion creates hot, expanding gas, which blasts out the rear of the engine—and the aircraft moves forward.

AMAZING ENGINES!

STEAM ENGINE

The world's most powerful steam engine was the River Don Engine, located in Sheffield, England. It had the power of 12,000 horses. It was built in 1905 and was used to power a steel mill until 1970.

JET ENGINE

The largest single jet engine is the General Electric GE90. It's so big a person can easily stand inside of it. Two GE90s are used to power the Boeing 777, at just under the speed of sound, for 6,000 miles (9,700 km). That is roughly the distance from Los Angeles, California, to Warsaw, Poland.

INTERNAL COMBUSTION ENGINE

The Wärtsilä RT-Flex96C is a diesel engine that powers giant container ships. It is the size of a large house, weighs as much as 300 elephants, and is as powerful as 107,000 horses.

ROCKET

Saturn V, the rocket that carried Apollo astronauts to the moon between 1969 and 1972, is still the most powerful rocket ever built—and it is the largest engine of all time. At liftoff it produced 66 times more thrust than the GE90 jet engine. The amount of power the rocket produced could power all the lights in New York City for 75 minutes.

ROCKET POWER

A rocket engine has no moving parts. Instead it has a combustion chamber where two fuels react when a spark is added. Hot gas is shot out of the rocket through an exhaust nozzle at its base, and that's what pushes the rocket upward. Because rockets don't need air to burn their fuel, a rocket keeps working when it leaves the atmosphere. No air-fed engine could work in outer space.

WORD CHECK

COMBUSTION: Another word for burning. Most combustion is a reaction between a fuel and the oxygen in the air.

PERSONALITY PLUS

The first engine was invented 2,000 years ago in Egypt by the mathematician and engineer Heron of Alexandria. His steam-powered machine was the aeolipile, which translates to "the ball of Aeolus," the Greek god of air and wind. The device had a boiler in its base, which supplied a flow of steam to a hollow sphere at the top. The sphere had two curved nozzles on either side, each facing in opposite directions. Jets of steam blasted out of the nozzles, making the sphere spin around. Heron showed his invention to his friends but never used it to power anything.

MARVELS OF ENGINEERING

Understanding the way forces work has allowed us to build some amazing structures. Early builders used natural materials such as stone, wood, and earth. Today's megastructures are made of tougher human-made materials, such as concrete and steel.

Bricks are blocks of baked clay, while concrete is a mixture of sand, water, and a powder called cement. When concrete dries in the air, the cement glues the sand together to create a rock-hard solid. Because it starts out as a gooey liquid, concrete can be molded into any shape before it sets. Brick and concrete can hold very heavy weight, but builders use steel, a stronger and more flexible alloy, for larger structures. Steel is mostly iron with small amounts of carbon and other substances mixed into it. Those additions make the metal super strong. It will bend but not break, and that gives large structures, such as bridges and skyscrapers, the strength they need to bear heavy weight.

DOME HOME

In the 1940s, there was a big housing shortage in the U.S. and homes needed to be designed and built quickly. Architect and inventor Buckminster (Bucky) Fuller had the bright idea to build dome homes out of triangle shapes, because triangles are twice as strong as rectangles. These big half-balls were stronger, lighter, and quicker to construct than most buildings. Fuller called them geodesic domes because the word "geodesic" means the shortest line between two points on a curved surface. Now they're mostly used as industrial buildings, stadiums, and greenhouses. These domes are also at playgrounds, because they're fun to climb.

ROCK OF AGES

The Pyramids at Giza are remarkable structures built almost 5,000 years ago. They have outlasted all of the other Seven Wonders of the Ancient World, which included the Lighthouse of Alexandria, the Temple of Artemis, and the Colossus of Rhodes. Why? Because the pyramid shape is one of the most stable forms of construction. The Great Pyramid, which is the biggest of the three, was built in 2589 B.C. and is almost solid rock. There are 2.6 million blocks of stone in it, and only three small rooms inside. At 481 feet (147 m) it was the tallest building on Earth for 3,800 years!

GEEK STREAK

It may look delicate, but the silk that spiders use to build webs is stronger than steel. If a thread of silk were as thick as a piece of steel wire, it would be five times stronger and weigh much less. That means a piece of spider's silk as thick as a pencil would be strong enough to stop a jumbo jet in mid flight! Scientists and engineers see spider's silk as a possible building tool of the future and have been trying to discover ways to make more of it. They have even given goats the genes for spider's silk in an attempt to try to have the goats produce it in their milk. Who knows? Some day we may even build our homes from it.

REACHING FOR THE SKY

The Burj Khalifa is the tallest building on Earth. It looms 2,717 feet (828 m) above Dubai, a large port city on the Persian Gulf, and can be seen by people living 59 miles (95 km) away. Like most skyscrapers, the Burj Khalifa is made from concrete and steel. At its center are tall concrete pillars, reinforced with bars of steel inside. Steel girders stick out from the pillars to make the 163 floors. Unlike a house, the skyscraper is not held up by its outer walls. Instead, the walls are vast panels of glass hanging on the outside of the building. The Burj Khalifa has 24,348 windows. It takes four months to clean them all.

WORD CHECK

ALLOY: A metal made by mixing two or more metals. Steel is an alloy of iron and carbon, brass is an alloy of copper and zinc, and bronze is an alloy of copper and tin.

TOOLS OF THE TRADE

Engineers can learn a lot from natural structures. For example, honeybees build lightweight but strong nests with six-sided rooms made of beeswax. These hexagonal cells are enclosed between thin walls called honeycombs. Engineers use the same honeycomb structure to build many things. The walls of spaceships have a honeycomb layer sandwiched between thin sheets of metal. This makes a wall that is just as strong as a solid one but much lighter. Other uses include racing shells and modern snowboards.

BUILDING BRIDGES

Stone and concrete alone are not flexible enough to build a long bridge. The weight of the bridge would be too much for it to support itself. One way to solve this problem is to support the structure with arches, like ancient Romans did when they built their viaducts. Instead of pushing straight down, the curve of the arch spreads the weight out to the two arch supports, so the bridge can cross larger spaces. The largest modern bridges do it another way. The road is hung, or suspended, from thick steel cables supported by sturdy columns. A suspension bridge, such as the Clifton Bridge in the United Kingdom (above), can cross deep rivers and leave room for ships to pass underneath.

LIGHTWEIGHT SUPERJUMBO

Building bigger planes creates bigger problems for engineers. The planes need to be strong enough to carry passengers but light enough to fly. The Airbus 380 superjumbo jet can carry more than 500 passengers and is so big it can't fit on a football field. Because steel is too heavy for a plane this size, billions of tiny carbon strands are glued and woven together to make carbon fiber, a substance that is as strong as steel with only a quarter of the weight. Carbon fiber is used to make many other things— from tennis rackets to canoes.

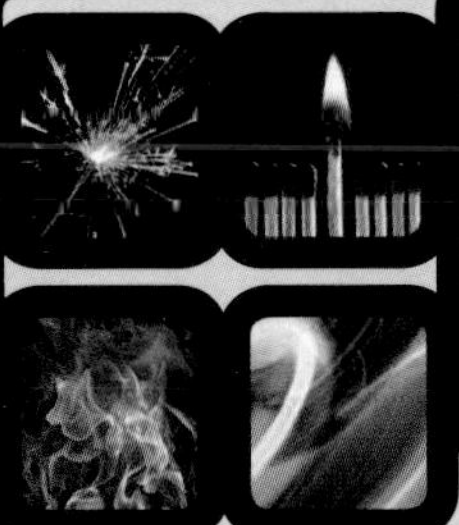

ENERGY

IT MAKES MATTER CHANGE

The universe is made of energy. All the atoms and particles in our bodies, and everything we see around us, are tiny packets of contained energy. Energy is what creates motion, heat, electricity, and sound. The chemical energy in our food is what keeps us alive.

Energy is mysterious stuff. You can't see it. You can only see what it does. Scientists describe energy as something that can do work. That doesn't mean it goes out and gets a job, though. The scientific idea of work is to transform matter by moving it from one place to another, or changing it in some way.

A machine is a device that can do work. Think of a crane lifting a crate or a saw cutting through a log.

The human body is a machine, too. Our food energy is put to work powering our heartbeat, firing our brain cells, and moving our hands, feet, legs, and arms.

Besides using energy to power our bodies, we also use energy to control our environment. Hundreds of thousands of years ago we learned to control fire—how to set it alight and keep it burning—and the energy from fire changed the way we lived. It kept us warm in winter, frightened away wild animals, and let us see in the dark.

Today, we've learned to control more than fire. We convert different kinds of energy into electricity, and we send that around the world to be used when and where we need it. Electricity is also made inside power plants, and most of them still use fire to do their job. This fire, or heat energy, comes from substances called fuels.

Nuclear power plants, like the one shown here, produce heat from radioactive fuels made from uranium and use that energy to power generators.

Fossil fuels, such as coal, natural gas, and oil, are burned, and their heat energy is also used for power.

But fossil fuels produce pollution that is damaging our environment, changing our climate, ruining soil and water, and causing illnesses. There are other sources of energy that are cleaner and safer.

We can make electricity from sunlight using solar cells in panels on rooftops and in vast arrays in desert fields. We can use geothermal energy from the volcanic heat deep underground. Giant turbines harness the power of the wind, and tidal and wave generators can tap the immense power of the oceans. Someday humans will learn to create energy the way stars do, through clean nuclear fusion.

We'll never run out of energy. We just need to discover the cleanest way to use it.

Did you know? If we covered an area the size of France, which is 341,754 square miles (885,000 sq km), with solar panels, we could power the entire world.

In this NASA photo of the sun's blazing surface, loops of plasma twist and turn as they zip back and forth along magnetic fields. Plasma is made of ions and electrons, and it's extremely energized, or hot. When plasma cools, it turns into the kind of matter we know on Earth as solids, liquids, and gases.

TYPES OF ENERGY

Energy cannot be created or destroyed, but it can be transformed into something else. The amount of energy in the universe today is exactly the same as it was when the universe began. In all that time, energy has been passed from one object to another, making some go faster or become hotter, and some go slower and become colder.

Adding energy can make an object break apart or combine with another substance to make something new. The natural events all around us are driven by transformations of energy: The gravitational energy of the moon is turned into the motion energy of the oceans. Plants, and other organisms, take the energy of the sun and the land and turn it into the chemical energy of sugars to fuel their growth. Coal and wood contain chemical energy that is turned into heat when they are burned. If you look for them, you will find different types of energy at work everywhere.

CONSERVATION OF ENERGY

The way energy behaves is governed by a set of rules called the laws of thermodynamics. The first law states that the amount of energy conserved in a system always stays the same—even though it may transform into different types of energy. Imagine someone cycling up a hill. Chemical energy from the rider's food is used to make the muscles contract and move the legs. Chemical energy has become kinetic energy. The rider's legs pump the pedals, transferring kinetic energy to them and to the back wheel of the bike. The bike moves up the hill with the kinetic energy it has received. Not all of the chemical energy ends up as kinetic energy, however. The rider's legs and body have gotten warm with the exercise, and warmth is given out as thermal energy. As the bike climbs higher, the kinetic energy is being converted to potential energy. When the rider reaches the top, he does not need to pedal anymore. He can use his potential energy to freewheel down the other side.

TYPES OF ENERGY

All energy is the same, but it is easier to understand by describing it according to the way it works.

KINETIC ENERGY

This is the energy of objects in motion. A rushing river or a spinning tornado are good examples of kinetic energy.

POTENTIAL ENERGY

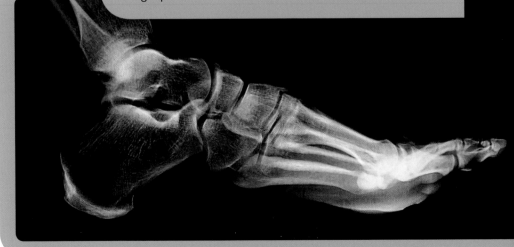

An object is said to have potential energy when it has the possibility of producing another type of energy. A storm cloud converts its potential energy to electrical energy when it releases a lightning bolt. The water at the top of a waterfall has potential energy that is converted to kinetic energy as the water falls to the river below.

ELECTRICAL ENERGY

This is the potential and kinetic energy carried by an electric current, which is a flow of charged particles. Electricity is very useful because it can be used to transport energy from one place to another, where it can be converted into another type of energy like heat, or thermal energy, from a heater.

THERMAL ENERGY

Thermal is another word for heat. Thermal energy is how we measure the kinetic energy of atoms and molecules. Every object contains some thermal energy. Thermal energy is actually the tiny vibrations and motions of the atoms inside an object. The faster the atoms move, the more heat they generate.

CHEMICAL ENERGY

This kind of potential energy is stored in the bonds that lock atoms together in a substance like a battery. When a chemical reaction causes the bonds to break, energy is released and the substance changes into something new, like electricity. When a car burns gasoline, the engine changes the chemical energy into kinetic energy, which makes the car move.

SOUND ENERGY

Sound, or acoustic, energy is carried by wave motions traveling through the air. The sound wave gets its energy by the motion of an object in the air—clapping hands, a slammed door, or a vibrating violin string for example. Sound energy can also travel through liquids and solids.

RADIANT ENERGY

This kind of energy is carried by radiation. Light is one kind of radiation; others include infrared, microwaves, and x-rays. Each type of radiation carries a specific amount of energy, and they all can travel through space.

PERSONALITY PLUS

James Prescott Joule (1818–1889) was an Englishman who wanted to make his brewery more efficient. When he compared the heating abilities of different water heaters, Joule found that the energy needed to heat water with an electrical heater was the same as the energy required to heat water by a machine that stirred it. Although the methods of heating were different, the amount of work being done was the same. A century later, a unit of energy, the joule, was named in his honor.

MEASURING ENERGY

Scientists have a simple word for the amount of useful energy given or taken away from an object: work. Work is using a force to move an object a certain distance. Imagine you have two boxes that you need to push across the room. One box is twice as heavy as the other. That means it requires twice as much energy, or work, to move the heavy box than the smaller box over the same distance. Whenever energy is transformed from one type to another, it is doing some kind of work. The amount of energy involved is measured in units called joules (J). One joule is roughly the energy needed to lift three apples, or to move one pound (.45 kg) a foot (0.3 m) in the air.

TOOLS OF THE TRADE

A sound pressure level (SPL) meter app uses the built-in microphone on a smartphone to measure the decibels, or noise volume, of sound energy.

LOL! 😄

Q: Why do transformers hum?

A: They don't know the words.

TRY THIS!

WHAT YOU NEED: A stopwatch, a scale, a tape measure, some stairs, a lot of energy

HOW LONG IT TAKES: 15 minutes

You can calculate your body's power with this simple experiment. First, weigh yourself in pounds. Then measure the vertical height—straight up from the bottom to the top of the stairs. Now, run up the stairs—several flights will make it more interesting—and time how long it takes to get to the top. Then calculate the energy needed to lift your body up the stairs by multiplying your weight by the height of the stairs. Divide the energy by the time of your run. This is the power of your body.

POWERING UP

The speed with which energy does its work is described as power. When a sprinter walks back along the track after finishing a race, she is using the same amount of energy as during the race. The work required to move her body is always the same. However, she did the work much faster during the race. The power used to move her body in the race is calculated by dividing the number of joules, or units of energy, by the time it took to use them. The unit of power is the watt (W); 1W is equal to 1J per second.

ENERGY THROUGH THE AGES

The modern world is hungry for power. Every hour we use 150 thousand trillion watts of it. This power is used to generate electricity; drive our cars, ships, and aircraft; and run the machines inside factories.

Our way of life depends entirely on generated power. For more than 300 years, 90 percent of our power has come from fossil fuels such as coal, natural gas, and gasoline. Pollution from fossil fuels damages the environment. The biggest problem is the way pollution is changing Earth's climate. Today, we are looking for new, cleaner ways of making power. Take a look at how people have used energy through the ages.

125,000 B.C.
The ancestors of humans learn to control fire. The heat and light from burning wood change the way people live and work forever.

25,000 B.C.
Wood fires are used to bake clay pots and jars, making them hard and waterproof.

6500 B.C.
Wood-fired furnaces are first used to smelt copper, and later, as hotter furnaces are developed, other metals such as iron.

4000 B.C.
Coal begins to be mined as a fuel in China.

3500 B.C.
The first carts are moved by muscle power alone. Then strong domestic animals, such as oxen and donkeys, are harnessed to pulleys and winches, and animal power is used to raise water from wells and haul heavy loads.

400 B.C.
Gears are invented in ancient Greece. These make use of mechanical advantage, which magnifies forces, making it possible for muscle-driven machines to move heavier objects than ever before.

100 B.C.
The Romans power their machines with large treadmills driven by slaves walking inside. Treadmills, for people and animals, remain a source of power for mills and early factories until the 18th century.

A.D. 27
The Roman architect Vitruvius invents the waterwheel, which harnesses the flow of water to produce a spinning motion that can drive machines.

A.D. 600
The windmill is invented in Persia. Like a waterwheel, the windmill converts the wind into a spinning motion.

1698
Thomas Savery invents the first steam engine to power water pumps in mines in southern England. Grateful miners call it "the miner's friend." Only one problem—it tends to explode.

1709
A new method of making iron using processed coal is developed in England. This leads to the industrial revolution and a huge increase in the use of coal as a fuel, first in Britain, and then around the world.

1859

The first oil well is drilled at Titusville, Pennsylvania, U.S.A., starting the modern petroleum industry.

1896

Henri Becquerel discovers radioactivity and has the idea of using it as a fuel.

1956

The first nuclear power plant for generating electricity opens at Calder Hall in England.

1860

Jean Lenoir invents the internal combustion engine, but it will be another 25 years before Karl Benz puts one in an automobile.

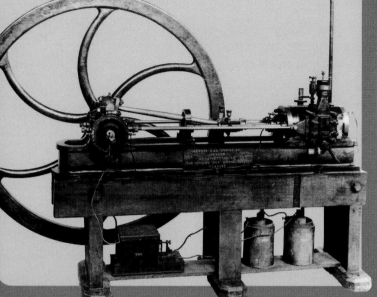

1882

Thomas Edison builds the first power plant that supplies electricity to customers in London, England. A similar plant opens in New York City a few months later.

1984

Solar Energy Generating Systems builds a solar power plant in the Mojave Desert in California. It uses the heat from the sun to generate electricity.

1960

A geothermal power plant using the heat released from volcanic activity underground is built at the Geysers, near San Francisco, California, U.S.A. This plant will become the world's largest geothermal power plant, with 22 separate generating sites.

1997

The world now uses 14.5 million tons (13.2 million t) of coal every year. That is twice the weight of the Great Pyramid in Egypt.

2003

The Three Gorges Dam opens in China. The dam uses the Yangtze River to generate 22,500 megawatts of power. This makes the Chinese dam the largest power plant on Earth.

2012

The Gansu Wind Farm opens in central China. It has around 4,000 wind turbines and produces 6,000 megawatts. More turbines will be added with the hope that by 2020, the wind farm will become the second largest power plant on Earth, after the Three Gorges Dam.

2015

The largest solar farm, using the light from the sun to generate electricity, is built in Los Angeles and Kern Counties, California. The Solar Star plant produces 579 megawatts, which can power 255,000 homes. At the same time, China, Australia, and Pakistan begin building solar plants that will power even more homes.

ANCIENT ENERGY

Why are coal, gasoline, and similar substances described as fossil fuels? A fossil is the remains of a living thing that has become buried underground. Over millions of years, the remains are converted to rocklike substances. Coal is the fossil remains of dead trees. Petroleum, from which we get gasoline and natural gas, is the remains of microorganisms that were buried under seabeds. The chemical energy stored in a body does not disappear when the organism dies. It is still there even after it has been transformed into a fossil.

HEAT

WORD CHECK

RADIATION: A transfer of energy through space. It does not have any weight or mass. Radiation includes all kinds of light such as visible light, radio waves, x-rays, and ultraviolet light.

People have been using heat from the beginning of civilization. Once Stone Age humans used the heat from fire to stay warm in winter, they were able to live in colder places. When heat was used to cook foods, people began to eat a wider range of plants and animals. Heat is still our main source of energy. The heat released from fuels provides about four-fifths of the world's electricity.

Although we've used heat for thousands of years, it took a long time to figure out what heat actually is. People once thought heat was an invisible gas that could flow in and out of objects, making them hot or cold. What we discovered was that heat moves in two ways: through thermal energy and infrared radiation. Thermal energy is carried by the atoms and molecules bumping into each other. Infrared radiation is invisible radiant energy that turns into heat when it hits molecules.

MEASURING HEAT

To understand heat, we need a way to measure it. Temperature measures the heat in an object on a scale divided into units called degrees. Temperature is indicated on an instrument called a thermometer (right). The Fahrenheit (°F) scale was invented in 1790 and is still used in the United States. Most of the rest of the world began using the Celsius (°C) scale in the 20th century, which says that water freezes at 0° (32°F) and boils at 100° (212°F).

TOOLS OF THE TRADE

The first thermometers contained a liquid such as colored alcohol or mercury that expanded when it was warmed and contracted when it got cold. This made it go up and down inside the thermometer showing the changes in temperature. Today, we use electric thermometers. They have an electronic component called a thermistor—the word comes from "thermal" and "resistor." The amount of electricity carried by the thermistor varies as it warms up or cools down, and that is used to calculate temperature.

CONDUCTION OF HEAT

Heat moves through solids by a process called conduction. Conduction is why the handle of a pan gets warm even though only the bottom is being heated. The heat from the cooktop transfers energy to the metal on the bottom of the pan. The atoms in this area start to vibrate more. As they vibrate, the hot atoms bang into cooler ones nearby, and that makes them move around more too. Gradually the heat energy is conducted away from the source of heat (the cooktop) and into all parts of the pan, including the handle. Metals are very good at conducting heat because their electrons can move around easily, carrying energy with them. This is why they often feel colder than other substances. The metal draws away the heat of your finger, so it feels cold. Plastics and wood do not conduct heat well, so they feel warmer to the touch.

PERSONALITY PLUS

English scientist William Crookes (1832–1919) discovered the element thallium and also studied the cathode-ray tube used in television sets. He invented the Crookes radiometer, known as a light mill. It looks like a lightbulb with four fan-shaped blades inside. One side of each blade is black, the other silver. When left in the sunshine, the fan spins. Today, the light mill is used to demonstrate how a heat engine runs by converting light energy into heat.

RADIATING HEAT

When you warm yourself by a campfire, you are feeling heat in the form of radiation. We cannot see it, but our skin can feel it. This heat radiation is called infrared. Unlike conduction and convection, infrared radiation does not need a substance to move through. For example, the warmth of the sun travels to Earth through the emptiness of space as infrared radiation and gets converted to heat when it hits the water in your skin.

THERMAL CURRENTS

Heat moves through liquids and gases in a different way than it does in solids. The atoms with a lot of thermal energy rise upward, and cooler atoms sink down to take their place. This creates a flow inside the liquid or gas called a convection current. That's what spreads the heat around water boiling in a pan. The same thing is happening on a huge scale in the oceans and in the atmosphere. Glider pilots will use thermals, or the upward drafts of air in a convection current, to lift their planes higher. The thermals are created by heat from the ground, which warms the air and makes it rise up.

BIG BODIES

Humans and many other animals are warm-blooded. We use our supply of chemical energy to keep our bodies at a certain temperature. On a cold day, we might shiver to warm ourselves up, while on a hot day we will sweat or pant to cool down. Staying at the right temperature uses up a lot of energy, but big animals, like bears and elephants, are able to do it better than small ones. Why? The surface area of a big object is small compared to its volume, so an elephant loses body heat much more slowly than a tiny mouse. The mouse must eat all the food it can find to have the energy to maintain its body temperature. If it goes without food, it cannot survive long. The elephant does not have this problem. It can get by just eating twigs and leaves. These do not contain much energy but the elephant's vast body uses it more efficiently.

REFRIGERATION

Nearly every home in the United States has a refrigerator, and a quarter of them have two. Because refrigerators are so common, we forget that they do something very unusual: They make things cold.

The laws that govern heat say that heat always moves from a hot object to a colder one. That is why a hot drink always goes cold—heat flows to the colder air around it. It also explains why you need to eat an ice-cream cone quickly. The air around it is warmer and gives the ice cream some of its heat, making the ice cream melt.

We have invented many ways of releasing heat so it can spread out and warm us. A wood fire is the simplest one, but electric heaters and home furnaces do the same thing. However, a refrigerator does the opposite. It is a heat pump that pulls heat out of food to make it colder than its surroundings.

WORD CHECK

HUMID: Having a lot of moisture in the air. The air before a thunderstorm can feel humid.

IN THE FRIDGE

Only the food compartments in a refrigerator are actually cold. The machinery at the back is warm because it pumps heat out of the food compartment through a series of pipes, and into the air. To chill the refrigerator, a pump pushes a liquid called a refrigerant through a tiny nozzle, making the liquid expand into a gas. Because it expands so fast, the temperature of the gas drops and becomes much colder than the food compartment. Following the rules of heat going from hot to cold, some of the heat from the food goes to warm up the gas. The gas is then squeezed again so it becomes a warm liquid. The liquid runs through pipes on the back of the refrigerator where it cools down, giving away its heat. Then the process starts all over again.

PRESERVING FOOD

Keeping food cold is the best way to keep it fresh. We can store a piece of food in the refrigerator for days and it will taste just as good as it would have if we'd eaten it as soon as we bought it. The cold preserves the food by slowing down the natural processes that make it go bad. If left at room temperature, germs and fungus that have settled on the food will grow much faster than they would at lower temperatures, making the food look moldy and smell nasty. Cooling food will slow the growth of organisms, but freezing the food will stop the germs from growing completely, so the food can be kept for weeks and still taste fresh when it is defrosted.

SUPERCOLD STATE

There are three states of matter: solid, liquid, and gas (see page 42). Plasma, which is a type of gas that can carry electricity, is often described as a fourth state. In 1995, two American scientists, Eric Cornell and Carl Wieman, created a fifth state. It is called the Bose-Einstein condensate, and it exists only at the coldest temperature possible: minus 459°F (-273°C). When Cornell and Wieman chilled a few thousand atoms of rubidium metal to this extremely low temperature, the atoms did something that surprised the scientists: They joined together and began working as a single piece of matter. The Bose-Einstein condensate can be created only under special conditions. But scientists believe it's worth the trouble. It helps them investigate how atoms work. This knowledge will help scientists create new materials for the future that seem like science fiction today.

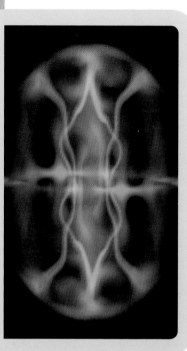

BIG CHILL

Refrigeration doesn't just keep food fresh. The same process is used to cool our houses. An air conditioner is like a refrigerator in two halves. The cold section is inside the house cooling the air, while the hot part is outside, pushing away the unwanted heat. Refrigeration is also used to cool the fuels of the most powerful space rockets. Fuels like oxygen and hydrogen are normally gases, but if they are cooled into a liquid, more fuel can fit into the rocket's tanks. Another use of cold is in magnetic resonance imaging (MRI) scanners in hospitals (above). These machines use giant magnets, which must be cooled down to work properly. So the insides of an MRI machine are cooled to about minus 450°F (-268°C), almost the same temperature as space.

COLD FEET

The male emperor penguin is the only animal to stay on land during the Antarctic winter, when temperatures drop to minus 40°F (-40°C) and the icy winds blow at hurricane speeds. If your body was exposed to these temperatures the heat from your bare feet would melt the snow into water, which would freeze again in seconds—and you'd be frozen to the spot! A penguin avoids this problem by refrigerating its feet. The blood vessels that carry cold blood out of the feet are wrapped around the ones that carry warm blood in. The cold blood coming from the feet cools down the warm blood from the body so it won't heat up the foot and melt the snow. At the same time, the warm body blood heats up the cold foot blood so it can reenter the body. Penguins get cold feet, but they like it like that.

PERSONALITY PLUS

In 1902, a young engineer named Willis Carrier was asked to solve a problem for a printing company in Brooklyn, New York. Their print room was so humid that the ink would not dry on the paper. Carrier solved the problem by building a machine for removing water vapor from air—and ended up inventing the air conditioner. The machine worked by chilling the air so the vapor turned into liquid water that collected in the machine. Later, Carrier sold his new air conditioners—and chilled out America.

ELECTRICITY

There are two kinds of electricity: static and current. "Static" means "still." In static electricity, a charge builds up in one place and stays there. When the charged particles move from place to place, it is called current electricity.

GEEK STREAK

A lightning bolt is pushed through the air by a force of 100 million volts. That is a million times more powerful than the voltage running through a TV or toaster in your house!

Static electricity was the first form to be discovered. The word "electricity" comes from the Greek word *electron*, which means "amber." Greeks discovered that when rubbed with a fur cloth, the yellow stone would emit a static charge. In the 1750s, American scientist Benjamin Franklin collected the charge from a bolt of lightning and showed that it was the same thing produced by amber—only much more powerful. A few years later, scientists figured out how to make electricity run in a continuous flow instead of in short sparks. This was current electricity, which is used today to power our lights, our appliances, our tablets, and smartphones.

MAKING A CURRENT

When one object has too many electrons and another has too few, the electrons can jump from one to the other to even out the numbers. This creates a spark. An electric current happens when the electrically charged particles keep moving. To make this continuous flow of electricity, the positive/negative imbalance between the objects needs to remain constant so the electrons will keep jumping from atom to atom. Besides being used in homes and appliances, current electricity is also powering our electric cars (below).

LOL! 😄

Q: What would you call a power failure?

A: A current event.

ELECTRIC FORCES

Electrically charged objects create a force. The force pushes away objects with the same charge and pulls together objects with opposite charges. This explains why dust sticks to a piece of charged amber and why rubbing a balloon will make it cling to your sweater. The rubbing gives the balloon extra electrons from the sweater, and so the two materials have opposite charges and they attract each other. Give your body a static charge, as this girl is doing by touching a machine that generates static electricity, and a weird thing happens: Your hair stands on end. This is because all of your hairs have the same charge, so they repel each other, giving you a very strange hairstyle.

WORD CHECK

ELECTRODE: A solid component of an electrical system that releases or receives an electric current

CONDUCTORS AND INSULATORS

Only certain materials carry, or conduct, electric currents. These materials are called conductors. Metals, such as copper and gold, are the best conductors. That's why the electrical wiring in a house is made from copper (gold is too expensive). The thick cables that carry electricity over power lines are made of aluminum, which is the best lightweight conductor. The best nonmetal conductor is graphite—the stuff in pencil leads—but most nonmetals are insulators, which means they block the flow of electricity. The difference between the two is this: The atoms in a conductor allow their electrons to move around; in insulators the electrons are locked in place. An electrical cable (left) is a good example of conductors and insulators at work. The copper core conducts the current, while the plastic insulators around it stop the current from leaking out.

VOLTAGE

Danger! High voltage! You may have seen these signs on power lines (right), but what do they mean? Voltage is the amount of energy an electric current carries through a substance. It is produced by differences in charge—the larger the difference, the higher the voltage. A low voltage is enough to push a current through a conductor, such as a copper wire, that has very low resistance, but not enough to get it through substances that have high resistance, such as wood, paper, and most plastics. Increasing the voltage increases the size of the current. If the voltage is high enough, it can force electricity through any substance. High voltage is dangerous because it can create sparks through the air (just like lightning) and send huge currents through a human body, which can be fatal.

TOOLS OF THE TRADE

The electric battery was invented in 1800 by Italian scientist Alessandro Volta. We get the word voltage from his name. Regular batteries today work in the same way as Volta's first system. Two electrodes, which are solid metals that are not alike, are made to react with a liquid acid. One solid gives electrons to the liquid solution, while the other takes them away. These reactions force the electrons to flow through the liquid solution between the solids, and they create a difference in charge between the top of the battery and the bottom. When both ends of the battery are connected to a conductor, a current runs through it. Eventually the chemicals run out and the reaction stops—and your battery is dead.

MEASURING CHARGE

We measure electric current in amps (A), which is short for "ampere." This unit is named after French scientist André-Marie Ampère, who, in the 1820s, figured out how electricity works. When a wire has a current of 1A, it means that about six billion electrons are moving through it every second. The more amps a current has, the more electrons (electrical charge) it carries. Amps measure the movement of not only electrons, but any charged particle. Electricity moves through metals as electrons, but in electrified liquids, the current is carried by ions. Ions are atoms that have lost or gained electrons, so they can have a positive or negative charge (see page 28). Both kinds of ions can be made to flow in a current.

FRANKENSTEIN SCIENCE

Remember that famous story about Dr. Frankenstein, the mad scientist who brought a monster to life using a spark of electricity? Of course that was all made up, but when the story was written in the early 19th century, many scientists were trying to do that for real. People believed that electricity was a mysterious life force found inside animal bodies. Electricity is indeed used inside our bodies to signal the nerves and brain, and to power our muscles, but we now know there is a lot more to it than that. Read on to find out about some odd and interesting discoveries with electricity.

1650s

German scientist Otto von Guericke invents an electricity generator that creates large static charges. When he rubs or spins around a ball of sulfur, it picks up a charge and produces sparks.

1700s

Englishman Francis Hauksbee builds an even more powerful static electricity generator by replacing the ball of sulfur with a glass sphere with most of the air sucked out. Spinning the sphere charges it, and Hauksbee finds that when he touches the charged glass, an eerie blue glow appears inside. This is the same effect that is used in modern fluorescent lightbulbs.

1730

In London, Stephen Gray shows that static electric charges can move through certain substances, but are blocked by others. This is the discovery of conductors and insulators. Gray performs the famous "Flying Boy" experiment to prove his findings. A young boy, lying flat, is suspended from the ceiling by silk ropes, which are good insulators. When Gray touches the boy's feet with a sulfur ball generator, the boy becomes charged with electricity. The boy then holds his hands over bowls of ripped paper fragments, and these magically rise up and cling to his body.

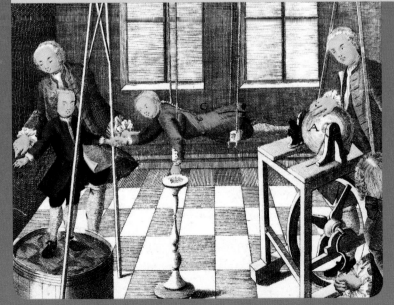

1740s

Electricity is used by showmen to perform magic tricks, such as setting candles on fire with sparks. One trick, popular for centuries, is a real-life "electric kiss." A young lady is charged with electricity, so when a young man gives her a kiss, sparks fly between their lips!

1745

Dutch scientist Pieter van Musschenbroek finds a way to collect large amounts of electric charge in special glass jars. They become known as Leyden jars, after the city where they were invented.

1752

American Benjamin Franklin uses a kite to lift a metal key and wire into a lightning storm. The electricity from a lightning strike travels down the wire and charges up a Leyden jar. This shows that lightning is just another form of electrical spark.

1780s

While investigating the muscles and nerves in a frog's legs, Italian biologist Luigi Galvani accidentally touches the brass hook holding the legs with a steel scalpel. He's amazed to see the frog's legs give out a spark and wiggle—even though they are cut off from the rest of the body! The chemicals inside frog legs work like the acid in a battery. The brass and steel create a circuit that produces a current of electricity that runs through the leg muscles, making them move. Galvani has discovered electric current, which he calls "animal electricity."

1800

Alessandro Volta creates "animal electricity" without animals. Instead, he uses a pile of two kinds of metal discs soaked in acid to produce an electric current. He names his invention the electric "pile" (below), but we remember it today as the first electric battery.

1803

Galvani's nephew, Giovanni Aldini, tours Europe showing what electricity can do. He uses electric currents to make frogs, as well as larger animals, appear to come back to life.

1818

English author Mary Shelley writes *Frankenstein*, a story of a doctor who builds a monster from body parts and brings it to life with the electricity from lightning. The book is one of the first science fiction stories, and the monster, sometimes known as Frankenstein, is now famous around the world.

1924

German scientist Hans Berger invents the electroencephalograph (EEG), a machine that measures electrical activity in the brain. The EEG shows that the brain produces a series of "brain waves" that change when people relax, sleep, or work hard. Almost 30 years later, chemists will discover how the body makes this electricity: The electric signals sent by nerves are produced by charged ions flooding in and out of nerve cells.

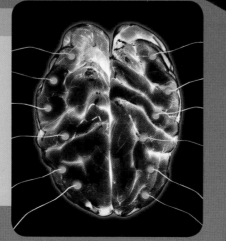

NUCLEAR POWER

Most fuels use a chemical reaction to release energy, like burning a log for heat. But when can a fuel produce heat without burning? When it is a nuclear fuel.

Chemical reactions involve two or more elements using the electrons on the outer edge of their atoms to bond together. The nuclear reactions we use to make heat and power—fission reactions—are different. They don't involve the electrons or electromagnetism. The nuclear reaction happens right at the center of the atom, in the nucleus. Only a certain kind of atom—a radioactive atom—can perform the type of nuclear reactions we use for our power plants. A radioactive atom is very large, with hundreds of protons and neutrons packed into its nucleus. That nucleus is unstable, so it's possible for some of the protons or neutrons inside to be broken away, or decay. When that happens, a huge amount of energy is released in the form of heat, light, and radioactivity.

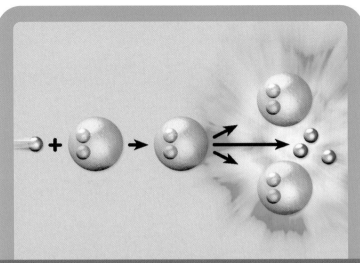

NUCLEAR FISSION

Nuclear fuel can be made to perform a powerful reaction called nuclear fission. That's when an atom from a radioactive metal, like uranium, is split into two pieces, releasing a huge amount of energy. Neutrons from the split then collide with other uranium atoms, making them split, too. This is called a chain reaction. When nuclear fission occurs very fast, it creates an immense explosion. This is what happens inside a nuclear bomb. Scientists have found a way to control the fission process inside nuclear reactors, so the chain reactions happen slowly and safely.

FUSION

About a tenth of the world's electricity is made from fission reactions in nuclear power plants. However, most of the energy being released in the universe today comes from another nuclear reaction: fusion. Whereas fission takes large atoms and splits them into two smaller ones, fusion does the reverse. It pushes two small atoms together to make one larger atom. Depending on the type of fuel used, this process gives out four times as much energy as fission, but it requires huge amounts of energy to make it happen. Fusion occurs in the center of stars, like our sun, where the pressure at its core is 250 billion times stronger than on the surface of Earth. So far, no one on Earth has been able to make a fusion reactor that produces more energy than it uses up, but new reactors are getting closer every day.

LOL!

Q: What did the nuclear physicist have for lunch?

A: Fission chips.

PERSONALITY PLUS

In December 1938, Austrian physicist Lise Meitner and her nephew Otto Frisch discovered what had been thought impossible: The atom could be split. They named the process "fission" and published a paper about their discovery in 1939. Meitner also showed that a tiny part of the atom's mass turned into energy and produced a huge amount of heat and radiation. This discovery led to the development of nuclear power and, to Meitner's dismay, the atom bomb.

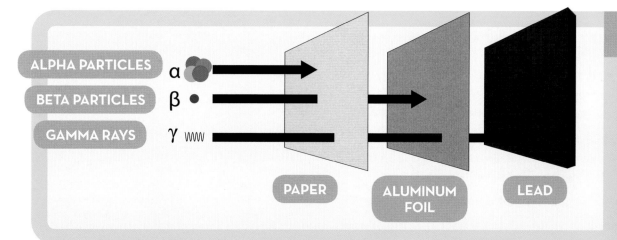

ALPHA PARTICLES α
BETA PARTICLES β
GAMMA RAYS γ

PAPER   ALUMINUM FOIL   LEAD

RADIOACTIVE RADIATION

There's a downside to making nuclear power with radioactive metals: radioactive radiation. All energy that travels as a wave through space is radiation, but only the radiation given out by radioactive metals like uranium and plutonium is radioactive. There are three kinds of radioactive radiation: alpha, beta, and gamma. All three contain a lot of energy. Alpha particles are caused by too many protons in the nucleus of the atom. Thin barriers, like the skin or paper, can block alpha waves. Beta particles are caused by too many neutrons in the atom's nucleus. Beta waves can pass through the skin and soft objects, but are blocked by metals. Gamma waves are the worst: They are an invisible high-energy light that can burn skin and blast through walls. Only thick lead shielding can stop them.

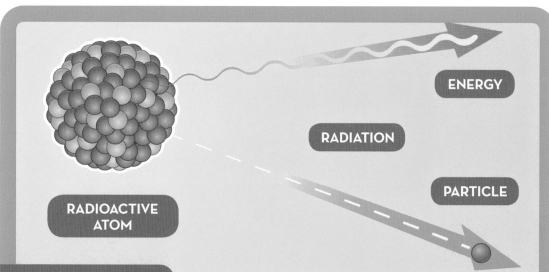

ENERGY

RADIATION

PARTICLE

RADIOACTIVE ATOM

RADIOACTIVE DECAY

Nuclear power would not be possible without a process called radioactive decay. Rocks and minerals contain tiny amounts of radioactive atoms, like uranium and thorium. Over time, the nuclei of these atoms break up, or decay, releasing smaller particles as well as heat and other forms of energy. Radioactive decay is a slow process. The heat energy it gives off is not enough to be useful. So to create nuclear power we refine radioactive metals like uranium into nuclear fuel.

WORD CHECK

RADIOACTIVITY:
Radiation that occurs when a nucleus is broken down into smaller particles

GEEK STREAK

A smoke detector is the most radioactive thing in your house. It contains a tiny amount of americium, an element with the atomic number 95 in the periodic table, which gives out a little radioactivity. The radioactivity electrifies the air inside the detector and when smoke gets in, it blocks the electricity—and sets off the alarm.

HALF-LIFE

Scientists know that an unstable atom is more likely to break up, or decay, than a stable one, but it is impossible to predict exactly when that will happen. In order to measure the time it might take, scientists decided to measure an atom's half-life, or the average time it takes for half of a radioactive substance to lose its radioactivity. Uranium (left) has a half-life of 4.5 billion years. That's also the current age of Earth, which means there is half the amount of uranium on the planet now than when it formed—the other half has decayed. Radon gas has a half-life of 4 days, while francium's is 22 minutes.

MAGNETISM

People have been aware of magnetic forces for more than 4,000 years. Magnetism was one of the first natural forces studied by scientists.

The word "magnet" comes from Magnesia, an ancient kingdom in what is now northern Greece. Some of the rocks there are natural magnets called lodestones. Lodestones contain a lot of iron, and iron is magnetic. Some other metals, like nickel and cobalt, can be magnetic, too, but iron remains the main ingredient in naturally occurring magnets. Most materials have all their electrons paired, so one electron cancels out the magnetism of the other and the total magnetic field is very small. But the metal atoms inside iron have unpaired electrons with their own north and south poles and magnetic force field. When the atoms line up together, the little forces they produce individually combine into one powerful magnetic force. Magnets may be ancient technology, but they are at the heart of modern life. They make our electricity, store our computer files, and point us toward the North Pole.

OUR MAGNETIC HOME

We live on a giant magnet. Planet Earth's core is made from a solid ball of hot iron that is spinning around inside an ocean of hot, liquid iron. This creates a superstrong magnetic field that surrounds the planet and reaches far out into space. A compass always points north because its needle is a magnet and it lines up with the magnetic field of the Earth—with one needle pointing north and the other south. Compasses have helped sailors navigate the seas for more than 1,000 years, and migrating birds and other animals use Earth's magnetic field to find their way as well.

FORCE FIELD

Magnets are surrounded by an invisible force field that is the space where the force of magnetism is located. The force field is strongest near its north and south poles. It comes out of the magnet's north pole and goes in through the south. In a simple bar magnet, the magnetic force field wraps around the magnet (below). In a horseshoe magnet, the poles are bent together, with the north pole on one end of the magnet and the south pole on the other. This creates a very strong force field between the two poles. If an object made of iron comes into the field, the force field pulls it to the magnet and makes it stick. If the force fields of two magnets meet, the north pole of one magnet will be attracted to the south pole of the other. However, when like poles are brought together, they push each other away.

TRY THIS!

WHAT YOU NEED: Some breakfast cereal with extra iron (check the package), a strong magnet, a strong ziplock plastic bag, a mortar and pestle (or something to grind the flakes), a sturdy bowl, a paper towel, water

HOW LONG IT TAKES: 2 to 3 hours

A little bit of iron in your food is good for you—it makes your blood healthy. Companies sometimes add extra iron to their cereals, and you can use a magnet to find it. First grind the cereal into a fine powder in a sturdy bowl. Put the cereal powder in the plastic bag and pour in enough water to cover it. Zip the bag shut and squish it all around. Drop in the magnet and squish some more. The magnet should collect dark grains around it. These are the iron flakes in the cereal. Fish out the magnet and set it on a paper towel. When it's dry, the iron should be easy to see on the magnet. You've just refined iron!

ELECTROMAGNETS

There are two kinds of magnets: permanent and electromagnetic. A compass needle and a horseshoe magnet are permanent magnets because they are always surrounded by a force field. Electromagnets get their magnetism from electricity. An electromagnet is a coil of electrical wire wrapped around a piece of iron or other magnetic metal. When a current runs through the wire, the movement of the electrons produces a magnetic field with a north and south pole, just like a permanent magnet. However, switch off the electric current and the magnetic field disappears. Electromagnets can be just as strong or stronger as permanent ones. They make it possible for junkyard cranes to lift and move heavy steel cars.

MAGNETIC MEMORY

Magnets are used in many electronic devices such as electric motors, generators, microphones, and loudspeakers, to name a few. One of the most important uses of magnets is in computer hard disks. A hard disk is a flat circle of magnetic material that is divided up into tiny sectors. Each sector can be magnetized or demagnetized by an electromagnet that moves above the disk on a device called a head. A computer file is stored by creating a one-of-a-kind pattern of magnetized and demagnetized sectors that can be read by the head—or erased and overwritten with a new pattern.

MAGNETIC TRAIN

The fastest train in the world can go 373 miles an hour (600 km/h) because of magnets. But you won't find it on a railroad track. In fact it doesn't ride on rails at all. A maglev train—short for "magnetic levitation"—is lifted off the track and propelled forward through the air by powerful magnetic forces. The maglev track is lined with electromagnets, as are the train cars. These repel each other, making the train float, or levitate, in midair. Magnets along the track move the train forward. They switch their north and south poles in a sequence, so some parts of the track are always pulling the train, while others are pushing it, which makes the maglev go very, very fast.

PERSONALITY PLUS

In 1600, English scientist William Gilbert was the world's leading expert on magnets and even wrote a book about how to make them. He told the reader to line up a piece of iron from north to south and tap it with a hammer while heating it gently. (Gilbert didn't know it, but the tapping gave the iron energy so the magnets could line up to produce the magnetic field.) Gilbert was also the first person to show that Earth was a magnet. He proved it by carving a mini version of Earth from a lump of lodestone. Then he placed a compass on the magnetic globe. Wherever he put it, the needle always pointed to the north pole of the lodestone—just like a compass did on Earth.

ELECTROMAGNETISM

For many years, scientists thought electricity and magnetism were two separate things. But in 1820, it was discovered that they are both created by a single process known as electromagnetism.

This discovery happened by accident while Danish professor Hans Christian Ørsted was showing his students how electric current could make a wire warm up and glow. During the demonstration, the needle of a compass on a workbench suddenly swung toward the electrified wire. When Ørsted turned off the current, the needle swung back to north. It was already known that electrified objects were surrounded by a force field—an electric field that repelled and attracted other charged objects. But Ørsted's discovery showed that electric currents also created a second field—a magnetic one that made the compass move. Understanding electromagnetism has changed the world. It is used to power electric motors, and it generates the electricity for our homes and offices.

ELECTRIC MOTOR

One year after Ørsted's discovery of electromagnetism, British scientist Michael Faraday made the world's first electric motor. He used two cups of mercury, each with a metal wire and a magnet inside. In the right cup, the metal wire hung loosely in the mercury, while the magnet was fixed in place. In the left cup, the wire was secured and the magnet floated loosely attached to a thread. When an electric current from a battery was applied to the wire, a circuit was created through the mercury, which is a good conductor of electricity. This created an electromagnetic field, which interacted with the magnetic field of the permanent magnet in the right cup, causing the magnet in the left cup and the wire in the right cup to turn. Today electric motors are used to power everything from the fan in a hair dryer, to golf carts, to high-speed trains.

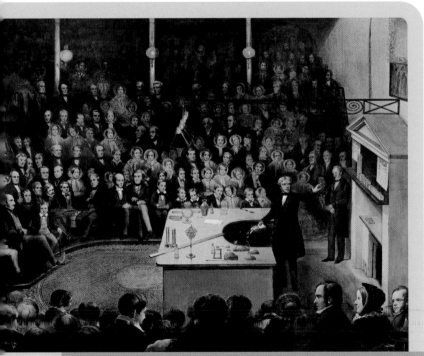

INDUCTION

Besides inventing the electric motor, Michael Faraday also made the biggest discovery in electromagnetism: the phenomenon of induction. The induction effect happens when you physically turn a wire in a magnetic field, and that motion is converted into electrical energy. It is the opposite of the motor effect, which is when an electrified wire is placed in a magnetic field and experiences a force and turns, converting electrical energy to motion. Without induction we could not make electric currents.

ELECTRICITY GENERATOR

An electricity generator is very similar to an electric motor, with a large magnet surrounding a loop of wire. But the generator requires an outside source of motion energy to make the wire spin. This can be as simple as a person cranking the handle of a windup flashlight, or kids pedaling the wheels of their bikes to charge their cell phones. As the wire moves through the magnetic field, its motion energy is converted into a force that pushes an electric current through it. The faster it spins, the stronger the current.

PERSONALITY PLUS

In 1831, Joseph Henry of the United States discovered induction at the same time Michael Faraday was announcing his findings in London. The two men are considered to be the founding fathers of the electrical industry and electrical technology. Henry used electromagnetism to design motors, generators, and the telegraph, where coded messages were sent down wires as pulses of electricity. He was President Lincoln's science advisor, and in 1846 became the first head of the Smithsonian Institution, which is now one of the world's greatest museums.

INSIDE A POWER PLANT

The purpose of power plants is to make electricity, and all but one do this by the induction effect, which uses moving magnetic fields to create electrical current. The exception is a photovoltaic solar system, which converts the energy of sunlight directly into electric current. Here are four types of power plants that harness a source of heat or motion and use that to spin a generator:

Thermal: These include all plants that burn a fuel, such as natural gas, oil, coal, wood, or garbage. Heat from the fuel is used to boil water into high-pressure steam that flows at great speed through a turbine. This is a fan-shaped machine with many blades that converts the forward blast of steam into a spinning motion—and that is what drives the generator.

Solar thermal: These power plants use mirrors or lenses to focus and concentrate the heat of the sun. That heat turns a liquid into a fast-flowing gas, which powers a turbine.

Nuclear: These work like thermal power plants, but the heat coming from fission reactions in nuclear fuel makes the steam.

Hydroelectric: A dam makes use of the natural flow of a river. The flowing force of the water is channeled through a turbine that spins the generator.

THERMAL   **NUCLEAR**   **HYDROELECTRIC**

SOLAR THERMAL

LOL!

Q: Why did the lights go out?

A: Because they liked each other.

TOOLS OF THE TRADE

Hybrid cars have two engines—one is gasoline-powered and the other is an electric motor powered by a battery. The electric motor gets the car moving and works best at low speeds. Once the car hits the highway, the gas engine takes over because it works better at higher speeds. This makes the hybrid more efficient than a regular car—but it doesn't stop there. When a regular car needs to slow down, its brakes grab the wheels to stop them spinning. This wastes all the energy used to make them turn in the first place. A hybrid car connects the braking wheels to a generator, and it uses that energy to make more electricity, which is stored in the battery.

TRANSFORMERS

The power lines that carry electricity across the country have huge currents running at very high voltages. These currents are way too powerful for everyday machines—they'd explode. So electric companies control the voltage with transformers, which use electromagnetic induction to increase or decrease the flow of current. Step-up transformers at power plants boost current to high voltage to send it long distances. Then step-down transformers in neighborhoods lower it for use in homes.

WORD CHECK

PHOTOVOLTAIC CELL: A panel, usually made of silicon, that converts sunlight directly into electricity (see page 128)

ELECTRONICS AND CIRCUITS

Electronics are the devices we use to make electrical currents do something useful for us, like amplify our voices or run a calculator. In electronics, the current often flows in a loop, or circuit.

A circuit begins with the current leaving a source of power, travelling through various components, and then returning to the power source again. The power source might be a battery or the electrical supply from a power plant. The components connected to the circuit could be something simple like a lightbulb or a toaster. Electronics are components that control the flow of electricity through the circuit. They can make it change direction, alter the current's strength, or even stop it completely. In an electronic circuit, the current not only supplies energy but also acts as a signal carrying information. These kinds of circuits are what control microprocessors and computers.

DIRECTION OF CURRENT

Benjamin Franklin was the first person to use the terms positive and negative to describe the way electricity moves through a circuit. He thought a current began at the positive terminal of a power source and ran to the negative one. Today, we describe it the other way: Negatively charged electrons, which carry the current, are pulled out of the negative terminal toward the positive one. That means an electric current flows from negative to positive.

MICROCHIP

The simplest circuits are made of wires that run from a power supply to its components and back. They are installed inside the walls and ceilings of every house. An integrated circuit, or microchip (above), does not use wires. Instead the whole circuit is made from a single piece of conductor—in most cases a small wafer, or chip, of pure silicon that can fit on a fingertip. The electronic components in the circuit are cut into the surface of the chip, as are the connections between them. The components are tiny—you need a microscope to see them—and there are many millions working together on a modern microchip!

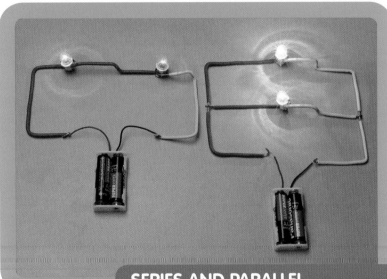

SERIES AND PARALLEL

There are two types of circuits: series and parallel. In a series circuit, the components—for instance, two lightbulbs—are connected in a row, one after the other. The voltage of the circuit will be split between the bulbs, so they'll each use half—and will glow dimly (above, left). If one of the bulbs burns out, that breaks the circuit and the other bulb will go out, too. However, in a parallel circuit, the circuit is divided into two branches, each with one bulb, and joins together again before returning to the power source. Each bulb gets the full voltage coming from the power source, so they glow more brightly (above, right). Plus, if one bulb goes out, the other will keep on working.

LOL!

Q: What did the baby lightbulb say to its mom?

A: I love you watts and watts!

CAPACITOR

The capacitor is a device that stores an electric charge so it can be used later. Capacitors are often a part of electrical circuits used in electrical devices, such as amplifiers and motion detectors. Capacitors come in all shapes and sizes, but they are basically constructed the same: A large surface of conducting material is sandwiched between insulators and rolled up tight. The capacitor stores a charge when connected to a power source. Once it's full, the charge stays inside even if the capacitor is disconnected. If wired to another circuit, the capacitor's charge floods out and provides a powerful but temporary surge of current. A camera flash is powered by a capacitor.

TOOLS OF THE TRADE

We are used to counting with 10 digits, 0 to 9, which is known as the decimal base. However, computers use just 2 digits, or the binary base. A circuit of transistors stores information as 1s and 0s, and that means a computer uses only these numbers to count. It takes a lot more digits to count this way:

DECIMAL	BINARY
0	0
1	1
2	10
3	11
4	100
5	101
6	110
7	111
8	1000
9	1001
10	1010
100	1100100

Each binary digit is known as 1 bit (1b) of information. Early computers used binary codes that had 8 bits or digits in them, and so 8 bits is known as 1 byte (1B). Sometimes 4-bit codes were used, or half a byte, and they were nicknamed "nibbles."

SEMICONDUCTOR ELECTRONICS

Most components in a modern electrical circuit are made from semiconductors, such as the metalloid (or chemical element) silicon. A semiconductor is a material that will conduct electricity in some circumstances but act like an insulator in others. Transistors are semiconductor components that work like switches: They can turn the current in areas of a circuit on and off. They can also store digital computer code.

WORD CHECK

TRANSISTOR: A small electronic device that is used to control the flow of electricity in electronic equipment, such as radios and computers

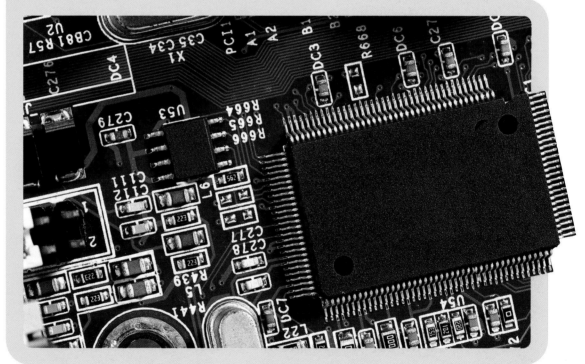

PERSONALITY PLUS

American engineer Gordon Moore (1929–) is famous for starting the Intel Corporation, one of the largest microchip makers in the world. Moore is also famous for "Moore's law," which essentially says that the number of transistors on a microchip would double every two years, which would double the processing speed. He said this in 1965, and his prediction has proved to be pretty accurate. In 1947 the first transistor was about an inch (2.5 cm) wide. By 1970 a computer chip that size had 2,300 transistors on it. Today it has more than 2 billion!

WAVE ENERGY

Nothing stays still in nature. From the tiny subatomic particle to the whole planet, energy travels around in the form of vibrations. These vibrations are called waves.

The most familiar waves are the ones that roll across the ocean, but sound is also a wave, as is light. When the ground shakes during an earthquake, it is because seismic waves from deep inside Earth are coming to the surface. All waves share the same characteristics and behave the same way. For instance, we all know the way a light wave reflects off a mirror. When a sound wave bounces off a canyon wall and comes back as an echo, that wave is being reflected in the same way. However, waves are not all identical. Each is produced by a different kind of motion.

TRANSVERSE WAVE

TYPES OF WAVES

There are two types of waves: transverse and longitudinal. Light moves as transverse waves. They vibrate up and down at right angles to the direction the wave is traveling, just like waves on the surface of the ocean. The second kind of wave, the longitudinal wave, is how sound travels through air, water, or rocks. Instead of vibrating up and down, the particles squeeze together and then spread out in the same direction as the wave's motion.

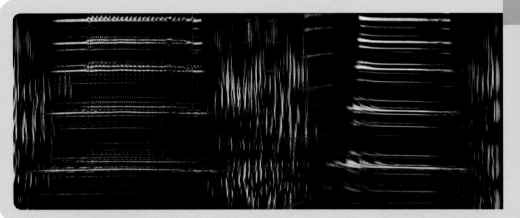

MEASURING WAVES

Every wave—no matter how it is moving—has two basic measurements. The first is wavelength. This is the distance from one crest to the next. The second is frequency, which is the number of wavelengths that the wave travels in a second. High frequency means it can repeat more wavelengths in a short distance, so it has a higher pitch, if it is a sound wave. Low frequency means it has a long wavelength. The call of the blue whale is a low-frequency sound wave (left) and can be heard for miles. Frequency is measured in hertz (H). 1H is one wavelength per second.

TRY THIS!

WHAT DOES A MIRROR DO?

WHAT YOU NEED: A mirror, some paper, colored pens

HOW LONG IT TAKES: Less than 15 minutes

Check out the way reflection works. First write a short message, such as "WHAT DOES A MIRROR DO?" and hold the paper up to the mirror. Can you read it? It's backward. Now try writing the question in reverse, and hold it up again. You should be able to read the reflection. (This is an easy way to write secret messages to a friend or write in your diary so no one can read it!) Now see if there are letters that look the same in the mirror as they do on the page. Also try drawing different shapes with different colored lines. How do they change when they are reflected?

REFLECTION

The simplest wave behavior is reflection. All waves reflect when they hit an impenetrable surface. When a light wave hits a mirror, the direction of the wave is measured according to an imaginary line coming straight out of the mirror at a right angle. This line is called the normal. If the light travels straight at the mirror along the normal then it will reflect straight back. If it arrives at an angle to the normal, it will reflect at the same angle—but on the other side of the normal. So light arriving from the left will reflect to the right. All waves reflect according to this simple rule. And it explains why a mirror image shows things backward, with the left and right swapping places.

INTERFERENCE

On a windy day, when there are lots of waves on the ocean, it can be hard to see single waves moving across the water. It might look like the water is just sloshing around. This is due to a wave behavior called interference. Interference occurs when two waves meet and join together. If the waves have the same wavelength and the crests and troughs all match up, then the two of them will merge into a single wave that is twice as high as the originals. If the same two waves were to meet, but the crest of one lined up with the trough of the other, then the two waves would cancel each other out. Normally, waves interfere less exactly than this and become jumbled together.

LOL!

Q: What did the receiver say to the radio wave?

A: Ouch! That megahertz!

GEEK STREAK

There are many benefits to using ocean waves to generate energy. It's renewable, unlike fossil fuels, such as coal and oil, which are in limited supply. It's clean. Wave generators turn waves into energy, while the burning of fossil fuels pollutes the air with chemicals. It's more reliable than solar energy, which is produced only when the sun shines. Waves create energy day and night.

DIFFRACTION

Have you ever wondered why you can hear noises coming from around corners? Or how light shining through a tiny hole can illuminate the entire room? The reason is a process called diffraction. Diffraction occurs when a sound or light wave passes through a gap that is smaller than its wavelength. The wave does not stop, but travels on to the other side, with the same frequency and wavelength. The only difference is that the wave now ripples out in all directions, where before it moved in one direction. It's as if the gap has made the wave start again from a single point.

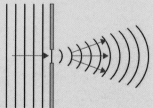

PERSONALITY PLUS

In 1935, American scientist Charles Richter (1900-1985) developed a way to measure the waves that make earthquakes. He called it the Richter scale. Earthquakes' waves are caused by rocks cracking deep underground. When the waves reach the surface, they make the ground shake, split, and ripple—which can cause terrible damage to cities. The Richter scale measures the power of the waves. Very strong quakes are rated as 9 on the scale. A quake rated as 1 is so small it can be detected only by machines. Each number on the Richter scale is 10 times more powerful than the number before it. So waves that are measured as a magnitude 8 quake are actually 10 times more powerful than ones that cause a 7 quake, and 100 times more than a 6 quake.

SOUND WAVES

Sound is a type of energy made by vibrations. It travels in waves through matter, such as solids, liquids, and gases, and can be heard.

Did you know we have sound wave detectors on our heads? Our ears convert sound waves traveling through the air into nerve signals that go to our brain. Ears can tell the frequency of a sound wave, how much power it has, and when both ears work together, where the sound is coming from. We communicate with sound, and it's also a big part of how we entertain ourselves. So it's no wonder machines like the telephone, the radio, and the phonograph are important inventions in history. Sound waves can also be used to detect objects in the dark, navigate under water, and see inside the body.

TOO LOUD!

We all understand that a sound can be quiet or loud, but what causes that difference? A piece of music has the same notes whether it's played loud or soft. Clearly, the wavelengths and frequencies have not changed, only the sound wave's amplitude, which is another name for the distance between the top and bottom of the wave. A sound wave with large amplitude is loud. But amplitude is not about height—it measures how much space, or volume, a sound wave takes up in the air as it travels. That's why we call loudness volume.

MAKING MUSIC

Pluck a string on a guitar. Sound waves come from the vibrating string and cause the air molecules around it to vibrate in a wave of compressions (when the molecules are close together) and expansions (when the molecules are spread apart). The musical note is a single, clear sound wave with a certain frequency. We hear high notes when the wave has a high frequency and low notes when it has a low frequency. Most other sounds, including voices, are a more complex mixture of waves that often change frequencies, but our ears detect them just as well.

WORD CHECK

SONAR: A device that uses sound waves to find things underwater. It is short for "sound navigation and ranging."

GEEK STREAK

When fire engines or police cars race to an emergency they often turn on their sirens. As they whiz past you, the whine of their sirens seems to drop in pitch. This is called the Doppler effect. As the siren comes toward you, its sound waves are squashed so they sound high-pitched. When it moves away, the waves are stretched, so the pitch drops.

RECORDING SOUND

Our ears detect sound by turning the motion of the air into a vibration of the eardrum, which is a delicate flap of skin deep inside the ear. Sound recorders do the same thing. The first device that could record sound—the phonograph—was invented in 1877 by Thomas Edison. The phonograph captured sounds, such as the language of Native Americans, with a trumpet-shaped horn that focused sound waves onto a tiny needle, causing it to wobble up and down (below). As it wobbled, the needle made a groove on a cylinder of soft wax. That groove was a solid, fixed version of the sound wave. To play the sound back, the needle ran back through the groove—wobbling again—and made the air vibrate in the horn. Out came the sound! Modern recorders use wobbling magnets to convert sound directly into electrical signals, which are then recorded as computer code.

TRY THIS!

WHAT YOU NEED: A paper clip, a foot (30 cm) or more of string or thread, a paper cup

HOW LONG IT TAKES: 30 minutes

Want to make a cup violin complete with a loudspeaker? Make a small hole in the bottom of the cup. Thread the string through it, and tie the top end to the paper clip inside the cup so it anchors the string on the bottom of the cup. Now grip the string below the cup with one hand and pull tight. Wet the fingers on your other hand, and pull your wet fingers down the tight string. It should make a buzzing noise, especially in the cup. The string vibrates as you pull on it, and that makes the air in the cup vibrate, too.

MAKE SOME NOISE!

Loudspeakers—from the huge ones at rock concerts to the little earpiece in your cell phone—use magnetic forces to amplify recorded sounds. The recorded sound arrives at the speaker in the form of an electric current, which rises and falls just like the sound wave it was copied from. The speaker has an electromagnet surrounded by a permanent magnet at its center. The electric current carrying the recorded sound electrifies the electromagnet, creating a magnetic force field that changes in a way that matches the sound wave. The electromagnet's field repels the permanent magnet, which makes the electromagnet wobble back and forth. The electromagnet is connected to a cone-shaped disk, which transfers the wobble to the air, creating sound waves.

ECHOLOCATORS

Ever wonder how submarines can travel through the deep, dark ocean without bumping into things? They use a detection system called sonar to know what is in the water around them. This system sends out a pulse of sound—it sounds like a ping—that travels through the water. (Sound travels four times farther in water than in air.) The ping reflects off solid objects, including the seabed, and travels back to the sub as an echo. The time it takes for the echo to come back tells the sonar operators how far away an object is. The echo also tells them what the object is made of, how big it is, and where it's going. Bats, whales, and dolphins use sonar to communicate, hunt for food, and find their way around in the dark.

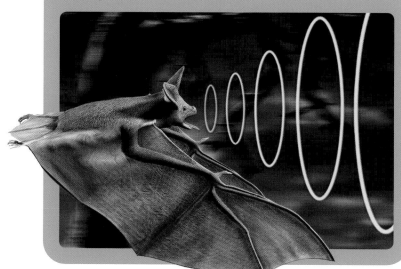

TOOLS OF THE TRADE

Doctors use sound waves to look at the heart and other soft organs inside our bodies. They're also used to look at unborn babies. Called ultrasound, these waves travel into the body and echo off the soft tissues inside. The echoes are picked up by the ultrasound machine, which converts them into a picture. Ultrasound waves are safe, painless, and too high-pitched for a human to hear.

121

LIGHT AND COLOR

Sunlight is a wave of energy that we can see. It travels from the sun and reflects off objects all around us.

Our eyes gather light waves and convert them into an image of dark and bright shapes that our brain sees as a house, a car, or a blade of grass. Sunlight appears to be white but in reality there is an entire rainbow of colors in its rays. When white light shines on the house, car, or lawn, the colors in the object that are not absorbed bounce back to our eyes. Then our eyes tell our brain that the house is yellow, the car is blue, and the blade of grass is green. Without light, there would be no color. In fact, there would be no sight at all.

SEEING COLOR

Light waves can be reflected or absorbed. When we see colors, we are actually seeing the light that wasn't absorbed. An apple appears red because it has absorbed every color except red. Since white light is the combination of all colors in the spectrum, snow appears white because it absorbs nothing and reflects all of the light. A piece of black paper looks black because it absorbs all light into the paper and none is reflected back out.

WORD CHECK

PIGMENT: A chemical substance that has a particular color

COLOR SPECTRUM

In the 1700s, Sir Isaac Newton shone light through a piece of cut glass, or prism, and discovered that sunlight could be separated into seven different colored rays of visible light. This color spectrum includes red, orange, yellow, green, blue, and violet—the colors of the rainbow (see page 125). What is it that makes light a different color? Its wavelength. At one end of the visible spectrum is red—it has the longest wavelength. At the other end is violet, with the shortest wavelength.

MIXING LIGHT

The three primary colors we see in light are red, green, and blue. Our eyes do the mixing. When red and green light waves are mixed together we see yellow light. Mix red light with blue and we see a pinkish red color called magenta. That's the color sometimes used to light a singer performing on stage.

LOL!

Q: What kind of bow can't be tied?

A: A rainbow.

INTERFERENCE PATTERNS

Colored light is made from waves, and like any wave they can interfere with each other. Interfering light waves create beautiful shimmering patterns—what you see on the surface of a soap bubble, or when spilled gasoline is floating on water. This colorful pattern is formed when white light (with all the colors) shines onto a thin film of gasoline. Some of the light is reflected straight back, but some of it shines through the layer of gasoline and hits the water underneath. This light travels just a tiny bit farther before it reflects back. Now we have two sets of light waves, with the second set being slightly out of step with the first set. That makes the waves interfere, and some color waves disappear while others are boosted. The result? A shimmering swirl of colors.

SCATTERING COLORS

If light coming from the sun is white, then why is the sky blue? Light waves scatter when sunlight hits the Earth's atmosphere. Blue light has more energy in it than other colors, so it is scattered more by the air, and it takes longer to reach the Earth's surface. This explains why sunlight seems to fill the air with light and isn't like a giant flashlight beam blasting down from space. What we see when we look up is all the blue light bouncing around the sky.

PAINTING WITH COLOR

The primary colors of light are red, blue, and green. But the pigments used to color inks, paints, and dyes have different primary colors: cyan (blue), magenta (a pinkish red), yellow, and black. Why different colors? Because paint and inks are not waves, but objects that absorb and reflect light. When the primary colors of light waves are combined, they become white light. When primary colors of dyes and ink are all mixed together, they form the color black.

TRY THIS!

WHAT YOU NEED: A thick card cut into a circle, colored markers, a sharp pencil (for spinning the top)

HOW LONG IT TAKES: 1 to 2 hours

Want to try mixing the colors of light? Make a color spinner. This is a top that has all of the colors in the spectrum on it. See what happens when it spins. Divide the card into six equal wedge-shaped sections. Color one section in each of these colors: red, orange, yellow, green, blue, violet (pale purple). Make a small hole in the center and push the pencil through so the tip is facing away from the colored surface. Spin the top—fast. What happens to the colors? They should merge together and become white (or perhaps a pale brown). Now try making different tops with fewer colors and see how they mix when you spin them.

BENDING LIGHT

Light is a wave that can be bent. When it's bent, interesting things happen.

In the vacuum of space, the speed of light is fixed. It doesn't change. But when a light wave enters a medium of different density, like air or water, it slows down. The change of speed is what causes the light to bend, or refract. This refraction is what causes a beautiful rainbow to arch across the sky, or a diamond to sparkle. Light refraction can also make you think you see water flooding across a highway, or a city floating in the air.

SPEED SHIFT

Light speed slows by a third in water, and by more than half when passing through a diamond, which is one of the hardest materials we know. The cut diamond refracts the light into all colors of the rainbow. Jewelers call this rainbow color "fire."

CHANGING POSITION

Refraction can be confusing. Imagine a cat eyeing a goldfish in a fishbowl. The light from the fish does not travel in a straight line to the cat's eyes. As it moves into the air, the light is refracted a little. However, the cat doesn't know this, and so it sees the fish under the water in a straight line from its position. Luckily for the fish, if the cat dives in to catch its prey, it will miss—the fish is actually located deeper down!

REFRACTION

Usually light travels in a straight line, but if it strikes a new medium, like water, it refracts, or bends. That's because part of the light wave strikes the water before the rest of it. When we look at a straw in a glass of water, the light from the top of the straw goes straight to our eye. But the light from the straw in the water bends, making it look like it's broken.

FOLLOWING A RAINBOW

When it is raining and sunny at the same time, look toward the sun and then turn around. Do you see a rainbow? Light from the sun has been reflected back at you by the raindrops. But the white sunlight is refracted as it goes in and out of the rainwater. Each color in sunlight refracts by a slightly different amount—red the least and blue the most. So the sunlight is split into the dazzling array of colors. The rainbow may be very close or miles away—but you'll never get close enough to touch it because it's not really there. It is just colored lights in the sky.

GEEK STREAK

A rainbow starts with white light, which is the combination of all the colors of light. When it passes through the prism of a raindrop, it is separated into the six colors of the rainbow: red, orange, yellow, green, blue, and violet.

WORD CHECK

MEDIUM: The substance a wave is traveling through. Ocean waves only move through water, but sound can travel through air, water, and even rocks. Light travels through any medium that is transparent, or see-through.

MIRAGES

You're riding in a car on a hot sunny day. "Stop!" you cry out. The road ahead looks covered in a shimmering pool of water. You've just seen a mirage, a trick of the light caused by refraction. Air of different densities, hot and cold, can refract light just like water. As the air above the ground becomes hot, it refracts the sunlight. The shimmering water is actually light from the sky. The opposite can happen if the air is cold above the ground, but warmer higher up. Light from a distant object on the ground—a tree, mountain, or even a city on the horizon—will look like it is projected into the sky.

PERSONALITY PLUS

Seven hundred years ago, most people thought a rainbow was the rim of the sun reflecting off a sheet of rain. A German monk named Theodoric of Freiburg decided to take a closer look. He made model raindrops out of large glass balls filled with water. Then he followed the path of light in the raindrop and learned that light was refracted three times: entering the raindrop, inside the drop, and exiting it. He also proved the colors of the rainbow were formed by the interaction of light with the water drops.

125

ELECTROMAGNETIC SPECTRUM

The electromagnetic (EM) spectrum includes radio waves, infrared light, ultraviolet (UV) light, and x-rays.

These forms of electromagnetic radiation are the same as visible light, just with different energy. We are unaware of most of this light because our eyes can't see it. We do, however, feel heat from infrared rays. Electromagnetic radiation is released when matter goes from a high-energy state to a lower energy state. The EM waves used to heat your food in a microwave oven are low in energy compared to visible sunlight, which is medium range. Other kinds of EM radiation, such as gamma rays, are really high energy, and can be produced by powerful explosions, burning stars, and lightning.

ELECTROMAGNETIC SPECTRUM

The electromagnetic spectrum is divided into sections according to the wavelengths of each type of radiation. Visible light falls in the middle of the spectrum. Radio waves and infrared waves have longer wavelengths, while ultraviolet, x-rays, and gamma rays have shorter ones.

X-RAYS
These powerful rays were discovered by the German scientist Wilhelm Röntgen in 1895. They have much higher energy and shorter wavelengths than ultraviolet rays. X-rays have enough energy to shine through soft objects, which is why they are used to take images of bones inside the body.

MICROWAVES
This type of radiation has wavelengths measured in inches. Microwaves are used in microwave ovens and to transmit cell phone calls and Wi-Fi signals.

VISIBLE LIGHT
This is the light we can see, such as sunlight, firelight, and electric lights. Visible light colors go from shortest wavelength to longest: violet, blue, green, yellow, orange, and red.

RADIO WAVES
These were discovered in 1887 by Heinrich Hertz, who made them in his lab by causing electricity to zap across a gap as a spark. Radio waves can have very long wavelengths up to hundreds of miles long.

INFRARED
In 1800, William Herschel measured the temperatures of light that had been split into colors. He found the hottest part was always an area of invisible rays just next to the red light. He called it infrared, which means "less than red." Its wavelengths are measured in fractions of an inch. Infrared cameras and goggles can see the heat emitted by people and animals at night. Infrared waves are also used in remotes.

ULTRAVIOLET
These rays are invisible to our eyes. They have a slightly shorter wavelength than blue and violet light—the name ultraviolet means "above violet."

GAMMA RAYS
The most high-energy and most dangerous waves in the EM spectrum, gamma rays are produced by nuclear reactions. They have tiny wavelengths about the size of an atomic nucleus.

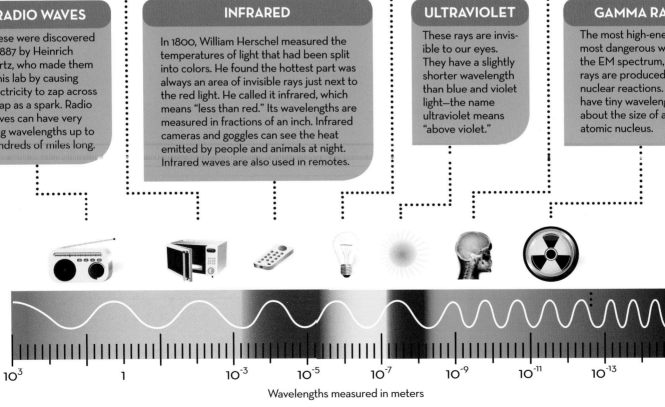

10^3 1 10^{-3} 10^{-5} 10^{-7} 10^{-9} 10^{-11} 10^{-13}

Wavelengths measured in meters

TOOLS OF THE TRADE

Wavelengths of high-energy radiation get so small that describing them as millionths of a meter is too complicated. So scientists use a unit called an angstrom (Å), named after Swedish scientist Anders Jonas Ångström. An angstrom is one ten-billionth of a meter. Visible light has a wavelength of around 5,000 angstroms, UV is 300 Å, while x-rays are around 5 Å.

WAVES AND PARTICLES

Electromagnetic radiation is a stream of photons, or packets of energy particles, traveling through space. It travels as a wave with up and down fluctuations of its electric and magnetic fields (see above). When the electromagnetic radiation contains a lot of energy, like x-rays, the wavelength of these fluctuations is small, and the frequency is high. Lower energy radiation, like radio waves, have longer wavelengths and lower frequency.

PACKETS OF ENERGY

How electromagnetic waves interact with atoms tells us a lot about the structure of an atom. Atoms have electrons moving around in their outer shells, and when energy is added, an electron can jump to a different position. Then it can jump back down again, releasing a packet of electromagnetic radiation called a photon. This packet of energy eventually hits another atom. The photon might be reflected—or bounce off—or its energy might be absorbed by the atom, and make another electron jump farther out from its nucleus.

ELECTRON

NUCLEUS

PHOTON

PROTECTIVE LAYERS

As well as visible light, the sun gives out a large amount of ultraviolet (UV) light. This high-energy radiation can damage the chemicals inside cells in your body and cause diseases, such as cancer. Darker skin offers some protection (it absorbs UV photons better than light skin) and so do sunblock lotions. But our best protection is high in the sky—a thin band of gas in the upper atmosphere called the ozone layer. Ozone is a special form of oxygen that filters out much of the dangerous UV arriving from the sun. In the last half of the 20th century, refrigerators and aerosol cans used gases that damaged the ozone layer, making large holes that let UV through. Today, those chemicals are banned and the ozone layer is slowly rebuilding.

PERSONALITY PLUS

Louis de Broglie (1892-1987) was the first person to suggest that particles, such as electrons, could act like waves. In 1924, this French scientist began to develop a system that showed that all particles, including electrons and quarks (found inside protons and neutrons) are not solids at all but a complex tangle of wavelike vibrations. The vibrations mean that a particle's position is never totally fixed—it is always shifting between different possible locations. This discovery helped establish a new way of describing our world, called quantum mechanics.

ELECTROMAGNETIC WAVES

Electromagnetic waves are produced by charges moving inside atoms. They create an electric field that then makes a magnetic field.

Visible light, radio waves, and x-rays are examples of electromagnetic waves and each has its own special properties. High-energy radiation, such as x-rays and gamma rays, can go through solid objects. Low-energy radiation, such as radio waves, bounces off nearly everything and can travel great distances on Earth because of this. Solar panels convert electromagnetic waves from the sun into electricity, without producing any pollution. Optical fibers use light waves to send messages at superfast speeds. Laser light waves can be found in everything from video game players to checkout scanners in grocery stores. Lasers cut sheet metal, guide missiles to their targets, and are used in laser tag.

SOLAR POWER

Electromagnetic waves from the sun are converted into electricity by solar panels, making clean energy. The solar panels on roofs (below) make use of the photovoltaic effect, which occurs when light shines on a particular type of solid, such as silicon. The light waves break chemical bonds and free up electrons that we can use in an electrical circuit. Solar panels were first used to power satellites and space probes. Then they became common in small electric devices like calculators. In 2015, Morocco took steps to become the world's solar superpower, building a 500,000-mirror complex in the Sahara, with plans for more.

WIRELESS COMMUNICATION

In 1901, Italian inventor Guglielmo Marconi (1874–1937) demonstrated that radio waves could be sent huge distances on Earth, even across the Atlantic Ocean. This is because radio waves bounce off the atmosphere, making them travel across the Earth and not fly off into space like other waves. This ushered in the modern age of telecommunication. Early radio signals were simple pulses of radio waves that spelled out the dots and dashes of Morse code. Later it became possible to alter the shape of the radio wave so it could carry sound information or any data. Today's cell phones send and receive messages as computer code in radio waves.

WORD CHECK

PHOTOVOLTAIC: A system that converts the sun's energy directly into electricity using a non-mechanical device, usually made from a combination of silicon and metals

MICROWAVES

When you pop a frozen dinner into a microwave oven you are cooking your meal with short-wavelength radio waves. The oven directs a powerful beam with a very specific wavelength, about 4.7 inches (12 cm), at the food. Microwaves at this wavelength transfer their energy to the water in the food, making those molecules very hot. The heat spreads through the dinner and cooks it. Different microwaves are used in radar signals, cell phones, and satellite communications.

TOOLS OF THE TRADE

Laser beams are also used as a way to communicate quickly. The fastest method is to shoot electromagnetic waves through optical fiber. These flexible strands of thin clear glass can carry anything from telephone calls and emails to streamed video around the world in a fraction of a second. Instead of being sent as electric current along a wire, the optical fiber transmits information as a laser beam—actually several beams at once. Each beam sends coded data as ultrafast waves, which can be decoded at the other end. Thick cables with hundreds of fibers bundled together run between cities and along the ocean floor. Each one can carry 10 million megabytes of data every second.

MEDICINE

X-ray machines were the first scanners that let doctors see inside the human body. The powerful rays shine through the skin and soft body parts but they can't get through hard bones. The rays cast a shadow on a screen behind the patient. This shadowy image is captured in a photograph, or x-ray image, that can show broken bones and other damage inside the body. More recently, x-rays and gamma rays have been used to burn away cancers and other tumors that can't be reached by regular surgery.

LASER BEAMS

Natural sources of light, like the sun or a flame, are made up of a jumble of wavelengths. However, a laser is a beam made up of just one wavelength of light. All of the light from a laser behaves in exactly the same way, so the beam stays tight as it reflects and refracts. A scanner in a store (left) flashes a laser at the bar code on an item and reads the price. A DVD player reads a movie file by reflecting a laser off the disc.

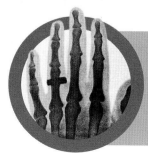

PERSONALITY PLUS

Anna Röntgen was the first person to ever have an x-ray taken when, in 1895, her husband beamed rays through her hand. The resulting picture showed the bones in her fingers and her wedding ring. She was shocked by the skeletal picture, and said, "I have seen my own death." In 1901, her husband, Wilhelm Röntgen, was awarded the first Nobel Prize in physics for his discovery of x-rays.

SPEED OF LIGHT

Light travels almost a million times faster than sound. If light were to travel in a circular path it would orbit the Earth seven and a half times in one second!

All electromagnetic waves in a vacuum, such as space, travel at the speed of light. In the 1600s people believed that light didn't travel, but was instantaneous. Italian scientist Galileo Galilei felt that it had to have some speed and tried to measure the time it took for a distant light to reach his eyes. His experiment failed because there was no way for him to measure such a short period of time. Today, physicists use lasers to measure the speed of light, which has been determined by the International Committee for Weights and Measures to be 186,282 miles per second (299,792 km/s).

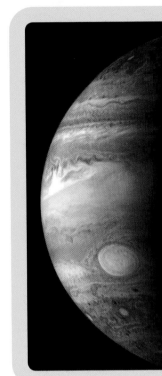

DISTANCE AND TIME

Because the speed of light is fixed in the vacuum of space, we can use it to measure distances. A light-year is the distance light travels in a year. The nearest star to the solar system, Proxima Centauri, is about four light-years away. The light from Proxima Centauri left the star four years ago, so what we see today is what the star looked like then. The most powerful telescopes can see more than 13 billion light-years away. The light from 13 billion light-years away shows us what the universe looked like when it was only a few million years old! That makes light a kind of time machine that lets us look into the past.

MEASURING LIGHT SPEED

The first person to measure the speed of light with any accuracy was the Danish astronomer Ole Rømer. In 1676, he saw that Jupiter's moon Io did not always appear in the sky at the same time. He knew that Io made its orbit around Jupiter every 1.65 days, but it showed up in the sky ahead of its expected orbit when the Earth was closer to Jupiter, and it came later when Earth was farther away. That was because the light from Jupiter took several hours to reach Earth. Knowing the distance to Jupiter and the difference in time, he thought he could calculate how fast light traveled. His answer was close to the modern figure for the speed of light.

BLACK HOLES

Light is affected by gravity. A black hole is an object in space that has the highest gravity of all. It can take up less space than a pinhead, but weigh more than our sun. (Some black holes weigh as much as a million suns!) The speed with which a rocket would have to fly to escape the pull of gravity if it was very close to a black hole would have to be faster than the speed of light. Nothing can go that fast. That means nothing can escape from a black hole—not even light itself. This is what makes a black hole black. No light shines out from it—it is completely dark and totally invisible at its center. However, the stars and other objects that get sucked into black holes get very hot as they fall in, and astronomers look for this hot halo to figure out where black holes are.

LOOKING AT LIGHT

Imagine you are in a car driving at night with the headlights on. You can see light coming from all directions—the stars in the sky, the lights from a stoplight up ahead, the headlights of oncoming traffic, and the lights from the cars behind you. All these light sources seem to be moving at different speeds compared to you. Scientist Albert Einstein explained that the speed of light is staying the same, but the space between you and the lights is being squeezed and stretched, the way the sound of a police siren is squeezed and stretched as it passes by you.

GEEK STREAK

The speed of light in air is only slightly slower than its speed in a vacuum. The speed in water is a third slower than in a vacuum; and the slowest speed of all is through a diamond. Inside this jewel, light slows to less than half its full speed.

BREAKING THE SPEED LIMIT

Light travels fastest through a vacuum, and slows down when it moves through things like air, water, or glass. However, it is possible for high-energy particles to appear to travel faster than light in these mediums. This creates a strange flash of eerie blue light, known as Cherenkov radiation. Flashes of Cherenkov radiation are produced by high-speed particles from space crashing into Earth's air. It also happens inside the reactors at nuclear power plants.

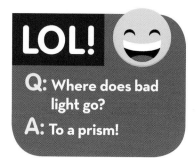

LOL!

Q: Where does bad light go?

A: To a prism!

LENSES

A lens is just a simple piece of curved glass or plastic, but when light is refracted by it, an image is formed.

People have been using lenses to magnify objects for more than 4,000 years. In the 13th century, Europeans put two magnifying lenses in a frame to create the first pair of glasses. In the 1600s, the first telescope was invented, which magnified an object more than 30 times its actual size. Now lenses are everywhere—in cameras, binoculars, projectors, and the peephole in your door. Lenses allow astronomers to peer through giant telescopes into deep space and scientists to examine tiny microbes invisible to the human eye through microscopes. The science that studies how lenses work is called optics.

CONVEX LENS

Most lenses have a convex shape, which means they curve outward like an eyeball. A convex lens is thick in the middle, which makes light rays that pass through it bend toward each other and meet. Where the light beams meet is called the focal point. A magnifying glass is a convex lens. The earliest convex lenses were made from carved crystals in Mesopotamia. They were used as "burning glasses" to focus sunlight into a white-hot beam that could light a fire.

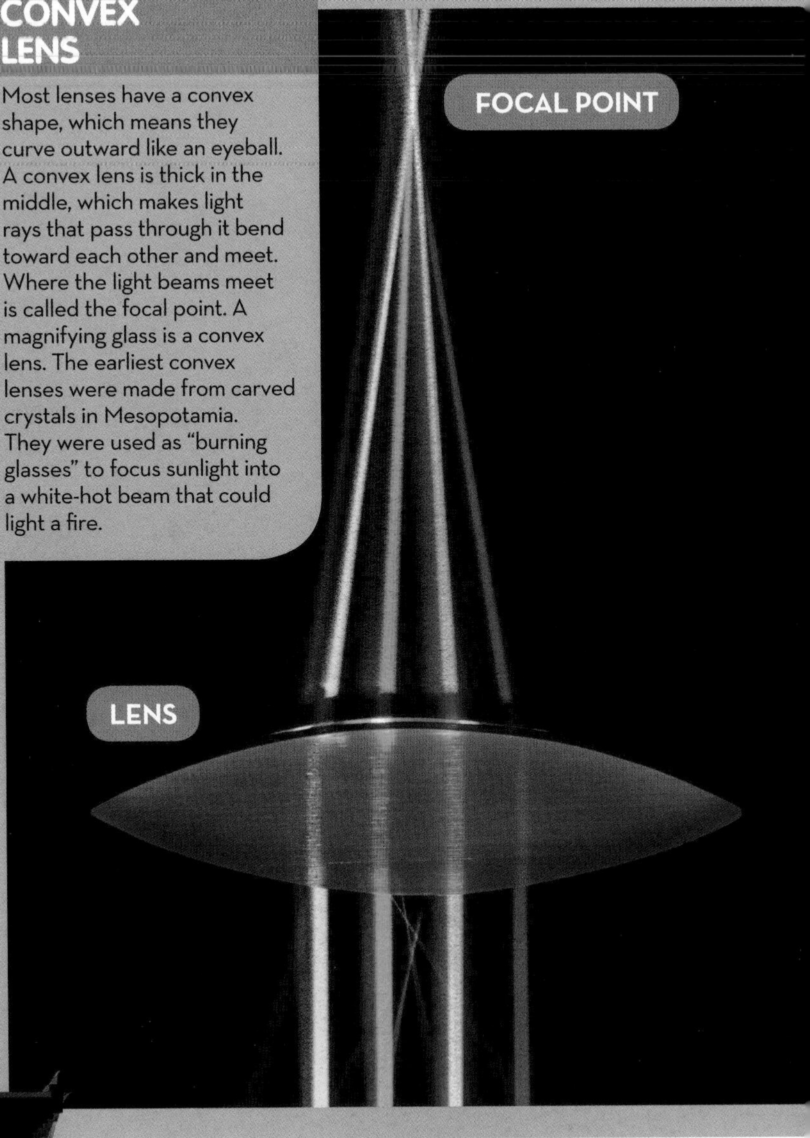

FOCAL POINT

LENS

CONCAVE LENS

A concave lens curves inward and makes light hitting it diverge, or bend outward. While a convex lens magnifies an image, a concave lens makes it look smaller. Concave and convex lenses are often used together in devices like movie projectors. The convex lens creates a magnified image and the concave lens allows the image to be projected onto a movie screen. Moving the second lens back and forth on a telescope, camera, or binoculars allows you to focus the image exactly where your eyes can see it best.

MAGNIFICATION

A convex lens can produce a magnified image of an object, making it appear much larger than it really is. For this to work, the object being viewed has to be near the lens and closer than the focal point.

PARABOLIC DISH

How do we listen to sounds or gather light waves from outer space? With a giant bowl-shaped device called a parabolic dish. This big dish is a giant concave lens that has a reflective surface that is used to collect light rays or project heat, sound, and radio waves. You'll see large parabolic dishes at radar stations and solar power plants. Many homes have smaller parabolic dishes on their roofs that are antennas for satellite TV systems.

LOL!

Q: What happened when the glass fell into the lens grinder?

A: It made a spectacle of itself.

ELECTRON MICROSCOPE

Magnifying with light has a limit. It is not possible for microscopes with curved lenses to make images of objects less than 300 billionths of a meter across. The problem is the wavelength of light is too big to reflect off such tiny objects. However, electrons have much smaller wavelengths, so scientists employ microscopes that use electric and magnetic fields instead of curved lenses to create images out of electrons. These electron microscopes allow them to peer inside living cells and view particles that are only a few atoms wide.

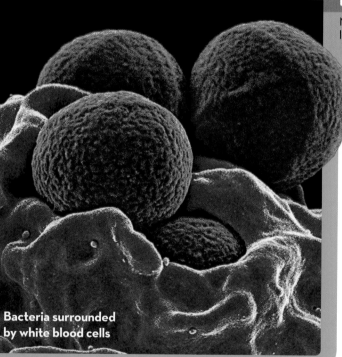

Bacteria surrounded by white blood cells

TOOLS OF THE TRADE

A microscope uses two lenses at either end of a tube. The first lens gathers light coming from the object being viewed and focuses it into a little image inside the tube very close to the second lens. The second lens magnifies this focused image so you can see its tiny details.

PERSONALITY PLUS

The founding father of the science of optics was an Arab named Ibn al-Haytham, who lived and worked in the 11th century. Most of his discoveries were made when he was in prison in Cairo, Egypt. (Al-Haytham had upset the caliph by boasting he could build a dam across the Nile River—he couldn't.) Al-Haytham was the first to prove that light beams travel in straight lines. This led him to figure out the law of reflection (see page 118). Al-Haytham also showed that light travels from objects to the eye. Up until then people thought that the eyes sent out a laser-like beam that scanned objects and picked up their reflections.

TRY THIS!

WHAT YOU NEED: A large jar, water, some small objects, such as coins or tiny seashells

HOW LONG IT TAKES: 15 minutes

To create your own magnifier, place the small objects on a table, take the lid off the jar, and turn it upside down over the objects. Now spoon as much water as you can into the hollow dip on the jar's base. The curve of the jar's base makes the water puddle work just like a convex lens. Look through your water lens and check out the writing on the coin or examine the delicate ridges on the seashell.

VISION

The human body has five main senses—hearing, smell, taste, touch, and sight.

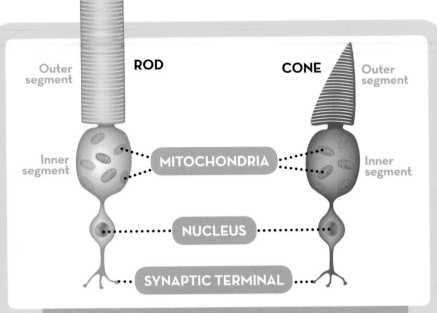

All of these senses are very important, but we probably rely most on our sense of sight. Beyond showing what is around us—things like food, objects, and other people—we use our vision for communication. People often make faces and gesture with their hands to add extra meaning to the words they use in a conversation. Human eyes work in the same way as those of other vertebrates, although other kinds of animals use a different vision system. All eyes in nature follow the same rules of optics as any other light-detecting device. In fact our eyes work very much like a camera, with a lens focusing light onto an image that forms on a light-sensitive surface. In a camera, that process creates a photograph. Our eye converts the image into a nerve signal that allows our brain to visualize the scene we are viewing.

RODS AND CONES

There are two kinds of retinal cells at the back of the eye: rods and cones. Each works like a dot on a TV screen, and the brain puts together an image from the pattern of dots it receives from each eye. Rods (named for their shape) produce a black-and-white image, and work best in the dark. Color images are detected by cone cells. Cones have different chemicals that respond only to blue, green, or red light, and work best in bright light. The main chemical in these retina cells is a pink-colored substance called rhodopsin. When light hits rhodopsin it produces a chemical change that sends a nerve signal from the eye to the brain.

ANATOMY OF THE EYE

The human eye is an egg-shaped sphere covered in a protective white layer called the sclera. An opening at the front, called the pupil, is surrounded by the iris, which can widen and tighten to make the pupil larger and smaller, and control how much light gets inside. The middle of the eye is filled with a clear jelly called the vitreous. The back surface is covered with the retina, which has light-sensitive cells that convert light beams into nerve signals and send them to the brain. Light coming into the eye is focused on the retina by a flexible clear convex lens.

WORD CHECK

RETINA: The light-sensitive layer of tissue at the back of the inner eye that acts like film in a camera. It receives light, converts it into images, and sends it to the brain.

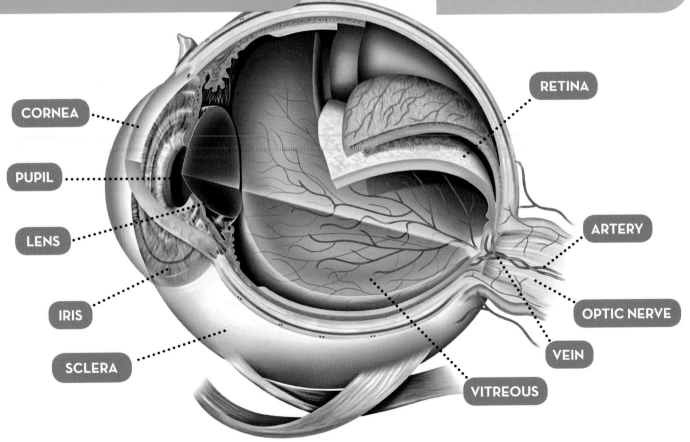

SEEING PATTERNS

What we see is not always what arrives in our eyes. The visual cortex—the region at the back of the brain that processes signals from the eyes—looks for recognizable patterns in the jumble of light hitting the retina. Some of the most important patterns are those made by faces. As this optical illusion shows, we sometimes get confused by patterns.

USING EYEGLASSES

Many people have problems seeing because their eye lenses can't form focused images. People who cannot focus on distant objects are nearsighted, or myopic, because they can see things that are near. Those who cannot see close up are farsighted, or hyperopic, because they can see far. The lenses in eyeglasses sit in front of the eyes to correct the problem.

TRY THIS!

WHAT YOU NEED: Your eye and this book

HOW LONG IT TAKES: 3 minutes

The nerves that carry signals from your retina run along the inside of the eye until they reach the large optic nerve that takes the information to the brain. Where the optic nerve pokes through the retina there is no room for rod or cone cells, so you cannot see with this bit of the eye. Follow this simple procedure to find the blind spot in each of your eyes:

Cover your left eye and look at the dot above with your right eye. Concentrate on it and don't look away. Now bring the book slowly toward your right eye. Keep looking at the dot but think about the +. And then suddenly—it disappears! This is because the light from the + is hitting your blind spot. Repeat the test but cover the right eye and look at the + with your left. Now make the dot disappear.

ANIMAL EYES

There are many different kinds of eyes in the animal kingdom. Jellyfish, sea stars, and flatworms can only tell the difference between light and dark by using ocelli, or "simple eyes." These are patches of light-sensitive cells on the body that don't have lenses and can't form images. Vertebrate eyes, found in fish, birds, and mammals, use retinas to capture images. Octopus and squid eyes are similar but evolved separately. We know this because the nerves carrying the images in vertebrate eyes run over the top of the retina, while in octopus and squid, those nerves are buried underneath. Insects and other bugs use compound eyes with hundreds of individual lenses. Compound eyes are very good at detecting movement—which is why a fly always sees the flyswatter coming!

GEEK STREAK

Largest eyes: A colossal squid's eyes are 11 inches (27 cm) wide, with a pupil 3.5 inches (9 cm) across. That helps it see in the deep, dark water.

Sharpest eyes: Eagles, falcons, and other birds of prey can see eight times farther than humans. They can spot a rabbit running across a field a mile (1.6 km) away.

Most number of eyes: Giant clams have thousands of tiny simple eyes running around the fleshy rims of their shells.

THE WORLD IN COLOR

We humans see the world in brilliant, vivid color. That's an ability we inherited from our primate ancestors. Like us, apes and other primates make images from the three colors of light picked up in the eye—red, green, and blue. They are especially good at seeing red and green light—and yellow, which is a mixture of those two colors of light. That helps them (and us) see if fruits and veggies are ripe and ready to eat. However, most mammals, like dogs, lions, and cows, only see with two colors—blue and yellow. Dolphins and whales view everything in black and white. Try to imagine what the world looks like to these other animals.

Binocular Vision

Our eyes point forward, with each eye looking pretty much at the same things at the same time. However, each eye sees the object in front of us in a slightly different position to the other one. Our brain uses these differences to calculate how far away everything is. This is called binocular vision, and it creates a very detailed, three-dimensional view of what is in front of us.

Horse Sense

We can't see something creeping up behind us—but a horse can. Its eyes point sideways so each one sees an almost complete view all the way to the back of its head. This is great for spotting danger. Unfortunately, it's difficult for a horse to see what's right in front of its nose!

A Dog's View

Though dogs can't really take a color exam, we know through their behavior that they are able to see shades of blue and yellow, but can't really see colors from green to red. The vision system that dogs and most other mammals use is called dichromacy, meaning "two colored." (Our vision uses trichromacy—three colors.)

Seeing Red—Not!

Everyone knows that bulls hate the color red. That's why they charge at bullfighters, right? Nope. In fact a bull cannot even see the color red. You could wave a green cloak at a bull and it would make him just as mad. The bull is reacting to the motion, not the color. It's best to stay still—or get out of his way!

UV Vision

Honeybees, like many insects, can see a fourth color—ultraviolet (UV) light. When we look at a flower under UV light we find it is covered in stripes that are normally invisible to us. Bees see the stripes and use them as a guide to the sweet nectar they've come to collect.

Heat Seekers

Snakes, like pit vipers and pythons, don't use their eyes to hunt for food—they use their noses. Sensitive pits on their snouts can detect the heat radiating off their prey. The pits work like an infrared camera to show the snake where warm-blooded animals are, even when they are hiding in thick undergrowth.

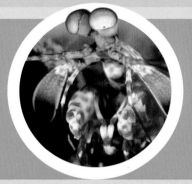

Best Color Vision

Mantis shrimps have the best color vision of all. Their compound eyes have 10,000 lenses and use 12 different light-sensitive chemicals to detect a vast array of colors. These big shrimps make their bodies glow and shimmer in the water, which is difficult for us to see—but other mantis shrimps can spot their friends easily.

Water Vision

Most fish and other water animals see in black and white. Underwater the sunlight always shines down from above, so it is light when you look up and dark when you look down. In this environment, color vision is not as important as being able to spot hunters attacking from the dark depths, or catching other animals swimming in the bright water above you. The best way to do that is to have sensitive eyes that pick up all kinds of light in the same way—and that's monochromacy, or black-and-white vision.

Bioluminescence

In very deep water, 3,000 feet (914 m) down, there's almost no light from the sun. It is pitch-dark even in the middle of the day. So, many deep-sea animals make their own light with a process called bioluminescence. They mix body chemicals together to make light—but no heat, unlike our lightbulbs—and use this to attract mates or lure their prey.

Headlight Fish

The headlight fish uses bioluminescence another way. It has a glowing patch of skin on its head that sends out red light into the water. No other fish can see this beam of light, but the headlight fish uses it like a searchlight to hunt down its food.

Color Blindness

Color-blind people can't see this number.

Though most of us see three colors, its not uncommon for a person to only see shades of two colors. Color blindness occurs when one type of cone cell in our eye doesn't work properly. Most color-blind people can't tell the difference between red and green; in rarer cases they can't see blue. One in 12 men is color blind; in women it's 1 in 200. (Amazingly, all male South American monkeys are color blind, but none of the females!)

PHOTOGRAPHY

Photography is the art of capturing light in a permanent image. Its main tool is the camera. In every camera, a lens focuses light from the outside onto a light-sensitive surface.

The word "photography" comes from Greek words meaning "drawing with light." Cameras don't actually draw, though. They collect the light that bounces off the objects in front of them. Inside the dark box of a camera's body, the light is focused on an electronic chip or on film. This records the light pattern, which can be turned back into an image on paper or on a screen.

French photographer Louis Daguerre made the first practical camera and explained it to an excited crowd in Paris in 1839. His photos, printed in black and white on metal plates, took a few minutes to record. In the late 1800s, George Eastman invented a plastic film that captured images quickly. Film cameras were popular until digital cameras, using light-sensing chips, overtook them in the early 2000s.

LIFE IN MOTION

Regular cameras record still images as photographs. Video cameras record a quick series of images that seem to move when they're played back. Each still image in a video is called a "frame." Video cameras usually record between 24 and 60 frames per second. To the human eye and brain, those rapidly changing pictures seem to be moving smoothly.

GEEK STREAK

More than 1.5 billion photos are posted to social media, such as Facebook and Instagram, *every day*.

INSIDE A DIGITAL CAMERA

When you take a digital picture, light reflecting from objects outside enters the camera through its lens. The lens focuses the light onto a mirror, which reflects it up to a viewfinder. This lets you see what the camera sees. Press a button, and the mirror flips out of the way. A shutter opens. The light hits a chip covered with millions of tiny, light-detecting sensors. These record the strength of the light as numbers that can be read by a computer.

FILM

Older cameras use film instead of chips to hold their images. Film cameras don't need electronics or computers to work. Instead, the focused light falls on strips of plastic that are coated with special chemicals. These chemicals get dark where the light hits them. To make a photograph, the film needs to be developed—it goes through another chemical process to print the image on paper.

PLAYING WITH PICTURES

Digital pictures are usually stored in a computer. Because each image is just a set of numbers to the computer, it's easy to change a picture using photo-editing software. Ordinary users might touch up a photo to remove freckles or brighten color. But a skilled computer user can do almost anything to a photo. She can make bodies look different, add people or take them out, or create a completely new background. Moviemakers use this kind of digital magic to make spaceships fly and dragons breathe fire.

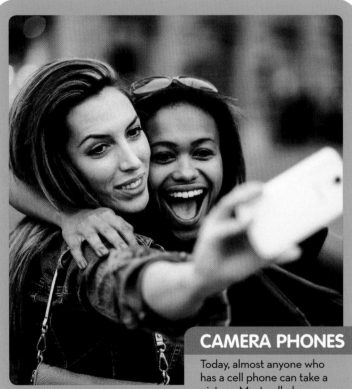

TOOLS OF THE TRADE

If you want to photograph something very big and far away, or very small and close up, many cameras let you change your lenses. Long telephoto lenses show you the details of distant objects. (Sports photographers often use these.) Macro lenses zoom in on tiny, close objects, such as insects or flowers. They project a life-size image onto the camera's sensor.

TRY THIS!

WHAT YOU NEED: A round box (such as an oatmeal or potato chip container), wax paper, a pencil or pushpin, tape, a towel

HOW LONG IT TAKES: 15 minutes

If you want to see an image on your own pinhole camera, carefully poke a hole in the bottom of your container with the pencil or pushpin. Tape wax paper over the open end of the container. Drape the towel over your head and the camera, leaving the pinhole end uncovered. Point the pinhole end at a bright scene. You'll see the image of that scene projected on the wax paper—upside down!

CAMERA PHONES

Today, almost anyone who has a cell phone can take a picture. Most cell phones have simple built-in cameras. A lens on the cell phone case focuses light onto a small sensor inside the phone. The image is stored in the phone's memory. Cell phone cameras are quickly surpassing all but the best cameras, though most professional photographers still depend heavily on large cameras for their superior optics.

WORD CHECK

SENSOR: Any device that senses something from the outside, such as light, sound, or motion, and reacts to it by sending a signal

TELESCOPES

A telescope is an instrument that gathers light (and other radiation) so we can see distant objects, such as stars. Telescopes can be as small as a baseball bat or as big as a spaceship.

A Dutch maker of eyeglasses, Hans Lippershey, invented the first telescope in 1608. His instrument, which used glass lenses to make faraway objects seem closer, was meant to be a spyglass for watching distant objects. But in 1610, Italian scientist Galileo Galilei built a better version and used his telescope to view the sky. He discovered four moons of Jupiter, as well as craters on the moon's surface. By 1668, another great scientist, Isaac Newton, invented a telescope that used mirrors instead of lenses to collect light. Today, both kinds of telescopes are still built. Those that use only lenses are called refracting telescopes. The ones with mirrors are called reflecting telescopes. Some telescopes use both mirrors and lenses.

Big modern telescopes don't collect just visible light. They use computer chips to detect all kinds of radiation, ranging from radio waves to x-rays and gamma rays.

REFRACTING TELESCOPES

The simplest kind of refracting telescope uses two lenses. The bigger one at the telescope's end is called the objective lens. It gathers light (let's say, from a star) and focuses it through a second lens in the eyepiece. You look through the eyepiece to see the star. One downside to simple refracting telescopes is that the image you see is upside down.

Most refracting telescopes have several lenses working together at the objective end. This helps create a clearer image. The bigger the objective lens, the more light the telescope gathers, and the more detail you can see.

WORD CHECK

REFRACTION: The bending of light as it moves from one clear material to another. In a refracting telescope, glass lenses change the direction of the light that passes through them.

REFLECTING TELESCOPES

Reflecting telescopes pick up light with a curved mirror instead of a lens. In a simple reflector, light enters the tube of the telescope and bounces off the objective mirror in the back to a second, angled mirror. This reflects the light up to lenses in the eyepiece, where you can look at the image. Just as with refracting telescopes, bigger is better when it comes to collecting light. With bigger mirrors, you'll see far-off objects more clearly.

LOOKING BACK IN TIME

In 2015, the W. M. Keck Observatory in Hawaii, U.S.A., confirmed the existence of the most distant galaxy ever found. It's called EGSY8p7 and is 13.2 billion light-years away. Because it has taken that long for its light to reach us, scientists are able to see back in time and observe how galaxies were formed when the cosmos were very young.

EYES IN SPACE

The air around Earth soaks up or blocks some of the radiation from space. To get a clear view of what's happening out there, dozens of telescopes have been sent into orbit. One of the most famous is the Hubble Space Telescope (above). Launched in 1990, it has produced spectacular images of distant stars and galaxies. There are no humans riding in the Hubble. Instead, sensitive chips record the incoming light and send it as a stream of numbers to Earth. Here, computers translate the data back into an understandable picture.

GEEK STREAK

With four telescopes working together, the Very Large Telescope can detect objects that are four billion times fainter than the naked eye can see.

OBSERVATORIES

To see really far into space, you need a really big telescope. The world's largest telescopes are housed in observatories on mountains and in deserts around the world. In those places, the air is clear and dry, which is good for seeing the sky. The Mauna Kea Observatories (right), on Hawaii's tallest mountain, hold 13 telescopes. Some see visible light, others see radio waves or infrared (heat). The Very Large Telescope (VLT), in Chile's Atacama Desert, has four huge telescopes that work together. The light beams they collect are combined in underground tunnels to create one big image.

TOOLS OF THE TRADE

Most people don't realize they might already own a telescope—two of them, in fact. Binoculars are nothing more than two short telescopes joined together. A typical pair will magnify objects seven times. You can use them to examine the craters of the moon or spot the big moons of Jupiter. With binoculars, you can even see another galaxy: Andromeda, more than two million light-years away.

PERSONALITY PLUS

German-English astronomers William (1738–1822) and Caroline Herschel (1750–1848) were a brother-sister stargazing team. Together they built hundreds of telescopes to William's design, with Caroline shaping the mirrors. Using one of these handmade instruments, William discovered the planet Uranus in 1781. Caroline went on to spot eight comets and a small galaxy.

SEEING THE INVISIBLE

All around us is an invisible world. It's made of things too small to see. From tiny microbes down to the basic building blocks of molecules and atoms, so much is hidden from the naked eye. We need microscopes to show us this world hidden from plain sight.

Three kinds of microscopes are used to see the tiniest objects. The most familiar kind is the light microscope, which shines light on a sample and magnifies it with lenses. But scientists can view even smaller items using streams of particles from electron microscopes. And some microscopes use pinlike probes to see what the eye cannot. On these pages, we'll show you what you can see with some special 'scopes.

The Naked Eye

What's the smallest thing your eye can see without a microscope? Most of us can see objects about one-tenth of a millimeter wide (or .004 inch). This is as wide as a fine human hair. It's about the size of the human egg cell, which is one of the only cells that can be seen with the naked eye.

HUMAN HAIR

How Small Is a Nano?

Scientists measure objects in meters. (One meter is 39.37 inches, or a bit more than three feet long.) The smallest things that we can see without help are measured in fractions of a millimeter, or thousandths of an inch. Once we start using microscopes, we have to use even smaller measurements—thousands and millions of times smaller. Most cells and bacteria are measured in micrometers. One micrometer is one-millionth of a meter. Viruses and molecules are even tinier, measured in nanometers, or one-billionth of a meter. Atoms can be measured in picometers—one-trillionth of a meter. Millions of atoms could fit into the period at the end of this sentence.

Light and Lenses

A standard microscope, like the kind in a classroom, shines visible light through a sample. Lenses then magnify the light from the sample as it reaches your eye, so that it looks bigger. A school microscope might be able to magnify something about 400 times. A good laboratory 'scope will magnify an object about 1,000 times. In this kind of microscope, a human hair would look about as wide as a cell phone.

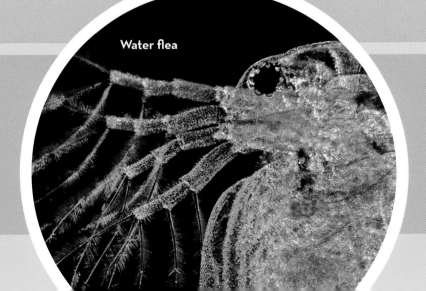
Water flea

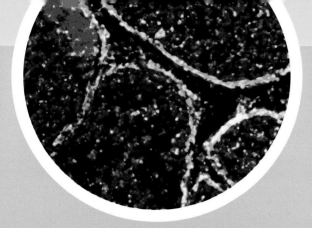

Looking for the Glow

A new kind of light microscope looks at samples that glow. The microscope shines a particular kind of light on a specimen, which absorbs it and starts to shine with its own light. This kind of glow is called fluorescence. Then the microscope sorts out the glowing light from regular light. This lets it see details that can't be seen in ordinary light. These microscopes are good for looking inside human cells.

Shooting Electrons

Electron microscopes can see much smaller objects than even the best light microscope. That's because they use beams of electrons, and electrons have wavelengths much smaller than the space between atoms. At the top of these big instruments is an electron gun. It fires a beam of electrons down a long tube. Magnets in the tube keep the beam focused on the sample at the bottom. There, the beam scans back and forth across the sample. As the electrons hit the sample, they give off signals that show up as an image on a computer screen.

Electron microscopes can magnify an object more than 500,000 times. They can reveal the fine details of insect eyes, grains of pollen, or tiny cells.

The egg of a butterfly perches on a plant.

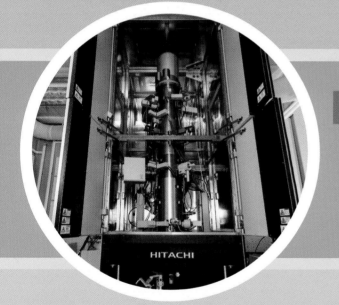

Going Big to See Small

In a special, extra-tall room at the University of Victoria in Canada is the world's most sensitive electron microscope, the STEHM. (That's short for scanning transmission electron holography microscope.) It's almost 15 feet (4.6 m) tall and weighs more than seven tons (6.4 t). Guided by 65 magnetic lenses, the microscope's powerful electron beam can detect a single atom. Scientists hope to use it to learn new things about chemistry, physics, and the human body.

Tiny Ups and Downs

With scanning tunneling microscopes (STMs), we can get 3-D images of objects down to the size of atoms. These 'scopes use a tiny probe like a pin, with a tip no bigger than a single atom. A current of electrons flows between the probe and the sample. As the probe moves over a sample, it scoots up and down over the atoms below it. Signals from the probe travel to a computer to create a map of the surface below.

STMs can not only make images of samples—they can also move atoms around, one by one. Playful scientists have spelled out their company name or even drawn little human figures by rearranging atoms as if they were the world's smallest balls.

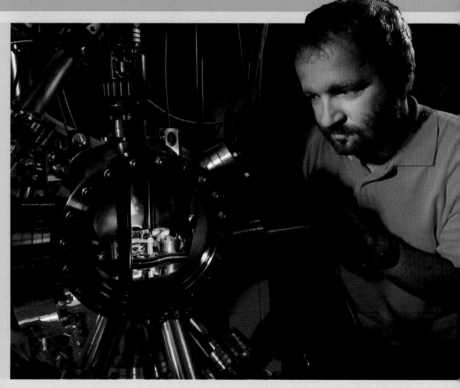

LITTLE CIRCUITS, MIGHTY MOTION

In the 19th century, the world worked on gears, steam, and human muscle. Huge, clanking machines ran factories. Locomotives delivered the mail across the country. People lifted, carried, and hammered parts together. Today, thanks to electronics, all that power fits in the palm of your hand.

Electronics is the science of sending electrical currents through circuits. Using digital code, those circuits can process information and send signals from one device to another. Electronic circuits are at the heart of computers, telephones, televisions, and radios. They control everything from toys to spacecraft.

Vacuum tubes, invented in the early 20th century, were the first practical electronic tools. Electricity flowed through wires inside the glass tubes, which then could strengthen and send out electrical signals. Early radios, televisions, and computers used vacuum tubes. But vacuum tubes were big and hot. In 1947, scientists at Bell Laboratories invented a much smaller, faster, and cooler device: the transistor. Transistors have tiny switches that direct electrical current and turn it on and off. They conduct electricity using a fraction of the energy of vacuum tubes. They can be combined on a single metallic chip with other circuits to run modern electronic devices, from cameras to computers to satellites.

Electronic circuits are particularly important in communications and computing. In radios, televisions, cell phones, and navigation tools, they send and receive signals using radio waves. They translate digital code into words and pictures that we can understand. That's because they use microprocessor chips. These chips have built-in circuits that can bring in information, turn it into an answer or a picture, and put it back out to the user. These chips can handle a computer's amazingly complex operations. They start up your computer and run programs that let you type, see videos, search the Web, and play games. In supercomputers, they go a step further. Microchips are linked together to help predict the weather and uncover the secrets of distant stars.

Electronics help save lives. Using computer chips, medicine has gone high-tech. Computerized scanning machines can see into our bodies to find broken bones. Robotic tools can perform surgery with greater delicacy than a surgeon's fingers. Electronic machines test our blood samples in a jiffy to count our blood cells and measure levels of vitamins and chemicals. And simple computer chips in wristbands can count every step we've taken to make sure we're getting our exercise.

Electrical currents run through an electronic circuit board like this to power everyday machines like the microwave that pops your popcorn. In complex laptops and robots, the circuits translate information into pictures, words, movement, and more.

RADIO WAVES

Radio waves are a kind of traveling energy. They can carry signals for radios, televisions, cell phones, and computer networks.

Radio waves, light, x-rays, and gamma rays belong to the same family. They are all forms of electromagnetic radiation that travel in waves at the speed of light. Radio waves are long, invisible, low-energy waves. From one wave top to the next they can be anywhere from a fraction of an inch to 60,000 miles (96,561 km) long. But as long as they are, you can't feel them. Radio waves pass right through many kinds of solid objects, including the human body. They bounce off anything that can carry electricity, from clouds to metal.

Some things naturally send out radio waves. Lightning in thunderstorms and stars such as the sun give off long radio waves that are detected by radio telescopes. But people also build all kinds of devices that use antennas to send and receive radio waves. Radio waves carry information around the world.

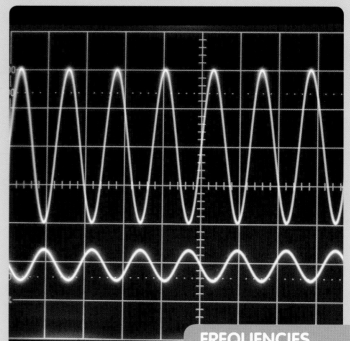

RADIOS

When we talk about "the radio" we usually mean a gadget that we listen to. Your radio picks up radio waves traveling through the air from a distant radio station. Those waves carry a signal and move at a particular frequency. At home, when you tune your radio dial to a station, the built-in antenna picks up that specific signal. The radio turns the signal back into sound.

FREQUENCIES

We often hear about a radio "frequency." What's that? It's how often the top of a wave passes a fixed point. Think about waves in the ocean. Long, slow waves might flow past a rock at the rate of one per minute. Short, choppy waves might roll past the rock as fast as ten per minute. That rate is their frequency.

Radio waves move a lot faster than ocean waves. Millions of radio waves can pass a fixed point in one second. Radio frequencies are measured in hertz (Hz), or waves per second. One hertz is one wave per second. One megahertz (MHz) is a million waves per second.

GEEK STREAK

Like light, radio waves will travel forever unless something stops them, such as a mountain or trees. Radio waves carrying television signals have been leaving the Earth for more than 70 years. That means our TV programs have reached planets 70 light-years away.

TELEVISION

Radio waves carry not just sound, but moving pictures—your favorite television show, for instance. Like radio stations, each television channel has its own frequency. Carrying coded video signals, the waves zoom to your house through the air or through cables underground. On your television or computer screen, the code gets changed back into pictures and sound.

CELL PHONES

Cell phones are radios that can both send and receive. They change the sound of your voice into an electrical signal and send it out in radio waves. The waves travel to cell towers and stations, and eventually to the cell phone you are calling. That phone receives the radio signal and changes it back into sound.

WI-FI

Many schools, homes, and businesses have Wi-Fi routers, devices linked to the Internet by a cable. Wi-Fi is short for "Wireless Fidelity." Routers are little radio transmitters. They can relay an Internet signal into the air using radio waves that travel about 300 feet (91 m). Your computer has a built-in radio antenna that picks up those signals and translates them from zeros and ones into information you can use.

TOOLS OF THE TRADE

Antennas that act as transmitters change electrical signals into radio waves and send them out. Antennas that pick up those waves and change them back into signals that can be understood are receivers. Most antennas are metal wires, rods, or dishes. The biggest ones are huge bowls that pick up radio waves from space. The smallest are little wires tucked inside cell phones.

PERSONALITY PLUS

German scientist Heinrich Hertz (1857–1894) was a smart but modest man who proved the existence of electromagnetic waves. While working as a physics teacher in Berlin, he built a simple radio transmitter and receiver in a corner of his classroom. With these, he was able to measure radio waves and show that they traveled through the air. Hertz thought his discovery wouldn't amount to much. When his students asked him what was next, he said, "Nothing, I guess." He was wrong. His work helped lead the way to the practical use of electromagnetism. Today, his name is given to the standard measurement of frequency (the hertz).

SATELLITES

WORD CHECK
ANTENNA: A device (such as a wire or metal rod) for sending or receiving radio or television signals

A satellite is any object, natural or artificial, that orbits a planet. Moons are natural satellites. People have built thousands of artificial satellites and launched them into space, where they circle the Earth.

The Soviet Union shot the first satellite, Sputnik 1, into orbit in 1957. The beeping, basketball-size metal sphere lasted only a few months before falling back to Earth. Today, about 1,200 working satellites orbit our planet. Countries such as the United States and China launch them regularly into space on rockets. Many old, inactive satellites are also still floating around the Earth. Satellites are amazingly useful in our daily lives. They relay telephone, radio, and television signals around the world. They watch the planet's weather and help us predict storms. They pick up distress signals from ships in trouble. And they track the position of planes, cars, and cell phones, so we can find our way to new places.

EARTHWATCH

With their sensitive cameras, satellites keep an eye on the Earth's oceans and forests, its weather, and its human activity. Satellites in high and low orbits spot hurricanes as they form. They observe coral reefs and polar ice to give us clues to climate change. And they help protect endangered ecosystems: Using satellite images, Brazilian police have discovered illegal logging activities in the Amazon rain forest—and they're going after the culprits!

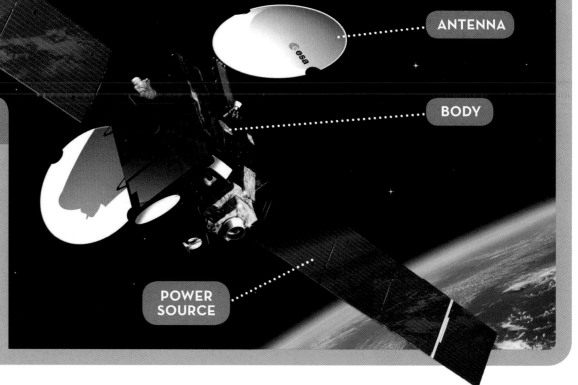

PARTS OF A SATELLITE

Satellites come in different sizes, but they all have a body, a power source, and an antenna. The body, called a bus, holds the satellite's science equipment and computer. Power often comes from solar panels that stick out like wings. These turn sunlight into electricity and use it to run the satellite. They also store some power in batteries to keep the satellite going when it's in the dark. The antenna sends and receives signals to stay in touch with Earth.

ANTENNA

BODY

POWER SOURCE

CROWDED SKIES

Many satellites circle the Earth on different paths, or orbits. Some are far out in space and some are closer to the planet. Some stay over the Equator and others swing around the North and South Poles. Satellites that always stay over the same spot on the Earth are called geostationary. Their orbits are about 22,000 miles (35,406 km) high. Satellites in low orbits, about 200 to 500 miles (320 to 800 km) high, don't stay over one place. They can zoom around the planet in 90 minutes, moving at 17,000 miles an hour (27,359 km/h).

GEEK STREAK

Planet Earth is surrounded by orbiting junk. Along with 1,200 or so active satellites, about 12,000 pieces of large and small trash litter Earth's neighborhood. These include nonworking satellites, old rocket parts, nuts and bolts, and one astronaut's glove.

YOU ARE HERE

Global positioning system (GPS) satellites tell us where we are, and how to get to the next place. Twenty-four of these satellites (and a few spares) orbit 12,645 miles (20,350 km) above the Earth. Each one has a very precise atomic clock. The satellites send radio signals down to GPS devices (such as those in cell phones) on Earth. The device uses its own clock to find out how long the signal took to arrive. That tells it the distance to the satellite. With four signals from four satellites, the GPS device uses geometry to figure out just where it is.

TRY THIS!

WHAT YOU NEED: A pair of binoculars and a clear night sky

HOW LONG IT TAKES: 15 minutes, if you know where to look for a satellite

Have you ever seen an unblinking point of light moving steadily across the night sky? That's a satellite! They are easy to see with the naked eye—you just need to know where to look. Binoculars will give you an even closer view. Many websites and apps, such as "Satellite Flybys," will tell you when and where to look in your location. If you want to see the International Space Station (yes, that's a kind of satellite), check in with NASA's "Spot the Station" website for the next appearance in your skies.

RELATIVITY IN ACTION

Einstein's theories of relativity seem strange and unreal, but without them GPS satellites wouldn't work. Relativity predicts that time passes a little faster on objects in orbit, such as satellites, compared to time on Earth. And so it does. Scientists have to slow down the atomic clocks on GPS satellites by 38 microseconds a day to match clocks on Earth. Otherwise, within a day, their positioning would be wrong by about six miles (9.6 km) and would get steadily worse.

TOOLS OF THE TRADE

Satellites can't launch themselves into space. They have to ride piggyback on a rocket, or launch vehicle. These rockets come in several parts, called stages. One stage holds the fuel that will lift the rocket off the ground. Another holds more fuel to help it reach space. The third holds the satellite itself. The two fuel stages break off and burn up in Earth's atmosphere when they are no longer needed.

COMPUTERS

A computer is an electronic machine that can store and work with large amounts of information. Computers can be stand-alone devices that we use for work, school, or play. They are also built into all kinds of everyday objects, from cars to phones.

Number-crunching machines have been around for hundreds of years. But computers really took off when microprocessor chips were invented in the 1970s. These little chips, printed with circuits, allow computers to run millions of calculations very quickly. With microprocessors, computers shrank from room-size monsters to slim notebooks.

Big or small, all computers follow the same four steps as they work. The first is input: The user uses a mouse, keyboard, voice, or finger to feed in information. The second is storage: The computer puts that information into memory. Third is processing: The microprocessor chip speeds through calculations to do the job you've asked it to do. The fourth is output: You see your results on a screen or printout.

ZEROS AND ONES

Computers work quickly and store lots of information because they translate everything into zeros and ones. This is called binary code. The letter "z," for instance, is 01111010 in binary code. Inside a computer, these zeros and ones are read as "off" and "on" by the switches on the microprocessor.

HARDWARE

All the parts of a computer that you can touch, from the outer case to the tiny wires inside, are called its hardware. Computers are complicated, but they all have the same basic pieces. The brain of any computer is its central processing unit, or CPU. This holds the microprocessor chip that runs the computer's calculations. Every computer also has memory. Laptops and bigger computers store information on magnetic hard drives. Smaller devices use portable memory chips.

LOL!

Q: What do you get when you cross a computer with a lifeguard?

A: A screen saver!

SOFTWARE

Without software, a computer would just be an expensive hunk of metal. Software is the set of instructions that tells the computer what to do. There are two main kinds of software. The operating system (OS) controls the computer's basic functions—input, output, processing, and storage. It starts up every time you turn on the computer. Applications (or apps) are programs that let you do specific tasks, such as word processing, browsing the Web, or playing games.

TABLETS

Tablets are mobile computers. Flat and lightweight, they are small enough to carry easily in one hand. You don't need a mouse or a keyboard to use a tablet. Instead, you simply touch its screen. Tablet screens have many thin layers. Your touch sets off a little electrical charge, which sends a signal to the tablet's chip. The chip recognizes your finger's location and starts the matching action, such as launching an app or typing a letter.

TOOLS OF THE TRADE

Devices that you attach to a computer to extend its use are called peripherals. Some, such as a keyboard or a mouse, input information to the computer. Others, such as a monitor or printer, allow the computer to output information. Peripherals connect to the computer though cables or radio signals.

GEEK STREAK

A powerful laptop computer can run billions of calculations per second. However, the top supercomputers leave laptops in the dust. A Chinese supercomputer known as Tianhe-2 can perform 33.86 quadrillion calculations per second. That's 33,860,000,000,000,000 in the time it takes you to say "quadrillion."

SUPERCOMPUTERS

To study the world's weather or a black hole, you need more than a normal computer. You need a supercomputer. A supercomputer is made from tens of thousands of processors, like the ones in this room, working together. Each processor solves one part of the problem. Supercomputers can fill a room and use enough electricity to power a small city.

PERSONALITY PLUS

American engineer Douglas Engelbart (1925–2013) entered the computer field when the machines were still being programmed with paper cards that had holes punched in them to give instructions to the computer. One day, he had a vision of himself in front of a computer screen filled with pictures that he could interact with. In 1968, at a demonstration now known as "The Mother of All Demos," he showed off his new invention, the computer mouse (left), and predicted a time when networked computers could share information. His work inspired the interactive computing that we now take for granted.

REVOLUTION IN COMPUTING

Counting machines have been around since ancient Chinese merchants totaled up sums with an abacus. However, modern inventions led to a revolution in computing. Electrical power allowed computers to count ones and zeros at lightning speed. Tiny chips, printed with circuits, sped up that counting and helped computers shrink to pocket size. And the Internet connected billions of users around the world.

Difference Engines

In 1821, English mathematician Charles Babbage (1791–1871), frustrated by the work of checking astronomy tables, exclaimed, "I wish to God these calculations had been executed by steam!" This gave him the idea for building a machine that would automatically perform and print out mathematical calculations. He designed three such machines between 1821 and 1849. Two were "difference engines" and one was an "analytical engine." These were the first computers. Babbage never finished building them. If they had been completed, they would have had thousands of moving parts and weighed about five tons (4.5 t).

ENIAC

The room-size Electronic Numerical Integrator and Computer (ENIAC) was the first all-purpose digital computer. Built in 1946, it weighed 40 tons (36.3 t) and had vacuum tubes as switches. It was used to predict the paths of artillery shells for the military. Also, it could be programmed with punch cards to do different jobs. ENIAC could perform 5,000 calculations per second—a big improvement on doing math by hand, but still a lot slower than even the simplest cell phone today.

Actual size

Computer Chips

Digital computers rely on electrical switches turning on and off to do their calculations. In 1971, scientists at the Intel Corporation managed to pack all those switches onto a tiny chip. Just one-eighth of an inch (3.2 mm) wide, the Intel 4004 microprocessor had as much computing power as ENIAC. Chips quickly became even smaller and faster. They allowed companies to build small, desktop-size computers for the first time.

Personal Computers

In 1977, the Apple II microcomputer went on sale. Designed primarily by Steve Wozniak, the desktop computer had a color display and was easy to use. It became the first truly successful personal computer, a device that the average person could use at home or at work. The Apple II was soon followed by the IBM PC, in 1981. This personal computer had its own operating system, PC DOS, that was different from Apple's software. The IBM PC became popular as a desktop computer for businesses. Over the next decades, Apple, IBM, and other personal computers became ever smaller and more powerful.

Computers to Go

The first personal computers were too heavy and bulky to be carried around. In 1981, Adam Osborne, a writer of computer books, invented the first successful portable computer. The Osborne 1 all-in-one device had a fold-out keyboard and a small, five-inch (12.7-cm) screen. Although it could be carried, you had to be pretty strong—it weighed more than 23 pounds (10.4 kg). Nevertheless, it led the way to smaller, lighter portables and laptops. Today, more laptops are sold than desktop machines. Some of them weigh less than 2 pounds (0.9 kg).

Connections

The beginnings of the Internet—the worldwide network that connects computers—go back to the 1960s. In those years, the U.S. Department of Defense linked some of its computers using a system called ARPANET. But the Internet we all use today didn't come into being until later. In the 1980s, British computer scientist Tim Berners-Lee, working in Switzerland at the European research lab CERN, worked out a way that all computers could communicate using a universal language. In 1991, the Internet became open to everyone.

On the Move

By 2007, a computer could fit into your hand and make a phone call, too. That year, Apple Inc. sold the first smartphone, the iPhone. These cell phones had touch-sensitive screens and contained programs that let the user send email, take a photo, and browse the Internet. Three years later, in 2010, Apple followed up with the iPad, a computer tablet. Other companies quickly launched their own versions of smartphones and tablets. With these mobile devices, anyone with a pocket could have a computer handy.

Quantum Weirdness

Some research labs are working on the next wave of computing machines—quantum computers. Normal computers store information in ones or zeros: bits. Using the laws of atomic physics, quantum computers would store information in ones, zeros, or ones and zeros at the same time: qubits. A quantum computer would be mind-bogglingly fast, able to crack difficult codes or solve hugely complex problems in biology. So far, scientists have built quantum computer chips with only a few qubits—but change comes fast in the computer world.

CELL PHONES

A cell phone is a portable telephone that sends messages with radio waves. "Cell" is short for "cellular." Cell phones use a cellular network. Their signals travel from one radio tower to the next. The area covered by each tower is its cell.

A cell phone is basically a two-way radio. Its built-in microphone changes the sound of your voice into electrical signals. The phone's computer chip then turns those signals into numbers. An antenna inside the phone sends the string of numbers to the nearest cell phone tower. Each cell tower hands off the signal to the next tower until it reaches the one closest to the person you are calling. That person picks up the call with the antenna in his phone.

Many cell phones today do a lot more than just handle phone calls. They send and receive text messages and photographs. They connect to the Internet for information and to GPS satellites to help us find our way. They are little computers that talk to each other and to us.

MESSAGES

Many people let their fingers do the talking when it comes to cell phones. Text messaging is a common use for mobile phones, particularly among younger Americans. In 2013, they sent an average of 67 texts per day. Formally known as SMS, for "short message service," a text message is particularly helpful when you need to communicate quietly. Many smartphone applications also support various kinds of instant messaging that can include pictures and videos.

FROM CAR PHONES TO SMARTPHONES

The first truly mobile phones were built into cars in the 1970s and '80s, but most people couldn't afford these big, fancy devices. Motorola engineer Martin Cooper made the first call on a handheld cell phone on April 3, 1973. With a battery that lasted only 30 minutes, his awkward invention weighed almost 2.5 pounds (1.1 kg). By the 1990s, cell phones had become small, lightweight, and available to the average person.

WORD CHECK

CELL: Comes from the Latin word *cella*, meaning an inside room or chamber. Cells in living tissues were so named because they looked like little rooms. The area covered by a cell phone tower's signals is called a cell because it's like a big, invisible room around each tower.

TOOLS OF THE TRADE

Cell phones, and other portable electronics, are powered by small but strong lithium-ion batteries. These lightweight batteries hold a charge for a long time. They can also be recharged when you plug the phone into an electrical outlet. But watch out! Lithium-ion batteries—and the cell phones that hold them—heat up with heavy use.

THE MOBILE WORLD

In just a few years, cell phone use has spread around the world. There are now more cell phones than there are people, because some people own more than one. In countries without good access to landline phones, cell phones have changed lives, as they are used to reach the Internet, make payments, and get health information. Breaking news about important events such as revolutions or earthquakes now flashes around the globe via text messages and cell phone videos.

FIND THE CELL TOWER

Cell phone towers can be hundreds of feet tall. Some communities find them ugly, and require the towers to be disguised in some way. Some have plastic branches or palm fronds attached so they look like odd, skinny trees. Others are hidden inside flagpoles, church steeples, or cactuses. If you pay attention while you're traveling, you can often spot these dressed-up towers.

DANGEROUS DISTRACTION

Talking or texting on a cell phone is distracting, and that distraction can be fatal. Even though they know it's dangerous, about half of young American drivers have texted while driving. About one-fourth of all drivers check the Internet while behind the wheel. Studies show that this distraction is even deadlier than drinking alcohol before driving. Cell phone use plays a part in up to half of all car accidents, causing thousands of deaths. Many countries and U.S. states ban cell phone use while driving. The moral: The message can wait. You are not a slave to your phone.

TRY THIS!

WHAT YOU NEED: A ruler, a friend, a cell phone, paper, a pencil

HOW LONG IT TAKES: 20 minutes

Grab a ruler and a friend, and test out the distracting effects of cell phone conversations. Here's how: Hold the ruler near its top so it hangs down. Ask your friend to hold her hand at the bottom, but not touching the ruler. Drop the ruler. See how far it drops before your friend catches it. Make a record of the inch line where her fingers grabbed it. Repeat this two more times, and record the average drop by dividing the total measurements by three. Now ask your friend to call someone on her cell phone and start a conversation. Repeat the ruler drop another three times. What's the new average drop? Is it farther than before? If it is, your friend's response time is slower—she's showing the effects of cell phone distraction!

GEEK STREAK

In 2014, Brazilian teenager Marcel Fernandes Filho set a world record for speed texting by correctly typing the following message in 17 seconds:

The razor-toothed piranhas of the genera Serrasalmus and Pygocentrus are the most ferocious freshwater fish in the world. In reality they seldom attack a human.

ROBOTS

A robot is a machine that can do a job that a person can do. Robots usually have moving parts. They can make simple decisions, but they can only do what they've been programmed to do.

When we think of robots, we usually picture a machine with arms, legs, and a face. But real robots don't usually look like people. They don't need to look human, because they're made to do things that humans can't or won't do. This includes repetitive or dangerous work: building cars, carrying boxes, or defusing bombs. Some are designed to visit places that human bodies can't explore, such as deep under the ocean or across the surface of Mars.

Many things that are easy for us are hard for robots. They have trouble picking things up without crushing them. They can't easily see the edges of objects—a robot has a tough time just folding laundry. And they're not too skilled at moving around on rough surfaces. Every year, though, robots get better at these tasks and become more a part of our daily lives.

WORKERS

Robots are most commonly used in car factories. They are programmed to do the same well-defined job, such as welding or painting, over and over again without tiring. This makes them valuable on the assembly line. Factory robots are usually fixed to the floor. They have one long arm that can twist, bend, and pick up heavy objects.

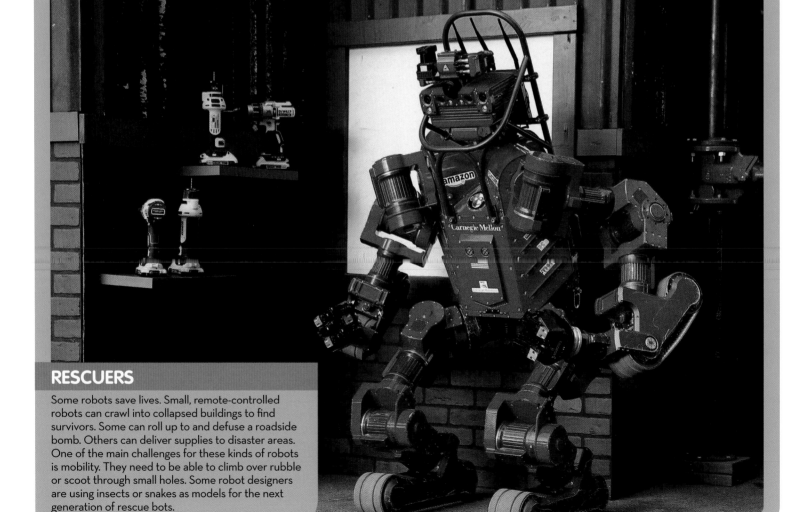

RESCUERS

Some robots save lives. Small, remote-controlled robots can crawl into collapsed buildings to find survivors. Some can roll up to and defuse a roadside bomb. Others can deliver supplies to disaster areas. One of the main challenges for these kinds of robots is mobility. They need to be able to climb over rubble or scoot through small holes. Some robot designers are using insects or snakes as models for the next generation of rescue bots.

EXPLORERS

In the crushing depths of the ocean, or in the airless reaches of outer space, robots are our eyes and ears. Robots connected to research ships have explored the unseen ocean floor. One of them, the Nereus, dropped into the seven-mile (11.3-km)-deep Challenger Deep trench in the Pacific Ocean and sent back pictures through a fiber-optic cable. Robotic rovers, trundling across the surface of Mars, dig up soil samples and search for signs of life.

NANOBOTS AND SWARMS

The next big thing in robotics may be the next small thing: nanobots and swarm robots. Inspired by nature, scientists are building tiny robots that imitate living creatures. Nanobots are microscopic robots made from organic molecules. Injected into an ailing body, they can detect disease or deliver medicine right where it's needed. Swarm robots are tiny, simple machines that behave like a swarm of bees or a colony of ants. Following simple programmed instructions, they work together to carry out surprisingly complex tasks.

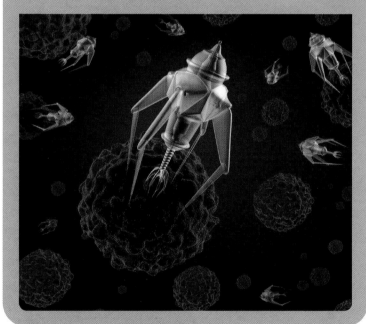

THINKING MACHINES

Will robots ever be as smart as humans? Could they ever replace us? Scientists who study artificial intelligence (AI) say that to think like humans, robots would have to do many difficult things. Without outside help, they would need to solve problems, make plans, recognize the world around them, be creative, and read and understand language, among other things. With real AI, you wouldn't know if the person you were talking to was a robot or a human. Robots are a long way from this state, but they are getting smarter every day.

WORD CHECK

ROBOT: A machine that can do the work of a person and that works automatically or is controlled by a computer. *Robot* means "hard work" in the Czech language, and came from the 1920 play *R.U.R.*, by Karel Capek. *R.U.R.* stood for *Rossum's Universal Robots*. In the play, the robots are factory workers that turn against their human masters.

GEEK STREAK

More than one million industrial robots work in factories around the world. They are greatly outnumbered by service robots: automated vacuum cleaners, lawn mowers, Lego toys, and the like. More than 17 million of these have been sold worldwide.

PERSONALITY PLUS

Scientist and writer Isaac Asimov (1920–1992) was a biochemist who wrote or edited more than 500 books of science and science fiction. In his short stories, he came up with the "three laws of robotics": 1. A robot may not injure a human being or, through inaction, allow a human being to come to harm. 2. A robot must obey the orders given it by human beings, except where such orders would conflict with the First Law. 3. A robot must protect its own existence as long as such protection does not conflict with the First or Second Laws. Asimov's logical rules for robots were a big influence on engineers as they began to build the first real robots.

Elephants roam the African savanna. African elephants are just one of the thousands of different kinds of mammals that call Earth home. In the early 1900s there were a few million African elephants. Today their numbers are declining, mainly due to illegal hunting, called poaching. Conservationists are working hard to protect them.

IT'S ALL AROUND
US!

From the **big bang** that created the cosmos to majestic elephants in Africa to tiny microbes that cover our skin, life thrives in our universe, on our planet, **and on us!** While physical sciences tell us how the mechanics of our world work, life sciences tell us about **the universe, our planet, the creatures around us, and our own bodies.**

THE UNIVERSE

BEYOND OUR EARTH

Planet Earth is a big place with beautiful lands, deep oceans, and ice-capped mountaintops. But our amazing home planet is just a small part of a larger solar system, which is part of a galaxy, which is part of an immense universe. Almost all of it is extremely far away and untouchable. Since the beginning of time, humans have studied the night sky to understand the space beyond us. We've named star patterns, used cycles of the moon to construct calendars, and determined the makeup of the sun. In recent centuries we've learned enough about space to plot trips to the moon and planets and even to map the universe. So how do we know what's out there?

The answer is light. Sunlight reflected from planets and moons reveals their surfaces. Light from stars billions of miles away reaches us here on Earth. Patterns in the spectrum of starlight—its rainbow of colors—tell us what gases make up the stars and how hot they are. Changes in light tell us how stars, planets, and comets are moving and whether they're zooming toward or away from us. The story of light is full of surprises. Astronomer Nicolaus Copernicus, watching the sun and planets, astonished the world in the 1500s by showing that the sun, not the Earth, was the center of the solar system. Telescopes that captured and magnified light revealed new planets and moons. Distant blotches of light turned out to be other galaxies, speeding away from us in an expanding universe. When the light from other stars dimmed and brightened a little, we learned that they, too, had planets circling them. Invisible forms of light—radio waves, x-rays, and gamma rays—even pointed the way to strange black holes.

Within the solar system, we've begun to add to what we've learned from our eyes and our telescopes by sending spacecraft to the moon and planets. These craft send back images to Earth. And still the surprises keep coming. Desertlike Mars might once have had flowing rivers. Rocky-looking moons turn out to have oceans under their surfaces. Tiny Pluto has tall mountains of ice.

In this section, you'll be introduced to what we know—and don't know—about the universe and our place in it. What you will likely discover is that the universe is stranger and more amazing than we ever expected.

Did you know?

Early Native Americans said that the whitish band across the night sky was spilled kernels from a bag of corn stolen by a mythical dog. Today we call it the Milky Way—home to perhaps 200 billion stars.

Like a string of sparkling diamonds, the Milky Way stretches across the sky over the desert of Bardenas, Spain. Scientists think that only 10 percent of the massive Milky Way is luminous, or glowing, matter like this. The other 90 percent may be dark matter.

THE BIG BANG

The big bang is the simple name we give to an amazing event: the beginning of the universe. In the instant of the big bang, all of space, time, matter, and energy appeared. The universe expanded outward at unimaginable speeds.

Astronomers know that the big bang happened because the universe is still spreading out in all directions. When they follow that expansion back in time—like running a movie in reverse—they can track the universe back to a single point, 13.8 billion years ago. Then, all matter was crammed into a tiny, hot, and dense dot known as a "singularity." Just why that singularity existed, and why it suddenly expanded, is still a mystery. Some scientists think the first expansion could also have created other "bubble" universes (right). The big bang can boggle the mind. We can't say what happened before the big bang, because there was no "before." Time did not exist until the big bang. We can't say what existed outside of the singularity, because there was no "outside." That tiny point was the whole universe.

THE FIRST MICROSECONDS

A whole lot happened in the first fractions of a second after the big bang. Basic physical forces, such as gravity, appeared. The tiny, hot universe went through a superfast expansion, called inflation. It grew to about the size of a grapefruit. Teeny subatomic particles called quarks (see page 25) popped into existence.

THE NEXT THREE MINUTES

Over the next few minutes, the growing universe cooled to a mere 1.8 billion°F (1 billion°C). Quarks combined into atomic particles such as protons and neutrons. The universe was a hot, seething mass of these particles (right). As their surroundings cooled, the particles began to combine into atomic nuclei and simple atoms.

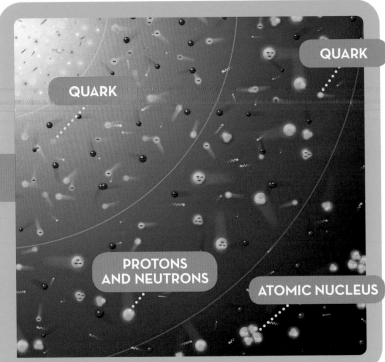

QUARK

QUARK

PROTONS AND NEUTRONS

ATOMIC NUCLEUS

THE NEXT 200 MILLION YEARS

The universe continued to cool off as it grew over the years. Atoms began to cling together in gases, mostly hydrogen and helium. Light started to shine from the gases as they clumped together pulled by gravity. These were the first stars (right).

WORD CHECK

BIG BANG: In 1949, astronomer Fred Hoyle was the first to use the phrase "big bang" to describe most astronomers' view of how the universe began—by expanding outward from that single dot of matter, the singularity. In fact, the big bang was neither big nor loud. It started off infinitely tiny and made no noise at all. Hoyle himself didn't believe in the big bang. He thought the universe had always looked the same, without a beginning or end.

MILLIONS OF YEARS MORE

Over the next hundreds of millions of years, stars and collections of stars—called galaxies—formed from condensing clouds of gas. These galaxies were smaller and closer than galaxies today. Often, they smacked into each other, creating more stars in the process.

TOOLS OF THE TRADE

We don't have any pictures of the big bang—but we do have some baby pictures of the universe! A space telescope called the Wilkinson Microwave Anisotropy Probe (WMAP) measured heat left over from the big bang. It was then able to make a map of the universe as it looked when it was 375,000 years old.

THE BIRTH OF EARTH

Over the next few billion years, the first big stars began to explode as supernovas (see page 166). From their cores, they sprayed heavy elements, such as iron and carbon, into space. These heavy elements collected around other stars and formed into planets. Our own planet Earth was born 4.5 billion years ago in the Milky Way galaxy. Today, the universe is cold and enormous, but still expanding.

GEEK STREAK

If the big bang isn't astounding enough for you, how about this: We might live in just one universe out of many. Some scientists believe that multiple universes popped into being in the early microseconds of the big bang. We can't see the others, but they could have completely different kinds of life-forms and ways of survival than our own.

163

GALAXIES

A galaxy is a vast collection of stars, gas, and dust, held together by gravity. Galaxies can be small, with just a few million stars, or giant systems with trillions of stars. The universe holds more than 100 billion of these huge star families.

We live in a galaxy we call the Milky Way. Shaped like a spiral, with long, curving arms, the Milky Way has about 200 billion stars. At its center is a dense block of stars and probably a massive black hole. The whole galaxy rotates around that center, including our solar system, which is about two-thirds of the way out on one of the spiral arms. Until the early 20th century, most people thought that our galaxy was the only one. In the 1920s, astronomer Edwin Hubble discovered that the glowing clouds scientists saw in their telescopes were actually other galaxies. Not only that, but many of them were moving away from us at high speeds. The universe was much bigger than we thought—and it was expanding.

VIOLENT GALAXIES

Galaxies like our own are fairly quiet places, spinning calmly through space. But other galaxies are wild and crazy. Some have a compact region known as a quasar. Quasars shoot out jets of intense radio energy at almost the speed of light. Astronomers think the energy comes from matter falling into a massive black hole in the quasar's center. Most quasars are in galaxies very far away, meaning they formed in the early years of the universe.

THE SUN

SHAPES AND SIZES

Many galaxies, like the Milky Way, are shaped like spirals, with long arms winding around the center. These arms often contain young stars still being formed. Galaxies come in other shapes, too. Elliptical galaxies are egg-shaped groups of older stars. Irregular galaxies are just what they sound like—odd-shaped. They contain stars of all ages, and lots of gas and dust.

WORD CHECK

GALAXY: To our ancient ancestors, the band of stars across the sky that we call the Milky Way looked like a trail of spilled milk. The Romans called it *via lactea* ("milk road"), and the Greeks knew it as *galaxias kyklos*, or "milky circle." From that Greek phrase we get the word "galaxy."

COLLIDING GALAXIES

Galaxies smack into each other all the time. In fact, our own Milky Way is busy gobbling up a dwarf galaxy called Sagittarius. Our galaxy's gravity is ripping Sagittarius apart and pulling long tails of stars out of it. When galaxies collide, they sometimes trigger a burst of star births as their gas clouds merge. At other times, one galaxy knocks another far into space like a bat hitting a baseball.

GEEK STREAK

Riding a spiral arm of the Milky Way galaxy, our solar system travels at about 500,000 miles an hour (about 800,000 km/h) as the galaxy spins. It takes about 225 million years for the system to make one complete galactic orbit.

GROUPS, CLUSTERS, AND SUPERCLUSTERS

Galaxies don't just float around at random. They tend to cling together in groups. Our own Milky Way is part of a collection of galaxies called the Local Group. Groups of galaxies can form larger assemblies, called clusters. Clusters sometimes stick together in superclusters—some of the largest structures in the universe. Scientists named this galaxy cluster RXJ1532. The elliptical galaxy at its center holds a supermassive black hole.

TRY THIS!

WHAT YOU NEED: A dark summer night (best away from city lights) and sharp eyes

HOW LONG IT TAKES: 10 to 15 minutes, or longer

In the right conditions, you can see part of the Milky Way galaxy stretching above you at night. You'll need the darkest surroundings you can find. Try to get away from city and house lights on a very clear night with no moon. Summertime is best. Let your eyes adjust to the dark and look toward the southern horizon. You should see a gorgeous, cloudy band reaching across the sky. This is the main section of the disk-shaped galaxy—the part that holds the most stars.

GALAXY CLUSTER RXJ1532

ELLIPTICAL GALAXY WITH BLACK HOLE

GALAXY

DARK MATTER

When astronomers measure the gravity in galaxies, they find that there's much more mass than can be accounted for by stars, planets, and gas. Galaxies hold some kind of invisible matter that greatly outweighs visible matter. Astronomers call this mysterious stuff dark matter, and they don't know what it is. It's not dust or dark stars or black holes. It might be tiny subatomic particles that we can't quite see—yet. One NASA scientist proposes that it looks like strands of hair.

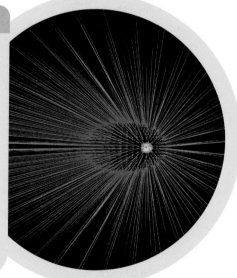

PERSONALITY PLUS

When Edwin Hubble worked at California's Mount Wilson Observatory, he had an unlikely helper: the observatory's janitor. Milton Humason (1891–1972) was a high-school dropout who worked as a mule driver bringing supplies up to the new observatory. He was fascinated by astronomy and took a job there as a janitor. Soon, the smart, hardworking man was given a job as an assistant to the astronomers. Over the years, he became a key part of the team that found the distances to other galaxies and proved that the universe was expanding.

STARS

They look like twinkling lights in the night sky, but up close, stars are huge, burning balls of hydrogen and helium gas. Our own sun is a star. All stars give off heat and light by fusing atoms together in their dense, hot cores.

Stars follow a life cycle from birth to death. They are born when clouds of gas are pulled together by gravity and collapse into dense spheres. As they condense, they heat up until fusion begins in their cores. Small to medium-size stars, like our sun, will glow steadily for billions of years. The biggest stars burn through their gas much faster and last only a few million years. A star's death depends upon its size. Lower-mass stars like the sun run out of energy, puff up for a while into a bright reddish star called a red giant, and then collapse into a small star that cools off, called a white dwarf. High-mass stars go out with a bang. They blow up as spectacular supernovas.

SUPERNOVAS AND LIFE

Before a massive star explodes as a supernova, the extreme pressure in its core squeezes atoms into heavier and heavier elements, such as carbon, oxygen, and iron. When the supernova explodes, it shoots those elements out into space. They float around in gases that eventually form new stars, planets, and life. The heavy elements in your body—carbon, nitrogen, oxygen, iron, and so on—come from supernovas. You are literally made from stardust.

NEUTRON STARS

After a supernova explodes, what's left of its core can become one of two things: a neutron star or a black hole. If the core was up to three times as massive as our sun, it becomes a neutron star. These superdense stars are only a few miles across, but they exert a huge gravitational pull. One teaspoon (4.9 g) of neutron star would weigh about 100 million tons (90.7 million t). Some neutron stars that rotate rapidly and emit beams of electromagnetic radiation are known as pulsars.

WORD CHECK

FUSION: Combining two different things so that they melt together. In atomic fusion, the kind that goes on in stars, the nuclei at the center of two atoms merge into one heavier atomic nucleus. This releases huge amounts of energy.

GEEK STREAK

Within a single day, an exploding supernova can become as bright as four billion suns.

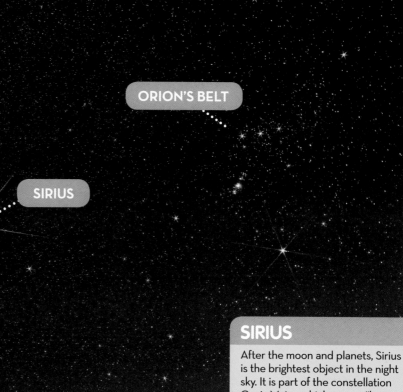

ORION'S BELT

SIRIUS

LOL!

Q: Where do you find black holes?

A: In black socks!

STAR-WATCHING

From the Earth, we can see a few thousand stars with the naked eye. Some are very bright, like Sirius, while others are dim, like Polaris, the North Star. How bright a star looks from Earth is called its "apparent magnitude." Some look bright only because they're close, or dim only because they're far away. A star's true brightness, as seen from a standard distance, is called its "absolute magnitude." Polaris is naturally brighter than Sirius—it has a greater absolute magnitude—but it looks dimmer to us because it's farther away.

SIRIUS

After the moon and planets, Sirius is the brightest object in the night sky. It is part of the constellation Canis Major, which means "larger dog," so it is sometimes called the Dog Star. Ancient Egyptians called it the Nile Star because it appeared in the eastern sky around the time of the annual flooding of the Nile River that irrigated Egypt's farmlands. Because it is so bright, the Greeks gave it the name Sirius, which means "glowing."

TRY THIS!

WHAT YOU NEED: A clear winter's night and a coat

HOW LONG IT TAKES: 20 minutes

Winter is the best time for finding Sirius. On a dark night, go outside and give your eyes time to adjust to the darkness. Now face south and you'll see three bright stars in a row. Those stars form the belt of the constellation Orion. Just down from the belt and to the east, you'll see Sirius, shimmering in the sky.

BLACK HOLES

When huge stars explode, leaving behind cores more than three or four times the mass of our sun, the cores turn into truly bizarre objects: black holes. When that much mass collapses in on itself after a supernova, nothing can stop it. It gets smaller and denser until it disappears from sight. It becomes a black hole. A black hole is infinitely small, but it contains all the mass of the original core. Its gravitational pull is so strong near its surface that not even light can escape.

PERSONALITY PLUS

Danish astronomer Tycho Brahe (1546–1601) was a colorful character. As a young man he lost part of his nose in a duel and wore a fake nose the rest of his life. He kept an elk as a pet. Tycho was also a great star-watcher. He changed the world of astronomy when in 1572 he saw a "new star" in the sky. This was actually a supernova. Tycho's discovery proved that skies were an active place, not a fixed sphere holding unchanging stars, as people had previously thought.

THE SUN

Our sun is a typical star, but to us it is unique. It is the center of our solar system, holding all the planets, asteroids, and comets in its gravitational grip. Its heat and light make life on Earth possible.

Compared to everything around it, the sun is enormous. It is more than 864,000 miles (1,390,000 km) wide and holds more than 99 percent of the mass in the solar system. If the sun were as big as a beach ball, the Earth would be the size of a pea. The sun doesn't have a solid surface. It's a swirling, stormy, superheated ball of hydrogen and helium gas. The temperature at its surface is 10,000°F (5500°C); its core is an unimaginable 27 million°F (15 million°C). Luckily for us, we're far enough away from the sun (92 million miles/148 million km) that we get just enough energy to sustain us. Scientists say we live in the "Goldilocks Zone," neither too cold nor too hot, but just right. Born about 4.6 billion years ago, the sun will last for about another 5 billion years before it swells into a red giant star (see page 166).

THE FUSION POWERHOUSE

The sun's heat and light come from fusion in its core, or center. Crushed by the intense pressures at the sun's heart, hydrogen atoms fuse into helium atoms. In the process, they release energy. This energy makes its way through the sun's body until it is released into space in the form of solar flares. Fusion eats up 600 million tons (544 million t) of hydrogen every second, but because the sun is so big, it will be billions of years before it runs out of fuel.

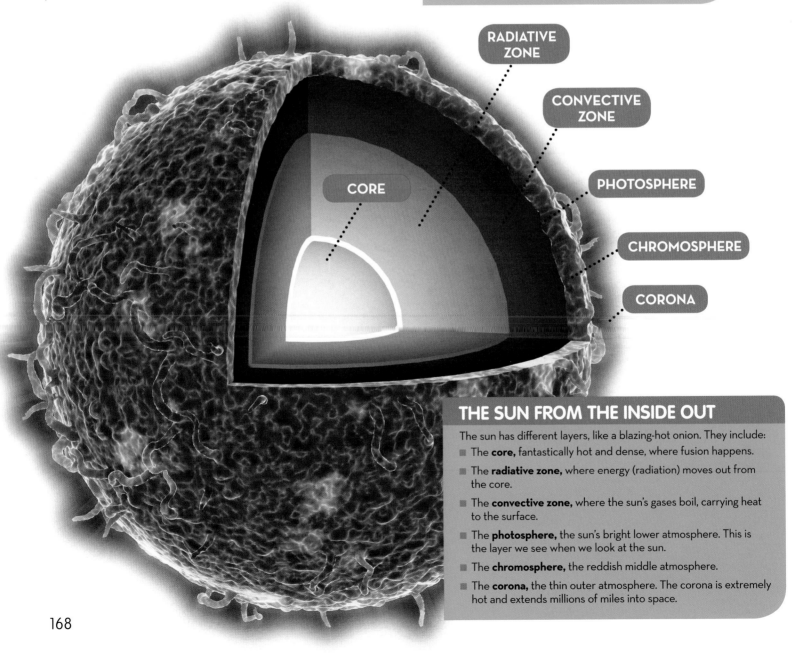

RADIATIVE ZONE

CONVECTIVE ZONE

CORE

PHOTOSPHERE

CHROMOSPHERE

CORONA

THE SUN FROM THE INSIDE OUT

The sun has different layers, like a blazing-hot onion. They include:

- The **core,** fantastically hot and dense, where fusion happens.
- The **radiative zone,** where energy (radiation) moves out from the core.
- The **convective zone,** where the sun's gases boil, carrying heat to the surface.
- The **photosphere,** the sun's bright lower atmosphere. This is the layer we see when we look at the sun.
- The **chromosphere,** the reddish middle atmosphere.
- The **corona,** the thin outer atmosphere. The corona is extremely hot and extends millions of miles into space.

SUNSPOTS

Astronomers have long known that the sun has dark spots that move across its surface as the sun rotates. In the 20th century, they realized that these sunspots are places where the sun's magnetic field is concentrated on its surface. The spots are cooler than the surrounding gases, so they look dark. Sunspots appear and disappear in regular 11-year cycles, going from fewer spots to more spots and then back again.

SOLAR STORMS

The sun is a stormy place. Different kinds of storms erupt from its surface when its gases twist and turn and heat up. Sometimes, the gases shoot out into space as solar flares. Other times, eruptions called coronal mass ejections (CMEs) shoot out huge balls of magnetic gas. They can shoot far enough to reach Earth's atmosphere, and then their magnetic particles can disturb our satellites, radios, and electricity.

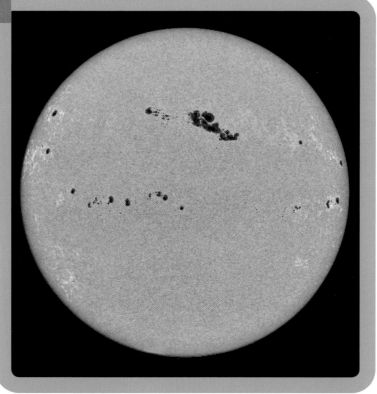

GEEK STREAK

A solar flare is a tremendous explosion on the sun. It happens when energy stored in magnetic fields is suddenly released. Surrounding materials heat to millions of degrees and produce a burst of radiation that can cause radio blackouts on Earth.

LOL!

I was up all night wondering where the sun had gone . . . and then it dawned on me.

SOLAR ENERGY ON EARTH

Earth receives only one-half of one-billionth of the sun's total energy. That's still more than 20 times the energy contained in all Earth's reserves of coal, oil, and natural gas. We use solar panels to turn the sun's energy into heat and electricity for homes, industrial plants, and more.

TOOLS OF THE TRADE

Floating in endless daylight, the Solar and Heliospheric Observatory (SOHO) is a space-based telescope that always watches the sun. SOHO orbits the sun just as the planets do. Its instruments have told us a lot about our star's structure, atmosphere, and storms. SOHO has also captured images of many comets that pass near the sun—including some that dive into it and never return.

PERSONALITY PLUS

For centuries, scientists struggled to understand how the sun could burn for so long without running out of fuel. In 1926, British physicist Arthur Eddington (1882–1944) used Einstein's new theories of relativity to answer this question. Working with Einstein's equations, he calculated how the sun continues to produce energy. He showed that the cores of stars, like the sun, are hot enough to fuse hydrogen into helium and release energy. Eddington was a good writer and funny, too. His books about science were popular with the public and helped explain the physics of stars so everyone could understand them.

CONSTELLATIONS

Our ancestors saw that stars seemed to form pictures in the sky. They called those pictures constellations, and gave them names from their myths and stories.

Today there are 88 officially recognized constellations. We call most of them by their old Greek and Roman names, but the Egyptians, Babylonians, Chinese, and other cultures had their own names for the same star patterns. Why were these constellations important? Because ancient astronomers noticed that they moved across the night sky in predictable ways. Seeing a certain constellation appear at a certain spot in the sky each season told a farmer when to plant or harvest a crop. And ancient sailors relied on the constellations to guide them home from their journeys across the seas. Desert peoples used them to find their way across the vast sands of the Sahara, which is why so many of the stars also have Arabic names.

THE BIG DIPPER

The seven stars of the Big Dipper are probably the most recognized in the sky. It has different names in different places: the French call it the Chariot; in the British Isles it's the Plough. In Africa it was known as the Drinking Gourd. Runaway slaves knew to follow it to freedom in the North before the U.S. Civil War.

The Big Dipper itself is a star pattern called an asterism within a larger constellation called Ursa Major, or the Great Bear. The Big Dipper is visible year-round, but knowing where it is in the sky can tell you what season you're in. It's highest in the sky in the spring and summer, and lowest in the fall and winter.

ORION, LORD OF THE WINTER SKY

Orion, named after a great hunter in Greek mythology, is one of the easiest constellations to spot. Look south in the winter and find the three bright stars that make up Orion's belt. On Orion's left shoulder is the orange star Betelgeuse (pronounced Beet-el-jooze). This red supergiant is one of the biggest stars in our galaxy. Hanging down from Orion's belt, where his sword might be, is a bright misty patch known as the Orion Nebula. New stars are being born in this region of hot gases.

WORD CHECK

ASTERISM: A group of stars not officially designated as a constellation but commonly known by most non-astronomers

LOL!

Q: Why didn't the Dog Star laugh at the joke?

A: It was too Sirius.

THE SIGNS OF THE ZODIAC

What's your sign? According to the beliefs of astrology, if you're born between late July and late August, you are a Leo (the lion), which means you are probably an outgoing, dramatic leader. The other 11 signs in the zodiac have distinct personality traits, too. Ancient astrologers weren't scientists, but they were observant and skillful sky-watchers. They saw that the sun, the moon, and planets traveled a curved path through the sky called the ecliptic, which means "the place where eclipses take place." They believed that this movement affected our personalities and our daily lives, depending on the position of the stars on the day and minute we were born. Over time they named the constellations along this imaginary line. So many were named after animals that they called the series of constellations the zodiac, which is Greek for "animal circle," or "zoo." The 12 constellations recognized by the ancients as part of the zodiac are Aries, Taurus, Gemini, Cancer, Leo, Virgo, Libra, Scorpio, Sagittarius, Capricorn, Aquarius, and Pisces. You may like to read your daily horoscope because it's fun, but just remember astrology is not a real science.

POLARIS, THE GUIDING STAR

The Big Dipper and Little Dipper rotate like riders on a merry-go-round circling a very bright star called Polaris, or the North Star. Polaris lies at the end of the "handle" of the Little Dipper. If you can see Polaris, you'll always know where you are because it sits directly over the North Pole. That's why for centuries Polaris has been a celestial compass for voyagers everywhere.

THE SOUTHERN CROSS

When you see the Southern Cross, you know you've crossed the Equator into the southern hemisphere. The longer bar of this kite-shaped constellation, also called Crux, points right at the South Pole. So it works just like Polaris, giving sailors and other voyagers south of the Equator a constant point of reference in the sky. Crux may be one of the smallest constellations in the sky, but it's so important for navigation that five countries have put it on their flags—Australia, Brazil, New Zealand, Papua New Guinea, and Samoa.

LITTLE DIPPER

POLARIS

BIG DIPPER

GEEK STREAK

The cave walls in Lascaux, France, are famous for the paintings made more than 17,000 years ago by early humans. Some of those drawings are thought to be pictures of the Pleiades and Hyades star clusters found in the constellation Taurus, making them one of the first star maps ever made.

PERSONALITY PLUS

The French astronomer Nicolas-Louis de Lacaille is credited with finding and naming 14 constellations in the southern sky between 1751 and 1753. He liked to name his constellations after things, instead of people and animals—which is why his constellations have names like Air Pump, Microscope, Telescope, Pendulum Clock, Chemical Furnace, Carpenter's Square, Painter's Easel, Mariner's Compass, and Sculptor's Workshop. When a fellow astronomer saw a chart of Lacaille's constellations, he commented, "It looks like somebody's attic!"

OUR SOLAR SYSTEM

Our solar system begins with the sun—our central star—and includes everything that circles around it. Eight planets, five dwarf planets, hundreds of moons, and countless asteroids and comets make up our solar system family.

All of these things formed from the same spinning cloud of gas and rocky dust about 4.6 billion years ago. Most of the gas pulled together into our sun, but much of the rest clumped up into planets and moons. The four planets closest to the sun—Mercury, Venus, Earth, and Mars—are smaller and rocky. The four outer planets—Jupiter, Saturn, Uranus, and Neptune—have big gas and ice bodies around a rocky core. Ancient sky-watchers named and tracked the five planets visible to the naked eye: Mercury, Venus, Mars, Jupiter, and Saturn. After the invention of the telescope, astronomers spotted Uranus, Neptune, and eventually Pluto and other dwarf planets. The 20th century brought us more knowledge, as spacecraft began to travel to planets and even land on their surfaces.

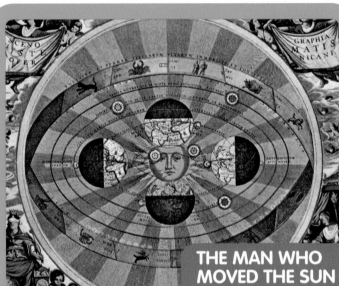

THE MAN WHO MOVED THE SUN

Until the 15th century, scholars believed that Earth was the center of the solar system. The ancient Greek scientist Aristarchus of Samos created a model of the solar system that placed the sun at the center, but that had been forgotten. Scholars thought the sun, other planets, and even stars circled around us. But in 1543, Polish astronomer Nicolaus Copernicus published a little book that proved Earth and other planets revolved around the sun. Many people, including religious officials, were unhappy at the idea that humans were not the center of the universe. Only in the 17th century, after telescopes were invented, did the sun-centered universe gain acceptance.

ORBITS

The solar system is in constant motion. Every planet orbits, or circles around, the sun in the same direction (counterclockwise, if you were looking from above). The planets' orbits are elliptical, like slightly stretched-out circles. Each orbit is one planetary year. Mercury, the closest planet to the sun, has a year just 88 Earth days long. Neptune, the farthest, takes more than 164 Earth years to complete one orbit.

WORD CHECK

ELLIPSE: In math, an ellipse is a curved shape with two focal points inside it. The total distance from both focal points to any point on the curve is always the same. Most ellipses look like ovals, but a circle is a special kind of ellipse in which both focal points are the same (the center of the circle). All planetary orbits are ellipses.

GEEK STREAK

Astronomers often measure distances in the solar system using astronomical units (AU). One AU is equal to the average distance between Earth and the sun, or 92,955,807 miles (149,597,870 km). The average distance from Neptune to the sun, for instance, is 30 AU. Multiply 30 by the distance above and you get nearly 3 billion miles (5 billion km)!

MOONS

Although Mercury and Venus lack moons, other planets make up for them by hosting lots of natural satellites. Earth has only one, but it's a big one. Mars has two little oddball moons. The outer planets have at least 170 among them, big and small. Some moons, such as Jupiter's Europa and Ganymede, have cold oceans under their surfaces. One, Saturn's Titan, has a thick but unbreathable atmosphere.

OTHER PLANETS, OTHER SUNS

Our planetary system is not the only one. In fact, astronomers estimate that our galaxy alone contains billions of planets circling its multitudes of stars. Using our best telescopes, we've been able to spot almost 2,000 planets around other stars so far. Many are gas giants like our Jupiter. Some are small, hot, and rocky. We don't know yet if any of them have life—but we're looking hard.

DWARF PLANETS

Five round, rocky solar system bodies that are too small to be planets, but too big to be asteroids, are known as dwarf planets. One, Ceres, lies between the orbits of Mars and Jupiter. The others circle the sun in the far icy reaches of the solar system, beyond Neptune's orbit. They include Pluto, once considered a planet, as well as Makemake, Haumea, and Eris. The last three are so distant that we've never gotten a good look at them.

LOL! 😄

Q: What should you do if you see a green alien from another planet?

A: Wait until it's ripe!

TRY THIS!

WHAT YOU NEED: Dark night during all the seasons, paper, pencil

HOW LONG IT TAKES: 10 to 15 minutes per night

Different planets are visible in the night sky at different times of the year. See if you can spot one on the next clear night. Record each spotting of Mercury, Mars, Venus, Saturn, and Jupiter. (You can track planet positions by month at astroviewer.com.)

Use these pointers to be sure it's a planet, not a star:

- Planets shine with a bright, steady light. (Stars usually twinkle.)

- Planets move against the background of stars from night to night.

- Planets are found only in a certain part of the sky, called the ecliptic. This is the same path followed by the moon and sun.

- Venus (shown above with Jupiter to its left) is the brightest planet in Earth's sky and the third brightest object we see after the sun and moon.

- Some planets have a distinct color. Mars is orange. Saturn is gold. Jupiter is bright white.

THE INNER PLANETS

The four planets closest to the sun are called the "terrestrial" planets—from the Latin word *terra*, which means "earth." Mercury, Venus, Mars, and our home planet Earth have much in common. They are relatively small and dense, with rocky surfaces. But only Earth (that we know of) has life.

When the inner planets first formed billions of years ago, they held lots of ice and gas. Then the young sun blasted them with radiation that blew away materials that were light, leaving behind rock. Early years for the inner planets were rough. Big rocks called meteorites bombarded them and left craters all over their surfaces. Over time, though, Venus, Earth, and Mars developed atmospheres. Weather, water, and volcanic eruptions smoothed out their surfaces. Only Mercury, which has almost no atmosphere, still shows the craters from its early history.

The only solar system body outside of Earth that humans have ever walked on is our moon. We have sent unpiloted spacecraft to all the inner planets and mapped their surfaces. Even so, we still have much to learn about our terrestrial neighbors.

MERCURY

Little Mercury, barely bigger than Earth's moon, is the closest planet to the sun. Pockmarked with craters, it has just a trace of an atmosphere. In the day, temperatures reach a scorching 800°F (430°C) on its barren surface; at night, they drop to a frigid minus 290°F (-180°C). Those days and nights are long, too. Mercury rotates slowly, so each complete day lasts 176 Earth days.

GEEK STREAK

Tiny Mercury has one of the biggest craters in the solar system: Caloris Basin. This is the mark left by a huge asteroid that hit Mercury with the force of a trillion hydrogen bombs. Shock waves from the impact traveled through the planet and wrinkled up the planet's surface opposite the crater, a landscape now known as the "Weird Terrain."

VENUS

The second planet from the sun, Venus is just slightly smaller than our planet. Like Earth, Venus has a thick, cloudy atmosphere. But under those clouds it's a different story. Venus is a toxic, crushing furnace. Its dense atmosphere traps heat, keeping temperatures at 864°F (462°C), hot enough to melt lead. Air pressure is 90 times that of Earth, enough to smash a human body. Those thick clouds do rain—but the rain is sulfuric acid. You really don't want to visit Venus.

WORD CHECK

ATMOSPHERE: From the Greek and Latin words for "vapor" and "sphere," it is the layer of gases surrounding a planet

TRY THIS!

WHAT YOU NEED: A clear morning or evening

HOW LONG IT TAKES: 10 minutes to search the sky

Venus was long known as the morning or evening star, notable for its brilliant white beauty in the twilight. Of course, it isn't a star at all—it's a planet—but morning and evening are the best times to see it. Look for it along the sun's path, about four hours before sunrise or four hours after sunset.

EARTH

Our home planet, the third from the sun, has just the right temperatures to keep water in its three forms—ice, liquid, and vapor—on its surface. Life on Earth was born in that water, on a planet that is two-thirds ocean. Earth's oxygen-rich atmosphere recycles the water and also protects us from meteors hurtling toward us and deadly solar radiation. Its big landmasses are in slow but constant motion, carried by rocky plates. It is the perfect home for the seven billion humans who scurry about its surface every day.

MARS

The fourth planet from the sun, Mars is half the size of Earth. It's a freezing cold, mostly dry world, with sand stained rusty red by iron. Its thin atmosphere and wispy clouds are made mostly of unbreathable carbon dioxide. Its landscape is dramatic: It has our solar system's largest volcano, Olympus Mons, and an enormous canyon, Valles Marineris, five miles (8 km) deep. Scientists once thought that slender tracks on the surface might be old streambeds, but in 2015 they discovered that the tracks are actually streams of water that appear when the temperature warms up and disappear when it's cold. Scientists are studying how this water can help support future life on Mars.

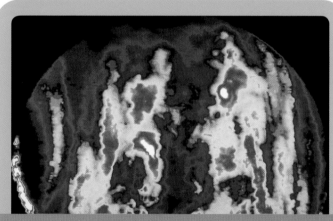

AIR TODAY, GONE TOMORROW

Venus, Earth, and Mars all have atmospheres, and yet each one is wildly different. On each world, the atmosphere began as gases leaking out from inside the planet. On Earth, green plants added oxygen. Earth's air keeps some heat trapped against the planet, but not too much. On Venus, carbon dioxide and steam combined to trap its heat like a greenhouse. The air got thicker and hotter. Mars had the opposite problem. In its early years it had thicker air and liquid water. Its light gravity, and maybe even meteor hits, let much of that air escape into space.

PERSONALITY PLUS

Percival Lowell (1855–1916), a wealthy American diplomat, did much to advance the field of astronomy in the United States. He founded an observatory in Arizona and launched the sky search that later found Pluto. However, his excitement over astronomy also led him astray. After reading a description of "channels" on the surface of Mars, he wrote three books claiming that these were in fact canals built by intelligent aliens. Astronomers went on to show that the supposed canals were just natural markings on a dry and lifeless planet—much to the disappointment of people who wanted to meet a real Martian.

EARTH

The third planet from the sun is different from the others. It's blue and white, a marbled mix of water and clouds. Earth is a warm, wet world whose waters have given rise to life.

Our world is the biggest of the inner planets. It's 7,926 miles (12,756 km) wide and not completely round, because it bulges a little at the equator as it spins. A shallow, moist atmosphere clings to the planet like a blanket. Under this atmosphere, about two-thirds of Earth is covered by a vast ocean. Earth didn't always look like this. When it formed billions of years ago, it was a red-hot, airless ball of rock. As it cooled, volcanoes and cracks in its surface released gases that began to form an atmosphere. Water vapor cooled into rain that filled up the first oceans. In time, early ocean plants released oxygen to make the atmosphere into the air we breathe today.

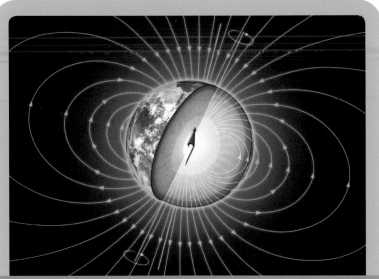

A MAGNET THE SIZE OF THE EARTH

Our planet (like some others) is surrounded by a gigantic, invisible magnetic field. This field is made by currents deep inside Earth's iron core. Just like a regular bar magnet—a rectangular magnet with a pole at each end—our planet's magnetic field has a north magnetic pole and a south magnetic pole. These poles are close to, but not the same as, the actual, geographic poles. We're lucky to have this magnetic shield—it protects our atmosphere from dangerous charged particles streaming out from the sun. It also gives us the northern lights, which is the dancing glow created when charged particles run down the magnetic field lines.

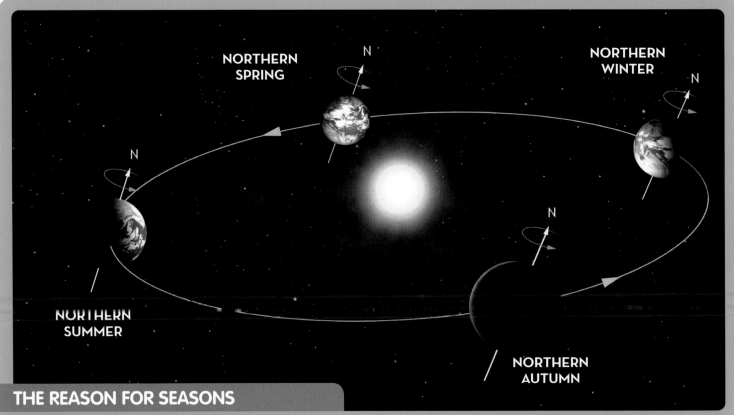

THE REASON FOR SEASONS

We have spring, summer, autumn, and winter because Earth leans to one side. Compared to the flat plane of its orbit, the planet's axis (the imaginary line through its North and South Poles) is tilted by 23.5 degrees. When the northern half of the planet leans toward the sun, that half gets more sunlight, so it's summer in the north. When the southern half leans toward the sun, that half gets more sunlight. It's summer in the south. In spring and fall, north and south get about the same amount of light.

WORD CHECK

EARTH: Every planet in the solar system is named for a god from classical mythology—except for Earth. Our own planet's name is taken from the ground beneath our feet. In Latin, *terra* means earth, or ground. In English, "Earth" comes from the Old English word *eorthe*—which also means earth, or ground.

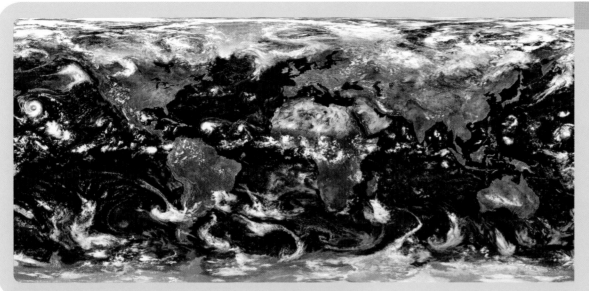

ONE BIG OCEAN

We have named the world's oceans as if they were separate bodies of water. However, Earth really has just one huge salty ocean, which covers 71 percent of the planet's surface. The Pacific, Atlantic, Southern, Indian, and Arctic Oceans are just labels for different parts of this single ocean. Without the ocean, humans couldn't survive. It is a storehouse of life and a kind of planetary safety net. It keeps extra carbon out of the atmosphere and continuously moves heat from warm to cold zones.

LAND ON THE MOVE

You can't feel it, but the very ground you stand on is moving. Earth's surface is broken into rocky plates that slowly shift around like huge, grinding puzzle pieces. Heat underneath the plates pushes and pulls them by a few inches each year. This motion creates mountain ranges, volcanoes, and ocean trenches. It also triggers thousands of earthquakes each year. Earth is the only planet in the solar system with this kind of plate movement, though other planets may have experienced it in the distant past.

THE LIVING WORLD

Earth is made of land, water, and air, but it's also made of life. A connected ecosystem of all living things, including plants and animals, makes up our planet's biosphere. Powered by the sun, the biosphere begins at the ocean floor and extends into the atmosphere at mountaintops. Bacteria, in the countless trillions, are the most common living thing in our biosphere. Humans are just a small part of the living world by number, but we have a huge effect on the world's resources.

TOOLS OF THE TRADE

Early scientists who studied Earth were often explorers who traveled the oceans and mapped distant lands. Today, we can see the whole planet from space using satellites. Each satellite has a different job. Some measure heat from the sun; others study cloud structures, ice sheets, ocean waves, rainfall, and even Earth's gravity field, which changes from place to place.

PERSONALITY PLUS

The Greek scientist Eratosthenes (276-195 B.C.) was a poet, mathematician, and librarian. Among other things, he figured out the size of Earth. Eratosthenes measured the angle of two shadows at high noon in Egypt—one in the city of Alexandria and the other in Syene, the ancient name for Aswan. Knowing the distance between the two cities, he used geometry to estimate Earth's circumference (the distance around the Earth) at about 28,000 miles (45,061 km). This isn't too far off from its real circumference of about 25,000 miles (40,000 km).

THE MOON

LOL!

Q: How does the man in the moon cut his hair?

A: Eclipse it!

Earth's moon is its close partner in the solar system. One-quarter the size of Earth, the moon is 238,900 miles (384,400 km) away—just a three-day flight by spacecraft! It is the only solar system body, aside from Earth, that humans have ever visited.

The moon orbits Earth every 27 days. Firmly gripped by Earth's gravity, it always presents the same side to us. We didn't see the moon's far side until the first spacecraft circled it. Our natural satellite is a patchwork of craters, mountains, and highlands. When astronomer Galileo Galilei first saw the moon through a telescope in 1609, he named its darker areas *maria*, or "seas," and the lighter places *terrae*, or "lands." We now know there are no seas on the moon, but Galileo's terms still exist in place-names such as the Sea of Tranquillity. Because the moon has no weather to erase its old craters, its surface is like a history museum that tells us about conditions in the early solar system.

FULL MOON

SUN

NEW MOON

NEW TO FULL AND BACK AGAIN

The moon is a rocky sphere, but to us on Earth it seems to change shape from night to night. That's because we see only the part that is lit by the sun. As the moon circles Earth every month, different portions of its surface catch the light. In the diagram above, the sun would be at bottom center. When the moon is between us and the sun, the side we see is completely dark. This is called the new moon. As the moon circles eastward away from the sun, the lit side grows from a crescent to a full moon, then wanes again to darkness in the second half of its orbit.

THE BIRTH OF THE MOON

Scientists aren't sure just where the moon came from. The main theory about its birth says that it was created by a huge collision. According to this theory, about 4.5 billion years ago a giant object the size of Mars crashed into the young Earth. The impact sent great chunks of Earth's crust and the underlying mantle flying into space. Gravity pulled them together to form the moon.

TOOLS OF THE TRADE

How do we know the exact distance to the moon? We ping it with lasers! American and Soviet space missions left reflectors on the moon's surface. Telescopes on Earth aim laser beams at these reflectors. By timing how long it takes for the beams to hit the reflectors and return— about 2.5 seconds—we get a very good measurement of the total distance.

WORD CHECK

LUNAR: "Lunar" means "of the moon." The word comes from the Latin word for moon, *luna*. The word "lunatic" also comes from *luna*. People used to think that the moon made you crazy.

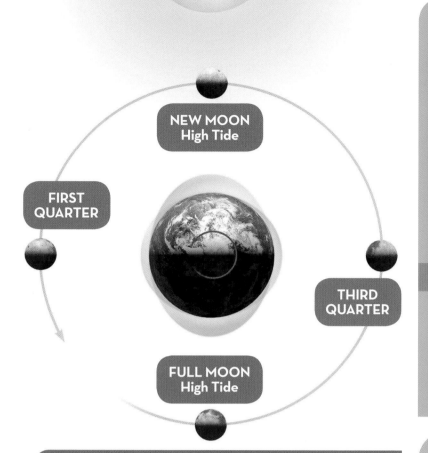

NEW MOON
High Tide

FIRST QUARTER

THIRD QUARTER

FULL MOON
High Tide

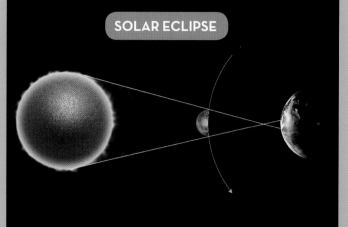

SOLAR ECLIPSE

SHADOWS FROM SPACE

Because the moon orbits directly between Earth and the sun, sometimes we're treated to a special event: an eclipse. There are two kinds of eclipses. A lunar eclipse happens when Earth passes between the sun and moon. Earth's shadow covers the moon and darkens it until it moves out of the shadow. A solar eclipse (above) occurs when the moon passes between the sun and Earth and its shadow falls on Earth. On the parts of Earth that fall into that shadow, it looks, for a little while, like the sun has been blotted out.

TWO HIGH TIDES

The moon's gravitational pull gives us high tides on both sides of Earth. Lunar gravity pulls on the ocean facing the moon, raising its water in a bulge. That's one high tide. Lunar gravity also tugs on the body of Earth itself, which moves toward the moon within its watery covering. The water on Earth's far side pulls away from Earth as it's left behind. That's the other high tide. The sun's gravity also adds a little to the tides, which is why we have very high tides when the sun and moon are lined up.

GEEK STREAK

Our moon is slowly leaving us. It moves away from Earth by about 1.5 inches (3.8 cm) every year. However, billions of years from now, the moon will run into the edges of the expanding sun. Then it will be pushed back toward Earth and break apart into many pieces. For a little while in the distant future, our planet will have rings made up of these moon pieces.

MOONWALKERS

On July 20, 1969, American astronaut Neil Armstrong (left) stepped out of the Apollo 11 lunar module onto the surface of the moon. He was the first human to walk on another world. In four short years, the Apollo space program landed 11 more astronauts on the moon. There, they collected moon rocks, set up scientific instruments, and explored in a rover. They even hit two golf balls over the dusty surface. In 1972, the Apollo program ended. No human has landed on the moon since then.

ASTRONOMY

The first sky-watchers didn't have telescopes, but they did have dark skies. No city lights blocked their view of the stars. So early people—shepherds on hills or priests in temples—knew the night sky well. The sun, the moon, the stars, and the five planets that they named were the known universe until the telescope was invented in the 1600s. Then we began to see farther and to discover new planets and stars. In the 20th century, spacecraft rocketed into space to add to our knowledge. Now we see a little more of the universe every year.

ca 2500 B.C.
The stone monument Stonehenge is built in England. Its stones may line up with the midsummer and midwinter sunrises.

ca 270 B.C.
Greek astronomer Aristarchus of Samos figures out that the Earth revolves around the sun.

ca A.D. 150
Greek-Egyptian astronomer Ptolemy writes the *Almagest*, the most important astronomy manual for the next 1,000 years.

250–900
Maya astronomers in Central America develop exact calendars and records of the movements of planets and stars.

1054
Chinese astronomers make note of an exploding star, the supernova that later produces the Crab Nebula.

1543
Polish astronomer Nicolaus Copernicus publishes *De Revolutionibus Orbium Coelestium (On the Revolutions of the Heavenly Orbs)*, which says that the Earth revolves around the sun.

1610
Italian astronomer Galileo Galilei is the first to use a telescope to take a close look at stars, the moon, and the moons of Jupiter.

1609
German astronomer Johannes Kepler publishes his first two laws of planetary motion.

1659
Dutch astronomer Christiaan Huygens publishes a description of the rings of Saturn, which he believes are a single solid object.

1687
English scientist Isaac Newton publishes his groundbreaking work, *Philosophiae Naturalis Principia Mathematica (Mathematical Principles of Natural Philosophy)*, which lays out his laws of motion and the law of universal gravitation.

1705
English astronomer Edmond Halley shows that three comets that appeared in 1531, 1607, and 1682 were really just one comet (now known as Halley's comet) that would return every 75 to 76 years.

1781
German-English astronomer William Herschel discovers Uranus, the first new planet to be found since ancient times.

1801
Italian astronomer Giuseppe Piazzi discovers Ceres, the first known asteroid (now considered to be a dwarf planet).

1846
Using calculations by French astronomer Urbain Le Verrier and British astronomer John Couch Adams to guide them, astronomers at the Berlin Observatory discover the planet Neptune.

1877

American astronomer Asaph Hall discovers Mars's two tiny moons, Phobos and Deimos.

1895

Inspired by science fiction, Russian inventor Konstantin Tsiolkovsky publishes the first formula for practical rocket engines.

1905

German physicist Albert Einstein publishes his special theory of relativity, which describes the link between space and time.

1916

Einstein publishes his general theory of relativity, which describes gravity in terms of the geometry of space.

1923

American astronomer Edwin Hubble shows that other galaxies exist outside our own Milky Way.

1929

Hubble discovers that the universe is expanding, carrying all galaxies away from each other.

1930

American astronomer Clyde Tombaugh discovers Pluto, which was then the ninth planet (now considered a dwarf planet).

1931

American physicist Karl Jansky launches the field of radio astronomy after he records radio waves coming from the Milky Way.

1957

Soviet engineers send the first artificial satellite into orbit, beach-ball-size Sputnik 1.

1961

Soviet cosmonaut Yuri Gagarin is the first person to fly in space, aboard the spacecraft Vostok 1.

1964

American radio astronomers Robert Wilson and Arno Penzias trace a steady hum in their telescope to radiation from the early years of the universe (the cosmic microwave background radiation). Their discovery helps to prove the big bang theory.

1967

British astronomer Jocelyn Bell discovers regular radio signals from space that turn out to come from pulsars, spinning neutron stars.

1969

American astronauts Neil Armstrong and Edwin (Buzz) Aldrin become the first people to walk on the moon.

1976

The Viking 1 and Viking 2 landers are the first U.S. spacecraft to land on Mars.

1990

The Hubble Space Telescope is put into orbit and begins to collect hundreds of thousands of images.

1992

Polish astronomer Aleksander Wolszczan discovers the first extrasolar planets (exoplanets), circling around a neutron star.

1998

Scientists studying distant supernovas discover that the universe is speeding up as it expands. The mysterious force behind this is named dark energy.

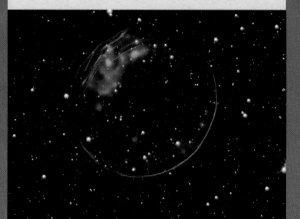

2004

NASA lands two rovers, Spirit and Opportunity, on Mars. The rovers send back evidence that water may once have flowed on the planet's surface.

2006

The International Astronomical Union writes a new definition of "planet" and names Pluto, Ceres, Haumea, Eris, and Makemake dwarf planets.

2014

The European Space Agency lands a small probe, named Philae, on the Comet 67P/Churyumov-Gerasimenko. It is the first time a spacecraft has made a soft landing—not destroying the craft—on a comet.

THE OUTER PLANETS

The outer solar system is a completely different neighborhood from the inner solar system. Four huge planets of ice and gas orbit there, far from the sun. In the outermost reaches, a vast ring of ice and rock holds four dwarf planets.

When the solar system formed from gas and dust, the sun's heat kept the inner planets dry and rocky. But farther from the sun, temperatures were cold enough that gases such as ammonia and methane could freeze into ice around a rocky core. As the young outer planets grew, their gravity pulled in hydrogen and helium gases that wrapped around them in deep, stormy atmospheres.

Jupiter is the king among these gas giants. It's bigger than all the other planets put together. All the outer planets have rings, but Saturn's are particularly bright and gorgeous. Uranus and Neptune are smaller worlds, but still enormous and icy in their distant orbits. The outer planets are rich in moons—170 of them at last count—some of which are as big as small planets themselves.

JUPITER

Enormous Jupiter could hold 1,400 Earths inside its gassy body. Orbiting 5.2 AU from the sun, it needs almost 12 years to complete one orbit. (Remember, one AU equals the distance from the Earth to the sun.) Its days are short, though, as Jupiter whirls around every 9.9 hours. Storms the size of the Earth swirl in its windy atmosphere. One huge storm, known as the Great Red Spot, has been visible for hundreds of years.

SATURN

Saturn's shining rings make it one of the most beautiful objects in the solar system. It's a giant planet, as big as 763 Earths, but not dense. If there were a bathtub large enough, Saturn would float in it. Saturn's orbit, 9.5 AU from the sun, takes 29 years, but like Jupiter it spins rapidly, so its day is only 10 hours long. Its seven rings, made of billions of icy and rocky particles, extend for hundreds of thousands of miles.

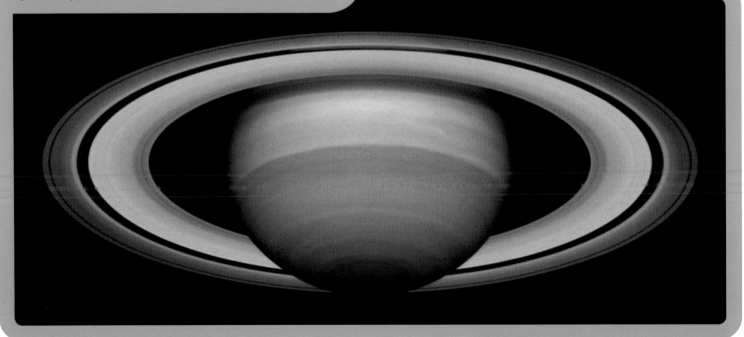

WORD CHECK PLANET: According to the International Astronomical Union, a planet must: (1) orbit the sun, (2) be round, and (3) have a clear orbit (not shared with other objects). Under this definition, Pluto isn't a planet, because it shares its orbit with other Kuiper belt bodies.

Q: What kind of music do you hear in outer space?

A: Nep-tunes!

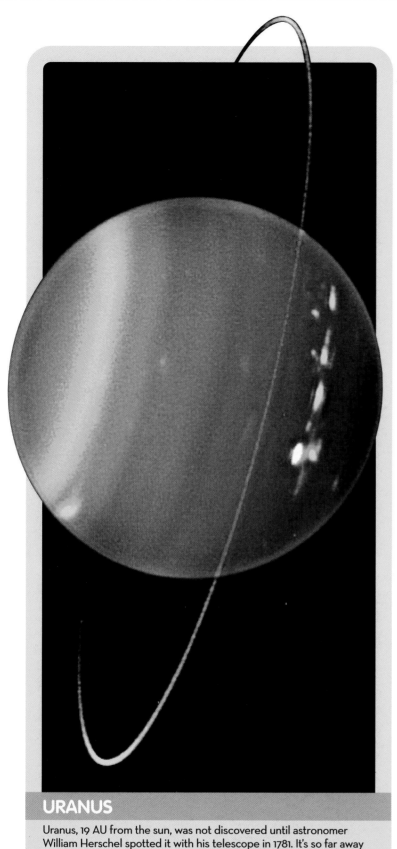

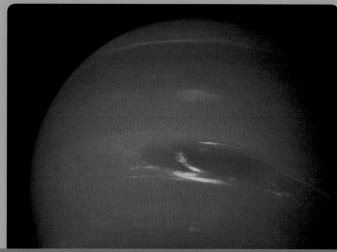

NEPTUNE

Neptune is so far away, at 30 AU from the sun, that we can't see it with the naked eye. It was discovered in 1846, after two mathematicians worked out its position based on its gravitational effects on Uranus. The blue giant is as large as 57 Earths and orbits the sun only once every 164 years. We don't know much about Neptune, but we do know it's stormy: The planet's winds whip around the planet at more than 1,200 miles an hour (2,000 km/h).

PLUTO AND ITS COUSINS

Once upon a time, Pluto was considered a major planet. The icy little world was discovered by telescope only in 1930, orbiting on average at 39 AU from the sun. In 2006, astronomers came up with a new definition for "planet," and Pluto was renamed a dwarf planet. It is in fact one of four dwarf planets, along with Eris, Makemake, and Haumea, that float within a distant ring of ice and rock at the far edge of the solar system. Known as the Kuiper belt, this ring holds hundreds of thousands of good-size rocky bodies.

TOOLS OF THE TRADE

Saturn's big moon Titan is a mysterious world with a thick, smoggy atmosphere. In 2004, we got our only look under its clouds when the Cassini space-craft dropped the Huygens probe (artist's rendering at left) onto its surface. Floating down under a parachute, the probe sent back images of lakes of liquid methane and dunes of carbon-rich sand.

URANUS

Uranus, 19 AU from the sun, was not discovered until astronomer William Herschel spotted it with his telescope in 1781. It's so far away that one orbit takes 84 years. As big as 63 Earths, Uranus has a rich blue color due to the methane in its icy atmosphere. Unlike any other planet, it spins on its side, with its poles facing toward and away from the sun. Some huge object must have slammed into it in the past and knocked it sideways.

PERSONALITY PLUS

Dutch scientist Christiaan Huygens (1629-1695) was a brilliant mathematician and all-around sharp guy. Among other things, he invented the first good pendulum clock. As an astronomer, he mapped the surface of Mars and was the first person to realize that the strange blobs that appeared next to Saturn in telescopes were actually rings. Huygens also believed that we would discover life on other planets, "equally good fitted worlds like ours."

ASTEROIDS AND COMETS

There's more to the solar system than the sun and planets. Hundreds of thousands of asteroids and comets also circle the sun. These small bodies are chunks of rock and ice left over from the formation of the solar system, billions of years ago.

Most asteroids are found between the orbits of Mars and Jupiter, a region known as the asteroid belt. The largest body in that belt, Ceres, has now been classified as a dwarf planet. Asteroids are also found in other parts of the solar system. They are lumpy, metallic rocks. Some are shaped like potatoes or dog bones. The biggest have their own tiny moons. Comets are similar to asteroids—they are solar system leftovers—but they come from farther out and hold a lot more ice. Sometimes they're called "dirty snowballs." Most comets orbit either in the Kuiper belt or in a very distant ring of icy objects known as the Oort cloud. A few zoom in close to the sun, flaunting a spectacular tail of gas and dust.

ASTEROID WATCH

In 1908, a huge explosion knocked down eight million trees in the remote forest of Tunguska, Russia. We now know that the blast was caused by a 120-foot (36.6-m)-wide asteroid that blew up in the atmosphere. Although such impacts are rare, observatories around the world track Near-Earth Objects (NEOs)—asteroids or comets that zoom close to Earth. To practice dealing with a close call, the U.S. space agency NASA is planning a mission in the 2020s in which an unmanned spacecraft (artist's rendering below) will practice grabbing a piece of an asteroid and sending it into orbit around the moon to keep it from smashing into Earth.

WORD CHECK

METEOR, METEORITE, AND METEOROID: What's the difference between these three things? A meteoroid is a rock floating in space. A meteor is a bit of space rock—a disintegrating comet or asteroid—that orbits the sun and may enter Earth's atmosphere. A meteorite is a space rock that has reached the ground.

REGULAR VISITORS: HALLEY'S COMET

Some comets are one-time visitors in our skies. If they start out in the very distant Oort cloud, they travel for millions of years before they swing around the sun and head back out into space. These are known as long-period comets. Other comets are regular visitors. These short-period comets come from the Kuiper belt near Pluto. They fall into regular orbits around the sun and show up in our skies at predictable times. The most famous of these is Halley's comet, which arrives every 75 to 76 years. Keep an eye out for its next appearance in 2061!

YOUR NAME HERE

People who discover asteroids are allowed to name them, as long as they follow a few rules from the International Astronomical Union. Most people name asteroids after themselves or their friends or colleagues. But some are more imaginative. Their asteroid names include Brontosaurus, Neverland, Purple Mountain, and Dioretsa (a backward-orbiting asteroid—get it?).

TRY THIS!

WHAT YOU NEED: Specific shower dates (see stardate .org/nightsky/meteors), a clear night away from city lights

HOW LONG IT TAKES: 10 minutes to hours (Wear warm clothes!)

A bright comet appears in the sky only every few years. But you can see pieces of comets light up the sky every year. These are meteor showers. Meteoroids are bits of disintegrating comets or asteroids that orbit the sun. Each year, the Earth passes through these bits. Some, called meteors, enter the atmosphere and burn up, looking like shooting stars. Look for the Perseid meteor shower, which are pieces of Comet Swift-Tuttle, every August. The Leonid meteor shower, caused by Comet Tempel-Tuttle, is a bright sight in November.

BUILDING WITH ASTEROIDS

As humans move out into the solar system in the future, they may turn to asteroids for their building materials. Many asteroids are rich in ice and in metals such as iron, nickel, and gold. Space miners could use the ice for water, air, and fuel. They could build mining stations and labs with the metal, like this model on an asteroid, seen from above. Some asteroids even have organic materials, such as carbon, that could be turned into fertilizer on space farms.

TRICKY LANDINGS

You might think it's hard to land a probe on a speeding comet. Well, it is—but in 2014 the Rosetta spacecraft managed to drop a probe, named Philae (right), onto the rough surface of Comet 67P/Churyumov-Gerasimenko after a 10-year trip. The little lander bounced twice on the comet's surface and landed in a shadow. For a few months it was silent, because it didn't have enough solar power, but when sunlight fell upon it again it woke up—just in time to see what happens when the comet starts forming its long, glowing tail.

EXPLORING SPACE

Only a few people have ever left our planet. However, we've been exploring space with our eyes and our spacecraft for a very long time. Each era of history has taught us more about our solar system, the stars, and the universe.

Early people were sky-watchers. Without electric lights to get in the way, societies such as the ancient Babylonians and Chinese knew the night sky much better than today's city-dwellers do. After the telescope was invented in 1609, new horizons opened up to astronomers. They discovered planets and moons. They saw that our Milky Way was just one galaxy among many, all of them sailing outward in expanding space. The truly hands-on era of space exploration arrived in the 20th century. Rockets, invented for use in World War II, were adapted for space flight after the war. The Soviet Union launched Sputnik 1, the first satellite, in 1957. Landers photographed the sands of Mars in the 1970s and spacecraft sped by remote Pluto in 2015—with many more missions planned for years to come.

AT HOME IN SPACE

Orbiting 240 miles (400 km) above Earth is a floating laboratory: the International Space Station (ISS). Since the year 2000 more than 200 people from around the world have lived and worked in the ISS. Among other things, they test how living creatures, from bacteria to lizards to humans, live and change in weightlessness. One day their research will help human crews as they voyage to Mars and beyond.

MISSIONS TO MARS

Missions to our neighbor Mars show all the different ways you can explore a world without sending human beings. In the 1960s we sent flyby missions, which scooted past but didn't land. Beginning in the 1970s we put spacecraft into orbit around the planet and sent landers to its surface, both studying its landscape. More recent landers and rovers (right) are rolling labs that have given us great images and information about the planet at ground level.

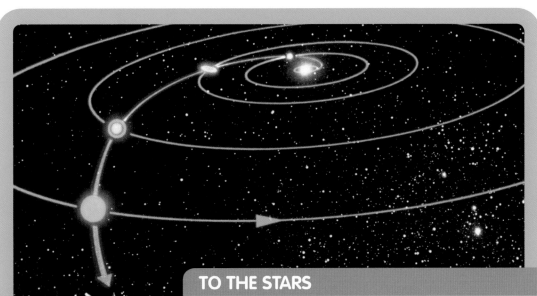

TO THE STARS

Wave goodbye to Voyager 1! This space probe, launched in 1977, has left the solar system altogether. It's still sending back information about interstellar space, though. Traveling now at 60,000 miles an hour (97,000 km/h) Voyager 1 will fly within 1.6 light-years of the star Gliese 445 in about 40,000 years. If aliens come across it, they could listen to the recordings on Voyager's gold-plated disk: sounds of whales singing, greetings in 55 different languages, and music ranging from Mozart to Chuck Berry's rock-and-roll.

WORD CHECK

SPACE PROBE: A space probe is any kind of robotic spacecraft that collects scientific information. Some probes fly by their target and take simple measurements. Others are more complicated landers or rovers that land on the surface of a different world and do experiments.

SURPRISING PLUTO

Until 2015, all we could see of faraway Pluto was a fuzzy gray dot in our telescopes. That changed when the New Horizons spacecraft, launched in 2006, finally flew past the dwarf planet after a three-billion-mile (4.8-billion-km) journey. The images New Horizons sent back to Earth were astonishing. The pale golden planet has a huge, heart-shaped plain and ice mountains 11,000 feet (3,350 m) high. Even more surprising, Pluto doesn't seem to have craters. That means that some kind of geological process, still unknown, is smoothing out its surface.

INTO THE RINGS

If it weren't for the Cassini mission, we wouldn't know how truly amazing Saturn is. The robotic spacecraft was launched in 1997. It arrived at Saturn in 2004 and is still orbiting. Among other things, it has discovered new moons of Saturn, dropped a probe onto the moon Titan, discovered oceans on the moon Enceladus, and studied the structure of Saturn's ring system. It has also sent us stunning images of the solar system's most beautiful planet.

PERSONALITY PLUS

French writer Jules Verne (1828–1905) never built a rocket ship, but he was a big influence on the first people who did. Verne trained to be a lawyer, but he loved writing much more—particularly a kind of writing he called "scientific fiction." His imaginative books about submarines, spaceships, and other devices that hadn't been invented yet inspired a generation of scientists. His 1865 novel *From the Earth to the Moon*, about a spaceship shot out of a cannon, was a favorite of scientist Konstantin Tsiolkovsky, who went on to work out the first practical methods of rocketry.

THE BIG PICTURE

If there's only one thing you know about the universe, it should be this: It's huge. Distances in the universe are enormous, immense, vast, whopping—indeed, astronomical.

The simplest way to measure the giant distances among the stars is in light-years. One light-year is the distance that light travels in one year, about 5.88 trillion miles (9.5 trillion km). In terms of light-years, just how big is the observable universe? Let's start with our moon. It's close: 1.3 light-seconds away. (That's 225,622 miles, or 406,696 km.) You could drive there if you had a special space-car and a few months.

Pluto? That's about 5 light-hours away (4.7 billion miles or 7.5 billion km). Much too far to drive. The nearest star, Proxima Centauri, is 4.2 light-years away (24.7 trillion miles or 40.1 trillion km). If we traveled at the speed of our fastest-ever space probe, Helios 2, we'd get there in 19,000 years or so.

The rest of the universe consists of other galaxies light-years away with their own massive stars of different sizes and temperatures, planets and moons, and asteroids and comets. On these pages you'll see some of the biggest objects in the distant space beyond us.

THE BIGGEST MOON

It's logical that our biggest planet, Jupiter, should have the biggest moon we know of: Ganymede. It's 10,273 miles (16,532 km) around at its equator, which makes it larger than either Mercury or Pluto. If it orbited the sun instead of Jupiter, it would be considered a planet. This giant moon has a thick icy shell over a salty ocean.

THE BIGGEST PLANET

Jupiter is big, but if you venture outside of our solar system you can find even bigger planets. The largest we've discovered so far is known as HAT-P-32b. It's twice as big as Jupiter and very hot. HAT-P-32b is so close to its sun, HAT-P-32, that it completes an orbit every two Earth days. Its broiling temperatures mean that it probably doesn't have life as we know it.

WORD CHECK

OBSERVABLE UNIVERSE: What do we mean by "observable universe"? We mean the universe that we can see in the light that reaches us from distant stars and galaxies. The farthest light we see left its stars 13.8 billion years ago, so 13.8 billion light-years is the size of the observable universe. However, since the light left those stars, the universe has continued to expand, carrying the stars with it. So by the time we see their light, the stars have moved farther away. We'll never be able to see them "now," because it takes so long for their light to reach us.

THE BIGGEST GALAXY

It's hard to measure galaxy sizes, but IC 1101 currently tops the list of supergiant galaxies. One billion light-years away, it is a golden, elliptical (oval) collection of one trillion stars. From its center to its outer edge it spans two million light-years: 40 times as wide as our Milky Way. It is probably made from smaller galaxies that collided and smooshed together. Now it's growing old, with few new stars being formed.

UY SCUTI

THE BIGGEST STAR

Stars are tricky to measure exactly, but the largest star we know may be UY Scuti, a red supergiant about 9,500 light-years away. UY Scuti is about 1,700 times as big as our sun, which would look like a pebble next to it. If UY Scuti took the place of our own star, all the planets out to Jupiter would be swallowed up in its fiery body.

VEGA

DENEB   ALTAIR

TRY THIS!

WHAT YOU NEED: A clear night sky in summer, away from city lights

HOW LONG IT TAKES: 10 to 15 minutes

The farthest star you can easily see with the naked eye is the supergiant Deneb. Look for it in the summer as one of three stars that make up the big "summer triangle": Deneb, Altair, and Vega. Look east in the sky and find brilliant blue-white Vega. Then look down and to the left and you'll see bright white Deneb. (Down to the right is Altair.) Astronomers think Deneb is about 1,400 light-years away. The light you see today left the star in the seventh century.

SLOAN GREAT WALL

THE BIGGEST WALL OF GALAXIES

One billion light-years from Earth is one of the largest structures in the universe: the Sloan Great Wall. It's a shining web of galaxies strung together in clusters and superclusters. From end to end it's about 1.4 billion light-years wide, which is one-sixtieth as wide as the entire observable universe.

TOOLS OF THE TRADE

It's hard enough just spotting Pluto in a telescope. How do we see planets in other solar systems, many light-years away? There are several ways to do this, but one of the simplest is to measure starlight. Instruments like the Kepler Space Telescope are very sensitive to light. If they see that the light from a distant star dims a little and then brightens again, they know that something has passed in front of that star and blocked its light. That "something" is very likely a planet.

189

LIFE ON EARTH

JUST LOOK AROUND YOU!

Earth boasts a spectacular variety of life, ranging from giant blue whales longer than a basketball court to tiny mites no bigger than pinheads that travel in the nostrils of hummingbirds. Even your own body is an ecosystem of life: About one thousand different kinds of bacteria live on human skin—and some of them live in just one area, such as behind your ear or on your elbow! And although there's now only one species of human, *Homo sapiens*, there are more than a million different species of insects. That includes some 400,000 different species of beetles alone!

Life is not only varied, it's also amazingly abundant. Just a teaspoon of soil, for example, may contain up to one billion bacteria as well as thousands of other microbes, tiny worms, and fungi. The Amazon rain forest of South America contains nearly 400 billion individual trees. Scientists estimate that there are about 10 billion billion ants on Earth—along with more than 7 billion humans!

Living things also exist nearly everywhere on Earth. Travel to the frozen reaches of the Arctic, and you'll find tiny ice worms that can survive only inside glaciers. Visit Yellowstone National Park, and you'll find one-celled organisms that live in scalding hot springs. The dark, cold depths of the ocean contain fish and crabs that can't live anywhere else on Earth.

To date, scientists have named about 1.3 million living things, or organisms. But they admit that there are many living things still waiting to be discovered. How many? Scientists estimate the number of species on Earth to be about 8.7 million, not including certain one-celled organisms. Though thousands of new species of insects, plants, and other living things are discovered every year, these researchers suggest that we have yet to identify more than 86 percent of Earth's land species and 91 percent of its ocean species. During the past half century, spacecraft have left our planet to explore distant moons, planets, comets, and asteroids. These spacecraft have sent back information that suggests life could exist in places other than Earth—perhaps in the icy ocean of Jupiter's moon Europa, or in undersea hot spots on Saturn's moon Enceladus. Other craft, such as the Mars rover Curiosity, have sampled actual scoopfuls of dirt for signs of life. Meanwhile, here on Earth, scientists continue to dig, dive, hike, and climb as they search for clues about the living things that call this planet home.

Did you know? Scientists estimate that about 12 species go extinct each day around the world. In 2010, axolotls were nearly extinct, but they're making a comeback.

This little swimmer, an axolotl, is sometimes called a "walking fish." It's not a fish at all, but an amphibian related to a salamander. Axolotls live only in two lakes in Mexico.

HOW **LIFE** BEGAN

Life appeared on Earth more than 3.5 billion years ago. The first single-celled living things developed in a harsh world of erupting volcanoes and a thick, hot atmosphere that crackled with lightning.

These single-celled organisms formed from simple molecules that existed in the ocean and other habitats. The simple molecules combined to form bigger, more complex ones—molecules that are the basic building blocks of living things.

Among these complex molecules are nucleic acids. They have the special ability to make copies of themselves. Two important nucleic acids that contain the "recipes" for making and maintaining living things are RNA and DNA.

The first single-celled living organisms were likely little more than blobs of complex molecules inside a film made of other molecules. This film, or membrane, gave them an inside and an outside. These early cells, called protocells, were able to grow and divide. Over time, protocells evolved into cells more like some of today's bacteria. Protocells called cyanobacteria layered with silt to form a kind of rock called stromatolite. Fossil stromatolites give a glimpse of life on Earth more than 2.5 billion years ago.

PRIMORDIAL SOUP

The chemicals needed for life may have first formed in warm seas. Lightning might have sparked a chemical reaction that filled the ocean with the first organisms, making it like a soup. This idea is called the "primordial (prehistoric) soup" hypothesis. Another hypothesis states that life first formed around hot-water vents deep in the ocean. Minerals at the vents formed thin mats of molecules called "biofilms." "Bio" means "life." Over time, the molecules joined to form complex molecules that became parts of living things.

RNA WORLD

One idea about how life began is called the "RNA world hypothesis." RNA stands for ribonucleic acid. Inside living cells today, RNA carries out jobs such as making proteins. But in the past, RNA may have been involved in the evolution of the first life on Earth. RNA can store information, such as the recipe for a living thing. It can also make chemical reactions happen. In this way, the first cells may have used RNA to reproduce themselves. At some point, DNA (deoxyribonucleic acid) largely took over this job.

EVOLUTION

How did we get from protocells to the marvelous animals and plants of today? This big change was made up of many, many small changes over many millions of years. This process is called evolution. Evolution starts at the level of the cell. A small change, called a mutation, can occur in a cell's genes, the parts that hold the DNA "recipe" for a living thing. This change can happen randomly—simply by accident. The mutation then gets passed on to new cells when the cell reproduces.

COOL EVOLVERS

As an animal evolves, mutations help it adapt, or adjust, to its surroundings. The mutations help an animal survive. That could include staying warm in cold weather, living without a lot of water in dry conditions, developing a special way to eat, or defending itself against predators looking for a meal. Check out these examples.

A hummingbird has evolved to have a superlong beak. This mutation has let it adapt to sip nectar from flowers. In the process, hummingbirds spread pollen so the flowers can make seeds. This partnership is an example of "coevolution."

A wasp has a painful sting. A hoverfly doesn't, but it has evolved to look like a wasp. Its disguise protects it from predators. Such "look-alike" pairings are called mimicry.

DIFFERENT PATHS

Two kinds of organisms could share a common ancestor, but may have evolved so much that they became extremely different from each other. For example, scientists have discovered that horses and lions likely share a common ancestor, the rat-size *Protungulatum donnae* (right), which lived millions of years ago. But horses evolved hooves while lions evolved paws. This process is called divergent evolution. Convergent evolution, on the other hand, is when two organisms that are not closely related evolve similar traits. Think of the wings of birds, bats, and butterflies!

FOSSIL DISCOVERIES

Fossils tell us a lot of what we know about ancestors of the plant and animal world. Fossils are the remains of organisms that lived more than 10,000 years ago. Dinosaur bones, footprints left by early humans, and ancient shark teeth are all examples of fossils. In 2011, scientists discovered fossils of bacteria that lived nearly 3.5 billion years ago. These "microfossils" were found in rocks in Australia.

GEEK STREAK

Some organisms have changed so little in millions of years that they're known as "living fossils." The tuatara, a lizardlike reptile found in New Zealand, is part of this group. It has hardly changed at all in the 200 million years separating it from its earliest ancestors!

NATURAL SELECTION

A genetic change is called a mutation. A mutation can help, harm, or not affect an organism's ability to survive and reproduce. If the organism survives and reproduces, the mutation is passed on to its young. If the organism has fewer offspring than ones without the mutation, or dies before reproducing, the mutation won't be passed on. Over time, this process of natural selection leads to a wide variety of living things—from microscopic germs to blue whales to the basilisk lizard (left), whose specialized feet let it run on water!

PERSONALITY PLUS

Charles Darwin (1809–1882) was a scientist who studied the natural world. His most famous research was a study of finches, a bird found in different parts of the Galápagos Islands. Based on his observations, he tested the hypothesis that one species evolved into another through natural selection. Today he is honored as "the father of evolutionary biology," and the body of knowledge he founded is called the "theory of evolution."

CLASSIFICATION OF LIVING THINGS

All living things are grouped into categories based on what they look like and how they're related to other kinds of life.

The system of classifying plants and animals is called taxonomy, and it works like this: Each kind of plant or animal is given a scientific name. The name is written in Latin so that scientists around the world can all identify it. This classification guides our understanding of the plants and animals around us. It also shows us how living things are related to ancient species that died out long ago—from tiny algae to massive dinosaurs.

Taxonomic classifications are linked to Earth's history and to the time periods when each living thing first appeared.

Scientists estimate that Earth formed some 4.5 billion years ago. The time between then and now has been divided into four periods called eras. Each era is millions of years long.

During each era, Earth developed certain climates, landforms, and life-forms. Some life still exists now as it once was. Some has changed, or evolved, over time, and some is gone forever. By looking carefully at fossils (see page 193), scientists can determine what Earth and its life-forms were like at different times.

Check out the eras and their related life-forms here. Together they make up the classification of living things.

CHANGING EARTH, CHANGING LIFE

Scientists think that more than 99 percent of all the species that have ever lived are extinct today. Over the billions of years since Earth was born, its climate and features have gradually changed, creating different habitats and climates that could support different kinds of life.

KING OF THE KINGDOMS

The biggest of all kingdoms is the animal kingdom. It makes up 75 percent of all life on Earth. Next comes plants, with 18 percent, and finally fungi, protists, and monerans, which together make up a tiny 7 percent.

TAXONOMIC LEVELS

The system of taxonomy classifies every living thing. In this system, different species and kinds of life are classified using seven different levels. Match these groups to the art below, from top to bottom.

FAMILY
Ursidae
(Pandas are in the Ursidae family.)

1. KINGDOM: The highest level of classification. The structure of an organism's cells is the basis for which of the five kingdoms it belongs to: animals, plants, fungi, protists, or monerans.

2. PHYLUM: The animal kingdom has some 20 different phyla. Vertebrates, or animals with backbones, are in a phylum called chordate. This includes dogs, birds, fish, and humans. Arthropods, another phylum, includes animals like scorpions or crabs, with outer shells and jointed legs.

3. CLASS: After phylum comes the level called class. All mammals are in the mammal class, within the phylum Chordata, within the animal kingdom.

4. ORDER: Just under class is the order. Artiodactyla, for example, is the order of even-toed hoofed animals, such as deer, cattle, and giraffes. Many of these are herbivores, eating mainly plants. The order Carnivora includes meat-eating mammals, such as tigers and lions.

5. FAMILY: Within each order are families. Under the order of carnivores is the family called Ursidae, which includes brown bears, polar bears, sloth bears, and giant pandas.

6. GENUS: A subgroup within a family. The genus name is written in italics. An animal from a genus can breed only with another animal in its genus. So within the Ursidae family, two bears of the *Ursus* genus, which includes brown bears and polar bears, would breed. But a polar bear wouldn't breed with a giant panda, of the *Ailuropoda* genus.

7. SPECIES: Each genus is divided into species. The species name is also written in italics. Under the *Ursus* genus, for instance, the species include brown bears (*Ursus arctos*), black bears (*Ursus thibetanus*), and polar bears (*Ursus maritimus*).

KINGDOM
Animalia

PHYLUM
Chordata

CLASS
Mammalia

ORDER
Carnivora

FAMILY
Ursidae

SPECIES
Ursus maritimus
(polar bear)

GENUS
Ursus

SUPER ANIMALS

What's the biggest group in the animal kingdom? The mighty insect. There are more than a million species of insects, from tiny termites to Australia's burrowing cockroach—a stunning three inches (7.6 cm) long. What's the smallest group? Mammals—with just 5,416 species.

NAME THAT LION!

All species are named with at least two names: The first is the genus; the second is the species. Sometimes there is also a subspecies name. A subspecies is a member of a species that might be isolated on an island or in mountains and breeds only with members of its group. For example, a lion is named *Panthera leo*. A subspecies, the Barbary lion of North Africa, is *Panthera leo leo*. The genus name is capitalized, the species is not. The names are italicized. To fully classify a lion, you need to include all its taxonomic levels: kingdom: Animalia (animals); phylum: Chordata (which includes vertebrates); class: Mammalia (mammals); order: Carnivora (carnivores, or meat-eaters); family: Felidae (all cats); genus: *Panthera* (great cats); species: *leo* (lions); and possibly the subspecies.

GEEK STREAK

Dinosaurs, which means "terrible lizards," are part of a big group of reptiles called Archosauria, or "ruling reptiles." Dinosaurs are classified into two orders, depending on the shape of their pelvis, the bone between the hips. Lizard-hipped dinosaurs, such as *Allosaurus* and *Tyrannosaurus*, had pelvises like today's lizards, as well as clawed feet. Bird-hipped dinosaurs had pelvises like the birds that fly through the skies today, as well as hoofed toes. Two examples were *Stegosaurus* and *Triceratops*.

ERAS OF EARTH'S HISTORY

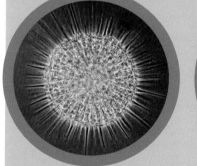

4.5 billion to 570 million years ago

570 million to 240 million years ago

240 million to 63 million years ago

63 million years ago to present

PRECAMBRIAN

Almost all of Earth's 4.5-billion-year history takes place during the Precambrian era. But it is so long ago and there are so few physical remains from it that scientists don't know much about it. They do know that life began then—tiny molecules developed into simple, single-celled life-forms floating in the ocean.

PALEOZOIC

As the Paleozoic era took hold, the number and kinds of species grew by leaps and bounds, from corals and jellyfish swimming in the warm seas to amphibians, which crawled out of the water onto land. The first land plants grew—including trees and mosses. Reptiles, the ancestors of dinosaurs, roamed the land.

MESOZOIC

During the Mesozoic era, dinosaurs ruled the Earth. The first mammals and birds appeared, and the first flowering plants grew. By the end of this era, the dinosaurs had become extinct. Snakes slithered, and marsupials—mammals with pouches, like kangaroos—came onto the scene.

CENOZOIC

Flowering plants flourished, and rodents and apelike primates roamed. Some five million years ago the first humanlike beings appeared. Gradually, supersize mammals such as woolly mammoths and saber-toothed cats became extinct, and today's life-forms took hold—like your dog, your mom's roses, and you!

PERSONALITY PLUS

Naturalist Carolus Linnaeus, born in Sweden in 1707, was the first to classify all life on Earth. His father, a Lutheran pastor, was also an avid gardener, and young Carolus quickly developed a love for plants and their names. When he went to the university to study medicine, he focused on collecting plants to learn all he could about their medicinal values. As a naturalist, he felt it was his duty to create a classification system for all living things that would reveal the order that God had created in the universe.

LIGHT, CHEMICALS, FOOD!

Plants, algae, and some microscopic organisms can make their own food from water and carbon dioxide, using sunlight as an energy source. This ability is called photosynthesis, which means "light put together."

Photosynthesis in a plant starts in the leaves. Leaves contain a green pigment called chlorophyll, which absorbs sunlight. The water needed for photosynthesis is soaked up by the plant's roots and sent to the leaves through a system of fine tubes. Meanwhile, carbon dioxide in the air enters the leaves through tiny holes in their undersides.

With all the ingredients in place, the energy in the sunlight captured by the chlorophyll fuels a chemical reaction. It causes water and carbon dioxide to combine and form a sugar called glucose. Oxygen and water are also produced as waste products. Most plants turn only about one percent of their absorbed light into stored energy. Some crops do better. Sugarcane turns about 8 percent of light into chemical energy, stored as sugar. That's why it's so sweet.

Algae and photosynthetic microscopic organisms don't have leaves, but they also use chlorophyll to capture the sun's energy.

Photosynthesis supports animal life, too. Animals either eat plants or other animals that ate plants. Animals also breathe oxygen produced by photosynthesis. Without photosynthesis, most life on Earth would disappear.

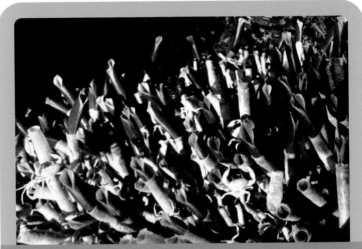

CHEMOSYNTHESIS

In 1977, scientists exploring deep parts of the ocean were astonished to discover animals living around vents in the seafloor that spouted hot water. This hot water was rich in minerals and chemicals containing sulfur. Bacteria around the vents used energy in these chemicals to turn water and carbon dioxide into glucose. They were the first organisms known to use chemosynthesis—the creation of food using chemical energy instead of sunlight. Giant tubeworms at seafloor vents don't have mouths or digestive systems. Instead, they store chemosynthesizing bacteria inside themselves. The bacteria "pay rent" by making food for the worms.

SEEING GREEN

Sunlight is made up of all colors of light. Chlorophyll absorbs mainly blue-violet and orange-red light. It doesn't absorb green light, however. Green light is reflected, which is why leaves look green. What about red or purple leaves, or brown seaweed? They contain chlorophyll, too. It's just hidden by other pigments, which soak up sunlight and then pass it along to the chlorophyll to use in photosynthesis.

WORD CHECK

CHLOROPLAST: Tiny parts in plants and algae that contains chlorophyll. "Chloro" means "green," and "plast" means "form."

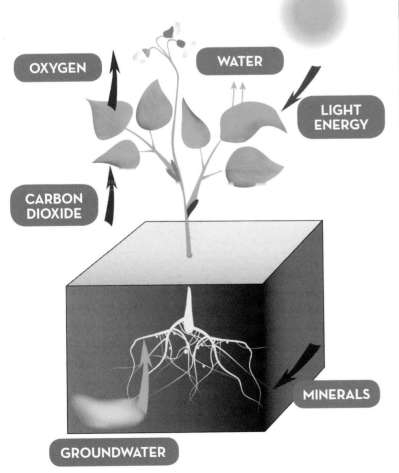

OXYGEN

WATER

LIGHT ENERGY

CARBON DIOXIDE

MINERALS

GROUNDWATER

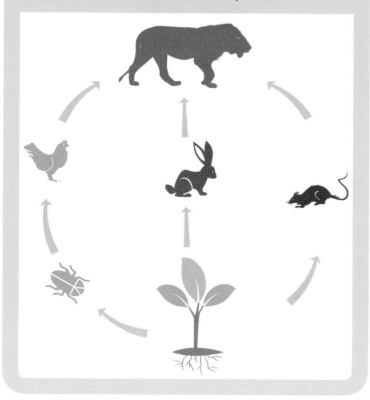

EATING GREEN

The emerald green sea slug eats seaweed and stores the chlorophyll in its body. The chlorophyll can make food for a few weeks and gives the slug its green color.

POWER SHARING

A variety of animals pair up with photosynthetic organisms. Coral polyps, for example, contain microscopic algae in the lining of their digestive system. The coral provides a safe home, plus waste products that are fertilizer for algae. The algae, in return, make food by photosynthesis, some of which is consumed by the coral. Coral also get their color from their algae friends. Sea anemones, jellyfish, and giant clams (above) also form partnerships with algae.

GEEK STREAK

A plant produces oxygen as a waste product during photosynthesis. But it also needs oxygen, just as you do, to break down food and get energy for life functions. So it stores some of the oxygen it produces during the day. At night, when it can't photosynthesize, it uses the oxygen absorbed by its leaves.

FOOD WEBS

Organisms that make their own food by photosynthesis or chemosynthesis are called producers. They produce food and use its energy to carry out life functions, such as growth and reproduction. This energy is passed along to consumers—the animals, fungi, and other organisms that eat them. The links between producers and consumers form a food web. Food webs exist wherever there are living things—on land, in water, and around hot-water vents on the deep seafloor.

TRY THIS!

WHAT YOU NEED: Two small planting pots with soil, two bean seeds, a shoebox, a window ledge

HOW LONG IT TAKES: About two weeks to sprout, longer to grow

Plant two bean seeds in separate pots. Put one on a window ledge that gets sunlight. Put the other under a box. The plant in the box will grow taller, but it will be pale and weak, while the plant that grows in the sunlight will be green and strong as its chlorophyll captures the sun's energy.

LOL!

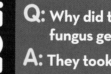

Q: Why did the algae and the fungus get married?

A: They took a lichen to each other.

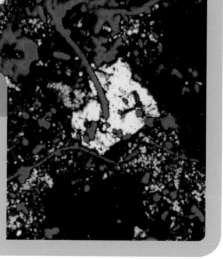

ROCK-EATING FOR ENERGY

Scientists have discovered bacteria living in rocks deep underground that use hydrogen, water, and carbon dioxide to get energy. They're called lithotrophs (the red growth at right), which means "rock-eaters."

197

NONFLOWERING PLANTS

The first plants grew on Earth more than 450 million years ago. These plants were nonflowering plants—plants that don't grow flowers to make seeds. Instead, many nonflowering plants reproduce by making spores.

A spore does not contain a supply of food, as the seeds of most flowering plants do. It's microscopic because it consists of just one cell, while a seed is made up of many cells. The tiny spores are contained in capsules instead of flowers. They're usually spread by wind. Some nonflowering plants, such as mosses, don't have roots or a system of water-carrying tubes inside them. Instead, they absorb water like kitchen sponges. Other nonflowering plants, such as ferns, have roots that soak up water from soil. The water then travels through tubes in the fern's leaves, just as it does in a flowering plant.

Many nonflowering plants grow in damp places, but others can survive in dry places. Mosses that grow in deserts, for example, go dormant during dry times, and look like they're dead. When rain finally falls, they quickly soak up water and spring back to "life."

FERNS

Ferns have roots and frilly leaves called fronds. They range from pea-size plants to treelike ferns that tower 65 feet (20 m) tall. The fern plant you see is actually the sporophyte. The spores are contained in dotlike capsules on the undersides of the fronds, called sporangia. Many ferns have tiny structures under their leaves that work like miniature catapults to fling their spores into the air. Then wind and water currents carry the dustlike spores away to grow in new places. A spore slowly develops into a tiny, heart-shaped plant, from which a new sporophyte grows. A new fern frond of most species starts out tightly curled up and slowly unrolls as it grows. The young fronds look like fiddleheads—and that's what they're called!

LIVERWORTS

Liverworts are closely related to mosses. Most liverworts look like leafy ribbons, but some are leafless plants that are flat and lacy. Species that look like chunks of liver inspired these plants' name. Like mosses, liverworts produce spores, which grow into larger green forms that produce little sporophytes. Liverworts were among the first plants to grow on land. Scientists have found fossil liverworts nearly 473 million years old.

MOSSES

Mosses tend to grow in thick clumps made up of many small shoots. They may look like mats or cushions and feel springy or velvety. Rootlike threads called rhizoids help them cling to ground, bark, rocks, and stone walls. A moss has a two-part life cycle: First, a spore grows into a leafy shoot. This plant then produces cells called eggs and sperm. When these cells meet, they combine to form a small sporophyte, which lives on its parent plant and forms new spores. A single capsule on a sphagnum moss contains from 20,000 to 250,000 spores. That's a lot—but only a very few will survive to grow into green shoots.

SEEDS BUT NO FLOWERS

Pines, hemlocks, spruces, firs, cedars—these familiar trees are nonflowering plants called gymnosperms. Unlike other nonflowering plants, gymnosperms make seeds. The seeds are produced in cones. Many gymnosperms have tough woody or papery cones. Some, such as junipers, have plump, fleshy cones. Gymnosperms were among the first plants to make seeds and have been around for about 300 million years. The world's tallest and biggest trees—coast redwoods and sequoias—are gymnosperms. The ginkgo is a gymnosperm that is often called a living fossil because there's very little difference between modern ginkgos and ginkgos that lived 200 million years ago.

WORD CHECK

SPOROPHYTE: The spore-producing stage in a nonflowering plant's life. "Sporo" means "spore," and "phyte" means "plant."

TRY THIS!

WHAT YOU NEED: A pad, a pencil, a field guide to help you identify cool nonflowering plants

HOW LONG IT TAKES: Up to an hour

Be a plant scientist, or botanist, in your neighborhood and look for nonflowering plants. Can you find moss growing on a tree or wall? A fern growing in shade? Horsetails growing in a ditch? Look for gymnosperms, too. Keep track of your finds in a notebook. A field guide will help you identify them.

HORSETAILS

Horsetails have hollow stems marked by joints. Spindly green hairlike branches stick out from the joints. The plants also produce stalks without branches that have conelike ends, which produce spores. Each microscopic spore is wrapped in four stringy "legs" called elaters. When the air is dry, the elaters unfold. They curl up when the air is damp. This movement helps a spore wriggle and sometimes jump to a new location! Horsetails contain silica, the same mineral used to make glass. The plants are nicknamed "scouring rush" because people have used them to scrub, or scour, pots.

GEEK STREAK

Mushrooms and other fungi were once considered to be part of the plant kingdom. Today they have their own kingdom. Like nonflowering plants, fungi make spores, not seeds. Unlike plants, they don't have chlorophyll and can't carry out photosynthesis. They lack roots. Instead, they have threadlike strands called hyphae that absorb nutrients.

PERSONALITY PLUS

German naturalist Engelbert Kaempfer (1651–1716) spent two years traveling in Japan studying the nation's history and its plants. He was also the first European to write scientifically about ginkgo trees. A ginkgo that grew from one of the seeds Kaempfer brought back home still stands in the Botanic Garden in Utrecht, Holland.

FLOWERING PLANTS

Flowers are structures grown by plants to make seeds. There are about 350,000 species of flowering plants alive today out of a total of about 400,000 known species of plants.

Look around in springtime, and you'll see flowers bursting into bloom. Flowers come in many sizes, shapes, and colors, but most flowers share a few basic structures. A typical flower has a female structure called a pistil. The base of the pistil is called the ovary and is where seeds develop. Sticking up from the ovary is a stalk that's capped with a part called the stigma.

Male flower parts called stamens surround the pistil. Each stamen has a sac called an anther at the top that makes dustlike particles called pollen. Pollen must land on a stigma and tunnel down into the ovary to fertilize the tiny "eggs," or ovules, inside it. The ovules then develop into seeds.

Flowers vary widely in how their reproductive parts are arranged. Some flowers, for example, have more than one pistil. Other plants grow separate male and female flowers.

POLLINATION

Pollen travels from flower to flower in many ways. Bees, bats, birds, and other animals pollinate between 80 and 90 percent of the world's flowering plants. Many plants attract these pollinators with scent and color, and provide a sweet liquid called nectar for them to drink. For instance, besides sipping nectar, a bee also stuffs protein-rich pollen into pockets on its legs to carry back to its nest. Some pollen sticks to its fuzzy body. When the bee visits another flower of the same kind, this pollen brushes off onto that flower's stigma. Other flowers' pollen is carried by wind or water. Some flowers can pollinate themselves.

SEEDS

After seeds form, a flower's ovary becomes a fruit. Some fruits form the large, tasty fruits we eat, such as apples and oranges. The seed itself is packed with nutrients. When a seed sprouts, the nutrients support the tiny seedling until it grows enough to start taking up water and producing its own food by photosynthesis.

BLOOMING SCHEDULES

"Annual" plants flower once and then die. These include pansies and snapdragons. "Perennials" live many years and keep growing new flowers, such as irises, daffodils, and tulips. "Biennials" produce flowers and seeds just once in two years. They include forget-me-nots and hollyhocks.

PERSONALITY PLUS

As a boy, George Washington Carver (1864–1943) tended a small but healthy garden. He was nicknamed "the plant doctor." Carver grew up to become a scientist. In his work, he helped improve farming methods to take care of the soil and boost crop growth. He also discovered more than 300 uses for peanuts!

SPREADING SEEDS

Some flowering plants depend on animals to spread their seeds. They may grow fruits for animals to eat. Then the animals spread the seeds in their droppings. Other seeds are sticky or bristly and cling to an animal's fur or feathers. Some seeds have wings, parachutes, or other structures that let the wind carry them to new locations.

WORD CHECK

PHOTOTROPISM: Movement toward or away from a source of light. "Photo" means "light," and "tropos" means "turn."

SEED LEAF

A seed contains either one or two small seed leaves, known as cotyledons. The number of cotyledons divides flowers into two main groups: monocotyledons, with one cotyledon, and dicotyledons, with two cotyledons. Grass and corn are both "monocots." Pansies and apple trees are examples of "dicots." Monocot plants have leaves with veins that run parallel to each other, like train-track rails. Dicots usually have netlike veins.

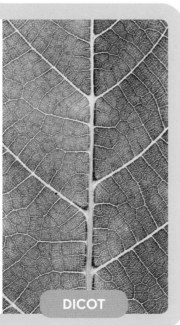

MONOCOT

DICOT

TRY THIS!

WHAT YOU NEED: A flower with a large head, such as a tulip; a knife (ask an adult to help cut it open)

HOW LONG IT TAKES: Up to an hour

Find a flower that you have permission to cut open. See if you can identify its pistil, ovary, stigma, stamen, and the anthers. Figure out if your flower comes from a plant that's a monocot or a dicot. Was it pollinated by an animal, wind, or water?

SUPER FLOWERS

WORLD'S SMALLEST FLOWER

The smallest flowers bloom on tiny *Wolffia* water plants, which are so little you could fit 5,000 of them in a thimble.

WORLD'S BIGGEST FLOWER

It belongs to the *Rafflesia* plant in Indonesia. It measures about three feet (1 m) across. Its strong, rotten-meat smell attracts pollinating flies.

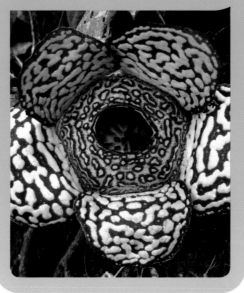

WORLD'S MOST FLOWER-FILLED

A sunflower is made up of a thousand or more tiny flowers. The smaller ones in the round center of the sunflower each form one seed—a favorite for snacks.

PLANTASTICS!

About 400,000 species of plants grow on Earth. They've all evolved to survive and thrive in different living spaces, or habitats. Some plants have evolved amazing adaptations that help them pollinate, spread their seeds or spores, and get the nutrients they need. Plants even fight back against the animals that would dare to nibble on them! They also make a variety of chemicals that can be used as medicines to fight diseases. Here are a few of the world's many remarkable plants.

Elephant Foot Yam

It's pretty to look at, but its powerful scent can send you running! Also called a stink lily, the elephant foot yam has a rotten-meat smell about as strong as the *Rafflesia* plant's (see page 201). Look for the elephant foot's maroon-colored flower and the knob jutting from the center. Its tube-shaped vegetable, grown underground like a potato, looks and tastes like a yam, but it's not related to other yams. It's one of the most popular foods in Southeast Asia and has been used for centuries by healers in India as a natural remedy for bronchitis, stomach aches, and more.

Venus Flytrap

An unsuspecting fly crawls onto the lip of a Venus flytrap. It brushes against sensitive bristles on the leaf. Snap! The leaf slams shut in less than one-tenth of a second, capturing the fly. Digestive fluids ooze out of the leaf. Within one or two weeks, the fly is digested, and the leaf will be ready to catch another meal. Venus flytraps grow wild in just a few marshy places in the southeastern United States. The soil they grow in is poor in nitrogen, so protein-rich snacks such as insects help flytraps get the nutrients they need.

Dodder

A dodder shoot sprouts from a seed, like many plants. But then the dodder does a very unplantlike thing: it swings in slow circles, as if sniffing the air—and in a way, it is! The dodder can sense chemicals given off by other plants. It selects a victim and twines around it, sinking rootlike structures into its stem. Then the dodder snaps its connection with the soil. After that, the dodder lives as a parasite on the other plant, sucking water and nutrients from it. Many dodder can cover a field in this way. No wonder farmers call the flower "witches' shoelaces," "strangleweed," and "devil's-guts"!

Mother-of-Millions

The mother-of-millions plant produces offspring by sprouting tiny "plantlets" on the edges of its leaflike stems. A single plant may produce as many as 600 plantlets this way! The plantlets fall off easily and take root. This species is native to the island nation of Madagascar. It became a popular garden plant, however, and was grown in other countries, where it escaped into the wild. The plant is poisonous and is a dangerous, invasive species in places such as Australia because cattle and sheep that eat it become very ill and often die.

Pitcher Plants, or *Nepenthes*

Throughout southeast Asia and Australia, insects tumble into pitchers grown by *Nepenthes* plants. The pitchers contain a pool of water. Insects, lured by the scent of nectar, check out the pitcher by crawling into it. There, they slide down the slippery sides into the pool. That's the signal for the plant to start making digestive juices to consume its prey. The insects may try to escape, but the fluids are sticky, and the rim of the cup is lined with toothy spikes! *Nepenthes* are often called pitcher plants or monkey cups. The biggest pitchers have been known to capture frogs and even mice.

Fishhook Barrel Cactus

The fishhook barrel cactus grows in deserts of the southwestern United States and Mexico. It bristles with sharp spines that are about three inches (7.6 cm) long. Each clump of spines contains an extra-large spine tipped with a sharp hook—the "fishhook" in its name. Its scientific name, *Ferocactus*, means "fierce cactus"! The big spines are fierce—they protect the plant from being chewed by rabbits and other animals. Smaller spines help shade the plant. Mule deer eat the cactus's fruit, however, and birds gobble up its seeds. In summer, the cacti grow bright yellow, red, or orange flowers.

Skunk Cabbage

One of the first plants to bloom in spring is the stinky, blotchy skunk cabbage. Skunk cabbage grows near streams, in marshes and wet woodlands, and in other damp places. It's able to make heat so it can emerge from frozen soil. The plant gets so warm it can even melt the snow around it! At first, skunk cabbage is just a purplish, hoodlike capsule, which slowly opens to reveal a spike covered with yellow flowers. It gives off a bad smell, which attracts insects that will pollinate it. Warm air rising from the flowers helps the smell drift up and out of their protective hood.

Walking Fern

The walking fern is named for its ability to spread by creeping across the ground. Its long, skinny leaves are its "legs." Wherever the leaf tips touch the ground, they take root. New leaves grow from the rooted tip. The original plant becomes surrounded by its offspring over time. This species also reproduces by making spores. Walking ferns often grow on moss-covered rocks and cliffs. The American walking fern grows in eastern Canada and in the eastern, southeastern, and central United States.

Madagascar Periwinkle

The cheerful flowers of Madagascar periwinkle brighten gardens worldwide. This plant also brightens lives because it makes chemicals that help fight cancer. People have used plants as medicines for thousands of years. Today, periwinkle is still used to make cancer-fighting drugs. Other medicines contain chemicals that are made in laboratories but are based on the structure and properties of chemicals discovered in plants.

TREES

What do oaks, pines, maples, and redwoods have in common? They are all trees—plants that have woody stems and live for many years.

Shrubs and many vines have woody stems and are perennial, too. The name "tree," however, is usually used for plants 15 feet (4.6 m) or more in height. A tree usually has a single main stem, or trunk, that rises well above the ground before it starts branching. A shrub usually branches out close to the ground and is shorter than a tree, and vines climb or cling to other plants.

Trees provide food and shelter for many species of animals. Trees provide people with lumber, paper, medicines, and many kinds of fruits and nuts. They also produce oxygen as they photosynthesize. More than 20 percent of the world's oxygen is given off by trees in the Amazon rain forest of South America alone.

Trees also provide shade and beauty. They help hold soil in place so rain doesn't wash it away. Their leaves even soak up pollution in the air. They take in carbon dioxide produced by human activities, such as driving cars and flying jets, and transform it into oxygen and sugar.

PHLOEM   **XYLEM**   **CAMBIUM**

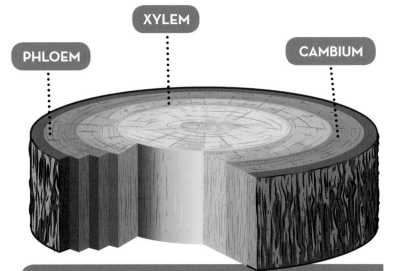

INSIDE A TREE

A tree's outer bark is made of dead cells. Underneath it, new bark grows in a living layer of cells called cambium. Cambium produces phloem and xylem. Phloem, which forms between the cambium and bark, carries nutrients, such as sugar, from the leaves to the rest of the tree. Xylem, which forms inside the cambium, carries water from the roots to the rest of the tree. Trees grow new xylem and phloem as they age. Old xylem forms tree rings that are visible when a tree is cut down.

BROADLEAF TREES

A broadleaf tree has wide, flat leaves. These leaves may be flexible and floppy, or firm and waxy. Like all leaves, their job is to make food, and being wide and flat is useful for soaking up as much sunlight as possible. Broadleaves that drop their leaves in autumn are called deciduous trees. They may turn brilliant colors as the chlorophyll in the leaves disappears and other pigments are revealed.

CONIFERS

Conifers are cone-bearing trees with needlelike or scaly leaves. Nearly all conifers are evergreen—trees that shed and grow new leaves year-round instead of losing them all in autumn. Their waxy, stiff leaves don't easily lose water in air, and they don't blow off in a winter wind like a broadleaf tree's would. That's why conifers thrive in cold northern lands and high on mountainsides, where they can photosynthesize all year round, even in weak winter sunlight.

PERSONALITY PLUS

Gordon Jacoby (1934-2014) was one of the first scientists to study rings in tree trunks to learn about the history of Earth's climate. His study of tree rings in boreal forests has revealed about 1,300 years of climate history. His worldwide study of tree rings also provided information on the paths of rivers and on earthquakes that occurred long ago.

BOREAL FORESTS

A coniferous forest is one that contains mainly conifers. About 17 percent of Earth's land area is covered by a coniferous forest that sweeps across northern North America, Europe, and Asia. Winter is long, dark, snowy, and very cold in much of this region, but conifers are well adapted to survive there. This vast forest is called the boreal forest, or taiga. *Taiga* is a Russian word that means "land of little sticks."

GEEK STREAK

Bananas don't grow on banana trees! A banana "tree" is actually a huge perennial herb. It grows from a short underground stem. Its false trunk is made of leaf stalks wrapped into a tight bundle. After the banana plant produces fruit, it dies. Later, a new plant sprouts from the stem.

TROPICAL RAIN FORESTS

Tropical rain forests grow in hot, wet regions near Earth's Equator. They're filled with evergreen broadleaf trees packed closely together. These rain forests cover only about 7 percent of Earth's land area but are home to about half of its plant and animal species. A single tall rain forest tree loses about 200 gallons (757 L) of water from its leaves into the air every year through evaporation, adding to the blanket of clouds that rain on the tropics and keep it warm and moist.

A banyan tree grows roots that dangle from its branches. The roots eventually take hold in the ground and turn into trunks. One huge banyan in India has more than 3,000 roots and trunks!

SUPER TREES

The world's tallest living tree is Hyperion, a coast redwood in Redwood National Park in California, U.S.A. The tree is 379.1 feet (115.5 m) tall.

Bristlecone pines can live for thousands of years. They're found in parts of the southwestern United States. One bristlecone still growing in California is 4,765 years old.

MICROBES

These tiny specks of life are found nearly everywhere on Earth. They exist in soil, air, water, and the outsides and insides of plants and animals.

Microbes are living things that are so small you need a microscope to see them. The world of microbes includes one-celled organisms such as bacteria and various kinds of fungi and algae. Microbes have been found in ancient rocks under the ocean and deep inside Earth. Scientists believe they've found bacteria trapped in salt crystals 250 million years old, some 1,850 feet (564 m) below Earth's surface in Carlsbad, New Mexico, U.S.A. Microbes are small but mighty. They break down the remains of dead plants and animals from insects to elephants. Some microbes cause disease—they're the ones we call germs. For instance, the itchy infection called athlete's foot is caused by a single-celled fungus. These microbes live in the nails, hair, and top layer of skin. Other microbes are used to make antibiotics, such as penicillin, to fight disease. Inside your body, helpful microbes digest food and produce some of the vitamins you need. There are about 100 million microbes living in and on you. They outnumber your own cells ten to one!

EUKARYOTES

A eukaryote is an organism made up of a cell or cells containing a "command center" called the nucleus. The nucleus controls the cell's growth and other functions. It is wrapped in a membrane, as are the cell's other tiny organs, called organelles. You are a eukaryote, as are plants and animals, because your cells contain nuclei. Many types of algae and fungi are single-celled eukaryotes.

PROKARYOTES

A prokaryote is a single-celled organism that has a central nucleoid, not a true nucleus like a eukaryote. Likewise, most of the parts inside it lack membranes. Its outer covering consists of a tough cell wall and a thinner cell membrane that lets substances move in and out of its liquid inside. Bacteria and archaea are in this group. Archaea are like bacteria, but their cell walls have different chemical properties. Bacteria and archaea create the beautiful colors of Grand Prismatic Spring in Yellowstone National Park, U.S.A. They thrive in the spring's super-hot waters.

NUCLEOID

CELL WALL

CELL MEMBRANE

LOL!

Q: Why did the computer sneeze?

A: It had a virus.

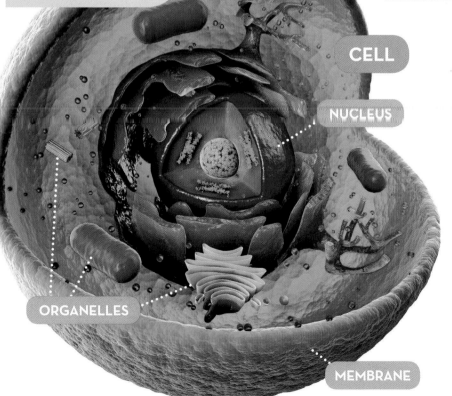

CELL

NUCLEUS

ORGANELLES

MEMBRANE

MICROBES: MENACING OR MEANINGFUL?

Viruses are microbes that must occupy other living cells in order to survive and reproduce. They cause colds, flu, and many other diseases. Other microbes produce delicious and helpful foods. Blue cheese, for example, gets its taste from a kind of fungus called mold. Yogurt, pepperoni, and sour cream are flavored by bacteria.

GEEK STREAK

Microbes are so small, they're measured in "micrometers" (also called "microns"). A micrometer is .001 millimeter, or 1/25,400 of an inch. An average microbe is less than 10 micrometers in size, but many microbes are smaller than one micrometer. Viruses are microbes so small that a thousand of them could fit in one bacterium.

WORD CHECK

ANTIBIOTIC: A medicine that kills bacteria or stops them from reproducing. "Anti" means "against," and "bios" means "life."

PROTOZOA

The word "protozoa" comes from Greek words that mean "first animals." The first scientists to see them through microscopes thought they were tiny animals. Many of them swim by lashing whip-like "tails" or waving hairlike strands called cilia. This group also includes amoebas, which move like drops of syrup running down the side of a pitcher. Protozoa are thought to be the oldest living things that consume food and turn it into energy.

FOOD FACTORIES

Some bacteria and archaea make their own food, as algae do, instead of consuming it. If they contain chlorophyll, they use sunlight and water to produce food, like plants do (see pages 196–197). Other microbes use energy from chemicals in their habitats instead of light. Microbes on the deep, dark seafloor, for example, use chemicals spewed out by hot-water vents. These microbes, in turn, are eaten by animals living in this harsh habitat.

PROTISTA

Protozoa and algae are placed in a group called Protista. Algae are plantlike organisms that make their own food. They range in size from single-celled microbes to long strands of seaweed that drift in the waves. Algae microbes form the green scum you find in and on ponds. Like plants, algae add oxygen to the atmosphere. In the ocean, algae form an important part of the food web. Diatoms are algae encased in delicate shells. The shells drift to the seafloor when diatoms die and are mined for many uses, such as adding scrubbing power to toothpaste!

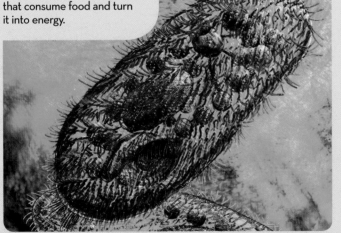

TRY THIS!

WHAT YOU NEED: A packet of baker's yeast, a cup of warm water, a pinch of sugar

HOW LONG IT TAKES: 5 to 10 minutes

Baker's yeast is a single-celled fungus added to bread dough. It makes bread rise because it gives off carbon dioxide as a waste product. Watch this microbe in action by adding baker's yeast and a pinch of sugar to a cup of warm water. As the yeast digests the sugar, it creates foam that bubbles on the surface.

PERSONALITY PLUS

Antonie van Leeuwenhoek (1632–1723) was a Dutch cloth merchant who made high-power magnifying glasses in his spare time. Using these handmade lenses, he became the first person to see bacteria and protozoa, which he called "very little animalcules." He reported his findings to scientists. Today, Leeuwenhoek is remembered as "the father of microbiology."

INVERTEBRATES
ON LAND

What do insects, spiders, and worms have in common? None of them has a backbone—or any bones at all! They're invertebrates—animals that lack a backbone made up of smaller bones called vertebrae. About 97 percent of animals fall into this group.

ABDOMEN **THORAX** **HEAD**

Some invertebrate animals, such as insects, have external skeletons. This skeleton, called an exoskeleton, contains fibers of a tough material called chitin. Hinges and flexible sections in the armor let the animal move its legs, antennae, and other body parts. Many invertebrates, however, lack exoskeletons. Some of these soft-bodied animals, such as snails, are protected by shells.

Insects make up the largest group of invertebrates by far. To date, scientists have described more than a million species. There are more species of insects than all other animal species combined. Most insects live on land or in freshwater. The same is true of arachnids, a group that includes spiders, mites, ticks, and scorpions.

INSECTS

All insects have an exoskeleton, six legs, and a body made up of three sections: a head, a middle part called the thorax, and an abdomen. Many insects have two pairs of wings. Others, such as flies, have one pair of wings, with the second pair forming little stalks that help it balance in flight. Insects molt, or shed, then regrow their exoskeletons as they grow because their tough armor can't stretch to fit.

SPIDERS

Spiders are arachnids—invertebrates that have eight legs and a two-part body. One of the two parts is the abdomen. The other half is a combined head and thorax, called a cephalothorax. The legs are attached to the cephalothorax. Spiders produce silk in abdominal glands. The silk oozes out of organs called spinnerets, which move to manipulate the silken threads. Many species use silk to make webs for catching prey. A spider may make a new web every day to replace a tattered one. It eats the old silk, which helps the spider recycle both nutrients and energy.

EARTHWORMS

Earthworms belong to a group of invertebrates called annelids, or segmented worms. Rings around the earthworm's body reveal the segments. All earthworms live on land, where they burrow in soil and eat and digest bits of plant material in it. Earthworms help nourish soil as well as loosen it up so water and air can enter. Most earthworms are small, but the giant Gippsland earthworm of Australia measures up to three feet (1 m) long. Earthworms churn up and turn over soil and leaf litter as they feed and burrow. An acre (0.4 ha) of farmland may contain 53,000 worms or more.

CENTIPEDES

Like insects, spiders, and scorpions, centipedes are arthropods—animals with a jointed exoskeleton. Centipedes have bodies made up of many segments, most of which have a pair of legs. Centipedes usually have between 30 and 50 legs, but some species have up to 350 legs! Centipedes eat insects, spiders, mice, and other small animals. Millipedes also have long, segmented bodies, but they eat plant material and have two pairs of legs per segment. The biggest centipede is the Amazonian giant centipede. It can be up to 11 inches (28 cm) long. Some cave-dwelling giant centipedes catch and eat bats.

BEETLES

This ladybug is one of about 400,000 known species of beetle. A beetle's front wings are strong covers that shield the hind wings when at rest.

LOL!

Q: What is on the ground and also a hundred feet in the air?

A: A centipede on its back!

SNAILS

A snail is a soft-bodied creature with a shell on its back. The snail can coil up and disappear inside. This invertebrate is a garden pest. Its rough tongue, called a radula, has a row of tiny teeth that scrapes the linings off leaves and flowers, destroying them. Some kinds of snails live on land, others in water. All snails are related to soft-bodied, shelled sea creatures called mollusks, which include clams and oysters.

GEEK STREAK

Nobody knows exactly how many individual insects inhabit Earth. Based on population counts in various studies, however, it's estimated that the world's insect population at any one time may be as much as 10 quintillion. That's a 10 followed by 18 zeros—about 143 million insects per person!

SCORPIONS

Like spiders, scorpions are arachnids. A scorpion's long abdomen ends in a venomous stinger called a telson. The venom is produced in a bulb-like part of the telson. The scorpion uses its venom to kill prey and protect itself from predators. Scorpions range in size from tiny species no bigger than jelly beans to African scorpions that measure up to eight inches (20 cm) long. Scorpions are burrowing animals that prey on insects and other small animals. Scorpions, in turn, are eaten by other animals, like mice.

PERSONALITY PLUS

Biologist Edward O. Wilson (1929–) has studied ants for decades. He discovered the first fire-ant nest in the United States as a high-school student. In the 1960s, he worked with other scientists to show that ants communicate using chemical signals. He describes ants and other invertebrates as "the little things that run the world."

OCEAN INVERTEBRATES

About 98 percent of all animal life in the ocean consists of invertebrates. They live everywhere from the seafloor to the surface of rocks on shore at the outermost edge of high tide.

The ocean is filled with invertebrates: giant clams with bathtub-size shells, sponges that look like pillows, and jellyfish that drift through the water like ghostly balloons with stinging tentacles for catching prey.

Invertebrates even build some of the ocean's habitats. Coral reefs, for example, are built by small animals called stony corals. A single stony coral is a polyp—a small, baglike animal with a mouth fringed with tentacles. Its other end is attached to a solid object, such as a rock. The polyp uses minerals it extracts from seawater to make a limestone cup around its body. Over time, old polyps die, leaving their stony skeletons in place. New polyps grow and add to the coral reef's size. Sponges, sea fans, sea snails, and many other invertebrates live on the reef.

WORD CHECK

CEPHALOPOD: A mollusk that has an obvious head and many arms. "Cephalo" means "head," and "pod" means "foot."

TOOLS OF THE TRADE

Bright lights on science equipment can scare off deep-sea invertebrates, like squid and octopuses, as well as other animals that live in darkness. So scientist Dr. Edith Widder (see opposite) invented a camera called "Eye in the Sea." It uses dim red light, which is invisible to these creatures. Dr. Widder also uses patterns of blue light to attract certain species into camera range.

PRETTY POLYPS

Sea anemones look like flowers, but they're actually polyps, like corals. You'll find them in coral reefs. They shoot out stinging tentacles to snare prey such as small fish and crustaceans. Believe it or not, jellyfish are related to anemones and corals (like this one). A jellyfish starts life as a polyp, but swims freely as an adult.

BIVALVES

Clams, oysters, scallops, and mussels are called bivalves. They have a two-part shell connected by a flexible hinge, and they filter food from seawater. Bivalves belong to a group called mollusks (see opposite).

SPONGES

Sponges were once thought to be plants, and it's easy to see why. These invertebrates don't have any nervous system or organs and spend their adult lives attached to a hard surface. Different species look like shrubs, antlers, cushions, tubes, fans, flowers, vases, and baskets. Most sponges feed by filtering bacteria and other small particles from seawater, but scientists have recently discovered a few species that have hooks for snaring tiny animals.

CEPHALOPODS: OCTOPUSES AND SQUID

Cephalopods are a kind of mollusk with big heads and long arms called tentacles. They also have a supply of ink that they squirt when danger is near. An octopus (below) has eight arms and a sharp beak. Octopuses range in size from species 0.6 inch (1.5 cm) wide to animals such as the giant Pacific octopus, which is up to 16 feet (5 m) across. Octopuses are famous for their ability to change the color, pattern, and texture of their skin to camouflage themselves. An octopus sucks up water and expels it quickly to zoom forward. A squid has 10 arms that are equipped with suckers. Two of them are extra-long tentacles with paddle-shaped ends. Like octopuses, squid can zip through the water using jet propulsion. One of the biggest species, the giant squid, measures about 40 feet (12 m) in length and has eyes as big as basketballs.

GEEK STREAK

The Great Barrier Reef is a series of coral reefs and islands that runs for about 1,250 miles (2,000 km) along the northeastern coast of Australia. It's so big, it can be seen from outer space. The reef system is home to more than 400 coral species as well as thousands of other kinds of animals.

MOLLUSKS

Mollusks are animals with soft bodies that aren't divided into sections like a crustacean or insect's body. Many mollusks, such as snails and clams, have strong, protective shells. Check them out:

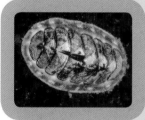

Chitons are flat, oval mollusks. Its shell is a series of eight overlapping sections called shell plates. It clings to rocks with its large, flat foot.

Sea cucumbers live on the seafloor where they feed on tiny animals and algae. A sea cucumber gathers its food with tentacles that surround its mouth.

Snails have a tongue-like radula lined with toothy spikes for dragging food into their mouths.

A **sea star** is an invertebrate with five or more arms. It uses the arms to open a clamshell just enough to slip its stomach inside and digest the clam!

CRUSTACEANS

On land, insects form the main group of arthropods. In the ocean, crustaceans are the ruling arthropods. Crustaceans have exoskeletons that contain tough fibers of chitin (see page 208). Unlike insects, crustaceans have two sets of antennae, which are located by their mouths. Lobsters, crabs, shrimps, and barnacles are well-known crustaceans. Like insects, crustaceans molt their exoskeletons as they grow. One of the largest crustaceans is the Japanese spider crab, which can have a leg span up to 13 feet (4 m) across!

PERSONALITY PLUS

Scientist Edith Widder (1951–) is a deep-sea explorer who specializes in studying bioluminescence—light that is produced by living things. In 2012, she became the first person to film a live giant squid in its natural, deep-sea habitat. Today she leads an association dedicated to ocean research and conservation.

FISH

Fish make up about half of the world's vertebrates, which are animals that have a backbone.

What do a shark, an electric eel, and a tuna have in common? They are all fish—animals with skeletons inside their bodies that are adapted to living underwater. Their ancestors, which lived more than 530 million years ago, were the world's first vertebrates.

Fish have fins for swimming, and most fish have skin covered with scales. Most also breathe through slits called gills, on the sides of their heads. Nearly all fish are also cold-blooded, which means their blood's temperature is set by the temperature of the water around them.

Fish come in an amazing variety of shapes, sizes, and colors. Eels are long and skinny, like snakes. Rays look like flying carpets. A sole looks like an old, flat slipper. Many fish, however, have a shape that's pointed in front and flat on the sides. This shape is perfect for swimming quickly and easily through water.

Fish are divided into three main groups: Cartilaginous fish have a skeleton made of cartilage instead of bone; bony fish have a skeleton made of bone; and lobe-finned fish are a group of bony fish whose fins contain muscle and bone, so the fins are stronger and more flexible than other fish fins.

PECTORAL FIN   DORSAL FIN

ANAL FIN

CAUDAL FIN

BONY FISH

Bony fish form the biggest group. They have hard skeletons made of bone, and most have scales on their skin. They have pairs of flexible fins that help them change direction quickly and easily as they swim. Most bony fish also have a gas-filled organ called a swim bladder. A fish can control how much gas is in its swim bladder in order to stay in one place in the water or to rise or sink.

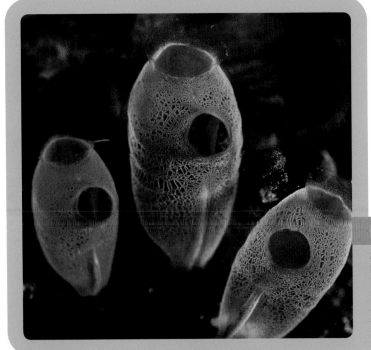

TOOLS OF THE TRADE

Ever listen to fish? Scientists do! More than 800 species of fish are known to make sounds. These sounds can be captured by a Marine Autonomous Recording Unit. The device sits near the seafloor, held in place by an anchor, recording sounds for several months at a time. Studying fish noises helps scientists learn what species are in a certain area.

BACK BASICS

Scientists once divided animals into two groups: vertebrates, which have backbones, and invertebrates, which don't. Today, fish and other vertebrates belong to the phylum Chordata and are known as chordates. At some point in their lives, chordates' bodies have a flexible rod, called a notochord. It forms early, when the animal is just a tiny clump of growing cells. It becomes part of the backbones in many animals. But some chordates, such as sea squirts, lose their notochords as they grow.

PERSONALITY PLUS

Dr. Sylvia A. Earle (1935–) is an oceanographer and explorer who has spent more than 50 years studying the ocean and its life. She has led more than 100 expeditions and spent more than 7,000 hours underwater. In 2012, she started a foundation called Mission Blue with the goal of protecting ocean areas from overfishing, pollution, and other threats.

CARTILAGINOUS FISH

Sharks, rays, and fish called chimaeras form a group called cartilaginous fish. They don't have bony skeletons. Instead, their skeletons are made of strong, rubbery cartilage—the same material that forms your ears. They have tough skin. A shark's skin is rough because it's covered with toothlike points called denticles. Cartilaginous fish don't have swim bladders. Sharks have a large, oily liver, which helps them float because oil is less dense than water.

BREATHING UNDERWATER

A fish needs oxygen, just as you do. Water, which contains oxygen, flows into a fish's mouth and through its gills. The gills contain thin tissues filled with blood vessels. These tissues absorb oxygen, which enters the fish's bloodstream. Some fish species, however, can get oxygen directly from air. Lungfish, for example, have swim bladders that work as lungs. Other species absorb oxygen through areas of skin on their bodies, mouths, and throats.

GEEK STREAK

Scientists have named about 30,000 species of fish. Every year, about 150 newly found species of ocean fish are added to the list. Many new species were discovered during the Census of Marine Life, which was a study that ran from 2000 to 2010. It involved about 2,700 scientists from more than 80 nations who researched ocean life and shared information.

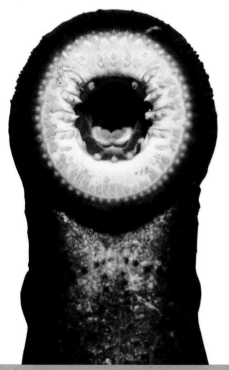

AMAZING FISH

Anglerfish live deep in the ocean in darkness. The female has a glowing "fishing rod" sticking out from her head to lure prey within reach of her giant mouth.

A clownfish lives among the poison-filled tentacles of an anemone on a coral reef. A gooey layer on the clownfish's skin protects it from the anemone's deadly sting.

Seahorses are unusual fish, and not just because of their shape. It's the males that give birth! They hold the female's eggs in their belly pouches until they hatch.

JAWLESS FISH

Jawless fish are fish that don't have biting jaws. This group includes lampreys and hagfish. A lamprey (above) clamps on to its prey with a suction-cup mouth and bores a hole in it with rasping teeth. Hagfish have slitlike mouths and toothy tongues. Jawless fish are slimy and don't have scales. Their skeletons are made of cartilage. Hagfish, however, don't have vertebrae, so many scientists think they don't belong in the vertebrate group.

REPTILES

Reptiles are vertebrate animals that can live on land and have skin that's covered in scales.

A turtle looks very different from a snake or a crocodile, but all three are reptiles. Scientists have named about 10,000 different reptile species. These reptiles range in size from lizards that can curl up on a penny to giants like the Komodo dragon, which can grow to be 10 feet (3 m) long!

Like fish, reptiles are cold-blooded. But their blood isn't always cold, so it's more accurate to call them ectotherms—animals that use their surroundings to control body temperature. Reptiles lie in sunlight to warm up, and go into burrows, water, or the shade to cool off. They can live in habitats ranging from wet jungles to hot, bone-dry deserts.

Many reptiles reproduce by laying eggs. These eggs have tough shells that protect them from drying out, so reptiles can lay eggs on land. Some reptiles give birth to living young.

SNAKES

Snakes are lizardlike, but they don't have legs. Instead, they use their muscular bodies to push against surfaces as they creep, climb, and burrow. Snakes flick their tongues to pick up any scents their nostrils might miss, and some species can also detect heat given off by prey. A snake can swallow animals larger than its head thanks to jaws that spread extra wide. Some snakes make deadly venom, which is injected into prey by biting. Spitting cobras spit venom from holes in their fangs—long pointed teeth—to defend themselves against predators. The venom stings the predator's eyes and can cause blindness.

GEEK STREAK

The world's largest living reptile is the saltwater crocodile, which lives in parts of India, Australia, and Southeast Asia. This species can measure more than 17 feet (5 m) in length and weigh more than 1,000 pounds (450 kg). They feed on water buffalo and other animals, large and small!

WORD CHECK

VENOM: A poison made by an animal that is injected into another animal through teeth or a sting

LIZARDS

Lizards make up more than half of all reptile species. Most lizards have four legs, though there are some legless kinds. Lizards eat a wide variety of food depending on their size and habitat. Small lizards catch insects. A chameleon catches prey by shooting out its long, sticky tongue at high speed. Chameleons change color to communicate with other chameleons and to camouflage, that is, to blend in with the background. Bigger lizard species feed on birds, frogs, fish, mice, and other reptiles. Some species, such as iguanas, eat fruits and leaves. The marine iguana of the Galápagos Islands chews algae off rocks!

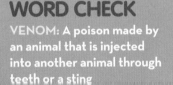

TRY THIS!

WHAT YOU NEED: A dark T-shirt; a light T-shirt; a hot, sunny day

HOW LONG IT TAKES: An hour

Some lizards turn dark to soak up more sunlight to get warm. They turn pale to absorb less sunlight. Put a dark T-shirt and a white T-shirt in sunlight and see for yourself which one feels warmer after an hour goes by. Which would you wear on a hot summer day?

CROCODYLIANS

The crocodylians are a reptile group made up of crocodiles, alligators, caimans, and gharials. They have strong tails, which push them through water as they swim. Their long snouts are lined with many teeth. Their eyes, ears, and nostrils sit on top of their heads, which lets them hide underwater while sneaking up on prey. Smaller "croc" species feed on frogs, fish, crabs, birds, and mice. Large species tackle prey as big as zebras and deer. Female crocodiles and alligators guard their nests and protect their babies. They even carry the little hatchlings carefully in their mouths.

THE TUATARA

The tuatara is a one-of-a-kind reptile. There is just one species, found only on small islands in New Zealand. The tuatara is often called a "living fossil" because it looks so much like its ancestors that lived millions of years ago. This reptile was at risk of going extinct by the end of the 1900s because cats and rats were eating their eggs and young. Efforts to remove these predators from the islands have helped save the tuatara.

LOL!

Q: What kind of photos does a turtle take?

A: Shellfies.

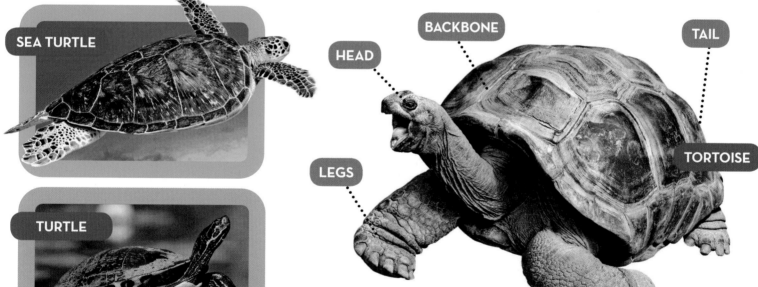

SEA TURTLE

TURTLE

HEAD **BACKBONE** **TAIL**

LEGS **TORTOISE**

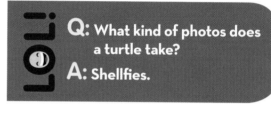

TURTLES

A turtle's shell is made of its backbone, ribs, and plates of bone fused together. Its head, tail, and legs stick out from openings in the shell. Tough scales called scutes cover the shell in most species, but some turtles have rubbery or leathery coverings instead. Tortoises are turtles with stumpy feet that live on land—even in deserts. Many turtles have webbed feet and live in water most of the time. Sea turtles have flippers. The leatherback sea turtle can measure up to six feet (1.8 m) long. Females migrate hundreds of miles back to the beaches where they hatched to lay their own eggs.

PERSONALITY PLUS

Dr. Archie Carr (1909–1987) was a zoologist who studied sea turtles. He discovered how green turtles traveled, or migrated, across the ocean to beaches where they laid eggs. He also showed how pollution harmed sea turtles and taught people how important it is to conserve wildlife and wild places. Carr's work helped create an organization dedicated to saving sea turtles.

AMPHIBIANS

Amphibians are vertebrate animals that generally divide their lives between living on land and in water. Most amphibians must reproduce and lay eggs in water, and many species grow up in water.

If you've ever seen a frog, you've seen an amphibian. There are more than 7,400 known species of amphibians. Like reptiles, amphibians are ectothermic. They sit in sunlight or on warm rocks to warm up. Unlike reptiles, most amphibians don't have scales. They have thin, moist skin, which oozes gluey mucus so they stay damp. Amphibians are able to breathe through their skin as well as their lungs—and some amphibians lack lungs and breathe only through their skin.

Most young amphibians look very different from their parents. As they grow, they change form by going through a process called metamorphosis. A frog, for example, starts life as a tadpole with gills, a long tail, and no legs. It grows legs and lungs and loses its tail as it becomes an adult.

GREAT PLAINS TOAD

The Great Plains toad lives in deserts, grasslands, and other habitats of the Midwest and western United States. It returns to water only to mate and lay eggs.

FROGS AND TOADS

Frogs and toads form a group of amphibians known as anurans. They are amphibians that lack tails but have long, strong hind legs. These legs make them powerful jumpers on land. Anurans that spend most of their time in water have webbed feet for swimming. Scientifically, frogs and toads are the same, but most people call smooth-skinned anurans "frogs" and ones with bumpy, dry, warty skin "toads."

POISON DART FROG

The skin of poison dart frogs makes a deadly poison. Their bright colors are a warning sign that tells predators that they better not eat them.

GEEK STREAK

The largest amphibian is the Chinese giant salamander. It can grow to be six foot (1.8 m) long! It lives in streams in parts of China but is endangered because it has been hunted for food. Scientists, zoos, and universities are working together on projects to help save this species.

SALAMANDERS AND NEWTS

Salamanders are amphibians that keep their tails as adults. They look a bit like lizards. Newts are a kind of salamander. Many eastern newts spend several years as a "red eft" (left) on land before becoming a green adult. The eft's orange skin signals that it's poisonous. They have rougher skin than other salamanders, and their tails are flat instead of round. Many salamanders mate and lay eggs in water, but some species live in water their entire lives. The axolotl salamander (see page 191) keeps its gills and its tadpole shape all its life. It looks as if it never grew up, but it's able to reproduce as an adult. Salamanders that spend their entire lives on land lay their eggs in damp places, such as inside rotting logs.

CAECILIANS

Caecilians are long, legless amphibians that many people mistake for a worm or snake. Their bodies are circled with rings. Some species have fishlike scales in these rings, but most caecilians have few scales or none at all. They have strong, bony heads that help them burrow. Some species live underground while others live in water. Small tentacles on their faces help them sense their surroundings and find prey. A species of caecilian found in Africa grows extra-thick skin to provide food for her young. The little caecilians have specially shaped teeth for feeding on the outer layer.

STAYING WET

Rain forests are great habitats for amphibians—but amphibians can survive even in deserts! They've evolved ways to survive in dry places or during droughts. In Australia, for example, the water-holding frog fills itself with water and then buries itself in the ground. There its outer layers of skin form a watertight cocoon. The frog can survive for two years as a buried water balloon! It emerges when rain falls again.

DISAPPEARING FROGS?

Frogs and other amphibians are very sensitive to changes in their habitat. Their thin skin absorbs air and water—and anything that's in it, such as pollutants. Most amphibians also need two habitats: a land-based one and a watery one. Nearly a third of all amphibians are in danger of dying out, and more than 100 species have gone extinct in the past 20 years alone. Pollution, disease, climate change, and habitat loss may all be part of the problem of amphibian extinctions.

TOOLS OF THE TRADE

A herpetologist uses a tool called a caliper to measure the length of an amphibian's body and legs. A caliper has a pair of jaws. One jaw stays in place while the other slides along a ruler. The animal being measured is placed between these jaws. Modern calipers have a digital display to show the measurements.

PERSONALITY PLUS

Robert C. Stebbins (1915–2013) was a herpetologist who wrote and illustrated books about reptiles and amphibians. His research included an important study of salamander species in California, U.S.A. He also worked to have laws passed to protect areas of deserts from off-road vehicles, which were destroying habitats of reptiles and amphibians.

BIRDS

There are more than 10,000 species of birds, but no matter how different they are, each one is a warm-blooded vertebrate with feathers, a beak, and wings.

Feathers! Birds are the only living animals that have these amazing adaptations. Feathers help a bird fly, attract a mate, and stay warm. Birds are "warm-blooded," or homeothermic. That means their bodies are able to make their own heat. A bird's feathers help hold in that heat and also keep cold air out. The bird world is filled with variety. It includes hummingbirds barely bigger than bumblebees, and ostriches that stand 9 feet (2.7 m) tall. Wings of different shapes give birds different flying abilities. The long, broad wings of an eagle help it soar in circles for hours on air currents that spiral up in the sky. The short, wide wings of a crow let it take off quickly and zip among branches. The sharply pointed wings of a falcon are for high-speed flying as it chases prey. The long, narrow wings of the wandering albatross let it soar for hours over the ocean without even flapping. Its wings stretch up to 11 feet (3.4 m) wide.

Some birds can't fly. Penguins, for example, swim as if flying underwater as they pursue fish. Ostriches run as fast as 43 miles an hour (70 km/h). Kiwis' wings are only an inch (2.5 cm) long, but they can dig burrows with their strong feet and claws.

FEATHER COLORS

Feathers not only keep a bird warm but make it fashionable, too! Some birds, such as whip-poor-wills, wear dull colors and blend in with their habitat. Other birds, such as parrots, are famous for their vivid colors.

FEATHERS

A bird has several different kinds of feathers. Flight feathers are stiff, strong feathers that are attached to its wing bones. The feathers that cover its body and give a bird its familiar shape are called contour feathers. Beneath the waterproof contour feathers are fluffy, soft feathers called down. Down traps air and helps keep a bird warm. Birds use their beaks to clean and comb their feathers because dirty feathers won't work well as raincoats or flight gear.

FEET

Feet are clues to a bird's lifestyle. Ducks, swans, geese, and other waterbirds have webbed feet that work as paddles for swimming. Eagles, hawks, and owls have strong, sharp-clawed feet for grabbing and killing prey. An osprey has spiky scales on its feet to help it grip slippery fish. Many birds have flexible toes for perching in trees. Most woodpeckers' feet have two toes pointing forward and two pointing backward, which helps them cling to tree trunks.

EGGS

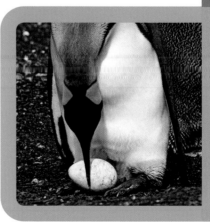

All birds lay eggs. Most birds take care of those eggs by keeping them warm. This behavior is called incubating. One or both parents incubate the eggs, depending on the species. Many birds also build nests for their eggs, while others lay them in burrows, in tree holes, or on cliff ledges. Emperor penguins keep their eggs on their feet, tucked under a fold of their belly!

PERSONALITY PLUS

Barbara Snow (1921–2007) and David Snow (1924–2009) were British ornithologists who studied birds in tropical forests. They were especially interested in the behavior of fruit-eating birds. Among the birds they researched was the oilbird, which lives in deep, dark caves and comes out only at night to eat fruit.

BEAKS

A bird's beak tells you a lot about how it lives and what it eats. A little warbler's thin, small beak is perfect for picking up tiny insects. A finch's stout beak is strong for crunching seeds. Shorebirds have long, thin bills just right for poking into wet sand and plucking out food. A hawk or owl's sharp, curved beak is adapted to slicing up mice and other prey.

WORD CHECK

ORNITHOLOGIST: A scientist who studies birds. "Ornith" comes from a Greek word meaning "bird."

BONES

Flying burns up a lot of energy, so birds that fly need to be lightweight. As a result, they've evolved hollow bones. Bigger bones in a bird's body, such as wing bones, may be crisscrossed with bars, or struts, that provide extra strength. But not all birds have lightweight bones. Penguins, for example, have solid bones. Being heavy is a plus for them while diving deep in the water to catch fish.

GEEK STREAK

Birds are actually feathered dinosaurs! Scientists have figured this out based on clues found in fossils of extinct dinosaurs. Some fossil bones have marks like those on modern bird bones that show where feathers are attached. Some fossils have been found with feather marks in the stone around them. Scientists have also tested samples of soft tissue from some dinosaur species' fossils and found that proteins in them closely match bird proteins.

SPEED KING!

The peregrine falcon hunts other birds. It dives down at a speed of 200 miles an hour (320 km/h) or more and grabs prey with its sharp talons. Peregrines are found on all continents except Antarctica.

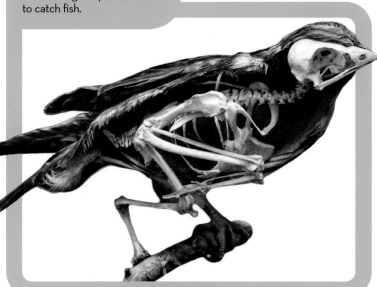

ATTRACTING MATES

Many birds brighten up springtime by singing. Males sing to attract mates and defend their territory from other males. Birds have many other ways of attracting mates. Sometimes they dance. Sometimes a male's feathers change to brilliant colors. The cassowary (right) is a large, flightless bird that lives in rain forests in Australia. The helmet-like crest on its head may be a decoration that helps the bird attract a mate.

TOOLS OF THE TRADE

Many birds travel, or migrate, between their winter grounds and their breeding grounds. Scientists who study how birds migrate often use a device called an Emlen funnel, made up of an upside-down paper cone in a cage. A bird is placed inside the cone. The paper records scratch marks made by the bird as it leaps and tries to take off in a certain direction. Scientists can use this device to test if birds are using star patterns or other cues to find their way.

UP CLOSE! PREDATORS AND PREY

A predator is an animal that hunts and eats other animals. The animals they eat are their prey. A hawk is a predator that seizes small prey, such as rabbits. A lioness is a predator that can take down large prey, such as a zebra. A praying mantis that grabs a cricket is also a predator catching prey. Predators play an important role in their habitats. Without predators, the numbers of prey animals, such as white-tailed deer, would become too large for their habitat. They would eat the plants and other food until there wasn't enough to support the population. Predators help keep a check on their numbers. Take a look at some predators that catch their prey in fascinating ways.

Sneaky Spider

Many spiders make silk and spin webs to catch insects. Bolas spiders, however, use their silk to make a kind of lasso! This spider dangles a line of silk in the air, with a sticky blob at the end of the line. At the same time, the spider produces chemicals that smell like scents given off by certain types of female moths. A male moth, attracted by the scent, flies to the spider. The bolas spider whirls the lasso with the sticky blob and catches the moth. Only the female bolas spiders hunt this way. The males are very small and eat flies smaller than themselves.

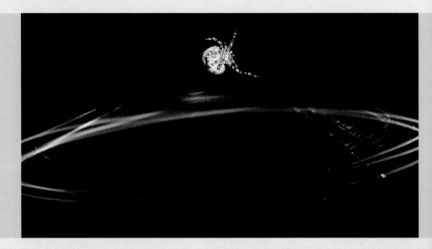

Darting Dragonflies

Dragonflies watch for prey, such as mosquitoes and butterflies, with huge eyes that are super sensitive to movement. They zoom after insects on wings that can carry them at speeds up to 30 miles an hour (48 km/h). They're very successful predators and catch their prey more than 95 percent of the time. Scientists have found that a dragonfly's eyes, wings, brain, and nerves can even calculate which way its prey will travel before it even starts to move in that direction. Then it adjusts its flight and veers to the spot where the prey will end up.

Snacking Snapper

The alligator snapping turtle is a big reptile—it can be more than two feet (0.6 m) long and weigh as much as 220 pounds (99.5 kg). It has a powerful, sharp beak and eats just about anything it can catch. It'll also eat any dead animal it finds. This turtle has a clever way of tricking fish into coming closer: It sits still and wiggles the pink, wormlike lure on its tongue. Curious fish swim up to its mouth to check out the "worm" and are quickly snapped up.

Aiming Archerfish

Archerfish turn into living water pistols to catch insects! A hunting fish aims at an insect perched on a stem above the water. It shuts its gills and then forces water out of its mouth. As it spits, the fish changes the shape of its mouth to control the speed of the squirt so that it packs the most force as it hits its target. Pow! The stream knocks the insect off its perch and into the water, where the archerfish gobbles it up. What makes the archerfish's skill extra amazing is that the fish must also deal with the way light bends when it enters water. It has to adjust its aim to make up for peering out of the water into the air.

Paddling Pelicans

A white pelican hunts by dipping its pouched beak into the water to scoop up fish and other prey. White pelicans may also hunt as a pack. The big birds form a curved line or a circle (shown at left). Then they beat their wings on the water to scare fish and herd them into shallow water. The pelicans surround the fish and scoop them up quickly and easily.

Patient Polar Bear

What does a polar bear eat? Anything it wants! And what it wants is seal blubber, the layer of fat right under the seal's skin. To catch its prey, a polar bear often waits by a ringed seal's breathing hole in the ice. A seal must come up for air every few minutes, but it has up to 15 breathing holes, so sometimes the bear must wait for many hours. When the seal finally pops up its head, the bear lunges and kills it with sharp teeth and claws. A polar bear can sniff out a breathing hole from a mile (1.6 km) away.

MAMMALS ON LAND

Mammals are warm-blooded vertebrate animals that grow hair and produce milk from special glands to feed their young. Scientists have named more than 5,000 species of mammals.

Hamsters, horses, hippopotamuses, and humans are all examples of mammals. Mammals' hair shows as much variety as birds' feathers do. Some mammals grow very thick fur. A very fuzzy rabbit, for example, may have more than 123,000 hairs per square inch (6.5 sq cm) on its body. Other animals, such as naked mole rats, have very little hair. Even sea mammals, such as whales, have hair at some point in their lives.

Nearly all mammals give live birth. All female mammals make milk for their young and care for them until they're old enough to find their own food. Baby pygmy shrews, for example, grow up in just three weeks. Baby chimpanzees, however, depend on their mothers for up to five years and stay with them for a few years after that, learning how to care for themselves as well as for their mothers' new babies.

PLACENTAL MAMMALS

The young of placental mammals grow inside their mother's body until they're ready to be born. They are attached to an organ called a placenta while they're inside her body. This organ is specially grown to link the young with the mother's bloodstream, which provides oxygen and nutrients. Cows, dogs, gorillas, and squirrels are examples of placental mammals. About 95 percent of all mammals are in this group.

BONIFIED BACKBONES!

All mammals have backbones built of separate connecting bones called vertebrae. But the number of vertebrae differs among species. Almost all mammals have seven vertebrae in their necks. The two-toed sloth and a sea mammal called the manatee have only six. Three-toed sloths have up to ten. The backbone is vital to all species. A bundle of nerves called a spinal cord runs through it. These nerves carry messages from the brain to the rest of the body.

MARSUPIALS

Marsupials are mammals that give live birth to tiny young that aren't fully developed. These young grow inside the mother's body for only a few weeks. After they are born, they move into a pouch on the mother's body. There they drink milk made by her body and keep growing until they're fully developed. Only then will they come out of the pouch. Kangaroos, opossums, and koalas are examples of marsupials. This baby kangaroo, or joey, is the size of a jelly bean at birth. It continues growing inside the mother's pouch. A joey starts exploring outside the pouch when it's about nine months old.

TOOLS OF THE TRADE

Scientists often put radio or satellite collars on wild mammals to study their travels. The collars send signals to radio antennas or to satellites orbiting Earth. Some satellite collars store information on the collars themselves. These collars are usually designed to fall off after a certain amount of time. They keep sending out signals so that scientists can track them down.

LAND AND WATER

Some mammals move easily on land and in water. The duck-billed platypus swims underwater, paddling with its webbed front feet and steering with its tail. Its sensitive bill helps it find worms and other food. A beaver (below) also moves between land and water with its webbed feet and a tail that steers. When danger approaches, it slaps the water with its broad, flat tail to warn others.

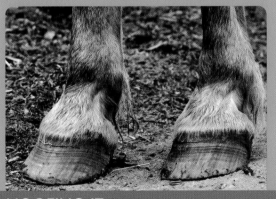

LARGE AND SMALL

The smallest living mammal is the Kitti's hog-nosed bat. It's also called the bumblebee bat, which gives you an idea of its size: barely an inch (2.5 cm) long! It weighs just .05 ounce (1.4 g). That's about as much as one dime! The largest living land mammal is the African elephant. A male of this species can stand 13 feet (4 m) at the shoulder and weigh up to 14,000 pounds (6,350 kg). That's almost as much as four cars.

HOT AND COLD

Scientists call warm-blooded animals "endotherms." "Endo" means "within" and "therm" means "heat." Mammals are endotherms because they make their own body heat. Like reptiles, however, a mammal can move between warm and cool places to help control its temperature. Unlike reptiles, many mammals can also sweat to get rid of extra body heat. Some mammals breathe heavily, or pant, to cool off. Mammals can also shiver to produce body heat when they're cold.

MONOTREMES

A handful of mammals lay eggs instead of giving live birth. They are known as monotremes. This word means "one hole." Monotremes, like reptiles and birds, have just one opening in their body's hind end. This opening is used for both ridding the body of waste and laying eggs. The platypus and echidna (right) are the only monotremes. They lay leathery eggs that hatch in about 10 days.

HOOFING IT

About a thousand species of mammal have hard tips on their feet called hooves. A horse has one hoof on each foot. Deer have two, and rhinoceroses have three. The hooves likely began as toes millions of years ago and gradually evolved into hooves.

PERSONALITY PLUS

Jane Goodall (1934–) is a scientist who began studying wild chimpanzees in Africa in 1960. She discovered that chimpanzees can make and use tools to catch food. Since 1986 she has devoted her life to educating people about wildlife conservation and working to protect both animals and habitats.

MAMMALS AT SEA

Mammals that live in the ocean are called marine mammals. Marine mammals include animals such as whales and seals.

Like land mammals, marine mammals are warm-blooded, and females make milk for their young. Many of them have hair, though some only have a little hair when they're first born and lose it as they grow. And even though they live all or part of their life in the ocean, they all breathe air.

Many marine mammals have bodies shaped so they slip easily through water. Dolphins, for example, are shaped like fish. Many marine mammals can also store extra oxygen in their blood and muscles so they can stay underwater longer.

Marine mammals must also cope with the cold. Most ocean water is chilly, and Arctic and Antarctic ocean water can be as cold as 28.4°F (-2°C), with ice bobbing at its surface! Many species have a thick layer of fat under their skin, called blubber, to keep them warm.

SEA COWS

Sirenians are often called "sea cows," and it's a good name for them! They are large, slow-moving animals that graze on water plants and seaweeds. Manatees are sirenians that live in warm Atlantic seas and the Gulf of Mexico. A Florida manatee can be up to 13 feet (4 m) long and weigh up to 1,300 pounds (600 kg). It uses its rubbery upper lip to gather its food. The dugong is a sirenian found in the Indian and Pacific Oceans. These marine mammals have flippers for front legs, and their tails work like paddles. They don't have thick blubber, so they need warm water. They never emerge onto land.

CETACEANS

Cetaceans are marine mammals that look the most like fish: whales, dolphins, and porpoises. These mammals' front legs have evolved into flippers. All that's left of their hind limbs are a few bones hidden inside their bodies. Like fish, they have fins on their backs. Their tails have fins that stick out sideways. Whales, dolphins, and porpoises all give birth underwater. Their young, called calves, are often helped up to the surface to catch their first breath.

PINNIPEDS

Seals, sea lions, fur seals, and walruses are pinnipeds. "Pinniped" means "fin footed" and refers to these animals' legs, which have evolved into fins for swimming. They hunt for food in the ocean but drag themselves onto land or floating ice to rest and give birth to young. Seals, sea lions, and fur seals all have blubber and fur to keep them warm. A walrus lacks fur, but its blubber can be four inches (10 cm) thick! A walrus's whiskers help it find clams and mussels in deep water. It uses its tusks to help pull itself out of the water onto the ice.

GEEK STREAK

The blue whale is the largest animal that's ever existed. It can be up to 100 feet (30 m) long—about three times as long as a school bus. Yet these giant mammals survive by filtering tiny krill from seawater! A blue whale may eat between 200 and 400 tons (181 to 363 t) of krill a day.

TOOLS OF THE TRADE

Dogs are land mammals—but they're being trained for whale research! The dogs sniff out whale droppings in the water, and scientists aim the boat in its direction to collect it. Substances in whale droppings can tell researchers about what whales are eating and if pesticides and other pollutants are being absorbed by the whales' bodies.

POLAR BEARS

Polar bears live in the Arctic, where they split their time between land and sea. Seals are their main food, and the bears hunt them from platforms of floating ice. Polar bears are often seen swimming hundreds of miles from land. They swim by paddling with their huge front paws, and holding their hind legs straight back to serve as rudders. Their paws have partly webbed toes. In winter, females give birth inside dens dug in the snow. A polar bear has both blubber and thick fur, which is actually colorless—it looks white because air spaces in the hairs reflect all the light hitting them.

SEA OTTERS

Sea otters live in the cold waters of the northern Pacific Ocean. They don't have blubber, but their thick fur keeps them warm and waterproof. A sea otter has up to one million hairs in one square inch (6.5 sq cm) of its furry body—more than you have on your entire head! Their webbed feet help them swim. A sea otter may float on its back while smashing a clam open with a rock on its chest. A sleeping sea otter floats on its back, too. A tangle of seaweed around its body keeps it anchored in place.

LOL! 😄

Q: What do polar bears eat for lunch?

A: Ice-bergers!

UP CLOSE! BIZARRE ANIMALS!

Animals large and small face challenges in their world. They have to find food and water while avoiding predators. They have to find mates and safe places for their young. On top of all that, they must cope with everything that the nonliving world throws at them, such as extreme heat, lack of water, or freezing cold. All animals have adaptations that help them survive. Some adaptations are body parts, such as colorful skin or sharp horns. Other adaptations are behaviors, such as digging a burrow to hide in or growling and baring teeth. Here are just a few of the many animals that have evolved some truly bizarre bodies and behaviors.

Amazing Aardvark

It's nighttime in southern Africa. A long-eared animal with a vacuum-cleaner nose sniffs its way along a trail. It's an aardvark—a mammal that feeds on ants and termites. It uses its huge front claws to rip open rock-hard termite mounds. It slurps up the insects with its sticky tongue, which is nearly 12 inches (30.5 cm) long. It also presses its piglike snout against holes in the mound and sucks the termites out of hiding—right into its snout. An aardvark may travel for miles in one night to find enough ants and termites for a meal.

Beetle Ka-Boom

The bombardier beetle is named for the way it "bombs" predators with a boiling-hot brew of poison! The beetle has two chambers in its hind end, called the abdomen. If the beetle is threatened by a predator, the chambers open so that the chemicals mix together and cause an explosion. The toxic, boiling fluid bursts out. The beetle aims its spray by twisting its abdomen.

Boxfish

Imagine living your life inside a box with just your face, arms, and legs sticking out. That's a bit like being a boxfish! These coral-reef fish have hard, boxy bodies that work like armor to protect them from predators. As if that weren't enough self-defense, their skin also oozes poison if they are scared. The poison keeps predators away and can even kill other fish swimming near them.

Roll With It

The three-banded armadillo is a mammal with armor-plated skin. If it senses danger, it rolls up into a ball. It curls up so tightly that it looks like a softball with scales. Other kinds of armadillos curl up, too, but not as completely as this species. Other animals that curl up to defend themselves include pill bugs, snakes called ball pythons, and anteaters called pangolins.

Itty-Bitty Bears

Tardigrades are invertebrates that are smaller than a sprinkle on an ice-cream cone. They're also known as water bears or moss piglets. By any name, they're tiny—but tough! Tardigrades normally live in mossy patches. But they can survive the superhot water of a hot spring or the freezing conditions of icy Antarctica. Tardigrades have even survived trips into outer space, where they were exposed to deadly radiation. The mini-beasts cope with tough times by curling up, drying out, and letting natural sugars replace the water in their bodies. They can survive for decades in this way.

Wee Wasps

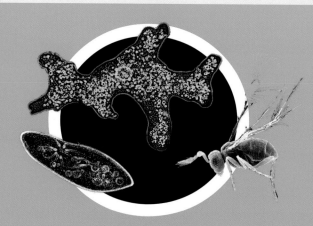

Ever have yellow-jacket wasps show up at a picnic? These big, buzzing bugs have cousins so small you often need a microscope to see them. The tiny wasps, which are shaped like their larger cousins, are parasites—they live inside other insects for a portion of their lives. One kind, the fairy wasp, lays its eggs in other insects' eggs, and its young eat the other insects' young after hatching. The tinkerbell wasp is just .01 inch (.25 mm) long—only 2.5 times as wide as a human hair. Another species, which lacks a common name, is smaller than some one-celled microbes!

Fancy Treehoppers

Treehoppers are insects that pierce the stems of plants and suck out their nutritious fluid. In many species, the front part of the thorax—the middle part of an insect's body—looks like a thorn, leaf, or twig. This disguise helps camouflage a treehopper from predators, such as hungry birds. Other treehoppers have "helmets" with bold stripes that break up their shapes, so they don't look like insects. The ant-mimicking treehopper is even more bizarre: It grows knobs that make it look like a stinging ant!

Beetle Beauty

The shiny metallic golden tortoise beetle changes color when it finds a mate or is alarmed by a predator. Young adult beetles are reddish brown and can change to a more orange or brown color with black spots. When older adults are resting or mating, they look like they've been spray-painted gold. The beetle's ability to switch colors appears to be caused by the special structure of the clear shell that forms a dome over its body. Tiny grooves run through the shell's layers. A red pigment flows in and out of the grooves, changing the way the glassy shell reflects light and shows the red color.

THE HUMAN BODY

THE AMAZING MACHINE

Your body is a collection of parts and processes that work together to keep you alive and well. The smallest bits of you are your body cells. There are about 37.2 trillion of them!

These cells aren't all the same. There are more than 200 different kinds of human cells, all performing different jobs. About 2 billion heart-muscle cells, for example, keep your heart pumping blood around your body. The blood itself contains about 25 trillion red blood cells, which are able to latch on to oxygen and carry it to all your other cells. Your liver, which contains about 240 billion cells, cleans your blood and recycles dead blood cells into digestive fluids.

Cells of the same type come together and form different kinds of tissue, which is the building material for all your organs and other body parts. Your stomach, for example, is made of layers of muscle tissue plus sheets of skinlike tissue, called epithelial tissue. Your skin includes epithelial tissue as well as strong connective tissue, which is like your body's version of superglue.

All those organs and body parts link up and form body systems. The skeletal system, for example, consists of the bones that form your body's framework. It's often paired with the muscular system, which is made up of the muscles attached to your skeleton. Your digestive system includes your stomach, intestines, and other organs that digest food. Your respiratory system, which includes your lungs, is in charge of bringing oxygen into your body and getting rid of a waste gas, carbon dioxide.

The collection of parts that forms the bodies of humans and other animals is called anatomy. When scientists compare the anatomy of different animals to see how they evolved, it's called comparative anatomy.

Your brain is the mastermind of your body. The brain makes the lungs expand with air and the heart pump blood. It houses memories, processes sounds and sights, smells and tastes, and is what makes you you. This big, complex brain is also what makes humans intelligent and imaginative enough to invent machines that can help scientists peer deep inside the human body and see how it works. This imagination also helps humans design amazing machines that examine the tiny proteins that contain the chemical codes for creating a human being.

Did you know? Your belly button is home to thousands of bacteria. They make up an ecosystem as big as a rain forest!

A break-dancer combines acrobatics with dancing by using highly trained muscle groups that include his arms, chest, abdomen, and legs. Break-dancers strengthen these muscles to increase the flexibility and balance they need to make handstands, headspins, and more at lightning speed.

229

SKIN, HAIR, AND NAILS

Your skin is much more than just a wrapper that keeps your inside separate from the outside! It's a complex organ that also happens to be your body's largest.

Your skin helps stop germs from entering your body. It turns sunlight into vitamin D, a nutrient your body needs. And it plays a very important role in helping your body regulate its temperature.

The skin you're in is made up of layers. The top layer is called the epidermis. Its surface is made up of dead skin cells. New skin cells form in the bottom part of the epidermis—about 500 million of them every day! Nails start to grow in the epidermis, over a platform called the nail bed.

Underneath the epidermis is the dermis. This layer contains blood vessels, sweat glands, and nerve endings, as well as strong, stretchy proteins that make skin both sturdy and flexible. The dermis also contains hair follicles, which grow hair.

KERATIN

Keratin is a tough protein made by your body. Skin cells grow keratin fibers that hook together to make skin stretchy and strong. Skin cells fill up with keratin as they get older. Your outermost skin cells are dead and keratin-packed, which gives you a tough, nearly waterproof covering. Keratin also forms your hair and nails. It's also the same material that makes up beaks, claws, feathers, hooves, and rhino horns! Humans, apes, and other primates are the only mammals with fingernails. Having fingernails instead of claws helps primates grasp objects.

SKIN COLOR

Your skin's color is created by skin cells called melanocytes. They're named after the pigment they produce, which is called melanin. One kind of melanin is brown-black. The other is red-yellow. Your skin's color depends on how much of each kind of melanin your melanocytes make. Skin also tans in sunlight thanks to melanocytes. They produce more melanin when they're exposed to sunlight because melanin helps protect skin from burning. (So does sunscreen. Remember to apply at least a 30 SPF!)

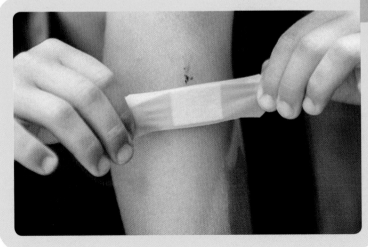

OUCH!

Scrape your skin, and your epidermis gets busy making new cells to cover that spot. Cut your skin more deeply, and your skin reacts more strongly. At first it bleeds, but then blood vessels shut down and stop the flow. Blood cells called platelets rush in to plug the cut. Proteins in your blood help form a clot and then a scab. White blood cells kill bacteria. Soon new skin starts growing, repairing the damage.

LOL! 😄

Q: What do you have when a rotten rabbit sits on your head?

A: A bad hare day.

GEEK STREAK

Got goose bumps? Mammals' fur and birds' feathers fluff up to keep them warm. "Goose bumps" are caused by your soft, thin body hair trying to do the same thing!

SKIN DEEP!

About 65,000 bacteria live on every square inch (6.5 sq cm) of your skin's surface. Another 6 million or so microbes live just under each of those patches! Scientists call these groups "vibrant" communities. Those bugs aren't diseases, they're just part of every healthy body.

TRY THIS!

WHAT YOU NEED: Your clean fingertips, an ink pad, paper

HOW LONG IT TAKES: 5 minutes

Fingerprints are the loops and ridges on your fingertips. Every person has his or her own unique set of fingerprints—even identical twins! Roll your fingertips on an ink pad and then press them on paper to make prints. Have other people make fingerprints the same way and then compare them to see the different patterns.

HAIR AND NAILS

Your hair is basically strings of dead cells filled with keratin! Each strand of hair starts off as a cluster of living cells inside a hair follicle. These cells are pushed up and out of the follicle as new cells form below them. By the time a hair pokes out of your skin, its cells are dead. That's why it doesn't hurt to get your hair cut. Your hair follicles are responsible for hair color, too. Cells in hair follicles produce melanin and add it to the hair as it grows. Your hair's color comes from melanin, just like your skin's color. Like hair, nails are made of dead, keratin-filled cells. It doesn't hurt to trim them, either. Your fingernails grow two to three times as fast as your toenails. A study published in 2009 also showed that nails grow faster now than they did 70 years ago. Researchers think that better nutrition may be part of the reason for the faster growth. It takes about six months to grow an entire fingernail.

SWEAT

Ever work up a sweat? Sweat is a mixture of water, salts, and other chemicals. It's produced by sweat glands, which are in the dermis layer of skin. You have about 2.6 million sweat glands. A square inch (6.5 sq cm) contains about 650 of them! Sweat helps cool down your body because the liquid water in sweat turns into a gas, called water vapor. This process, called evaporation, uses heat—and it gets that heat away from your skin. That's how the evaporation of sweat whisks away heat and cools you. You produce about two cups (0.5 L) of sweat a day, and even more if it's hot or if you exercise.

WORD CHECK

HAIR FOLLICLE: A sac in the outside layer of skin from which a hair grows. The word comes from the Latin *follis*, meaning "bag."

231

MUSCLES AND BONES

Bones provide a stiff, strong framework for your body—the skeleton. Muscles are attached to bones and pull on them to make them move. Your skeleton has many joints that work like hinges to let you bend and twist.

Our bones and muscles work together to keep us moving. They're what make it possible for you to run, jump, do a cartwheel, and paint a picture. The human skeleton is made up of 206 bones. Bones contain a large amount of hard minerals called calcium phosphate and calcium carbonate paired up with a tough protein called collagen. Together, these substances make a bone hard and strong as well as a little bit flexible so that it doesn't snap like a dry twig. Bones contain living cells, which make new bone material and break down the old. Bones also have nerves and blood vessels, and they have muscles attached to them. The muscles you use for moving are called skeletal muscles. Skeletal muscles are attached to bones by tough cords called tendons.

INSIDE A BONE

Your skeleton makes up about 14 percent of your body's weight. That's less than your skin, which makes up about 16 percent. Bones are light for their size because they aren't solid, compact bone all the way through. They are filled with spongy bone, which is strong but lighter in weight. Some bones also contain a jellylike substance called red marrow, which makes new red blood cells for the body.

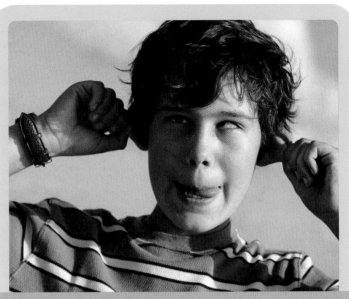

CARTILAGE

Your nose and ears are flexible because they're made of cartilage. Cartilage is rubbery but strong. It wraps around the ends of bones where they meet at joints. There it cushions the bones and also helps them glide smoothly instead of rubbing. Disks of cartilage also work as shock absorbers between the vertebrae in your spine. Injured cartilage heals slowly because it doesn't have a blood supply, as bones do.

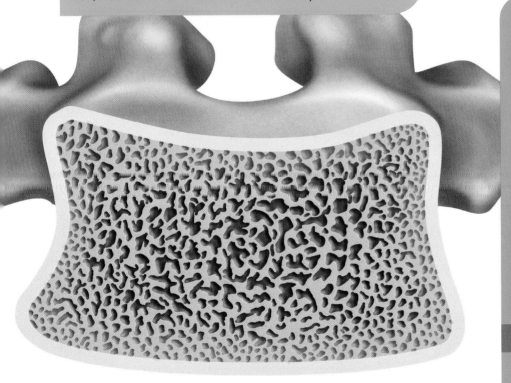

BROKEN BONES

A broken bone heals similarly to cut skin. A blood clot forms in the break. White blood cells arrive to fight infection. Then the healing begins: Strands of collagen knit the break together, and new bone begins to grow. A cast is often used to hold a broken bone still so that it heals properly. Keeping the bone still also makes it hurt less. A simple broken bone can heal in as little as two months.

PULLING POWER

A muscle can't push on bones to make them move. It can only pull. You can feel this action in your upper arm when you lift your forearm, or in your thigh when you lift your lower leg. The muscle doing the pulling bunches up, or contracts. The muscles in your face pull on skin to make you grin or raise an eyebrow. To lower your limbs or drop your smile, the muscles simply relax.

MUSCLE TYPES

You have about 650 skeletal muscles—the ones that make you move. These muscles look like bundles of fibers because they're made up of long, spindly cells bunched together. Your body also contains smooth muscle, which is made up of shorter cells. Sheets of smooth muscle line your blood vessels and digestive system. Your heart contains cardiac, or heart, muscles, which aren't found anywhere else in your body. They pulse regularly to keep your heart beating. Muscles make up about 30 to 40 percent of a woman's body weight. A man's muscles make up about 40 to 50 percent of his weight. By comparison, an elephant's trunk contains 16 big muscles and about 150,000 smaller bundles of muscles. It doesn't contain any bones or cartilage.

WORD CHECK

TISSUE: A group of cells that work together to perform a function, such as muscle tissue

TRY THIS!

WHAT YOU NEED: A clean chicken bone, a mason jar with a top, vinegar

HOW LONG IT TAKES: A week

Check out how a bone is made of both stiff and flexible substances by putting a clean chicken bone into a jar filled with vinegar. Screw the lid on tightly. Let the jar sit for a week. The vinegar, which is an acid, will react with calcium carbonate in the bone, weakening it. After a week you should be able to bend the bone easily!

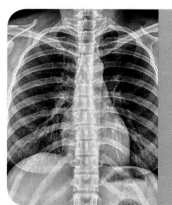

TOOLS OF THE TRADE

German scientist Wilhelm Röntgen discovered x-rays in 1895. X-rays pass through tissue such as muscle and skin, but are absorbed by bones. As a result, the bones show up as dark areas in a final film or computer image. Today, doctors still use x-rays to examine bones and teeth.

PERSONALITY PLUS

Guillaume-Benjamin-Amand Duchenne (1806–1875) was a French doctor who studied disorders of the muscles and nerves. He discovered that smiling made eyes crinkle at their corners, but only if they were real smiles, not faked ones. Today, such an "honest" smile is known by scientists as a "Duchenne smile."

THE BRAIN AND NERVOUS SYSTEM

Who you are and everything you do is packed into a mushy pink-gray organ in your head: your brain. The brain is your body's control center and holds all of your thoughts, feelings, and memories. It receives information and sends out messages to the rest of your body through fibers called nerves. Your brain and nerves together make up the nervous system.

The brain sits inside your built-in helmet, the skull. It perches on top of your body's main nerve, the spinal cord. The spinal cord is protected by your backbone's vertebrae. Along its length, 31 pairs of nerves stream out from it and lead to your arms, legs, and body. These nerves branch out into smaller nerves that are in contact with your muscles, glands, and other body parts. Your brain sends messages along your nerves to tell muscles to move. It also receives messages sent by your body. Some of those messages come from your body's sense organs, such as your eyes, ears, tongue, nose, and skin.

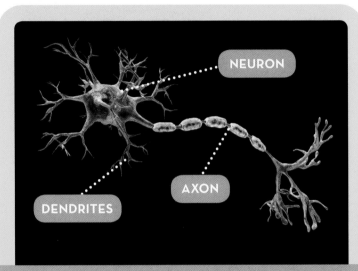

NEURONS

Nerves are bundles of nerve cells, called neurons. A single neuron looks sort of like a centipede. It's made up of a cell body with a long, thin stalk called an axon. Stringy strands called dendrites radiate from the cell body. The axon is tipped with as many as 10,000 dendrites or more. The entire neuron is wrapped up in a protective fatty covering. Your brain contains about 86 billion neurons.

THE BRAIN

More than 80 percent of your brain is made up of the cerebrum. This is the "thinking" part of your brain. It also processes information that arrives from your senses. It even helps you plan and perform motions, such as throwing a ball. Another important part, the cerebellum, helps you balance and coordinate your muscles. Last but not least, the medulla controls processes such as breathing and digesting.

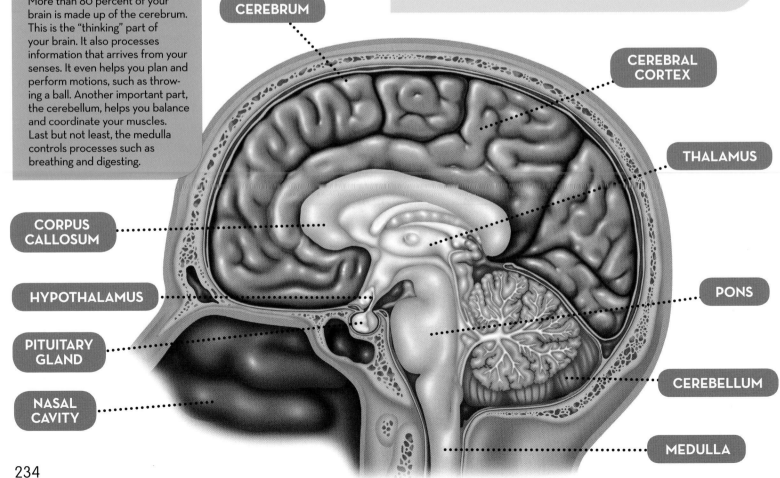

CEREBRUM
CEREBRAL CORTEX
THALAMUS
CORPUS CALLOSUM
HYPOTHALAMUS
PONS
PITUITARY GLAND
CEREBELLUM
NASAL CAVITY
MEDULLA

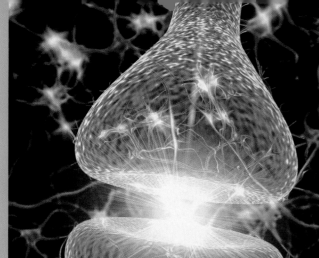

SENDING A SIGNAL

A message travels through a neuron in the form of electricity. It zips from the cell body to the tip of the axon. To reach the next neuron, the electrical signal must jump a gap called a synapse. It does this by causing chemicals to flow out of the axon. These chemicals seep across the synapse and reach the dendrites on the next neuron, where they spark the next electrical signal. Your brain produces enough electricity to power a 15-watt lightbulb. A signal from your brain to a muscle can zip along at 250 miles an hour (402 km/h). But if you stub your toe, the pain message trudges along at just 3 miles an hour (4.8 km/h).

LOL! 😄

Q: What is smart rain called?

A: A brainstorm.

HORMONES

Your brain crackles with electrical signals, but it also uses chemical signals, called hormones, to send directions. Hormones travel in the bloodstream but are made in the brain. The pea-size pituitary gland (see diagram opposite) makes hormones that control growth and reproduction. It takes its orders from another brain part, the hypothalamus, which uses hormones to tell it when to make hormones. Your hypothalamus and a few other brain parts form the "limbic system," which controls emotions such as joy and fear. It also helps form memories.

GEEK STREAK

A human's brain weighs about three pounds (1.4 kg). An elephant's brain can weigh four times as much! But brain size is not a direct measure of intelligence. Scientists who study animal thinking test animals to see how they solve problems. Some animals are tested to see if they recognize themselves in mirrors. As it turns out, elephants really are highly intelligent. So are big-brained dolphins. But animals with much smaller brains, including chimpanzees and dogs, score high marks, too.

PILOT AND AUTOPILOT

Your brain and spinal cord form your central nervous system. Together, they sort and make sense of all the information that's brought to them by your peripheral nervous system—the nerves in the rest of your body. The peripheral nervous system has two main parts: the somatic nervous system, which you control when you want to dance or run or throw a ball, and the autonomic nervous system, which works on its own to handle tasks such as making your heart beat faster or the pupils of your eyes widen.

RIGHT BRAIN, LEFT BRAIN

The nerves from the left and right sides of the body crisscross before they enter the brain. So when you move your right foot, the signal comes from your brain's left side! You may have heard people say that if you're creative you are "right brained" and if you are mathematical you are "left brained." The brain's left side is in charge of most of your speaking and math skills. The right side plays a large role in creative tasks, such as painting. But no one is either one or the other!

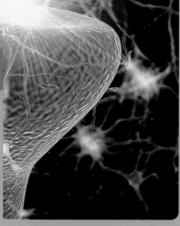

WORD CHECK

CORPUS CALLOSUM: A wide bundle of nerve fibers that connects the left and right sides of your brain, allowing them to work together so you can function. It's Latin for "tough body."

235

THE HEART AND CIRCULATORY SYSTEM

Your heart pumps around the clock, year in and year out. It started beating even before you were born. The heart's job is to pump blood through your body, nonstop, so that every cell gets the oxygen, nutrients, and water it needs to work properly—and to keep you working properly.

B lood is made up of a yellowish fluid called plasma mixed with different kinds of blood cells. Red blood cells are the ones that carry oxygen. The red color comes from a protein called hemoglobin, which is rich in iron. Iron and oxygen link up easily, which enables red blood cells to take oxygen from your lungs and carry it to your cells. Your blood travels through your body in tubes called blood vessels. This system of blood vessels that carries blood to and from your heart and through your body is called the circulatory system. Laid end to end, your blood vessels would circle the Earth two and a half times!

Arteries deliver oxygen-rich blood from the heart to the body.

Veins deliver oxygen-poor blood from the body to the heart.

The aorta, the biggest artery, branches into smaller arteries.

HEART

ARTERIES

The heart needs blood to work, just like any other organ. It gets blood from coronary arteries and veins, which twist all around its surface; in turn it sends blood out to the rest of the body. Veins are blood vessels that carry oxygen-poor blood to the heart, and most arteries carry oxygen-rich blood away from the heart. Arteries have strong, stretchy walls that contain muscles. The biggest artery is the aorta, which exits the heart's left side. Blood is pumped into this artery at a speed of nearly one mile an hour (1.6 km/h). The aorta branches into smaller arteries, which branch into even smaller arteries. The carotid arteries are a pair of large vessels that carry blood to your brain and face.

YOUR HEART

Your heart is actually a double pump. The left side receives blood from your lungs. This blood is rich in oxygen, and it's pumped out to the rest of your body. The heart's right side receives blood after it has circulated through the body. It pumps this blood with less oxygen to your lungs, where the blood picks up a fresh supply of oxygen. Your blood makes a complete round-trip through your body about once every minute.

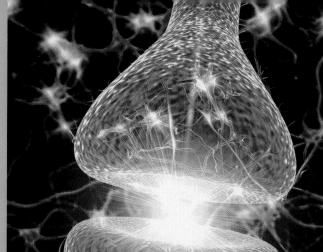

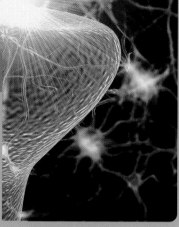

SENDING A SIGNAL

A message travels through a neuron in the form of electricity. It zips from the cell body to the tip of the axon. To reach the next neuron, the electrical signal must jump a gap called a synapse. It does this by causing chemicals to flow out of the axon. These chemicals seep across the synapse and reach the dendrites on the next neuron, where they spark the next electrical signal. Your brain produces enough electricity to power a 15-watt lightbulb. A signal from your brain to a muscle can zip along at 250 miles an hour (402 km/h). But if you stub your toe, the pain message trudges along at just 3 miles an hour (4.8 km/h).

LOL!

Q: What is smart rain called?

A: A brainstorm.

HORMONES

Your brain crackles with electrical signals, but it also uses chemical signals, called hormones, to send directions. Hormones travel in the bloodstream but are made in the brain. The pea-size pituitary gland (see diagram opposite) makes hormones that control growth and reproduction. It takes its orders from another brain part, the hypothalamus, which uses hormones to tell it when to make hormones. Your hypothalamus and a few other brain parts form the "limbic system," which controls emotions such as joy and fear. It also helps form memories.

GEEK STREAK

A human's brain weighs about three pounds (1.4 kg). An elephant's brain can weigh four times as much! But brain size is not a direct measure of intelligence. Scientists who study animal thinking test animals to see how they solve problems. Some animals are tested to see if they recognize themselves in mirrors. As it turns out, elephants really are highly intelligent. So are big-brained dolphins. But animals with much smaller brains, including chimpanzees and dogs, score high marks, too.

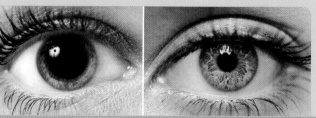

PILOT AND AUTOPILOT

Your brain and spinal cord form your central nervous system. Together, they sort and make sense of all the information that's brought to them by your peripheral nervous system—the nerves in the rest of your body. The peripheral nervous system has two main parts: the somatic nervous system, which you control when you want to dance or run or throw a ball, and the autonomic nervous system, which works on its own to handle tasks such as making your heart beat faster or the pupils of your eyes widen.

RIGHT BRAIN, LEFT BRAIN

The nerves from the left and right sides of the body crisscross before they enter the brain. So when you move your right foot, the signal comes from your brain's left side! You may have heard people say that if you're creative you are "right brained" and if you are mathematical you are "left brained." The brain's left side is in charge of most of your speaking and math skills. The right side plays a large role in creative tasks, such as painting. But no one is either one or the other!

WORD CHECK

CORPUS CALLOSUM: A wide bundle of nerve fibers that connects the left and right sides of your brain, allowing them to work together so you can function. It's Latin for "tough body."

THE HEART AND CIRCULATORY SYSTEM

Your heart pumps around the clock, year in and year out. It started beating even before you were born. The heart's job is to pump blood through your body, nonstop, so that every cell gets the oxygen, nutrients, and water it needs to work properly—and to keep you working properly.

B lood is made up of a yellowish fluid called plasma mixed with different kinds of blood cells. Red blood cells are the ones that carry oxygen. The red color comes from a protein called hemoglobin, which is rich in iron. Iron and oxygen link up easily, which enables red blood cells to take oxygen from your lungs and carry it to your cells. Your blood travels through your body in tubes called blood vessels. This system of blood vessels that carries blood to and from your heart and through your body is called the circulatory system. Laid end to end, your blood vessels would circle the Earth two and a half times!

Veins deliver oxygen-poor blood from the body to the heart.

Arteries deliver oxygen-rich blood from the heart to the body.

The aorta, the biggest artery, branches into smaller arteries.

HEART

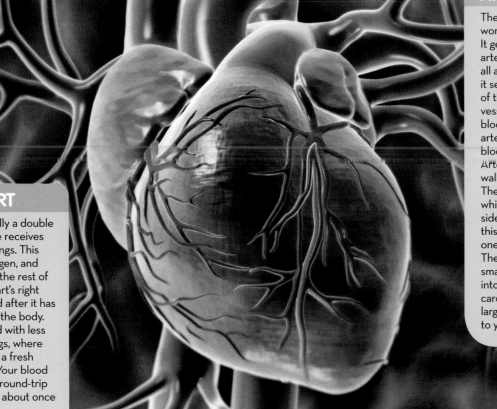

ARTERIES

The heart needs blood to work, just like any other organ. It gets blood from coronary arteries and veins, which twist all around its surface; in turn it sends blood out to the rest of the body. Veins are blood vessels that carry oxygen-poor blood to the heart, and most arteries carry oxygen-rich blood away from the heart. Arteries have strong, stretchy walls that contain muscles. The biggest artery is the aorta, which exits the heart's left side. Blood is pumped into this artery at a speed of nearly one mile an hour (1.6 km/h). The aorta branches into smaller arteries, which branch into even smaller arteries. The carotid arteries are a pair of large vessels that carry blood to your brain and face.

YOUR HEART

Your heart is actually a double pump. The left side receives blood from your lungs. This blood is rich in oxygen, and it's pumped out to the rest of your body. The heart's right side receives blood after it has circulated through the body. It pumps this blood with less oxygen to your lungs, where the blood picks up a fresh supply of oxygen. Your blood makes a complete round-trip through your body about once every minute.

WHITE
BLOOD CELL

PLATELET

RED BLOOD CELL

BLOOD SUPPLY

A blood cell makes about 250,000 round-trips in your body. Then it dies. A large organ called the liver helps rid your body of the dead blood cells. Meanwhile, your bone marrow is busy producing new blood cells—about two million every second! There are about five million red blood cells in just one drop of blood. Altogether, your blood is about 7 percent of your total body weight. Red blood cells make up about 45 percent of blood. Blood's other main cells are white blood cells, which fight disease. Platelets help form blood clots.

BLOOD PRESSURE

Blood pressure is the force pushing on blood vessels as blood flows through them. The force is highest when the heart beats fast. It's lower when the heart relaxes.

CAPILLARIES

Arteries get smaller and smaller until finally they become capillaries. A capillary is a blood vessel that's finer than a human hair, with a wall that is only one cell thick. A line-up of 3,000 red blood cells measures just an inch (2.5 cm). Yet these tiny cells can only fit through skinny capillaries one at a time! Capillaries are where oxygen, nutrients, and water seep out of the blood and into body cells. Waste material from cells also enters the bloodstream in capillaries. Finally, the capillaries link your arteries with blood vessels that are called veins.

GEEK STREAK

Bigger animals have slower heart rates than smaller animals. The average heart rate for a human at rest ranges from 60 to 100 beats per minute. A blue whale's car-size heart beats just 6 times per minute, while a mouse's tiny heart beats from 400 to 700 times per minute!

TRY THIS!

WHAT YOU NEED: Two fingers, your wrist, a timer

HOW LONG IT TAKES: A minute

You can feel your heartbeat in parts of your body where arteries run close to the skin. These spots are called pulse points. Gently place two fingers on the inside of your wrist to feel your pulse. Count the beats per minute. This is your resting heart rate.

UP CLOSE! ANCIENT MEDICINE

njuries and illnesses troubled people in ancient times just as they do now. Even prehistoric people tried to cure disease. Scientists have found neatly made holes in ancient skulls that are clues to early surgery. People in ancient times worked hard to find out what caused sickness and how to cure it, even though they had very limited medical knowledge and tools. Today, scientists and doctors have amazing tools, such as x-ray machines and CT scanners, to help them diagnose diseases and find cures. They benefit from knowledge that was gathered over hundreds of years by people in ancient times.

Egypt's Magic Spells

In the past, most people wrongly believed that magic and evil spirits played important roles in people's health. Researchers have found magic spells on ancient Egyptian scrolls (rolled-up sheets of paper made from a plant called papyrus). The spells of course didn't work!

Healing Honey

We know that ancient Egyptians also used everyday materials to take care of injuries and illness, because other ancient scrolls found by researchers contain instructions on how to care for injuries and damaged teeth. Doctors treated these problems even if they didn't always know why the remedies worked. For example, wounds were often covered with honey, which helped bandages stick and also seemed to speed healing. Today, we know honey contains ingredients that can kill some germs.

Call the Doctors in Greece

The ancient Greeks gave our knowledge of health a boost about 3,500 years ago. That's when a doctor named Hippocrates and his students began teaching that diseases were caused by problems in parts of the body, and were not punishments handed out by angry gods. Hippocrates used his senses to observe and study the human body and illnesses.

Top Docs

Hippocrates based his teachings on the work of an earlier Greek, Alcmaeon, who wrote about medicine and realized that our brains are where we think. Later, a Greek doctor named Dioscorides wrote five books filled with information about using plants and other materials as medicines (right).

Plant Medicine

Doctors in the Islamic world—countries in the Middle East—discovered new ways of practicing medicine. They used the medical texts of the Greeks and also came up with new treatments. They found ways to remove just the parts of plants that actually make medicines instead of simply mashing up an entire plant to give to a patient.

The First Hospitals

Islamic doctors created hospitals for treating patients, with strict rules for cleanliness. New doctors were trained in the hospitals. Hospital workers also kept careful records of patients' treatments. The earliest known Islamic hospital was in Baghdad, Iraq, about 1,200 years ago. The city had about 800 doctors. Islamic doctors did research in hospitals, too. In the 1200s, for example, an Arab doctor named Ibn al-Nafis figured out how blood circulated in the body. European doctors didn't know about the Islamic doctors' discoveries. It wasn't until 1628 that the English doctor William Harvey presented his own research on circulation. Islamic doctors also produced medical books that were later used in Europe.

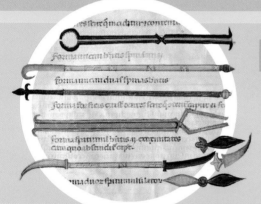

Early Surgery

Islamic doctors also found new ways to perform surgery. An Arab doctor named Abu al-Qasim al-Zahrawi wrote an encyclopedia about surgery and surgical tools, as well as the treatment for more than 300 diseases. He also explained the use of a material called "catgut" to make stitches in the body during an operation. Catgut, which is tough threads of material made from the intestines of sheep, cattle, and other mammals (but not cats!), dissolved naturally in the body after doing its job of holding the edges of wounds together. It was widely used until the mid-1900s, when it was replaced by synthetic materials in most countries.

Leonardo da Vinci's Human Body

Leonardo da Vinci (1452–1519) was an Italian artist and sculptor. One of his most famous paintings is the "Mona Lisa." But Leonardo is also famous for his scientific mind. He had a talent for designing machines and buildings. He also studied nature closely to see how it worked. This interest led Leonardo to study human anatomy. He turned his studies into detailed sketches. He drew human bones, muscles, and internal organs such as the heart and brain. He also drew the first scientifically accurate picture of the human spine. One of his collections of sketches is called "Anatomical Manuscript A" and contains more than 240 drawings, including the arms, chest, and neck.

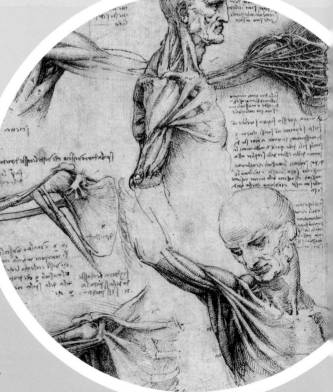

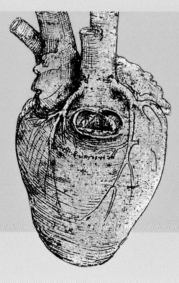

Leonardo's Heart

Today, scientists still marvel at Leonardo's drawings of anatomy. They compare them side by side with images taken by modern medical devices, which show just how accurate Leonardo's sketches are. His sketch of a heart even comes close to showing how it pumps—more than a century before scientists figured out this process. He drew four chambers in the heart at a time when people thought it had only two, and understood that the chambers worked in pairs. Leonardo even made a glass model of a cow's heart and pumped liquids through it to study their swirls and currents.

239

LUNGS AND BREATHING

Breathing brings air into a pair of organs in your chest called your lungs. Your body needs air because air contains oxygen, which cells use to break down sugars and produce energy.

Breathe in. Breathe out. Then repeat! You do this 20,000 times or more each day—and even more if you run, climb, swim, or otherwise get moving.

Air enters your body through your nose and mouth and flows down a tube called the windpipe. It's sucked into your lungs thanks to muscles in your ribs and a big muscle under your lungs called the diaphragm. These muscles contract, which makes your chest's interior expand and pulls in air. When these muscles relax, your chest's interior shrinks and air whooshes out of your lungs. Your lungs get rid of carbon dioxide, a waste product left over from the energy-making process.

But lungs aren't like balloons being filled up and emptied. They're spongy organs with a network of tubes running through them. They also have a lot of blood vessels, because blood picks up and transports oxygen to the body's cells.

UP THE NOSE

Air usually enters the nose, unless you're working hard and breathing through your mouth, too. The nose warms and moistens the air. It also works as an air filter. Sticky mucus traps dust, germs, and other things you don't want in your lungs. Tiny hairs called cilia wave and push mucus out of the nose and into the throat. Then the mucus is swallowed or coughed out. Sometimes particles tickle the inside of the nose and trigger an explosive sneeze. Your nose also contains cells that sense smells in the air you breathe. You often lose this sense temporarily when a cold makes your nose's lining swell up.

INTO THE PIPES

Air from your nose flows into your lungs through your windpipe, which is also called the trachea. This tube is up to six inches (15 cm) long in an adult. The trachea splits into two branches called bronchi. Each branch, called a bronchus, enters a lung, where it splits into smaller tubes called bronchioles. If you turn a picture of this system upside down, it looks like a tree, which is why it's called "the bronchial tree." If you laid out the bronchial tree in an average pair of lungs end to end, it would measure about 1,500 miles (2,414 km)!

TRACHEA

BRONCHIOLES

BRONCHUS

AIR BUBBLES

Hanging on the ends of the bronchial tree's smallest bronchioles are clusters of grapelike bubbles. These bubbles are called alveoli. Alveoli are microscopic balloons made of incredibly thin material just one cell thick. The walls of the tiny capillaries that wrap around them are just as thin. Their thinness allows oxygen to slip out of the alveoli into the blood, and allows carbon dioxide to leave the blood and enter the alveoli to be breathed out, or exhaled. If all the alveoli in an average pair of lungs were flattened out, they'd cover almost half of a tennis court. A baby starts life with up to 50 million alveoli. An adult's lungs contain 300 million to 500 million alveoli and sometimes even more.

IN THE AIR

The air you breathe is made up of many gases besides oxygen. Only about 21 percent is oxygen. Most of the air—about 78 percent—is nitrogen. The rest is made up of many different gases, including a small amount of carbon dioxide. The air you breathe out contains about 15 percent oxygen, because your body doesn't absorb all the oxygen in each breath. About 5 percent of the air breathed out is carbon dioxide. Your exhaled breath also contains water vapor from inside your warm, moist lungs. This gas turns into a liquid when it hits cold air, and you can "see your breath."

AIR HEAD!

Your brain sends signals to your muscles to make you breathe regularly so you don't even have to think about breathing. It also keeps track of how much carbon dioxide is in your blood. If the carbon dioxide level gets too high, your brain automatically triggers you to breathe. But your body needs some carbon dioxide in your blood to work properly. That's why a frightened person who breathes super quickly and loses too much carbon dioxide may be told to breathe into a paper bag. The bag holds carbon dioxide from the person's breath. Then the person breathes the carbon dioxide back in, helping the level go back to normal. A yawn is an extra-deep breath inhaled through a wide-open mouth. Scientists don't yet know why we yawn.

TOOLS OF THE TRADE

At a checkup, your doctor may clamp a probe on your finger to measure your blood's oxygen level. The probe senses the difference in color between bright, oxygen-rich blood in arteries and darker, oxygen-poor blood in veins. It's a quick way to see how well your respiratory system is working.

PERSONALITY PLUS

In 2015, Professor Daniela Riccardi and a team of scientists in England and the United States revealed a new discovery about the lung disease called asthma. Asthma causes a person's bronchial tubes to swell up, making breathing difficult. Riccardi's team found sensors in a person's airways that react when dust or pollen irritate lungs. This discovery may lead to new, better medicines for controlling asthma.

FUELING YOUR BODY

Digestion is the breaking down of nutrients in food, such as proteins, fats, and carbohydrates, into simple substances that your body can use for energy, growth, and repair.

Chomp! You bite into a sandwich. Your teeth munch, crunch, and mash the food. With that one bite, you're starting the process of digestion.

Food travels through your body in the digestive system. By the time you're an adult, your digestive tract is about 30 feet (9 m) long. Along this route, your sandwich is turned into mush. Enzymes are added to break nutrients into bits your body can absorb. Your blood then carries the nutrients to your cells. The cells use some nutrients to produce energy. Other nutrients become building blocks for new cells and tissues.

How long this journey takes depends on what you eat. Fruits and vegetables, for example, are digested more quickly than meat. A meal usually takes a day or two to digest. Anything that can't be digested is pushed out of the body as waste called feces, or poop.

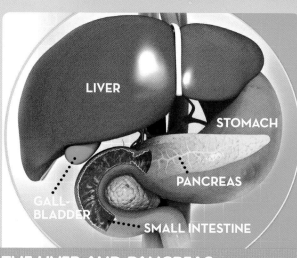

THE LIVER AND PANCREAS

The liver is a big, rubbery organ near your stomach. It tackles many jobs, such as processing nutrients for their next uses, storing extra sugars, getting rid of worn-out blood cells, and making a fat-dissolving digestive fluid called bile. Bile is stored in a sac called the gallbladder, which empties into the small intestine. Meanwhile, the sausage-shaped pancreas makes enzymes that digest carbohydrates, proteins, and fats. They flow into the small intestine, too. Unlike most of our organs, the liver has the rare ability to grow back if damaged by disease or injury. A piece of the liver transplanted into the body grows to full size in just three weeks.

INTO THE STOMACH

The esophagus leads to your stomach, which is a stretchy, muscular pouch. It squeezes the food, churning and mixing it into a thick soup called chyme. Glands in the stomach's wall add digestive juices that start breaking down fats and proteins. Other enzymes continue to break down carbohydrates. The stomach also produces a strong acid, which helps digest protein and also kills germs. A layer of mucus protects the stomach wall from the acid. Its wall absorbs some substances, such as water, simple sugars, and medicines such as aspirin.

DOWN IN THE MOUTH

Teeth turn your food into a mushy blob you can swallow. Sharp front teeth slice the food while bumpy teeth on the sides grind it. The tongue tastes food and moves it around. Glands in your cheeks and jaw and under your tongue produce saliva, or spit. Your salivary glands can start making spit just by you smelling food! You produce up to six cups (1.5 L) of saliva a day—nearly enough to fill a big soda-pop bottle. Saliva moistens the food and also contains enzymes that start digesting it. When you swallow, food leaves your mouth and is pushed down a tube in your throat called the esophagus.

WORD CHECK

MICROBIOME: All the microorganisms, usually referring to bacteria, in a human body. "Micro" means "small," and "biome" is a place where organisms live.

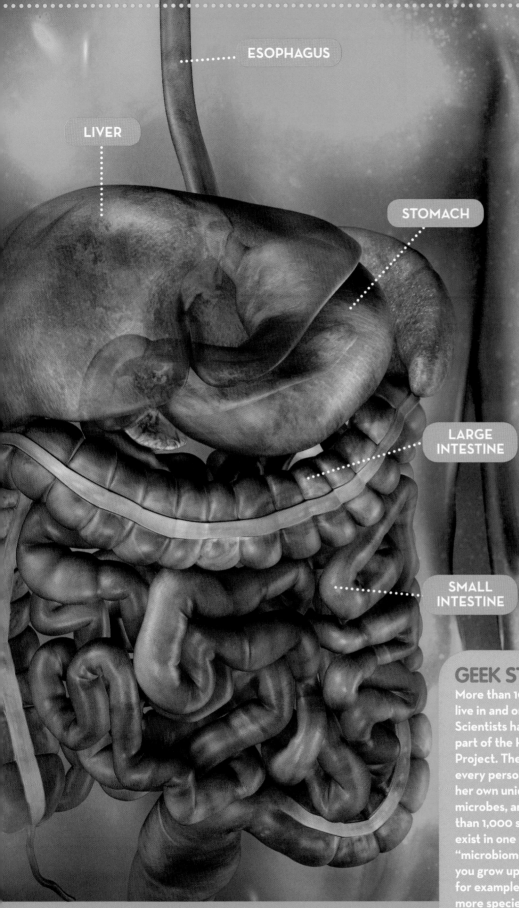

ESOPHAGUS

LIVER

STOMACH

LARGE
INTESTINE

SMALL
INTESTINE

NEXT STOP:
SMALL INTESTINE

Chyme from the stomach is squeezed into the small intestine. This "small" organ is a muscular tube about 10 feet (3 m) long in an adult—and up to 21 feet (6.5 m) long if stretched! It produces enzymes that continue digestion. A meal spends three to five hours being digested in your small intestine. Muscular contractions push it on its way and slosh it around. Nutrients from the food are absorbed by the millions of finger-like bumps, called villi, that cover the small intestine's walls. This organ also receives digestive juices from the liver.

THE LARGE INTESTINE

By the time a meal reaches the large intestine, most of its nutrients have been absorbed. But it still contains water, which is soaked up by this organ. The large intestine is wider than the small intestine, but it's only about 5 feet (1.5 m) long. It's divided into three sections called the cecum, colon, and rectum. The large intestine is also filled with trillions of microbes. They break down tough material, such as fiber, and any remaining proteins. They also make B vitamins and vitamin K. At the end of the large intestine, anything left over is stored as feces, which are emptied from the body.

GEEK STREAK

More than 100 trillion microbes live in and on the human body. Scientists have studied them as part of the Human Microbiome Project. They've found that every person has his or her own unique mix of microbes, and that more than 1,000 species may exist in one person. Your "microbiome" also changes as you grow up. Younger people, for example, are home to more species of microbes than elderly people.

PERSONALITY PLUS

Ivan Pavlov (1849–1936) was a Russian surgeon and scientist who studied the digestive system. He showed how nerves, behaviors, sights, sounds, and smells were affected when digestive juices flowed out of glands, and how much juice was made. He won the Nobel Prize for physiology and medicine in 1904.

GOOD NUTRITION

Nutrition is a combination of the foods you eat and the nutrients they become in your body. A plate of salad, a glass of milk, and a taco are filled with nutrients, but your body can't use them until you digest the food. Digestion breaks complex molecules in food into nutrients that can be absorbed by your blood and carried to cells.

Getting good nutrition means eating foods rich in nutrients. Different foods contain different amounts of nutrients, so it's important to eat a variety of foods, too. Scientists have studied what's in food and which foods keep people in good health. This knowledge has been used to help people figure out how to eat a nutritious, balanced diet. Scientists have found that fruits and vegetables should make up half of your daily food. The other half should be divided between proteins, such as eggs, fish, or meat, and grains, with a small amount of dairy products.

PROTEINS

Your hair, skin, muscles, red blood cells, and other body parts—right down to the tiny organelles in your cells—are made mostly of protein. Protein is the main building material in your body. During digestion, enzymes break protein in food into smaller parts called amino acids. (The enzymes themselves are made of protein.) Protein supplies energy, as well as vitamins and minerals such as iron. Your body can make some amino acids but must get the rest from food. Eggs, fish, chicken, meat, and milk products contain lots of protein. So do nuts, seeds, and beans.

FATS

Fats are made of molecules called fatty acids. Some fats, such as butter, are solid at room temperature. Fats that are liquid at room temperature are called oils. Scientists call them both "lipids." In your digestive system, enzymes start breaking down lipids in your mouth and finish the job in the small intestine. Your body uses lipids to build the "wrappers," or membranes, around cells and the coverings of nerve cells. Extra lipids are stored as fat that can be used later for energy. You need only small amounts of fat in a balanced diet. Good sources include fish, nuts, and cooking oils such as olive oil and canola oil.

CARBOHYDRATES

Rice, potatoes, and wheat contain lots of starch. Starch is a complex carbohydrate, meaning it is made up of sugar molecules strung together in long, complex chains. Foods with complex carbohydrates, like whole wheat bread, provide vitamins, minerals, fibers, and some protein. Complex carbohydrates help build cells and tissues. Digestive enzymes break down complex carbohydrates into simple carbohydrates. These are natural sugars, such as glucose, and they are what make foods such as berries taste sweet. Glucose is used by cells in chemical reactions that release energy.

"EMPTY" CALORIES

Potato chips, cake, candy, soda, and other snacks are often called "junk food." That's because they contain lots of energy in the form of calories, but not many nutrients. Calories in junk food come mainly from solid fats, such as butter, and added sugars. You can find out what's in a food by reading its nutrition label. A healthy diet can include a little junk food, but it shouldn't take the place of nutrient-rich foods. You can make easy switches to replace "empty" calories with nutrient-rich calories, such as eating unsweetened applesauce instead of applesauce with added sugar.

GEEK STREAK

It takes two enzymes to turn starch into simple sugar in your body. The first is amylase. It's found in spit and also in juices made by your pancreas. Amylase turns starch into a sugar called maltose. But maltose is still too big to be absorbed into your blood. So a second enzyme, maltase, splits each maltose molecule into two molecules of a sugar called glucose.

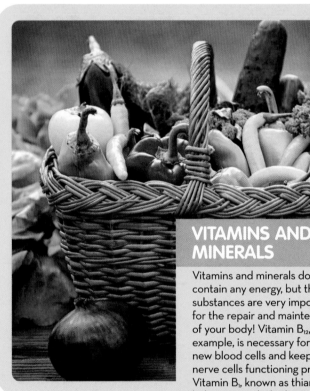

VITAMINS AND MINERALS

Vitamins and minerals don't contain any energy, but these substances are very important for the repair and maintenance of your body! Vitamin B_{12}, for example, is necessary for making new blood cells and keeping nerve cells functioning properly. Vitamin B_1, known as thiamine, helps turn carbohydrates into energy. The mineral calcium, found in milk and dark green vegetables, keeps bones and teeth strong. The mineral iron gives red blood cells the ability to carry oxygen. Carrots, kale, and other bright orange or dark green vegetables and fruits contain lots of vitamin A, which keeps your skin and eyes healthy.

WORD CHECK

LIPID: A fatty, waxy, or oily chemical compound that comes from a living thing and doesn't dissolve in water

TRY THIS!

WHAT YOU NEED: A cup of water, a spoonful of vegetable oil, a few drops of dish soap

HOW LONG IT TAKES: 5 minutes

Your body can't digest fats and oils until they've first been broken into microscopic drops. Bile from your liver does this job. Then enzymes work on the droplets. You can imitate bile's action by mixing a spoonful of vegetable oil in a cup of water. They won't stay mixed if you stir them, but the oil will blend in if you add a few drops of dish soap.

PERSONALITY PLUS

James Lind (1716–1794) was a British doctor. In his time, sailors often suffered from a disease called scurvy, which made them tired and weak and caused their gums to bleed. Lind noticed that sick sailors recovered from scurvy after they ate oranges and lemons. By 1795, the British navy started bringing fruits and juice on long voyages to prevent this sickness. It wasn't until 1928 that scientists discovered vitamin C, which is plentiful in oranges and lemons.

UP CLOSE! THE GENE SCENE

What color are your eyes? Is your hair curly or straight? How tall are you? Basically everything you can see in the mirror—as well as your invisible insides—is the product of a long, skinny molecule called DNA. DNA stands for "deoxyribonucleic acid" and is found in nearly every cell in your body. It is shaped like a ladder that twists around and around to form a spiral and holds instructions— passed from parents to child—that make each human being different.

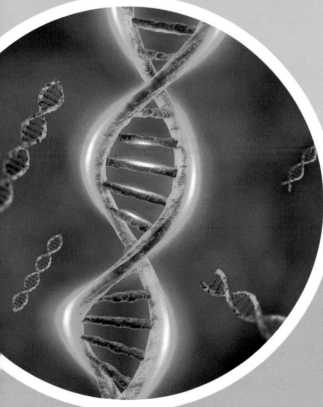

DNA Up Close

DNA is made up of smaller molecules called nucleotides. Each nucleotide is also made up of three smaller molecules. One molecule is a sugar. The second is a phosphate—a molecule made up of the elements oxygen and phosphorus. The third molecule is a base that contains nitrogen. There are just four kinds of bases. They link together in pairs to make the "rungs" of the DNA ladder, while the sugars and phosphates form the sides.

If you could remove all the DNA in just one of your cells and iron it flat, it would measure more than six feet (2 m) long. How does something that long fit in a tiny cell? For one thing, it scrunches up very tightly, like kite string wrapped around a handle. Plus, your DNA is chopped up into smaller lengths called chromosomes. Each chromosome is made of protein and contains a single DNA molecule. You have a total of 46 chromosomes in nearly every cell. They're bundled into 23 pairs.

Genes Are Geniuses!

Each of your 46 chromosomes is divided into smaller sections called genes. Genes contain instructions that control the building, growing, and functioning of your body. Every gene holds a "recipe" for making a particular molecule of protein. Scientists have found that humans have about 20,500 genes.

Many scientists who study genes try to figure out what jobs those genes do. One gene, for example, is known to make a protein that helps develop nerves, muscles, and bones. Another gene is the plan for making a hormone called insulin. Insulin helps people control how much sugar is in their blood.

Your Genome = You!

Your personal collection of genes is your "genome." It's a recipe for you! That recipe is one of a kind (even if you have an identical twin). But you also share more than 99 percent of your genome with other humans. The human genome, after all, contains lots of basic instructions for making an organism become a human instead of a jellyfish or a lion, as well as instructions that make brain cells, muscle cells, and more. But that small bit—less than one percent—makes a big difference. It's what makes each human an individual.

Human Code

In 1990, scientists began work on a project to "spell out" the entire human genome. This project involved slicing strands of human DNA into very small pieces. The pieces were placed in a jellylike substance. Then electricity was sent through this material, which caused the DNA to spread and separate so its transverse bands (its "rungs" made out of bases) could be seen. Scientists, with the help of computers, carefully figured out the order of the rungs and what base pairs they contained. This process is called "sequencing." It produced a lot of data: The human genome contains about three billion base pairs!

The Human Genome Project finished in 2003. Scientists now use this "map" of the genome to find out more about DNA and human diseases. Scientists have also decoded other genomes, including those of chimpanzees, bonobos, and gorillas. They've discovered that humans share about 99 percent of their DNA with chimps and bonobos, and about 98 percent with gorillas.

On the Trail of DNA

Many scientists have worked to crack the code of the human genome. The journey began with figuring out the structure of DNA. Here are a few of the scientists who paved the way.

■ **Rosalind Franklin** (1920–1958) was a British scientist who used x-rays to photograph DNA. Her photos showed a DNA molecule's shape for the first time. The image made it possible for other scientists to work out the structure of DNA.

■ American scientist **James Watson** (1928–) and English scientist **Francis Crick** (1916–2004) figured out that DNA was shaped like a twisting ladder. They called the shape a "double helix." They showed how either helix could be used as a blueprint to make the other helix. This was an important discovery that showed how DNA made copies of itself. They won the Nobel Prize for Physiology or Medicine in 1962 for their work.

■ American scientist **Francis Collins** (1950–) directed the Human Genome Project. He has made important discoveries in finding genes that cause diseases such as cystic fibrosis, which harms the lungs and other internal organs. Understanding genes that cause diseases or make people more likely to get them will help scientists find ways to prevent or fight these diseases.

■ American scientist **J. Craig Venter** (1946–) discovered a new, faster way to locate genes on chromosomes. In 1995, he and his team of scientists were also the first to sequence the genes of a free-living microbe. (Before that, the only organisms that were sequenced were germs that existed in other organisms.) Venter also led a project to sequence human genes alongside the Human Genome Project.

REPRODUCTION AND GROWTH

Your genome is one of a kind—but it's created from two other genomes. Those genomes belong to two people: your parents. Half of your 46 chromosomes come from your mother. The other 23 chromosomes come from your father.

A brand-new cell containing these 46 chromosomes has to divide to create two new cells. The DNA inside it has to copy itself so that the new cells have chromosomes, too. DNA copies itself by "unzipping," which makes it look like a ladder split in half right down through all the rungs. Every pair of nucleotides is separated.

Each half of a nucleotide contains one of the four bases. The bases' names are symbolized by letters: A (adenine), T (thymine), C (cytosine), and G (guanine). Each base matches up only with one other kind. A always pairs up with T, and C always pairs up with G. They fit together like keys in locks.

The two halves of an unzipped DNA molecule can make their other halves. Enzymes help bring new nucleotides to match up along the entire length of the two halves—and ta-da, there are two double helixes where there was just one before!

DNA, MEET RNA

A DNA molecule contains codes for proteins, but it needs help to actually make proteins. That's where RNA comes in. RNA stands for ribonucleic acid. The first copy of a portion of DNA is actually a strand of RNA. This RNA is a "messenger" that travels out of the nucleus. The messenger RNA's information is then used to make the new proteins. These new proteins are put together in cell parts called ribosomes.

ADENINE (A)

CYTOSINE (C)

GUANINE (G)

THYMINE (T)

THE FOUR BASES

The four bases that form DNA's nucleotides are A, C, G, and T. These four letters form the "words" that are genes. Every word tells how to make one kind of protein. All the genes are copied when a new cell divides to form more new cells. Cells in your body that are already functioning as special cells—such as nerve cells, or skin cells—can make only the proteins they need by unzipping and copying just a small section of a chromosome. Human protein-making genes range in length from just 500 letters to as many as 2.3 million letters. Most human genes are about 3,000 letters long.

WORD CHECK

PUBERTY: The growth that happens during the teenage years that turns children into adults

MESSENGER RNA

CELL NUCLEUS

X AND Y

"Boy or girl?" is often the first question people ask when a baby is born. Out of a baby's 23 pairs of chromosomes, 22 pairs are the same in both boys and girls. But pair 23 is different. In a girl, pair 23 is made up of two X chromosomes. Two X chromosomes together carry genes that determine female traits. A boy, however, has one X chromosome and one Y chromosome. Even though it's paired with an X chromosome, the Y chromosome contains genes that produce male traits.

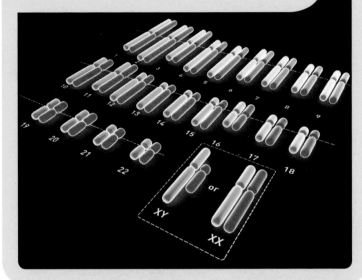

LOL!

Q: What's a chromosome's favorite item of clothing?

A: A pair of genes!

CHEMICAL MESSAGES

A human's growth from one cell to trillions of cells is an amazing process. Some of that growth is controlled by hormones, which are chemicals produced in the body. Your pituitary gland, for example, is a pea-size organ that sits under your brain near the nose. It produces many hormones, including a growth hormone that makes children get taller as they get older. The pituitary gland also signals other organs in the body to make hormones, such as the ones that start puberty in teenagers. Hormones cause girls' and boys' bodies to grow and change rapidly between the ages of about 10 to 15. Genes that exist at birth trigger the pituitary gland to start this process.

OLDER AND OLDER

Humans continue to change as they grow older. Scientists are studying aging to find out just why the body tends to become weaker as it ages. It was long thought that aging happened because of wear and tear on the body. Today, scientists are studying genes for clues about aging. Our DNA may become damaged over time, causing aging. Another theory is that cells can divide only a certain number of times to make new cells.

GEEK STREAK

Chromosomes are protected at each end by DNA strings called telomeres. Telomeres keep chromosome ends from fraying and losing genetic information. Telomeres grow shorter each time a cell divides. Scientists are studying telomeres for clues to aging.

PERSONALITY PLUS

Dr. Anne Brunet leads a team of scientists at Stanford University in California, U.S.A., who study genes. They are researching a new field called epigenetics. This is the study of how living things sometimes inherit traits that are not "coded" in their genes. Instead, these traits seem to be linked to chemicals that help control how genes are turned on and off, or "expressed," in the body.

FIGHTING DISEASE

The immune system protects your body against viruses, bacteria, and other germs. If germs do make you sick, your immune system attacks them. It can even create special forces to fight specific germs.

Your body is great at running, repairing, and refueling itself. But even the healthiest body gets sick sometimes. That's when your immune system steps in to get you back on track. Your skin is your first line of defense. One of its jobs is to keep out germs in the first place. Its tough outer layer is like a brick wall, and it also produces oil that makes its surface slightly acidic, which repels germs. The linings of your nose and internal organs ooze sticky, acidic mucus that stops germs. Even tears and saliva contain chemicals that kill germs.

Germs that get past these barriers are attacked by your immune system. Among the first responders are your white blood cells. They travel in your blood, where they surround and gobble up any germs. The immune system is quick to identify proteins that aren't part of your body and attack them.

ANTIBODIES

Your body kills many germs before they have a chance to cause harm. But sometimes, new germs that your body's never met before make you sick before your immune system figures out how to resist them. That's when blood cells called lymphocytes spring into action. They "tag" the germs and destroy them, which starts your recovery. Just as important, they leave behind proteins called antibodies. These antibodies will recognize the germs quickly next time and attack them immediately. Cells in your bone marrow produce millions of lympho-cytes every minute. The lymphocytes travel throughout your body to seek out and destroy germs.

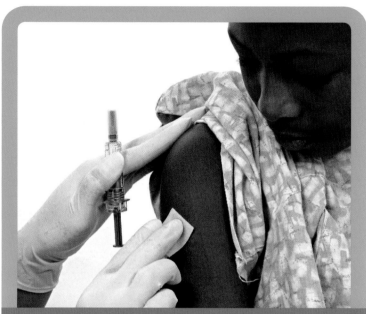

GETTING A SHOT

Some diseases can be largely prevented by getting a "shot," or dose of vaccine. A vaccine is made out of weakened or dead disease-causing organisms. It's injected into the body, where your immune system reacts to it by producing antibodies. If your body ever gets infected by the actual microbes that cause disease, the antibodies recognize them and alert your immune system to fight them right away. Babies naturally get many antibodies from their mothers. Later, vaccines from the doctor help protect them against diseases such as polio, measles, and mumps.

GEEK STREAK

Gene therapy offers a possible way to treat genetic diseases that happen when genes aren't working as they should (see opposite). It involves putting new genes into a person's cells to replace the mutated ones causing a disease. Cystic fibrosis, for example, is a genetic disease that causes a patient's lungs to fill up with thick, sticky mucus. In 2012 and 2013, some patients who inhaled a dose of DNA molecules containing normal genes found their lungs worked slightly better. Scientists are experimenting with gene therapy for this disease and many others.

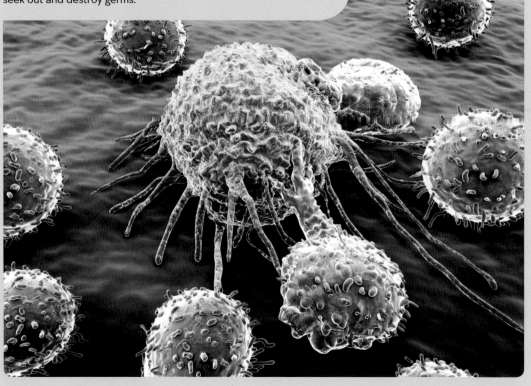

GENETIC DISEASES

A genetic disease is caused by one or more genes that don't work as they should because a person's DNA was changed or copied improperly. This change is called a mutation. Mutations can happen on their own or be caused by forces such as x-rays. The mutation is passed along to offspring. Diabetes can be caused by a mutation on chromosome number 5. It affects levels of sugar in the blood. People with diabetes help control their disease by choosing foods carefully. Sometimes a mutation on a chromosome from one parent is balanced out by a healthy chromosome from the other, so the child carries genes for the disease but doesn't suffer from it.

TOOLS OF THE TRADE

Some vaccines can be sprayed into the nose. A few are swallowed. But most vaccines are injected into the body. The vaccine is delivered through a needle attached to a pump and tube called a syringe. Researchers are developing a new needle-free shot called a jet injector. This device forces the liquid inside it to flow right through the skin without a needle's help.

COLDS AND "THE FLU"

Achoo! Why isn't there a single vaccine for the common cold? Because colds can be caused by more than 200 different viruses. A virus is a microscopic organism that invades living cells and causes infection. A vaccine against one cold virus would not stop a cold caused by another virus. However, there are vaccines that help prevent influenza, or "the flu," which attacks the respiratory system. The flu is caused by fewer viruses. They change over time, however, so people need a new shot every year. Resting and drinking lots of fluids helps patients recover from the flu and keeps them from growing weaker.

EBOLA

In 2014, a terrible, rare disease called Ebola swept across parts of Africa, killing more than 11,000 people. Ebola is caused by a virus and kills many of its victims, who suffer fever, muscle pain, rashes, stomach sickness, and bleeding. The virus was first discovered in 1976. It can be caught from infected fruit bats and apes and then spread from person to person. Lack of medical supplies and staff in some countries made it difficult to care for patients in the 2014 outbreak, though doctors and nurses came from around the world to help. Scientists are currently testing two vaccines to prevent Ebola.

PERSONALITY PLUS

Scottish scientist Sir Alexander Fleming (1881–1955) discovered the powerful germ-killing substance called penicillin in 1928. The "aha!" moment occurred when he saw penicillin mold growing on a plate of bacteria and noticed it killed the germs. Penicillin was one of the first antibiotics and is still used today.

PLANET EARTH

OUR LIFE-GIVING WORLD

From its burning hot core to the chilly darkness of its upper atmosphere, planet Earth is the ultimate recycler. It pulls its rocks—even its continents—deep into the superhot center of the planet, reshapes them, and returns them to the surface. It cycles its water through oceans, air, and rivers in an endless loop. Its plants and animals take in and release the air we breathe. Heat from the sun, plus heat from inside Earth, provides the energy to keep these cycles going for billions of years.

Our planet stays in restless motion because it's not a solid ball of rock. Like a (really big) peach, Earth has a solid center; a thick, soft middle; and a thin skin.

At Earth's very center is its inner core. Made of solid iron and nickel, the inner core is heated to a blistering 9000°F (5000°C). It doesn't melt, though, because it's compressed by the weight of the planet all around it.

Surrounding the inner core is the outer core. This, too, is mostly iron and nickel, and very hot. Its rock is liquid because it's not under as much pressure as the inner core.

Around the outer core is the mantle. It is the thickest part of Earth, about 1,800 miles (2,900 km) deep. The mantle is solid rock, but so hot that it flows like a thick, gummy liquid.

Earth's rocky, breakable crust rides on top of the mantle. At its bottom is a slippery layer called the asthenosphere. Over millions of years, continents slide around on the asthenosphere, smashing into each other and pulling apart. This movement causes mountains to rise, earthquakes to rumble, and volcanoes to spew out hot rock that has melted in the motion.

Earth doesn't stop at its surface. The atmosphere covers it like a misty cloak. Its lowest layer is the moist, windy air that humans breathe that extends hundreds of miles into space.

Living on the boundary between rock and sky are all the plants and animals that make up Earth's biosphere. This interconnected system of life is as much a part of Earth as its mountains and oceans.

In this chapter, you'll see what shapes our lands and seas. You'll find out about Earth's ancient history and the dinosaurs that once lived here. You'll learn about threats to the planet's oceans and air—and how to deal with them. You'll see how our planet is a unique, active, life-giving world.

Did you know? Earth's rapid rotation and its iron-nickel core create a powerful magnetic field. Like a shield, the field protects Earth from solar winds, which can cause electrical failures.

The Stromboli volcano, on an island in Italy, is one of the most active volcanoes on Earth. It has been continuously erupting for more than 2,000 years! Because its jets of lava can be seen for great distances at night, it's called the "Lighthouse of the Mediterranean."

EARTH ON THE MOVE

Earth is an active planet. Pieces of its surface slide slowly around like giant plates. At their edges, mountains rise up and valleys break open. Earthquakes ripple through the ground and volcanoes erupt. This powerful process of plate motion, known as plate tectonics, shapes Earth.

Earth's thin, rocky surface, the lithosphere, is broken into 12 major plates and several minor ones. The plates float on top of the mantle, which is rock so hot that it flows slowly, like a very thick liquid. Heat from inside Earth rolls through the mantle and pushes the plates from underneath like a conveyor belt.

Some plates are thousands of miles wide. Others are just a few hundred miles across. They carry continents and ocean floor. The North American plate, for instance, holds most of the North American continent and part of the Atlantic Ocean. Plates move slowly, just a few inches a year, about as fast as your fingernails grow. Over time, though, that adds up. Throughout Earth's history, landmasses have traveled all over the planet, meeting up and moving apart in a great dance of continents.

MATCHING FOSSILS

How do we know that the continents fit together like a puzzle, long ago? Rocks give us one clue: The same kinds of rocks are found along the matching edges of North America, Greenland, and Europe, for instance. Fossils provide another clue. The prehistoric fern *Glossopteris* (below) is found across South America, Africa, Antarctica, and Australia, lands now separated by oceans. Fossils of *Mesosaurus*, an early reptile, link southern South America and southern Africa.

PANGAEA

About 225 million years ago, most of the land on Earth was smooshed together into one landmass we call Pangaea (from the Greek words for "all lands"). On this supercontinent, the lands that later became North America, Europe, South America, Africa, Eurasia, Australia, and Antarctica were all snuggled together. As years went by and plates shifted, Pangaea broke apart. Its landmasses moved north and south, east and west. But if you look at the coasts of South America and Africa, you can still see where the old pieces fit together.

TOOLS OF THE TRADE

Scientists can go to sea to spot plate movements. They tow a device called a magnetometer behind their ship. This measures magnetism in the rocks of the seafloor around plate edges. Magnetic patterns in the rocks show the scientists how the seafloor is spreading over time.

WORD CHECK

TECTONICS: From the Greek word *tekton*, meaning "builder." Plate tectonics build the planet, raising up mountains and carving out oceans through the movement of Earth's plates.

PULLING APART

When two plates move apart, the widening crack between them is known as a divergent boundary. Melted rock rises up through the crack and cools to form new land. Both the Atlantic and the South Pacific Oceans have divergent boundaries down their middles. New ocean floor is being created in their rifts, or cracks. Sometimes plates pull apart under landmasses, too. Then the ground splits open in a rift valley on top of Earth, like this one.

SCRAPING PAST

Sometimes plates don't pull apart or smash together, but scrape past each other in different directions. Their meeting place is called a transform boundary. The rough, scraping movement creates cracks and ridges in the land around it. Sometimes pressure builds up and releases along a transform boundary, triggering an earthquake. California's famous San Andreas Fault (below) marks one such boundary, where the North American plate moves south and the Pacific plate moves north.

LOL!

Q: What did the ground say to the earthquake?

A: You crack me up.

PUSHING TOGETHER

When two plates press into each other, their meeting place is known as a convergent boundary. If an ocean plate meets a continental plate, the heavier ocean plate usually slides under the edge of the continent. If two continental plates meet, often they just crumple up, creating mountain ranges. The powerful forces involved when plate smashes into plate can give rise to volcanoes or earthquakes.

GEEK STREAK

The city of San Francisco sits mainly on the North American plate, which is moving south. Los Angeles sits mainly on the Pacific plate, which is moving north. In about 10 million years the two cities (if they still exist!) will meet up.

THE OCEAN FLOOR

The ocean floor is a place of huge mountains, steep canyons, rumbling volcanoes, and wide, flat plains. The ocean's deep water hides the world's longest mountain range and even the tallest mountain.

Scientists started to closely study the ocean floor less than 200 years ago. In 1872, a ship called the H.M.S. *Challenger* set sail from England. The crew's mission was to collect information about the ocean, including the mysterious, deep ocean floor. The scientists aboard *Challenger* dropped long lines, nets, and other devices into the ocean to collect samples from the ocean floor. They hauled up strange deep-sea fish as well as rocks and mud. They measured how deep the floor was. Among their discoveries was the deepest trench on Earth: Mariana Trench. In 1875, they recorded a depth of 26,850 feet (8,184 m) along the trench, but still did not reach its deepest part. Since that time, new technology has helped reveal the world hidden beneath the waves. Submersibles and remote-control cameras give scientists a close-up view. Satellites help create oceanwide maps.

ATLANTIC OCEAN FLOOR

MID-OCEAN RIDGES

The world's longest chain of mountains runs across the ocean floor. It's the mid-ocean ridge, a series of mountain ranges that wind around the world like the seam on a baseball. Added up, they span about 40,390 miles (65,000 km). A mid-ocean ridge forms in places where the ocean floor splits apart, with each side moving in opposite directions. Hot, melted rock underground flows up to fill the space. This process is called seafloor spreading.

CONTINENTAL DRIFT

The ocean basins formed as a result of continental drift (see page 254). Today, the Atlantic Ocean and the Arctic Ocean are slowly growing wider while the Pacific Ocean's basin shrinks. In the Indian Ocean, scientists have detected earthquakes possibly caused by a plate breaking up.

PERSONALITY PLUS

Jacques Piccard (1922–2008) and Don Walsh (1931–) were the first people to visit Earth's deepest spot: the Challenger Deep in the Pacific's Mariana Trench. The two scientists sank to the bottom in a bathyscaphe, a type of submarine. It took about five hours to complete the downward journey of 35,814 feet (10,916 m). Film director James Cameron also visited Challenger Deep in a specially designed submersible in 2012.

TRENCHES

Plates don't always slip smoothly past each other as they travel. Their edges can get stuck, and often grind against each other. This rough motion causes earthquakes. An oceanic plate can also slide under another plate in a process called subduction. In some parts of the world, oceanic plates slide under continental plates. This subduction creates a deep canyon, called a trench, in the ocean's floor. The mantle above a subduction zone melts in some places and forms molten rock, called magma. This magma creates volcanoes on the continent next to a trench.

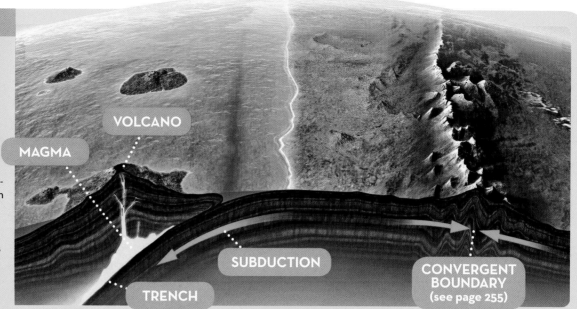

MAGMA

VOLCANO

SUBDUCTION

TRENCH

CONVERGENT BOUNDARY (see page 255)

HOT SPOTS

The Hawaiian Islands were formed by a hot spot in the Pacific Ocean floor. Hot spots are deep wells of magma that sit in some parts of the ocean floor, far from the mid-ocean ridge. A hot spot erupts over and over again over long spans of time. The lava piles up and forms a mountain. This mountain can grow tall enough to rise above the waves and form an island. A chain of islands may form over millions of years as the ocean plate slowly passes over the erupting hot spot. Volcanoes still erupt on some Hawaiian islands. The hot spot is now busy building a new undersea volcano in the chain.

GEEK STREAK

Earth's tallest mountain is Mauna Kea, a volcano that forms part of Hawaii's "Big Island." Mauna Kea's base is on the seafloor, but its peak is in the clouds, measuring 13,796 feet (4,205 m) above sea level! From top to bottom, it's 32,696 feet (9,966 m) tall—about 0.7 miles (1.1 km) taller than Mount Everest, the tallest mountain on land.

WORD CHECK

HYDROTHERMAL: Having to do with hot water. "Hydro" means "water," and "therm" means "heat."

HYDROTHERMAL VENTS

In 1977, scientists exploring in the Pacific Ocean discovered a weird world where superhot water shot from cracks in the ocean floor. Minerals in the jets of water made them look like clouds of smoke. The water was heated by magma under the floor. Bacteria living around these "hydrothermal vents" used energy from chemicals in the water to make food, much as plants use energy from the sun. Tubeworms living around the vents contain billions of bacteria in their bodies. They get nutrients from food made by the bacteria. Fish, crabs, and octopuses that have adapted to the depths survive by eating other vent creatures.

TOOLS OF THE TRADE

An echo sounder is a device on a ship's underside used to measure distance underwater. It gives off sound waves. Then it receives the echoes that bounce back from the ocean floor. This method is called sonar, which stands for "sound navigation and ranging." A scientist uses data, such as how long it took to hear an echo, to figure out the distance. The information can be used to map the ocean floor.

257

VOLCANOES

As you read this, 10 volcanoes are erupting around Earth. Any landform that sends out lava, ashes, or gas—whether it's a mountain or a sunken crater—is a volcano. Volcanoes play an important part in recycling rock and building new soil. They can also wipe out human life in the blink of an eye.

Volcanoes appear when magma, hot melted rock from Earth's mantle, rises up through a crack or vent in Earth's crust. This often happens at the edges of tectonic plates. Where two plates pull apart, magma usually bubbles up peacefully. More violent volcanoes arise where two plates collide. We can see this around the edges of the Pacific Ocean. Thousands of volcanoes line the coasts of North and South America, Japan, and Indonesia, where plates meet. This volcanic zone is known as the "Ring of Fire." Sometimes volcanoes also pop up over hot spots, places where plumes of magma punch through the middle of a plate like a hot needle.

RIVERS OF LAVA, CLOUDS OF ASH

Some eruptions release red-hot, glowing rivers of lava. The lava can spray up from the vent like a fountain before running down the slopes of the volcano. As it cools, it turns into solid rock. More dangerous than lava flows are explosive eruptions of gas, rock, and ash. These pyroclastic ("fiery fragment") eruptions can blow the entire side off a mountain. Superheated gas and rock fly away at hundreds of miles an hour, burning and burying everything in their path.

MAGMA AND LAVA

Magma causes explosive eruptions because bubbles of hot gas, such as water vapor, are trapped in it. As magma rises up through the crust, the gas expands. The foamy magma can erupt suddenly from a vent like soda from a shaken soda bottle—only far more destructive and powerful. Once magma reaches the surface, it gains a new name: lava.

SHIELD VOLCANOES

Built up by layers of lava, shield volcanoes are big, wide, and low. They look like a warrior's shield resting on the ground. Some of the world's most famous shield volcanoes are in the Hawaiian Islands. Mount Kilauea, on the island of Hawaii, is one of the world's most active shield volcanoes. It has been erupting for more than 30 years.

GEEK STREAK

In 1883, a volcano on the Indonesian island of Krakatoa erupted in a series of huge explosions. The noise was so loud that it was heard almost 3,000 miles (4,800 km) away after traveling for four hours. Scientists believe it was the loudest sound in modern history.

WORD CHECK

VOLCANO: A vent in Earth's crust. The ancient Romans believed that the god Vulcan, a blacksmith, lived under an island near Sicily. They said that smoke and ash from the island's volcano came from Vulcan's forge. They named the island Vulcano, which gives us our word "volcano."

STRATOVOLCANOES

Stratovolcanoes are the classic tall, pointy volcanoes. They are made from layers of lava and ash. Stratovolcanoes often produce violent, explosive eruptions. Mount St. Helens in Washington State, U.S.A., is a famous example. In 1980, an enormous eruption blasted the top off the volcano, killed 57 people, and buried miles of countryside under ash and rock.

CALDERA COMPLEX

Beautiful Yellowstone National Park, in the United States, rests on top of a supervolcano. This huge volcano is not a mountain, but a flat caldera complex. Shallow depressions in the ground, such as Grand Prismatic Spring (below), mark the places where Yellowstone has erupted in the past. Ash from these eruptions spread across thousands of miles. Sitting over a huge magma chamber five miles (8 km) deep, Yellowstone is still active and dangerous.

EARTHQUAKES

Planet Earth has the shivers. Three million times a year, somewhere in the world, Earth's crust suddenly shakes. That's an earthquake. Most of the time, earthquakes are too small to be felt. But big earthquakes can cause enormous damage.

D eep in the ground, rocky plates are grinding past or into one another. Often, they get stuck. Pressure builds up in the rocks until something breaks. The pressure is released and the rocks go *boing!* They rebound, sending waves of motion through the surrounding land. These waves can travel for thousands of miles, making the ground above them ripple and sway.

Most earthquakes happen along the edges of tectonic plates. The Ring of Fire region (see page 258) around the edge of the Pacific Ocean is notable for its earthquakes (as well as volcanoes).

The most dangerous aspect of an earthquake is not the shaking ground, but the earthquake's side effects. Collapsing buildings, landslides, and the huge waves called tsunamis cause most of an earthquake's damage and destruction.

STRIKE-SLIP FAULT

SEISMIC WAVES

MEASURING EARTHQUAKES

The size of an earthquake—the amount of energy it releases—is called its magnitude. The bigger the magnitude, the bigger the earthquake. Magnitudes were first measured by the Richter scale (see page 119). The height of an earthquake's largest wave was recorded on an instrument called a seismograph. Waves below 5 on the scale were minor. At 7, they were major.

Today scientists use the moment-magnitude scale (MMS) instead of the Richter scale. The MMS measures wave height and also the total energy an earthquake releases. The scale also tells us how much the rock around a fault was moved during the quake. The MMS can measure an earthquake's energy output up to 9.5.

WHOSE FAULT IS IT?

Earthquakes often happen around faults in the ground. This doesn't mean the ground has done something wrong. In geology, a fault is a crack in the earth along which blocks of ground are moving in different directions. In either a normal fault or a thrust fault, the ground on one side of the fault is rising higher than the other. In a strike-slip fault (above), one side is moving to the left while the other side is moving to the right. The 810-mile (1,300-km)-long San Andreas Fault in California, U.S.A., is an example of a strike-slip fault.

WORD CHECK

TSUNAMIS AND TIDAL WAVES: Tsunamis are often called tidal waves, but the two things are very different. The word "tsunami" is Japanese and means "harbor wave." It refers to the series of waves, sometimes huge, caused by an earthquake. Tidal waves are just what they sound like: waves caused by tides. These shallow waves are normal and not usually destructive.

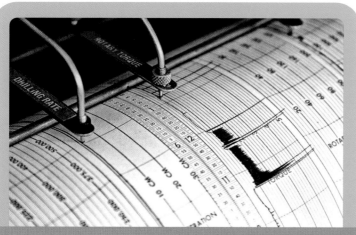

SEISMIC WAVES

The energy released by an earthquake travels in seismic waves. (The word "seismic" comes from the Greek word *seismos*, which means "earthquake.") The waves start at the earthquake's center, or focus. Some rumble along the surface of the ground. Others wiggle straight through Earth. After a big earthquake, Earth can vibrate for days.

NAMAZU THE EARTHSHAKER

According to Japanese myths, earthquakes were caused by the giant catfish Namazu. Most of the time, Namazu was motionless, because the god Kashima kept him pinned down with a giant rock. But when Kashima got distracted and let down his guard, Namazu would thrash his tail in the mud and shake the earth.

TSUNAMIS

When an earthquake suddenly shifts the ocean floor, that motion can cause a series of dangerous waves known as a tsunami. These waves roll harmlessly through the ocean until they approach land. As the ocean gets shallower, they pile up into walls of water. In 2004, a magnitude 9.1 underwater earthquake set off a tsunami that killed 230,000 people around the Indian Ocean. Some areas, such as the Hawaiian Islands or the coasts of Chile and Japan, have warning systems to tell people when a tsunami is coming.

GEEK STREAK

The most powerful earthquake in modern history rocked Chile in 1960. With a magnitude of 9.5, the quake knocked down buildings, started landslides, and triggered a tsunami that traveled all the way across the Pacific Ocean. No one knows the exact death toll, but several thousand people were killed.

TOOLS OF THE TRADE

Even if they're on the other side of the planet, scientists can measure an earthquake using a seismometer. A seismometer is bolted to the ground. Dangling inside it is a weight. When the ground shakes, the body of the seismometer shakes, too, but the weight hangs motionless. The machine records the difference in motion between the shaking body and the dangling weight to trace the waves of an earthquake.

ROCKS AND MINERALS

Rocks seem unchangeable, but in fact they are always being recycled into new forms. This process is called the rock cycle, and it forms three different kinds of rocks: sedimentary, metamorphic, and igneous.

Weathering—the effects of rain, wind, ice, and plants—breaks rocks into pieces. Water and wind carry the pieces into the sea. There, new layers press down on the older layers until they turn into sedimentary rock. As Earth's plates move and sink, some rocks are carried underground. Strong pressures and high heat squeeze them into metamorphic rock. These rocks in turn can melt underground and become hot, liquid magma. When magma cools, it turns into igneous rock. Movements of the Earth can carry these rocks to the surface at different points in the process. There, weathering starts the cycle all over again.

IGNEOUS ROCK

When Earth was young and its hot surface began to cool down, igneous rocks were the first to appear. Igneous rocks are formed from melted rock that cools and becomes solid. They can be made from lava flowing out of volcanoes or from magma deep within Earth. The granite that makes up many of our mountains is an igneous rock.

WORD CHECK

SEDIMENTARY: Made from materials that sink to the bottom of a liquid and sit there. The word "sediment" comes from the Latin word sedere, which means "to sit." Sedimentary rocks are made from hardened sediment.

SEDIMENTARY ROCK

Sand in a desert, broken stones on a hill, bits and pieces of shells and plants—all these things can be washed into streams and rivers as sediment. Floated downstream and dropped onto the ocean floor, they slowly turn into solid, sedimentary rock. Most of the rock we see on Earth's surface is sedimentary. It might hold fossils, shells, or footprints. Sandstone, limestone, and shale are common sedimentary rocks.

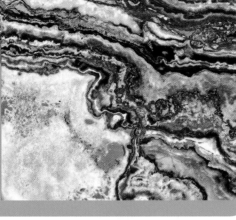

METAMORPHIC ROCK

As tectonic plates dive deep underground, they can carry rock into regions of intense heat and pressure. The heat and stress change the minerals inside the rocks. Under great pressure, limestone, a sedimentary rock, turns into the metamorphic, or transformed, rock marble. Granite, an igneous rock, becomes the metamorphic rock gneiss (pronounced "nice").

PRECIOUS MINERALS

People highly value some minerals for their beauty, rarity, or usefulness. Gemstones such as diamonds or sapphires are minerals in their pure, crystal form. Precious metals such as gold and silver are minerals found in cracks threading through rock underground. Other minerals, such as quartz, copper, or lead, are used in everything from glass to wiring to batteries.

TOOLS OF THE TRADE

Serious geologists all carry rock hammers, magnifying glasses, and little bottles of acid with droppers to see what minerals are contained in a rock. If they are looking for carbon, for example, they place a small drop of weak hydrochloric acid on the rock. If the rock holds minerals with carbon, the acid will make it bubble and fizz.

EAT YOUR MINERALS!

Your body is full of minerals. Without them, you would die. Salt helps your body balance its fluids. Calcium builds healthy bones. Iron carries oxygen in your blood. Your body makes some minerals naturally. Others, you have to eat. Don't worry—you don't have to chew up rocks. Minerals are part of the plants and animals that we eat in our regular diet. You have to take in just a tiny amount to stay healthy.

TRY THIS!

WHAT YOU NEED: A couple of different clean rocks and a coin

HOW LONG IT TAKES: 10 minutes

Geologists measure the hardness of minerals using the 10-point Mohs scale. The softest rocks are 0, and the hardest ones—diamonds—are 10. Run your own test with some clean rocks and a coin. Slide the coin against each rock and see if it leaves a scratch. Coins measure 3 on the Mohs scale. If it leaves a mark on the rock, the rock is softer than the coin and less than 3 on the scale. If the coin can't scratch it, the rock is harder than a 3.

AGES OF THE EARTH

From its fiery birth, the Earth has gone through many changes. Geologists have created a kind of calendar that divides Earth's history into distinct time periods. But instead of covering 12 months, the geologic time scale spans 4.5 billion years.

Until the 1700s, most people thought Earth was a few thousand years old. They believed that all animals appeared in their present forms at the same time. Then scientists who studied rock formations pointed out that they contained layers. Newer layers of rock were laid down on top of older layers. This process had to have taken a very long time. In the 1800s, people who uncovered fossils in various layers of rock realized that these were extinct animals that lived a long time ago. You could tell how old the rock was by the kind of fossil that appeared in it.

These clues and others led to the geologic time scale. The scale is divided into eons, eras, periods, and epochs. Each division is linked to a particular set of fossils (or lack of fossils). These divisions show the changes that have happened, which are really slow by human standards. It takes many generations of lifetimes before any noticeable change takes place. Yet in geologic time, Earth is constantly changing and evolving.

FOSSILS

Without fossils, we would know very little about the history of Earth. Fossils are the remains or the prints of plants or animals from long ago, preserved in rock. Usually fossils show just an animal's hard parts—its skeleton or shell. Sometimes, though, rocks preserve delicate details of feathers or skin. Because fossils are destroyed in the heat that shapes igneous or metamorphic rocks, almost all fossils are found in sedimentary rocks.

ALL HISTORY IN A YEAR

Compared to geologic time, humans have lived on Earth for the blink of an eye. If you think of Earth's history as a single year, the first single-celled life appears around the end of February. Not until September do we see multi-celled life. Dinosaurs appear in early December and die out suddenly on December 26. Humans don't show up until 11:58 p.m. on New Year's Eve.

February 27	September 1	December 1–26	December 31
SINGLE-CELLED LIFE	**MULTI-CELLED LIFE**	**DINOSAURS**	**HUMANS**

JAN	FEB	MAR	APR	MAY	JUNE	JULY	AUG	SEP	OCT	NOV	DEC

Precambrian era — Paleozoic era — Mesozoic era — Cenozoic era

THE AGE OF OLD LIFE

The Paleozoic era spanned about 300 million years. It began with a great increase in animal species. The seas filled with trilobites and mollusks. Plants spread over the land. The first four-legged creatures walked out of the waters. At the end of this era, something happened to wipe out almost all animals in the sea.

THE AGE OF DINOSAURS

The Mesozoic era, almost 200 million years long, hosted the planet's biggest animals. Reptiles and dinosaurs ruled the land. Pterosaurs soared through the air and mosasaurs hunted the oceans. The era ended 65 million years ago, when all dinosaurs except birds suddenly became extinct—possibly after an asteroid hit Earth.

GEEK STREAK

Some parts of the geologic time scale are measured in billions of years. At the other extreme is the epoch we live in now. The Holocene epoch, which began about 11,000 years ago and continues to today, represents just one two-millionth of the age of the Earth. During this mini epoch, mammoths, mastodons, saber-toothed cats, and giant sloths became extinct. Glaciers retreated around the world. And all human civilization, with cities, farms, and written records, began.

WORD CHECK

GEOLOGY: Comes from two Latin words: *geo*, "Earth," and *logia*, "speech." Geology means speaking about or studying the Earth.

THE AGE OF MAMMALS

The Cenozoic era picks up after the end of the dinosaurs and continues to the present. Although mammals were around before the era began, they spread out and developed new forms during this time. Horses, elephants, cats, and mammoths appeared. Whales swam the oceans. Some apes came down from the trees and evolved into upright, talking human beings.

PERSONALITY PLUS

Mary Anning (1799–1847) was one of the world's great fossil discoverers. The daughter of a poor cabinetmaker, she was raised near the fossil-rich cliffs of Lyme Regis, England. At the age of 10, she and her brother had already discovered a beautiful ichthyosaur fossil (an early ocean reptile). In 1823, she uncovered the first complete plesiosaur fossil (another ocean reptile). To earn money, she sold most of her finds to collectors. She rarely got credit for her discoveries, because she was a working-class woman and was not allowed to join scientific societies. Even so, many of the time's leading scientists consulted with her. She is now recognized as one of England's most important paleontologists.

THE AGE OF DINOSAURS

The Mesozoic era—often called the Age of Dinosaurs—began and ended with disaster. At the end of the previous era, the Paleozoic, something killed almost all the animals on the planet. At the end of the Mesozoic, almost 200 million years later, another mass extinction wiped out the dinosaurs. But in between, dinosaurs and giant reptiles ruled Earth. The first dinosaurs evolved from small, two-legged reptiles. Over time, they grew into many different species, large and small. Dinosaurs were warm-blooded animals that laid eggs and often traveled in herds. Some ate plants, while others were fearsome meat-eaters. Overall, they were very successful animals. If not for the catastrophic event that caused their sudden extinction, they might still be here.

Lizard-Hipped Dinos

Dinosaurs belong to one of two groups, based on the shape of their hip bones: lizard-hipped or bird-hipped. Lizard-hipped dinosaurs included both meat-eaters and plant-eaters. Some of the biggest animals were in this group. Long-necked sauropods such as *Brachiosaurus* or *Diplodocus* would have shaken the ground when they walked. Luckily for smaller animals, these were plant-eaters. But huge meat-eaters also prowled during the later Mesozoic era. Fast-moving, two-legged predators such as *Giganotosaurus* and *Tyrannosaurus rex* had powerful jaws that could deliver a killing bite.

Bird-Hipped Dinos

Bird-hipped dinosaurs were all plant-eaters. They include some of the oddest-looking creatures of the dinosaur age. The first dinosaur ever identified, *Iguanodon*, was part of this group. So were heavily armored dinosaurs, such as *Stegosaurus* and club-tailed *Ankylosaurus*. Many bird-hipped dinosaurs also had curious skulls, such as the bone-headed *Pachycephalosaurus* and three-horned *Triceratops*. *Parasaurolophus* had a duck-billed mouth and a curved, hollow crest. It may have used this crest as a trumpet to call others in its herd.

Flying Reptiles

While dinosaurs ruled the land, reptiles still ruled the sea and sky. Through much of the age of dinosaurs, pterosaurs flew overhead. Some of these flying reptiles were as small as sparrows. Others were huge. *Quetzalcoatlus* was the largest flying animal ever known. Its 36-foot (11-m) wingspan was as long as a school bus. Pterosaurs were not birds, but they had many features in common with birds. Their bones were light and hollow. They had large brains and keen eyes. They could soar with their long, slender wings, but could also flap them in powered flight. Some were covered with hair, which may have kept them warm.

Swimming Reptiles

Swimming through the oceans of the dinosaur age were reptiles of various shapes and sizes. Ocean-going crocodiles patrolled the seas. Plesiosaurs as long as whales flew through the water on paddle-like limbs. Pointy-headed ichthyosaurs, looking like modern dolphins, chased fish. Toward the end of the age, huge, toothy mosasaurs preyed on fish, ancient mollusks called ammonites—and other reptiles.

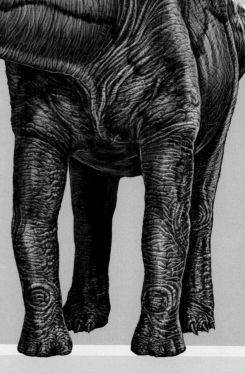

Biggest of the Big

How big were the biggest dinosaurs? We're not sure. We don't have many complete fossils of the giant creatures. However, most scientists believe that the biggest dino we know of, so far, was *Argentinosaurus*. We have only one partial skeleton of this long-necked plant-eater, but it's a doozy. The animal was about 130 feet (40 m) long and weighed about 80 to 90 tons (72 to 81 t). That's as long as four fire trucks lined up end to end, and as heavy as 15 elephants.

What Killed the Dinosaurs?

Dinosaurs, most ocean reptiles, and many kinds of plants became extinct 65 million years ago. For a long time, the reason for this was a mystery. Now we are pretty sure that it was because a giant asteroid hit Earth. One clue is the large amounts of a metal called iridium found in 65-million-year-old rocks. Iridium is rare on Earth but more common in asteroids. Another clue comes from images showing a huge impact crater under Mexico's Yucatán Peninsula. The crater is 65 million years old. A big asteroid impact would have kicked up so much dust that Earth's climate would have changed. The blast could have triggered wildfires and acid rain. It's possible the big dinosaurs could not adapt to this quickly changing world and died out.

The Dinosaurs' Children

Although most dinosaurs were wiped out at the end of the Mesozoic era, one branch of their family tree survived. This branch included birds. Today's birds evolved from small, meat-eating dinosaurs about 150 million years ago. (Curiously, they evolved from lizard-hipped dinosaurs, not bird-hipped dinosaurs.) The earliest birds had claws and teeth, like dinosaurs, but feathers like modern birds. Most of them were large shorebirds who spent a lot of time on the ground or in the water. After the big dinosaurs disappeared, birds evolved into many species. They lost their teeth and claws and became the skilled, graceful fliers we see today.

LANDFORMS

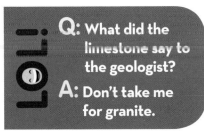
Our planet has its ups and downs. Its land rises and falls in mountains and valleys, deserts and canyons. Powerful forces are at work carving out these landforms. One force comes from inside the planet: The clash and rip of huge tectonic plates creates mountains and rift valleys. Other forces sweep across the planet's surface. Weathering and erosion from wind, water, and ice break down rocks and carry them away.

These processes can completely change the landscape over time. Colliding plates can raise mountains from a flat plain. Glaciers, wind, and water will smooth the mountain's edges and carve out valleys. Landslides drag rocks and soil downhill. Over time, a high, jagged mountain range like the Himalaya will turn into a low, rounded range like the Appalachians.

Living creatures also play a part. Plant roots break rocks into bits. Tiny animals such as worms churn rocks and plants into soil. Humans plow the soil into farms, cut through mountains to make roads, and dam up rivers to create new lakes.

VOLCANIC MOUNTAINS

Where hot, melted rock—magma—boils up through Earth's crust, volcanoes are born. Cooling magma and piles of ash can build up rapidly into mountains. Some are sharp cones, while others are gentle mounds. Some are extinct and not likely to erupt again. Hundreds of others have been active more recently. Famous volcanic mountains include Mount Fuji in Japan, Mount Vesuvius in Italy, and Mauna Loa in Hawaii, U.S.A., which is the world's tallest mountain when measured from its base on the seafloor.

FAULT-BLOCK MOUNTAINS

Where tectonic plates pull apart, the crust above them stretches out. Rocks in the crust get thinner and crack into faults. Some blocks, or chunks, of the crust sink down into valleys. Others rise up into mountains. The low-lying Death Valley, in California and Nevada, U.S.A., was formed by slipping blocks of rock. So were the steep Sierra Nevada mountains in the American West and the Harz Mountains in Germany.

GEEK STREAK

For millions of years, the Colorado River cut away at the rock of the Colorado Plateau. At the same time, geologic forces were raising the plateau. The result is a plunging ravine known as the Grand Canyon. At 277 miles (446 km) long, 1 mile (1.6 km) deep, and 18 miles (28.9 km) wide at its widest point, it is one of the biggest canyons in the world. The Grand Canyon also cuts through time. Its exposed layers of rock hold fossils that date long before the dinosaurs. At the lowest level are fossil plants more than one billion years old.

CARVED BY WIND AND WATER

When you look at a rock formation such as Delicate Arch in Utah, U.S.A., you would swear it was carved by human hands. But these rock arches and bridges are natural formations. Arches are made of rock that has been worn away by wind or water. Over time, the softer sections of the rock get carried away. The harder parts remain, standing above their surroundings in towers, arches, and windows.

IN THE DARK

Caves are natural openings in the ground. Some are modest holes just big enough for a bear. Others extend for miles in an underground maze. Caves are found in many kinds of rock, but the most common kinds appear in limestone. These are formed by rainwater dripping through the ground. The water mixes with carbon dioxide to form carbonic acid. Drip by drip, year by year, the acid eats away at the underground rock to hollow it out. Inside the cave, minerals in the dripping water gradually grow into hanging stalactites and the stalagmites that rise from the floor beneath them.

WORD CHECK

EROSION: The slow destruction of rock by wind, ice, or water. The word comes from the Latin verb *erodere*, "to eat away."

FOLD MOUNTAINS

When tectonic plates collide, the crust around the collision can wrinkle up like a sliding bath mat. Under tremendous stress, the rock bends and folds into mountains. Fold mountains are among the tallest in the world. The Himalaya in Asia, the Alps in Europe, and the Andes in South America are fold mountains.

PERSONALITY PLUS

Swiss scientist Louis Agassiz (1807–1873) was a famous teacher, expert in animal classification, and paleontologist. He saw that existing glaciers leave behind marks, such as long scratches in the ground, and boulders carried from far away. These marks also appeared on land without glaciers. He concluded that glaciers must have covered large areas of land in Europe and North America in a long-ago ice age. For this, and for his many other discoveries, he is considered one of the great scientists of the 19th century.

THE ATMOSPHERE

Earth's atmosphere is much more than the air we breathe. It is also a warm blanket that keeps the planet at just the right temperature. It is a shield that protects us from dangers from space. Its winds and weather touch all life on Earth.

EXOSPHERE

THERMOSPHERE

MESOSPHERE

STRATOSPHERE

TROPOSPHERE

The atmosphere is a mixture of gases: mostly nitrogen (78 percent) and oxygen (21 percent), plus small amounts of other gases, such as carbon dioxide and water vapor.

Living things recycle the air. Plants take in carbon dioxide and release oxygen. Animals take in oxygen and release carbon dioxide. The atmosphere has five layers, and we live at the very bottom.

Almost all the action happens in this layer, called the troposphere. Here, where the air is thick and damp, we find most clouds and weather. Above it lie the stratosphere, mesosphere, thermosphere, and exosphere. In these layers, the air thins out until it vanishes into outer space.

LOTS OF LAYERS

Of Earth's five layers of atmosphere, the troposphere is closest to Earth. It is seven miles (11 km) high and where weather happens. Next comes the dry air of the stratosphere, where commercial jets often fly to avoid strong air currents below. The mesosphere is where meteors evaporate. It is the coldest layer—so cold it freezes water vapor into ice clouds. The thermosphere is the hottest layer in the atmosphere. It is where the International Space Station orbits Earth and where the aurora borealis (northern lights) occurs. The exosphere, where the air is so thin it blends with outer space, is the farthest layer of Earth's atmosphere. Here's where you'll find many of Earth's orbiting satellites.

TOOLS OF THE TRADE

Have you ever accidentally let go of a helium balloon and seen it soar away into the sky? Atmospheric scientists do this every day, on purpose. They release large, white weather balloons carrying instruments called radiosondes into the air. The balloons zoom up to about 100,000 feet (30,000 m) before they pop and drop the radiosondes to the ground. Each one has a pre-addressed envelope so that the finder can send it back to the scientists who launched it.

EARTH'S FIRST ATMOSPHERE

When Earth first formed, the hot young planet had no atmosphere at all. As volcanoes began to erupt, they spewed out gases such as carbon dioxide, nitrogen, water vapor, and methane. Animals as we know them today could not have survived, because there was no oxygen to breathe. About 2.5 billion years ago, blue-green bacteria, often called blue-green algae, began to flourish in the oceans. They took in carbon dioxide and water and released oxygen. Over millions of years, the atmosphere changed into the oxygen-rich blend we have today.

THE GREENHOUSE EFFECT

Our planet stays warm enough for life, but not too warm, thanks to the greenhouse effect. As the sun shines on Earth, some of its heat is bounced back into space. Some heat is also absorbed by the ground and water, then released back into the air. Certain gases in the air, such as water vapor and carbon dioxide, trap this heat against Earth, just as a greenhouse traps heat inside its glass panes. The greenhouse effect is a natural process, but it can get out of balance. In the years that humans have been burning fossil fuels for power, they've been adding more greenhouse gases such as carbon dioxide to the air. These gases are trapping too much heat and changing our climate. Countries are now working on ways to reduce the amount of greenhouse gases they add to the air.

SUN

EARTH

ATMOSPHERE ⋯⋯

LIFE IN THE AIR

All kinds of life float or fly through the atmosphere, using its winds to travel around Earth. The bar-headed goose, named for the black bars on its head, is the highest-flying bird. It can soar right over the Himalaya at 21,000 feet (6,400 m), almost four miles high. Tiny, dustlike orchid seeds travel long distances on the wind and take root on remote islands. Plant pollen and spores from fungi ride the wind to new homes. Microbes might be the loftiest life-forms of all. They've been found in the stratosphere, 12 miles (20 km) high.

THE WALL OF AIR

The atmosphere is all that stands between us and some of the more dangerous aspects of outer space. Ultraviolet (UV) radiation in sunlight would give us cancer if all of it reached Earth's surface. However, a layer of ozone—a special kind of oxygen—in the stratosphere soaks up most of the UV rays before they reach the ground. Just above the stratosphere, the mesosphere catches incoming meteoroids. Almost all of them slow down and burn up in this chilly layer of the atmosphere.

PERSONALITY PLUS

Austrian skydiver Felix Baumgartner (1969–) knows firsthand what the stratosphere looks like. On October 14, 2012, he rode a helium balloon 24 miles (39 km) up into thin, cold air. Wearing a pressurized suit, he jumped out of the balloon's capsule and plummeted to the ground, opening a parachute after four minutes and landing on his feet in New Mexico, U.S.A., five minutes later. In his fall, he reached speeds of 843 miles an hour (1,357 km/h), faster than the speed of sound.

GEEK STREAK

Without the heat of the sun, our atmosphere would freeze into oxygen and nitrogen snow. The 5,000 trillion metric tons of air around us would collapse into a pale blue snowdrift 330 feet (100 m) deep around the world.

BLUE SKIES, RED SKIES

Why is the sky blue—except when it's red, or yellow? The sky is colorful because of the way air breaks up incoming light. White sunlight is actually made of all the colors of the rainbow. As it enters the atmosphere, air molecules and little particles of dust and water scatter the sunlight into colored rays. The color blue scatters the most, so the sky looks blue. At sunrise or sunset, sunlight travels through a thicker layer of the atmosphere close to the ground. Blue light is scattered away completely, but red and yellow light stay in the sky.

THE OCEAN

LOL!

Q: How can you tell the ocean is a friendly place?

A: Because it always waves at you!

The ocean covers nearly three-quarters of Earth's surface. It contains about 97 percent of all the water on Earth.

Look at a globe or a world map. See all that blue? It's mostly ocean. This water, which is salty, fills huge basins in Earth's crust and surrounds the continents.

The world's ocean is usually divided into five named oceans: the Pacific, Atlantic, Indian, Arctic, and Southern. The Pacific Ocean is the biggest. All the continents could easily fit into it. The Arctic Ocean is the smallest. It surrounds Earth's North Pole. In winter, chunks of floating ice cover much of the Arctic Ocean's surface.

The ocean affects your life in many ways, even if you don't live near it. About half the oxygen you breathe is produced by tiny, photosynthesizing organisms in its waters. Most of the rain and snow falling on land starts out as water vapor from the ocean. The ocean also stores heat in summer, which cools off nearby land. In winter, the ocean slowly releases its heat, which helps keep nearby land warmer.

CURRENTS

A current is water that flows in the ocean. A surface current (red labels below) is a river of water at the ocean's surface. Surface currents flow for hundreds of miles. They help carry heat around the world when they flow from warm tropical places to cooler places near the North and South Poles. The Gulf Stream is a strong, fast current that carries warm water near Florida up the east coast of North America and into the chilly northern Atlantic Ocean to Europe. Some currents team up to form loops, called gyres, which circle around an entire ocean (blue labels below). These gyres travel in a clockwise direction north of the Equator and counterclockwise south of the Equator.

WAVES

Winds blowing across the ocean pull and push on its surface. This energy sets the water in motion. The wave of energy travels through the water and causes it to rise and fall. Gentle breezes simply make the water ripple. Strong waves create sharp peaks with white caps. The biggest waves form in places where winds travel very long distances across the ocean. Waves crash on shore when they meet the shallow seafloor, which slows them down. Big storms that occur thousands of miles away create large, powerful waves.

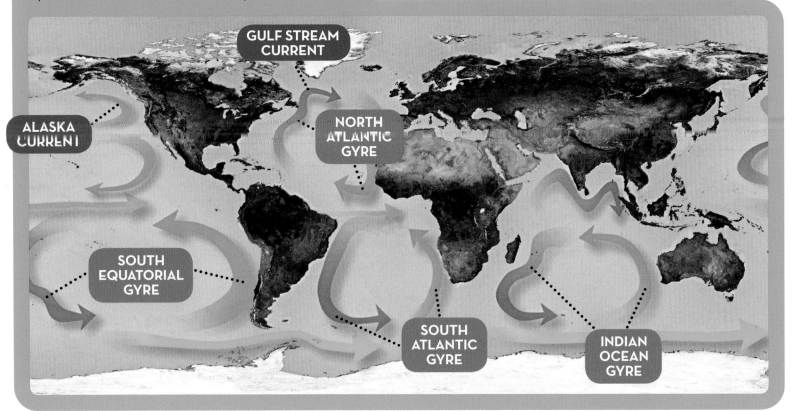

GULF STREAM CURRENT

ALASKA CURRENT

NORTH ATLANTIC GYRE

SOUTH EQUATORIAL GYRE

SOUTH ATLANTIC GYRE

INDIAN OCEAN GYRE

TIDES

A tide is a regular rise and fall of the ocean's surface along a coast. Many coasts experience two high tides and two low tides a day. At high tide, the water reaches far up on the shore. During the next six hours, the ocean drops back until it hits its lowest point at low tide. Then the tide starts creeping in again. Tides are caused by the gravity of the sun and moon pulling on the water. The moon is smaller than the sun, but it's much closer to Earth. As a result, it pulls more strongly on the ocean than the sun does.

WORD CHECK

SCUBA: An air-supply system used by divers while underwater. "Scuba" stands for "self-contained underwater breathing apparatus."

TOOLS OF THE TRADE

Scientists who study the ocean use submersibles to explore deep places. Submersibles are small submarines with very strong walls that won't cave in under great pressure. A submersible is also equipped with lights, cameras, and tools for collecting samples. The first submersible, called *Alvin*, has been carrying scientists deep undersea since 1964.

SEA POWER

The ocean's energy can be used to produce electrical power on land. Some wave-power equipment takes energy from waves on the ocean's surface. Other devices use changes in pressure deep underwater as a wave goes by. Wave energy is still mainly in the testing stage. A few nations produce some electricity by harnessing the energy of tides. The world's first tidal power station began producing electricity in 1966. It stretches across the mouth of the Rance River in France (above). A highway runs along the top of it.

PERSONALITY PLUS

Jacques Cousteau (1910–1997) was a French ocean explorer, inventor, and filmmaker who produced movies about ocean life. He was the co-inventor of the Aqua-Lung, a device for breathing underwater while scuba diving. He helped design underwater structures for oceanographers to live in while exploring. His work helped gain protection for whales and other endangered sea creatures.

OCEAN LAYERS

The ocean is divided into layers from the top down. The top layer is a sunlit zone about 650 feet (200 m) deep. Sunlight beams into this area, so organisms that carry out photosynthesis can live here. The ocean gets darker and colder as it gets deeper. The pressure grows, too, because of the heavy weight of all the water above it. Animals in each layer have adaptations for surviving the cold and pressure. Many deep-sea creatures are able to produce light. A lanternfish is dotted with light-producing organs. The light attracts prey and may also be used for communication.

THE WATER CYCLE

The water you drink today might once have quenched a dinosaur's thirst. That's because there is no new water on our planet. Instead, all of our water moves from ocean to air to ground and back to ocean in an endless exchange called the water cycle.

Heat from the sun powers the water cycle. The cycle doesn't have a beginning or end, but let's start with the oceans, which hold almost all of Earth's water.

Heat evaporates some ocean water, changing it into water vapor. The damp gas rises into the atmosphere. As it rises into cooler air, it condenses into clouds. Clouds drop the moisture back to the earth as rain or snow.

Much of this rain and snow goes right back to the ocean. Some freezes into glaciers and polar snow. The rest falls across the ground, running down hillsides as rivers, filling up lakes, and feeding plants and animals. Evaporation then lifts water into the air again. Each year, the cycle moves about 152 quadrillion gallons (575 quadrillion L) of water.

SNOW WONDER

Snowflakes grow out of water droplets in clouds. When the temperature is cold enough, the droplets freeze into tiny ice particles. The particles stick together and become ice crystals. When they get heavy enough, they fall. If snowflakes hit warmer air, they turn back into rain. If it's cold down below, they stay as snow. Snowflakes have a wide variety of shapes, but they always have six sides. When ice builds into a snowflake, that's the only way the ice crystals can fit together.

PERSONALITY PLUS

Wilson Bentley (1865–1931) was raised on a farm in the snowy town of Jericho, Vermont, U.S.A. After receiving a microscope for his 15th birthday, he started examining snowflakes close up. He figured out how to connect the microscope to a camera and set it up outside in the cold. Handling snowflakes with a feather, he took photo after photo of individual flakes. In 5,000 pictures, no two snowflakes were alike. Bentley's patient work earned him the nickname "Snowflake" Bentley.

WATER TO VAPOR

Evaporation is the magic wand that changes water into gas. It begins with heat, as sunlight warms water on Earth. Heat makes the water molecules jump around. After a while, the bonds between the moving molecules snap. The molecules float free, rising into the air as water vapor. Water can also evaporate from plants through open pores on the underside of leaves. This is called transpiration.

WATER RETURNS TO THE EARTH AS RAIN

WATER EVAPORATES

WORD CHECK

WORD CHECK

TRANSPIRATION: The act of releasing water vapor from a plant's pores. Plants pull in water through their roots and release it into the air through their leaves. The word comes from the Latin words for "to breathe through."

CLOUDS

Clouds are huge, fluffy storehouses of rain and snow. They are formed by rising masses of moist air. When the air reaches cool temperatures, its water vapor condenses into little drops of water. The drops cling together to form clouds. High, chilly cirrus clouds are made of ice crystals. Low-level cumulus clouds can gather into towering structures that bring rain, lightning, or hail.

FROM CLOUDS TO RAINDROPS

When water vapor condenses into water drops in a cloud, it has to condense around something. That something is usually a bit of dust or salt floating in the cloud. Water surrounds the little particle in a tiny cloud droplet. The droplets bump into each other and merge to make bigger drops of mist or drizzle. When the drop gets big enough, it falls as a raindrop. Small raindrops are perfectly round as they fall. Bigger ones flatten out on the bottom like a hamburger bun.

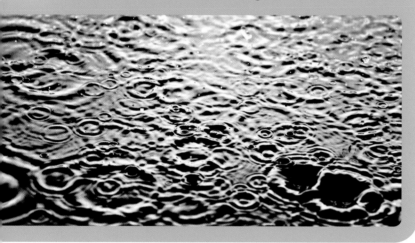

TRY THIS!

WHAT YOU NEED: A plastic cup, water, ice

HOW LONG IT TAKES: 15 minutes

Want to make it rain? It's easy to get condensation started at your own kitchen table. Take a plastic cup and fill it halfway up with ice. Add water until it's almost full. Make sure the outside is dry, set it on a counter, and wait 15 minutes. What do you see? The outside of the cup is now wet. The frigid cup cooled the air around it, and water vapor in the air condensed onto the cup.

GEEK STREAK

What are the rainiest places on Earth? The current ruler of rain is the village of Mawsynram, in northeast India. It receives a whopping 467 inches (11.9 m) per year. The award for most rain in one day goes to the French island of Réunion in the Indian Ocean. It was hit with 71.9 inches (1.8 m) in 24 hours during a tropical cyclone in 1966.

WHERE'S THE WATER?

Almost all of Earth's water—96.4 percent—is stored in the ocean as salt water. Most of the remaining freshwater is frozen into glaciers and polar ice caps. Some is also trapped underground as groundwater. All the liquid freshwater on the planet's surface, from the mighty Amazon River to the Great Lakes, makes up only 1/150 of one percent of all water. Most of that is used in farming. Not much is left for humans to drink or wash with. In some parts of the world, freshwater is rare and precious.

WEATHER

LOL!

Q: What's the opposite of a cold front?

A: A warm back!

Step outside: Is it sunny? Rainy? So cold you can't feel your nose? Whatever is happening in the air around you at the moment is the weather.

Weather is different from climate. Weather describes changing, local conditions. It varies from place to place and from moment to moment. Climate describes long-term weather patterns.

The sun is the engine that moves the weather. Sunlight heats Earth unevenly. Air at the Equator is hotter than air at the poles. Land heats up faster than oceans. As air warms, it rises. Air pressure in the warm air mass drops. When air cools down, it sinks. Pressure in cool air increases. Winds blow these warm and cool air masses around. Where they meet, weather can be unpredictable and stormy.

Weather scientists, called meteorologists, break down weather into six parts: temperature, air pressure, wind, humidity (moisture in the air), precipitation (rain or snow), and cloudiness. Put these six things together and you have a good idea of what it will feel like when you step outside the door.

TOOLS OF THE TRADE

Barometers are weather instruments that measure air pressure—the weight of the atmosphere. A traditional barometer is a tube that's open at the bottom and closed at the top, sitting in a bath of mercury. As air pressure pushes down on the mercury, the mercury rises into the tube. Numbers on the side of the tube give the air pressure reading. Most modern barometers have a small metal box inside that's attached to a spring. When pressure rises, the box is squashed inward. When pressure falls, the box pulls outward. This box is attached to a pointer, which swings around to the correct pressure number on the barometer's face. Rising pressure usually means good weather is moving in. Dropping pressure can mean rain.

WARM FRONTS

Is a warm front moving in? Pull out your umbrella! A warm front is the leading edge of a warm air mass. When a warm air mass runs into a cool air mass, the lighter warm air slides up over the heavier cold air. As it rises, the warm air cools off. Clouds thicken up as the water vapor in the warm air mass condenses into raindrops or snow. Get ready for some steady precipitation.

GEEK STREAK

January 22, 1943, was a crazy day in Spearfish, South Dakota, U.S.A. At 7:30 a.m., the temperature was a frigid minus 4°F (-20°C). Two minutes later, it had risen to a fairly mild 45°F (7.2°C)—49 degrees F (27.2 degrees C) higher. But the warmth didn't last. By 9:30 a.m., temperatures were back to minus 4°F (-20°C), a world-record temperature change.

COLD FRONTS

Cold front on the way? Get under cover! A cold front is the leading edge of a mass of cold air. When a cold air mass meets a warm one, the heavier cold air shoves its way under the lighter warm air. Pushed quickly into the cooler atmosphere, the warm air can form tall storm clouds. Gusty winds pick up on land as thunder, lightning, rain, and snow sweep through.

NATURE'S FORECASTERS

Sorry—groundhogs cannot predict the weather. But nature gives us other clues to the forecast. Your hair gets curlier in humid weather, so a case of the frizzies means a muggy day. Pinecones open when dry weather's coming and clamp shut when rain is on the way. And as the saying goes, "a ring around the moon means rain soon." High, icy cirrus clouds can reflect moonlight in a halo. These clouds often move in ahead of rain.

PREDICTING THE WEATHER

Predicting the weather is a tough but important job. Weather forecasts don't just tell us if it's going to rain tomorrow. They also help us prepare for dangerous storms such as hurricanes or tornadoes. Meteorologists put together a lot of information to make a forecast. They use weather instruments to measure air pressure, temperature, humidity, and more. Satellites send them pictures of clouds from above. Radar measures the movements of rain and wind. All this data and more goes into high-powered computers that help forecasters predict tonight's thunder-storm or tomorrow's sunny day.

WORD CHECK

PRECIPITATION: The general word for any kind of moisture falling from clouds, which includes rain, snow, hail, and sleet. It comes from the Latin words meaning "to throw headfirst."

FOG

Have you ever stepped out into such dense, foggy weather that you could hardly see your feet? Fog is like a cloud on the ground. It often occurs at night, when the ground cools off quickly and the moist air above it condenses into floating droplets. Valleys collect fog in places where cold, dense air sinks down into low spots. Fog rarely lasts all day. As the sun heats the air, dry air flows into the fog and erases it.

PERSONALITY PLUS

You might know Thomas Jefferson (1743-1826) as the writer of the Declaration of Independence and as the third U.S. president, but he was much more than that. Jefferson was an eager amateur scientist who studied plants, animals, fossils, and weather. He kept daily records of temperature and rain no matter where he was. On the day he signed the Declaration, he took his thermometer with him to Philadelphia and recorded the temperature four times.

CLIMATE

Weather is what happens in the atmosphere over a short period of time in a certain place. Climate is what happens in the atmosphere across a large area over very long periods of time.

Weather changes from day to day. It can even change from morning to afternoon on just one day! Your climate, however, does not change this quickly. It's measured in decades and even centuries, not days and weeks.

If you live in a tropical climate, for example, a rainstorm wouldn't surprise you. A tropical climate is warm and wet all year. A snowstorm, however, would be quite a shock! But you'd expect snow to fall if you visited Earth's North or South Poles.

Climate is determined largely by an area's location on Earth, because different areas receive different amounts of sunlight. Places near the Equator, for example, receive direct sunlight year-round and are hot as a result. Distance from the ocean also influences climate. So does height above sea level.

DRY CLIMATE

The subtropics lie alongside the tropics. They have a dry climate because air masses above them are dry—they've dumped all their rain on the tropics. Many deserts are in the subtropics. Deserts also form on coasts swept by cold ocean currents. The cold water chills the air and sends fog over the land, but not rain. Places far away from coasts can also be dry because the air loses its moisture before it reaches them.

Mountains may be rainy on one side and have a desert on the other. The dry climate of Death Valley in the southwestern United States is caused by mountains to its west.

TEMPERATE CLIMATE

A temperate climate is marked by changing seasons. Earth's tilt causes lands in the temperate zone to get much less direct sunshine for part of the year, which causes cooler temperatures. Temperate climates are affected by the ocean, too. Heat stored in the ocean helps keep places along coastlines warmer in winter than places farther inland. An ocean-warmed temperate climate is known as a maritime climate, while the inland place has a continental climate. The leaves of many deciduous trees in continental temperate zones turn vivid colors in fall and then fall off before the long, cold winter begins.

POLAR CLIMATE

Polar bears and penguins live at opposite ends of Earth, where they've adapted to life in the coldness of the polar climate. Many animals and plants live on the tundra, a region of short summers with lots of daylight and winters with long nights. Ice sheets cover the coldest polar regions, and sea ice floats in the Arctic Ocean at the North Pole. Many mountain peaks have polar climates, too. Climates around the world are affected by ice sheets, which reflect lots of sunlight back into the atmosphere. Without them, Earth would absorb all the heat energy in that sunlight and get warmer.

WORD CHECK

ICE SHEET: A glacier that covers more than 19,000 square miles (50,000 sq km) of land. Greenland and Antarctica are both covered by ice sheets.

MICROCLIMATES

A "microclimate" is a mini climate—an area where the climate is different from the larger area around it. It can be as small as a garden patch beside a house that stays warmer at night than the rest of the yard. It can be as large as an entire valley, which may be colder than surrounding areas because cold air is denser than warm air—so it sinks into the bowl of the valley. Water can create microclimates. For example, cold winds blowing across a lake pick up water vapor, which becomes snow that falls on one side of the lakeshore and not the other.

TOOLS OF THE TRADE

Scientists learn about Earth's past climate by drilling into its glaciers and ice sheets. The drills are long spinning pipes that tunnel through the ice with sharp blades or heat. Cut ice collects inside the pipe. These cylinders of ice, called ice cores, contain air bubbles, dust, and other particles with information about the atmosphere of the past.

GEEK STREAK

The climate of the Atacama Desert in Chile is so dry, it almost never rains. Moist air masses drop their rain on the west side of the Andes Mountains, leaving nothing for the desert. The desert city of Arica gets less than .02 inch (.05 cm) of rain a year.

TROPICAL CLIMATE

Earth's tropical zone lies along the Equator, where sunlight shines for about 12 hours a day year-round. Rain forests grow in tropical lands where rainfall is steady throughout the year. In some places, there is a wet and dry season. India, for example, is soaked with rain by warm, wet winds blowing off the Indian Ocean in summer. The winds reverse in winter, which causes a dry season. A tropical rain forest receives more than 70 inches (180 cm) of rain per year.

THREATENED ATMOSPHERE

Global warming is leading to climate change. In some places, climate change may cause droughts; in others, it might mean bigger storms and floods. Some places may grow cooler while others grow warmer.

The atmosphere is Earth's blanket. Water vapor, carbon dioxide, and other greenhouse gases keep Earth warm by preventing heat from radiating away from the planet into space.

But over the past 200 years, carbon dioxide levels in the atmosphere have gone up. The biggest increase has occurred in the past 50 years. This global warming is caused by the burning of fossil fuels such as oil, gas, and coal. Burning fuel releases carbon into the air, where it combines with oxygen to produce carbon dioxide. In addition, burning fossil fuels increases pollution and causes acid rain to fall.

Scientists have tracked Earth's temperature change by examining weather records dating back to the mid-1800s. Since that time, Earth's average surface temperature has risen by 1.4 degrees F (0.8 degrees C).

AIR POLLUTION

Air pollution also harms the atmosphere. Gas-powered vehicles, for example, produce a deadly gas called carbon monoxide. Power plants and industries that burn fossil fuels release sulfur dioxide and nitrogen dioxide. Burning wood releases harmful chemicals and tiny particles that damage lungs. Particles of lead, mercury, and other heavy metals pollute air, too. Clouds of pollution called smog often cover cities. Air pollution causes millions of deaths a year. In China alone, it contributes to the deaths of about 4,400 people a day. Many people wear masks to filter out the pollutants.

TOOLS OF THE TRADE

Devices called scrubbers are used in many smokestacks to trap pollutants. The "scrubbing" is done by using fluids to dissolve waste gases and filter them out, or by using substances that chemically react with pollutants. Many old power plants lack scrubbers, but new laws to stop pollution from drifting from one state to another might require them to be added.

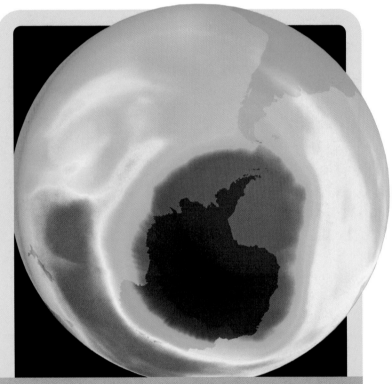

OZONE HOLES

In the 1970s, scientists noticed that chemicals called chlorofluorocarbons, or CFCs, had damaged Earth's ozone layer (see page 55). The ozone layer thinned mainly over the Arctic and Antarctica. CFCs were used as cooling materials, called refrigerants. Aerosol spray cans used CFCs, too. Very quickly, many countries agreed to cut back or completely stop using CFCs. This agreement, called the Montreal Protocol, went into effect in 1987. Scientists figured out how to replace CFCs with substances that didn't harm the ozone layer. These "ozone holes" still exist, but scientists predict they will shrink in the future.

GEEK STREAK

Sea ice covers large parts of the Arctic Ocean, especially in winter. Over the past 30 years, however, the amount of sea ice has shrunk. Less ice forms in winter, and more ice melts in summer. Less summer ice makes life difficult for polar bears in some areas, because they travel on sea ice to hunt seals.

ACID RAIN

Burning fossil fuels adds sulfur and nitrogen compounds to the atmosphere, where they react with water, oxygen, and other substances to produce sulfuric acid and nitric acid. Then these acids fall to the ground in rain. This "acid rain" washes aluminum out of soil and into the water, where it harms fish. Acid rain also washes away soil nutrients needed by plants. It harms forests, lakes, and other habitats—even old stone buildings and the painted surfaces of cars. Antipollution laws have helped cut down on acid rain.

CHANGES AT SEA

Global warming has affected the ocean, too. Water expands, or takes up more space, when it's heated, so as surface waters have gotten warmer, the height of the ocean's surface has risen. Melting glaciers and ice sheets add to the rise in sea level, resulting in the flooding of low-lying coasts and islands. This melting also means less snow and ice to reflect sunlight away from Earth, which causes the climate to warm even more. In turn, warmer water may also make storms such as hurricanes more powerful.

CLEANING UP THE AIR

In 1970, the U.S. government passed the Clean Air Act. This law aimed to clean up the atmosphere by reducing pollution given off by vehicles, power plants, and industries. Today's cars run about 99 percent cleaner than cars made in 1970. Factories are now built according to rules for pollution control. Power plants that burn coal use devices to capture much of the pollution instead of releasing it into the atmosphere. This hospital in Mexico City, Mexico, has a wall that helps clean the air. Its tiles contain materials that turn pollutants into less harmful substances. Sunlight powers the reaction.

PERSONALITY PLUS

Dr. James E. Hansen (1941–) is an American scientist who has studied physics, astronomy, and the climate. In 1988, Hansen spoke to the U.S. Congress about how human activity was affecting the atmosphere and causing the climate to grow warmer. His words helped make people worldwide more aware of the issue of global warming. Today, he continues to study climate change.

WINDS, STORMS, AND FLOODS

Wind is air that moves because of differences in atmospheric pressure. Atmospheric pressure is the weight of air above a place on Earth. Air moves from areas of high pressure to areas of low pressure.

The movement of air in the atmosphere creates everything from warm spring breezes to whistling winter winds. Differences in pressure are caused by the way the sun heats Earth. The tropics, for example, are bathed in sunlight year-round. The land, heated by the sun, warms the air above it. The warm air rises because it becomes less dense. Then cooler, denser air rushes in to take its place.

These huge, moving "packages" of air are called air masses. Most of the air in an air mass is similar in temperature, pressure, and amount of water vapor. One air mass, for example, may be full of air that's warm and wet. Another air mass may contain cold, dry air. Places where different air masses meet are called fronts (see page 276).

THUNDERSTORMS

A thunderstorm forms in places where warm, moist air rises and cool, dry air sinks. That place might be along a front, or where ocean air meets air over land. Vapor in the air cools and turns into water droplets, which form a tall, bulging thundercloud. The constant rising, falling, cooling, and heating of the air causes the cloud to have a different electrical charge at its top and bottom. The result is the giant zap we know as lightning. About 100 lightning bolts strike Earth every second. A bolt heats the air as it sizzles through it. The air quickly expands and then condenses, making the crash of thunder.

STRONGER STORMS

Many of today's "superstorms" are caused by extremes of weather. But climate change may cause stronger storms, floods, heat waves, droughts, and other events in parts of the world in the future. That's the view of a scientific organization called the Intergovernmental Panel on Climate Change (IPCC). Climate scientists use computers to predict how the climate will change as global warming raises the temperature of both atmosphere and ocean. People living on low-lying ocean islands say that flooding during storms has increased over the years. They are concerned that the floods are due to higher sea levels caused by melting polar ice caps.

WORD CHECK

SUPERCELL: An extreme thunderstorm with rotating winds that have a strong upward pull, or updraft. Supercells can become tornadoes.

HURRICANES

With winds that whirl at speeds of 74 miles an hour (119 km/h) or more, a hurricane is the most powerful of storms. Hurricanes form over warm, tropical water. High-pressure air starts to whirl around an area of low pressure. A typical hurricane is about 300 miles (483 km) wide but can be much bigger. It pushes water ahead of it as it barrels across the ocean. The water becomes a raging flood when it hits land. Satellites help meteorologists keep track of storms at sea. The images and information they gather are used to predict where a hurricane is heading and where it might come ashore.

TORNADOES

A tornado is a whirling funnel of wind that stretches from a thundercloud to the ground. The winds pick up dirt, raindrops, and other substances that give the wind funnel color so you can see it. Wind in a tornado can reach speeds of 120 miles an hour (180 km/h) or more—some have spun as fast as 300 miles an hour (500 km/h). Tornadoes cause terrible damage as they travel across land, ripping roofs off houses and tossing cars around like toys. Meteorologists use radar to watch storms that may produce the funnel-shaped tornadoes so they can warn people.

BLIZZARDS

A blizzard is a winter storm with winds that blow more than 35 miles an hour (56 km/h) for at least three hours. These winds whip up clouds of snow that make it impossible to see more than a quarter mile (0.4 km) away. Really strong blizzards may bring even faster winds and reduce how far you can see to nearly zero. A huge blizzard dropped more than two feet (0.6 m) of snow on central and eastern parts of Canada and the United States in January 2015, bringing traffic to a halt and shutting down entire cities.

TRY THIS!

WHAT YOU NEED: A thunderstorm, a pencil, a stopwatch, a calculator

HOW LONG IT TAKES: Once the thunderstorm has begun, no time at all

Sound travels more slowly in air than light does, and you can use that difference to figure out the distance between you and a thunderstorm. When you see lightning, start counting seconds with the stopwatch. Stop when you hear thunder. Divide the number of seconds by five. The result is roughly how many miles away the lightning struck. (Divide by three if you prefer kilometers!)

PERSONALITY PLUS

Sir Francis Beaufort (1774–1857) was an admiral in Great Britain's Royal Navy. He first went to sea when he was only 14. In 1805, he created a wind scale based on sailing conditions at sea. The scale ranked winds from "calm" to "hurricane." Today, the Beaufort Wind Scale also includes conditions on land.

WEATHER FORECASTING

Many people find out if it's going to rain or shine by looking up a weather forecast. This forecast is prepared by weather scientists, or meteorologists, who use computers to process information gathered by satellites and other scientific instruments. But people living in ancient times needed to predict weather, too. Farmers had to know if it would be rainy or sunny so they could plant and harvest crops successfully. Sailors needed to know about storms at sea and how winds would blow. For hundreds of years, people looked to the sky and the world around them for information about weather. Over time, they invented weather instruments we use today, too.

Sky Signs

Weather happens in the sky, so the sky is a logical place to look for weather signs! Cloud types and shapes provide information about winds high in the atmosphere and how much moisture is in the air. A towering white cloud on the horizon, for example, is a thundercloud bringing lots of rain. Cirrus clouds, composed of long, wispy streamers, are usually white and predict fair weather. By watching their movement you can tell what direction weather is coming from. Cirrus clouds moving south may indicate a cold front moving in from the north.

Color Clues

Sky color is a weather sign, too. For example, the old saying "Red sky at night, sailor's delight; red sky in the morning, sailor's warning" is often correct. The setting sun's light looks red because it's shining on dust particles floating in dry air between it and you. But if the red sky is fire-engine red, there might be lots of water vapor instead of dust, so rain may be on the way. A red sky in the morning may mean that good weather has already moved on and rainy weather will follow.

before A.D. 1
Weather vane in use in ancient Greece

1607
Thermoscope, an early thermometer, invented by Galileo Galilei (Italy)

1714
Mercury thermometer invented by Daniel Gabriel Fahrenheit (Holland)

mid-1400s
Hygrometer, which measures water vapor in air, invented by Nicholas of Cusa (Germany)

1643
Barometer, which measures air pressure, invented by Evangilista Torricelli (Italy)

Smoke Signals

People long ago noticed that weather affects how chimney smoke rises. Rising smoke meant good weather, but smoke that flattened out and spread sideways meant bad weather. Today we know that a layer of warm, moist air makes smoke spread out without rising, and that rain is probably on its way.

Ropes, Moss, Hair, and Seaweed

"Moss dry, sunny sky. Moss wet, rain you'll get." This old weather saying is based on truth: Moss soaks up water from the air. So does seaweed. In ancient times, people near seacoasts knew that seaweed lying on a shore felt damp if the air was humid and rain was on the way. Sailors noticed that ropes shrunk in damp air. Human hair does, too!

Animal Antics

In the past, people often linked odd animal behavior with changes in the weather. A pig carrying sticks in its mouth or a cat scratching a table leg was thought to be a sign of rain. Most animal weather sayings aren't true, though many kinds of animals do become restless before storms. A few sayings have some basis in fact. Bees, for example, often stay near their hives if rain is on the way.

Winter Worries

Will winter be harsh or mild? Many people think nature is full of signs that can predict a very cold, long winter. Among these signs are mice moving into a house, spiders making extra-big webs, extra-thick husks on corn, extra-thick fur on animals, squirrels gathering lots of acorns, and thin brown bands on woolly bear caterpillars. Scientists say these "signs" actually show what the past was like, not what the future will be. Animals that are well-nourished, for example, are healthy and grow thick coats. Longer-living spiders are large by fall and spin big webs. And the older a woolly bear caterpillar is, the wider its brown band will be.

Superstitions and Magic

Hundreds of years ago, most people believed events in nature were caused by magical beings. The Maori people of New Zealand, for example, believed dewdrops on grass were tears shed by a god. The ancient Egyptians believed a god rolled the sun across the sky. The ancient Greeks believed that a god named Zeus controlled the weather and flung lightning bolts when he was angry.

1837

Telegraph, which sent weather information quickly over long distances, invented by Samuel Morse (United States)

1929

First radiosonde (weather balloon) launched by Robert Bureau (France)

1989

First use of **Doppler radar** to forecast weather (United States)

1846

Cup anemometer, which measures wind speed, invented by John Thomas Romney Robinson (Ireland)

1960

First **weather satellite** launched (United States)

285

BIOMES

A biome is a large community of living things that share similar climate and living conditions around the world.

You know your address and your town—but do you know your biome? A biome is known as a major life zone. For example, a desert biome is a life zone with a hot, dry climate. Desert biomes are found in North and South America, Africa, Asia, and Australia. Experts count five major kinds of biomes: aquatic, desert, forest, grassland, and tundra. Some of them are divided into two or more kinds and may be named after the main types of plants that grow in these conditions. The hot, wet tropical rain forest biome, for example, is named after the thick, moist forests that grow well in this zone. The coniferous forest biome is named for the conifers, or cone-bearing trees, that live in this zone. Each biome is made up of a variety of smaller communities called habitats. A habitat is a place where organisms live. It's made up of all the living and nonliving things that make it "home, sweet home" for an organism. For example, a pond is a duck's habitat. It provides food, water, shelter, and a place to raise young that is just right for a duck. The duck, in turn, has evolved so that it is suited, or adapted, to living in a pond.

HABITATS
Every biome contains one or more kinds of habitats. A habitat is a place where a living thing finds everything it needs to exist: water, food, shelter, and a place to raise its young. A human family's habitat is their home and neighborhood—including a school and grocery store. Different creatures have different needs for food, water, and shelter, so each kind of animal or plant has a specific kind of habitat. A frog lives in a wetland habitat, where it shelters near a pond or stream, eats insects, and lays its eggs in or near the water. A moose lives in an evergreen forest, where it shelters in brush and eats vegetation. Moss is a plant that thrives in a cool, dark, moist habitat like a rain forest or swamp.

ECOSYSTEM
A biome is a supersize version of an ecosystem—a community of living and nonliving things that share a collection of habitats. A seashore ecosystem, for example, includes habitats that are close to the water and habitats higher up on shore that may get splashed by seawater every now and then. A habitat at the water's edge may include crabs that nibble on seaweed as well as seabirds that eat crabs.

A pool of seawater among rocks is a miniature ecosystem. It contains plant-eaters and predators as well as hiding places and shady shelters for these organisms.

PERSONALITY PLUS
Ernst Haeckel (1834-1919) was a German scientist who studied ocean invertebrates and wrote about evolution. In one book, he invented the word "ecology" to describe the relationship between living things and their habitats. He added the Greek word *oikos*, which means "home," to the word *ology*, which means "study of."

Smoke Signals

People long ago noticed that weather affects how chimney smoke rises. Rising smoke meant good weather, but smoke that flattened out and spread sideways meant bad weather. Today we know that a layer of warm, moist air makes smoke spread out without rising, and that rain is probably on its way.

Ropes, Moss, Hair, and Seaweed

"Moss dry, sunny sky. Moss wet, rain you'll get." This old weather saying is based on truth: Moss soaks up water from the air. So does seaweed. In ancient times, people near seacoasts knew that seaweed lying on a shore felt damp if the air was humid and rain was on the way. Sailors noticed that ropes shrunk in damp air. Human hair does, too!

Animal Antics

In the past, people often linked odd animal behavior with changes in the weather. A pig carrying sticks in its mouth or a cat scratching a table leg was thought to be a sign of rain. Most animal weather sayings aren't true, though many kinds of animals do become restless before storms. A few sayings have some basis in fact. Bees, for example, often stay near their hives if rain is on the way.

Winter Worries

Will winter be harsh or mild? Many people think nature is full of signs that can predict a very cold, long winter. Among these signs are mice moving into a house, spiders making extra-big webs, extra-thick husks on corn, extra-thick fur on animals, squirrels gathering lots of acorns, and thin brown bands on woolly bear caterpillars. Scientists say these "signs" actually show what the past was like, not what the future will be. Animals that are well-nourished, for example, are healthy and grow thick coats. Longer-living spiders are large by fall and spin big webs. And the older a woolly bear caterpillar is, the wider its brown band will be.

Superstitions and Magic

Hundreds of years ago, most people believed events in nature were caused by magical beings. The Maori people of New Zealand, for example, believed dewdrops on grass were tears shed by a god. The ancient Egyptians believed a god rolled the sun across the sky. The ancient Greeks believed that a god named Zeus controlled the weather and flung lightning bolts when he was angry.

1837

Telegraph, which sent weather information quickly over long distances, invented by Samuel Morse (United States)

1929

First radiosonde (weather balloon) launched by Robert Bureau (France)

1989

First use of **Doppler radar** to forecast weather (United States)

1846

Cup anemometer, which measures wind speed, invented by John Thomas Romney Robinson (Ireland)

1960

First **weather satellite** launched (United States)

BIOMES

A biome is a large community of living things that share similar climate and living conditions around the world.

You know your address and your town—but do you know your biome? A biome is known as a major life zone. For example, a desert biome is a life zone with a hot, dry climate. Desert biomes are found in North and South America, Africa, Asia, and Australia. Experts count five major kinds of biomes: aquatic, desert, forest, grassland, and tundra. Some of them are divided into two or more kinds and may be named after the main types of plants that grow in these conditions. The hot, wet tropical rain forest biome, for example, is named after the thick, moist forests that grow well in this zone. The coniferous forest biome is named for the conifers, or cone-bearing trees, that live in this zone. Each biome is made up of a variety of smaller communities called habitats. A habitat is a place where organisms live. It's made up of all the living and nonliving things that make it "home, sweet home" for an organism. For example, a pond is a duck's habitat. It provides food, water, shelter, and a place to raise young that is just right for a duck. The duck, in turn, has evolved so that it is suited, or adapted, to living in a pond.

GEEK STREAK
Big cities are habitats that can create their own climates. These "urban heat islands" are warmer than areas around them. A hot summer day can be up to 27 degrees F (16.6 degrees C) warmer in a city. The extra heat comes from many sources: vehicles such as cars and buses, warmth from heated buildings and air conditioners, even the body heat of many people living in one place. Planting trees and creating parks helps cities keep their cool.

HABITATS

Every biome contains one or more kinds of habitats. A habitat is a place where a living thing finds everything it needs to exist: water, food, shelter, and a place to raise its young. A human family's habitat is their home and neighborhood—including a school and grocery store. Different creatures have different needs for food, water, and shelter, so each kind of animal or plant has a specific kind of habitat. A frog lives in a wetland habitat, where it shelters near a pond or stream, eats insects, and lays its eggs in or near the water. A moose lives in an evergreen forest, where it shelters in brush and eats vegetation. Moss is a plant that thrives in a cool, dark, moist habitat like a rain forest or swamp.

ECOSYSTEM

A biome is a supersize version of an ecosystem—a community of living and nonliving things that share a collection of habitats. A seashore ecosystem, for example, includes habitats that are close to the water and habitats higher up on shore that may get splashed by seawater every now and then. A habitat at the water's edge may include crabs that nibble on seaweed as well as seabirds that eat crabs.

A pool of seawater among rocks is a miniature ecosystem. It contains plant-eaters and predators as well as hiding places and shady shelters for these organisms.

PERSONALITY PLUS

Ernst Haeckel (1834–1919) was a German scientist who studied ocean invertebrates and wrote about evolution. In one book, he invented the word "ecology" to describe the relationship between living things and their habitats. He added the Greek word *oikos*, which means "home," to the word *ology*, which means "study of."

NICHE

A niche in your home is a little space that's just right for an item or two. In a habitat, a niche is an organism's place, or job, in that habitat. A turkey vulture, for example, fills a niche as a scavenger—an animal that eats what's left of dead animals after predators finish feeding. It lives in grassland and forest biomes where its habitats include farms, roadsides, and landfills. This species plays this role throughout North, Central, and South America, where it lives in similar biomes and habitats. In Africa, that niche is filled by other vulture species. Vultures even occupy different niches at a feeding site. Scientists who studied vultures in Peru found that certain species arrived and ate first, while other species arrived later.

A MOUNTAIN OF BIOMES

Biomes form bands around Earth because temperatures and rainfall change as you move north and south. The tropical forest biome wraps around Earth's Equator. Cold, snowy polar biomes sit like caps on Earth's north and south ends. A tall mountain also displays these bands. A journey up a mountain may begin in a temperate forest of trees that lose leaves in the fall. Higher up the slope is a coniferous forest. Then these trees dwindle, and you're in a tundra biome filled with low-growing shrubs. Finally, you reach a cold alpine biome of gravel and snow and hardly any plants. A sky island is an ecosystem on a mountain that sits far away from other mountains. In 2015, scientists discovered seven new frog species in a Brazilian sky island. They're found nowhere else.

WORD CHECK

TUNDRA: The coldest biome, with little rain and few plants and animals. Its name comes from the Finnish word *tunturia*, or "treeless plain."

SYMBIOSIS

Different species in an ecological community may be closely linked as partners in the competition for survival. This partnership is called symbiosis. A lichen, for example, is made up of a fungus and a species of algae. The fungus forms the strands of a lichen's structure and provides a habitat for the algae. In return, the algae makes food by photosynthesis. Both species benefit. If only one did, this symbiosis would be called commensalism—a partnership in which only one species benefits, but the other isn't harmed. Parasitism is a kind of symbiosis in which one species benefits but the other is harmed. A flea, for example, is a blood-sucking parasite.

THREATENED BIOMES

Worldwide, habitats and species are threatened by habitat loss, deforestation, pollution, overuse, and other problems. Many people are working to find ways to conserve habitat while using resources, such as fish and forests, in a sustainable way.

In early fall, black-and-orange monarch butterflies are on the move in North America. They're heading south for the winter. Western monarchs spend winter in California, some Eastern ones in Florida, but the rest fly to spruce forests in Mexico. There they will crowd into treetops to survive the cold season. In spring, they'll fly north again to lay eggs.

The monarchs' Mexican migration, however, is threatened by deforestation—the cutting of trees. People living in the monarchs' winter habitat cut trees to sell for lumber and to clear land for farming. Researchers are trying to find a way to balance the needs of both butterflies and people. The monarchs' challenge is just one chapter in a story unfolding across Earth.

FORESTS FOREVER?

Forests are not only habitat for wildlife, but also for people. About 1.6 billion people depend directly on forests for resources such as food and fuel. Forests also play an important role in Earth's water cycle. Plant and tree roots keep soil from washing away in heavy rainfall and clogging rivers. And all 7.4 billion of us depend on forests for some of the oxygen we breathe. Every year, however, up to 58,000 square miles (150,219 sq km) of forests are cut down or burned. That's enough to cover the entire U.S. state of Illinois. Fortunately, the rate of forest loss has slowed since 2010. In some places, people are helping replant forests.

MANY MOUTHS

Earth is home to more than 7 billion people. By 2050, the total world population may be as high as 9.6 billion! That's a lot of people to feed. Already about 40 percent of Earth's surface is used for growing crops and raising farm animals. Turning more wild land into farmland will cause habitat loss—and that can turn many organisms into endangered species. An endangered species is one that becomes so rare, it is in danger of becoming extinct, or gone forever.

WORD CHECK

SUSTAINABILITY: Using water, air, land, and other parts of the environment so that they will be able to support both humans and other organisms now and in the future

GEEK STREAK

Grasslands are one of Earth's most threatened biomes. For example, they once covered about 40 percent of the United States, but now cover barely 5 percent. Most of these grasslands, called prairies, were plowed for planting crops. As a result, populations of birds that nest in grasslands have dropped sharply.

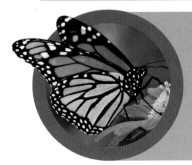

PERSONALITY PLUS

Dr. Fred Urquhart (1912–2002) was a Canadian scientist who started tagging monarch butterflies in 1937 to find out where they go in winter. Years later, he enlisted volunteers to help tag and track monarchs. Finally, in 1975, a volunteer found the monarchs' hideaway in Mexico's mountain forests. Dr. Urquhart urged governments to protect the monarchs' forests and also reduce pesticide use.

SAVING SPECIES

Overhunting, overfishing, and habitat destruction can cause species to become extinct. Scientists estimate that about 40 percent of frogs and other amphibians are in danger of extinction. Also at risk are about 31 percent of cactuses, 26 percent of mammals, and 13 percent of birds, among others. Preventing their extinction will require protecting habitat, stopping pollution, and enforcing strict laws to control hunting or collecting these species. Endangered species can be saved. Gray whales nearly went extinct about a hundred years ago because humans overhunted them. Laws were passed to protect the whales, and today there are from 19,000 to 25,000 of them.

PLANTING THE FUTURE

It's possible to grow food and support wildlife at the same time. Instead of cutting trees down for farmland, farmers can plant coffee trees (left), for example, to grow in shady rain forests. Many people buy "shade-grown" coffee to help conserve rain forests.

SAVING THE SEAS

The ocean is threatened by pollution. Every year, people dump millions of tons of plastic trash into it. Climate change is making the ocean warmer and more acidic. Some fish are in danger of going extinct because so many have been caught, or "overfished." About 100 million sharks, for instance, are taken from the ocean each year. These important predators help keep the numbers of smaller predators from growing too large. Today, many nations are setting up marine protected areas to help save habitat and control fishing. Many people are also working to slow climate change and stop plastic pollution.

CORAL CRISIS

A healthy coral reef is filled with many kinds of coral and fish. Scientists say that 75 percent of coral reefs are threatened habitats. Coral-reef fish suffer from overfishing—they're caught as food or for sale as pets. Without parrotfish, who eat the reef's algae, the algae can grow out of control and smother the reef. Reefs are also damaged by boats, fishing equipment, and pollution. "Bleaching" is another enemy. It occurs when coral polyps get sick and lose the colorful algae that live inside them and make food for them. Water that's too warm or salty, or that gets too much sunlight, can cause bleaching.

TOOLS OF THE TRADE

Scientists are using drones to keep track of deforestation—the cutting down and burning of forests. New, inexpensive drones fly over the landscape and film it. This close-up view gives a clearer picture of what's happening on the ground than a space satellite can. Drones also help scientists count wild animals.

CONSERVATION

Conservation means using Earth's resources wisely while also taking care of air, water, land, and living things in ways that let ecosystems continue to work well.

The old saying, "Waste not, want not" is a smart one: It means you won't run out of what you need if you don't waste things. This idea is an important part of conservation.

We need the natural world every bit as much as other species do. Yet humans have hurt Earth by polluting it, destroying habitats, wasting resources, and driving species to extinction. But humans can figure out ways to undo much of this damage and prevent it in the future. We're figuring out new ways to produce energy that doesn't pollute as much, to grow more food without using more chemicals, and to raise endangered animals and set them free in their natural habitats.

Conservation efforts can be as big as an organization with millions of members or as small as your school or home—or even just you! Everything you do to help take care of your habitat is conservation at work.

PARKS AND PRESERVES

Parks and preserves conserve ecosystems and wildlife. The world's first national park, Yellowstone National Park in the northwestern United States, is famous for bison herds. As many as 60 million bison once roamed North America, but they nearly became extinct due to overhunting in the 1800s. Today, nearly 5,000 bison live wild in Yellowstone thanks to laws and protection from illegal hunting, called poaching. Another 50,000 live on other parks, preserves, and private lands. Other species and habitats around the world are protected the same way.

CLIMATE CONTROL

Writer Bill McKibben wrote about climate change in a book called *The End of Nature* in 1989. He's still writing about it today. McKibben is also an activist—a person who works to cause a change in society. Activists hold marches, or big gatherings called rallies, to show support for change. McKibben helped start an organization called 350.org. People in more than 188 countries work with 350.org to stop the use of fossil fuels and educate people about climate change.

TRY THIS!

WHAT YOU NEED: A notepad and a pencil

HOW LONG IT TAKES: 10 minutes

Make a list of the "energy vampires" in your home. They're electronic devices that use electricity even when they seem to be off. They include devices with digital clocks as well as ones you turn on with a remote. Check chargers, too! A cell phone charger, for example, uses electricity if you leave it plugged in after you're done charging your phone. Think about unplugging devices when they aren't in use.

MEETING OF MINDS

In 2015, nearly every country in the world took part in a big meeting in Paris, France, known as the United Nations Climate Change Conference. Set up by the United Nations, the meeting was attended by 195 nations. Its mission: to come up with plans to control climate change, protect forests, save species, and make it possible for every person on Earth to lead a healthy, safe life. Young and Future Generations Day featured workshops in which youth representatives planned solutions to climate change. When the summit ended, all 195 countries had agreed to immediately begin to reduce their carbon output.

GEEK STREAK

Earth is home to about 1.5 million known species and millions not yet discovered. But this biodiversity is threatened by an extinction rate 100 or more times larger than before 1800. Scientist Edward O. Wilson, who writes about biodiversity, warns "we should preserve every scrap of biodiversity as priceless while we learn to use it and come to understand what it means to humanity."

SILENT SPRING?

Environmentalism is the effort to stop pollution and conserve habitats by working for better laws and protection of lands and species. It's often called the "environmental movement." In 1962, the book *Silent Spring* by biologist Rachel Carson (1907–1964) made people realize the dangers of the pesticide DDT. Carson wrote about how DDT in the environment collected in animals' bodies over time, slowly poisoning them. Birds with heavy loads of DDT laid eggs with weak, easily broken shells. DDT was banned in the United States in 1972.

WORD CHECK

BIODIVERSITY: The variety of life in a habitat or biome. Healthy ecosystems depend on biodiversity to work properly.

BETTER CITIES

Many towns and cities grow larger over time. If this growth isn't planned carefully, the city spreads haphazardly across the countryside around it. Habitats are paved over, broken up, or completely lost. This unplanned growth is called urban sprawl. With urban planning, however, a city can be designed so that people live close to jobs and shops or can use trains, buses, and bikes to travel, instead of cars. Urban planning also includes parks and other green spaces.

PERSONALITY PLUS

Dr. Eugenie Clark (1922–2015) was a marine biologist who studied sharks. She spoke to world leaders about creating marine protected areas. "Those of us who love the sea wish everyone would be aware of the need to protect the sea," she said. Today, scientists continue to study ocean animals at the marine laboratory she started in Florida, U.S.A., in 1955.

GLOSSARY

ILLUSTRATION OF VIRUS H1N1

Acceleration: Increase in velocity, which means traveling at increasing speed in a straight line

Acid: A chemical compound that has a lot of hydrogen ions. It dissolves in water, tastes sour, and neutralizes bases. Oranges and vinegar are acids.

Alkali: A base that can be dissolved in water. This compound turns blue with litmus paper and reacts with an acid to form salt and water.

Alloy: A metal made by mixing two or more metals. Steel is an alloy of iron and carbon; brass is an alloy of copper and zinc.

Alveoli: Tiny, thin-walled sacs inside the lungs where oxygen and carbon dioxide can enter and exit the bloodstream

Amino acids: Special organic molecules found in every cell of your body and all living things. They make protein for survival.

Ammonia: A colorless gas that is a compound of nitrogen and hydrogen

Anatomy: A branch of science that studies the body structure of humans, animals, and other living organisms

Antibiotic: A medicine that kills bacteria or stops them from reproducing. "Anti" means "against," and "bios" means "life."

Antimatter: Every particle of matter has a corresponding antiparticle with an opposite charge. Protons have antiprotons; neutrons have antineutrons. When matter meets antimatter it's called annihilation.

Artery: A blood vessel that carries oxygen-rich blood away from the heart

Arthropod: An invertebrate animal with an exoskeleton, jointed legs, and a body that is divided into sections

Asteroid: A small rocky object orbiting the sun. A large number of asteroids are found between the orbits of Mars and Jupiter.

Atmosphere: The layer of gases that surround a planet. Atmospheres can be thick or thin and of different kinds of gases. They're held in place by a planet's gravity.

AEROSOL CANS OF SPRAY PAINT

Atom: The smallest part of matter. It is made up of electrons and a nucleus containing one or more protons and neutrons.

Atomic number: Every element is an atom with a unique atomic number. The number represents the number of protons in the element's atom.

Bacterium: A single-celled microbe that does not have a nucleus

Base: The chemical compound that is opposite of an acid. It has a lot of hydroxide ions. Baking soda is a base.

Big bang: The phrase used by astronomer Fred Hoyle in 1949 to describe the beginnings of the universe. (In fact, the universe started off infinitely tiny and made no noise at all.)

Binary code: A system used in computer programs that represents letters and numbers as 0s and 1s

Biodiversity: The variety of plant and animal life in a habitat or biome. Healthy ecosystems depend on biodiversity to work properly.

Biofuel: A fuel that is made of plant material or animal waste

Biome: A region on Earth with similar climate, animals, plants, and other organisms

Biosphere: The zone on Earth where life is possible

Caldera: A circular, steep-walled basin that marks the spot of a volcanic eruption

Calorie: A unit of heat used to indicate the amount of energy that food will produce in the human body

Capillary: A blood vessel that links an artery and a vein

Carbohydrates: Molecules made up of sugars, which are substances made out of carbon, hydrogen, and oxygen

Carbon: A chemical element, abundant in the Earth's crust and necessary for life

Carbon dioxide: A colorless, odorless gas, vital to life on Earth

Carnivore: An animal that eats meat

Cartilage: A tough, flexible substance that forms part of many animals' skeletons and the entire skeleton of some animals, such as sharks

Catalyst: A substance that changes the rate of a chemical reaction but isn't used up in the process

Cell: The smallest unit in a living organism; also the area covered by a cell phone tower's signals

Cephalopod: A mollusk that has an obvious head and many arms, such as an octopus. "Cephalo" means "head," and "pod" means "foot."

Chemosynthesis: The process of making food by using energy from chemical reactions instead of sunlight

Chitin: A hard substance that is part of an insect's exoskeleton or the shell of a crustacean

Chlorophyll: A green pigment in plants, some algae, and microbes that captures sunlight for use in photosynthesis

Chordate: An animal that at some point in its life has a flexible rod in its body called a notochord. Fish, reptiles, amphibians, birds, and mammals are chordates.

Circuit: The path followed by an electric current

Comet: A small, icy body orbiting the sun

Commensalism: A kind of partnership in which only one species benefits, but the other isn't harmed

Composite: A material made up of two or more substances

Condensation: The change of water from its gas form (water vapor) to its liquid form (water)

Constellation: One of 88 groups of stars that seem to form a shape in the sky

Convective: Carrying heat from one place to another. In the sun's convective zone, currents of gas carry heat from the inside to the surface.

Convergent boundary: A place in the Earth's crust where plates push together

Coronary: Pertaining to the arteries that surround and supply the heart with blood

Cosmic ray: High-energy charged particles from outer space that travel at the speed of light

Cotyledon: A small leaf inside a seed; also called a "seed leaf"

Crust: Earth's thin outermost layer

Cyclotron: A particle accelerator that works by making beams of particles spin around in a circle faster than they've ever gone before

Dendrochronology: The study of tree rings to find out about the past. "Dendro" means "tree," and "chron" means "time."

Dermis: The layer of skin below the epidermis

Digital: Relating to signals or other information in the form of binary code

Divergent boundary: A place in the Earth's crust where plates pull apart

DNA: Deoxyribonucleic acid, a complex molecule shaped like a spiraling ladder that forms genes

Ecosystem: A community of all living things—plants, animals, and other organisms—in a particular area

Ecotherm: An animal that uses its surroundings to control its body temperature. Called "cold-blooded," ecotherms include fish, reptiles, and amphibians.

Electrode: A solid component of an electrical system that releases or receives an electric current

Electromagnetic: Relating to electricity and magnetism. An electromagnetic force holds negatively charged electrons around a positively charged nucleus.

Electron: A subatomic particle with a negative charge. Electrons spin in an orbit around the nucleus of an atom.

Elements: The simplest materials made up of atoms. They cannot be divided into anything else. There are 94 elements found in nature, and they are what make up matter.

Endotherm: An animal that produces its own body heat. Called "warm-blooded," endotherms include mammals, birds, and some fish.

Energy: What gives matter the ability to do something like move, change shape, or be warm. Scientists call energy the ability to do work.

Enzyme: A complex protein produced by living cells that acts as a catalyst and speeds up the rate of chemical reactions in plants and animals

Epidermis: The top layer of the skin

Eukaryote: An organism made up of a cell or cells containing a nucleus

Evaporation: The change from liquid into gas, like water to water vapor

Fault: A crack in the Earth along the length of which sections of ground are moving in different directions

Fission: A nuclear reaction in which the nucleus of an atom splits into smaller parts, releasing large amounts of energy

Fossil fuel: Coal, oil, or natural gas that was formed deep in the Earth from dead plants or animals

Frequency: The number of times that the top of a sound wave passes a fixed point

Fulcrum: The place where you rest the lever to move it up and down. A fulcrum is at the center of a teeter-totter.

Fusion: In atomic fusion, when the nuclei at the center of two atoms merge into one heavier atomic nucleus. This releases huge amounts of energy.

Galaxy: A system of stars, interstellar gas, dust, and dark matter held together by gravity

HOT EMBERS IN FIRE

Gamma ray: Light with the shortest wavelength and highest energy in the electromagnetic spectrum

Gene: A part of a cell that controls or influences the appearance, growth, and function of a living being

Genome: All the genes in an organism

Geology: The word comes from two Latin words: *geo*, "Earth," and *logia*, "study." "Geology" means speaking about, or studying, the Earth.

Glacier: A very large area of ice that moves slowly down a slope or valley over a wide area of land

Gland: An organ that produces substances that are either released from the body (saliva, sweat, or tears) or are released into the body to help the body work and grow

Glucose: A kind of sugar

Gluons: The particles that hold quarks tightly together, like glue

Gravity: One of the four fundamental forces of nature, which causes every object that has mass to exert a pull on every other object

Habitat: A place that provides food, water, and shelter for an organism

Herbivore: An animal that eats plants

Herpetology: The study of reptiles and amphibians. "Herpeto" comes from the Greek word that means "creeping thing."

Hertz: A measurement of the number of radio waves per second

Hormone: A chemical produced inside the body that tells your body how to work and grow

Humidity: The amount of water vapor in the air

Hydrogen: A colorless, odorless gas; the most abundant substance in the universe

Ichthyology: The scientific study of fish. *Ichthus* means "fish," and *logos* means "study" in the Greek language.

Inert: Something that is motionless and not involved with anything around it

Infrared: The scientific name for the radiation we feel on our skin as heat

Invertebrates: Animals without a spinal column

Keratin: The main structural material that makes up the outer layer of the skin

Laser: A device that generates a focused beam of light that can cut, drill, and read bar codes and CDs

Lava: Hot molten rock erupting from a volcano

Light-year: A unit of distance that is equal to the distance that light travels in one year: 5.88 trillion miles (9.46 trillion km)

Lipid: A fatty, waxy, or oily chemical compound that comes from a living thing and does not dissolve in water

Magma: Hot melted rock from the Earth's mantle

Mammal: A warm-blooded vertebrate animal that grows hair and, if female, produces milk from special glands for its young

Mantle: The layer of the interior of the Earth between the core and the outer crust

Marsupial: A mammal, like a kangaroo or a koala bear, that gives birth to partly developed young that continue their growth in a pouch in the mother's body

MALE PANTHER CHAMELEON

GLOSSARY

Mass: The amount of matter, or number of atoms, in an object

Matter: Anything that has mass and takes up space

Medium: What a wave is traveling through. Ocean waves move through water, but sound goes through air, water, and rocks; light travels through transparent things.

Membrane: A thin wall that separates the inside of a cell from the outside

Metamorphic rock: A rock whose original structure has been changed by high pressure, high temperatures, or both

Meteoroid, meteor, and meteorite: A meteoroid is a rock floating in space. A meteor is a shooting star and is called a meteorite when it reaches the ground.

Microbe: A single-celled organism too tiny to see without a microscope. Some microbes can cause disease, while others are important for life.

Microbiome: A collection of all the genes in a person's population of microbes. "Micro" means "small," and "biome" is a place where organisms live.

Microorganism: A living thing with just one cell in its body. It is too small to see without a microscope.

Microprocessor: A computer processor contained on a chip

Mineral: A nonliving solid found in nature and made of one or more elements

Molecule: Two or more atoms that have bonded together

Mollusk: A soft-bodied animal, such as a slug or a clam, with a body that isn't divided into sections

Neuron: A nerve cell

Neutrinos: The smallest known particles of matter

Neutron: A subatomic particle with no electric charge. It's found in the nucleus of all atoms, except hydrogen.

Nucleic acid: Acids found in cells that form RNA and DNA

Nucleus: The inner core of an atom

Nutrients: Substances that the body needs for health, such as fats, proteins, and carbohydrates

Orbit: The path of one object around another, such as the Earth traveling around the sun. One complete revolution is an orbit.

Organelle: One part of a cell that has a very specific function. The nucleus is an organelle. A chloroplast is an organelle that converts sunlight to energy in plants.

Organism: A living thing

Ornithology: The study of birds

Ozone layer: A region in the second layer of the Earth's atmosphere that absorbs most of the sun's damaging ultraviolet radiation

Paleontologist: A scientist who studies life in past geologic times

Parasite: An animal or plant that lives in or on another animal or plant and gets its food or protection from it

Particle: Any of the basic units of matter or energy, such as a molecule, an atom, a neutron, proton, or electron

Particle accelerator: A giant machine that makes atoms rev up and travel at almost the speed of light, and then smashes them together

Phloem: A layer of tree bark that carries food made by leaves to other parts of the tree

Photosynthesis: The process in plants and other organisms that converts sunlight into energy and releases oxygen into the atmosphere

Phototropism: The movement toward or away from a source of light, as when sunflowers turn toward the sun. "Photo" means "light," and "tropos" means "turn."

Photovoltaic cell: A panel, usually made of silicon, that converts sunlight directly into electricity

Phytoplankton: Microbes that float near the surface of the ocean and make food by photosynthesis

Piezoelectricity: Electricity produced in certain objects when they are twisted, bent, or pressed

Pigment: A chemical that has a particular color. This natural

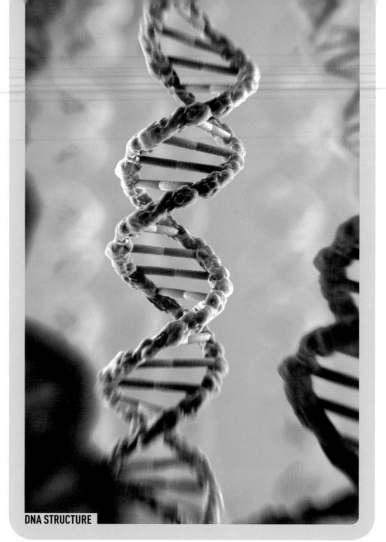

DNA STRUCTURE

substance gives skin and hair their color. Pigment is added to paints to make them a specific color.

Pistil: The part of a flower in which seeds form

Plastic: Able to be molded, stretched, or otherwise formed into a new shape

Platelets: Colorless blood cells that help blood to clot and stop bleeding

Plate tectonics: The movement of Earth's plates that builds the planet, raises up mountains, and carves out oceans

Pollen: Dustlike specks made by a flower's stamen that combine with a flower's egg cells to make seeds

Polymer: Large molecules made up of repeating units

Positron: An antimatter electron that has a positive charge

Precipitation: Any kind of moisture falling from clouds. It includes rain, snow, hail, and sleet.

Predator: An organism that kills and eats other organisms. A lion, for example, is a predator. Zebras and antelope are among its prey.

Prism: A clear object with at least two flat sides at an angle that refracts light

Properties: The characteristics that belong to a substance, such as its color and hardness, how heavy it is, or whether it forms compounds easily

Protein: A substance found in food such as meat, eggs, milk, nuts, and beans that is important for growth and other functions in living organisms

Protocell: A very simple structure made of a membrane that contains RNA (ribonucleic acid). "Proto" means "first." It is thought to have evolved into the first cell.

Proton: A tiny particle of matter that has a positive electric charge and is found in the nucleus of an atom

Protozoa: Single-celled organisms that can't make their own food

Pulsar: A spinning neutron star that gives off regular pulses of radio waves

Quantum: The smallest amount of a form of energy. Quantum physics is the science that studies how matter and energy behave at the smallest levels.

Quark: The very small particle that makes up protons and neutrons. There are six kinds of quarks: up, down, top, bottom, strange, and charm.

Quasar: A distant, very bright galaxy that sends out radio waves

Radiation: Energy that travels in the form of invisible waves or particles. It does not have any weight or mass and includes visible light, radio waves, x-rays, ultraviolet light, and gamma rays.

Radioactivity: Radiation that occurs when the nucleus of an atom is broken down into smaller particles

Radio wave: An electromagnetic wave that is often used to carry signals, such as for television broadcasts or cell phones

Reactor: A device that releases nuclear energy

Refraction: The bending of light as it moves from one clear material to another

Respiratory: Describes the body parts involved in breathing as well as the process of breathing itself

RNA: Ribonucleic acid, a complex molecule that contains information for making proteins

Router: A device that links computers to the Internet by a cable

Satellite: Any object, natural or artificial, that orbits a planet

Scuba: An air-supply system used by divers while underwater. "Scuba" stands for "self-contained underwater breathing apparatus."

Sediment: Particles or grains of weathered rock and debris that sink to the bottom of a liquid and sit there. From the Latin *sedere*, which means "to sit." Sedimentary rocks are hardened sediment.

Seismic: Relating to earthquakes or other waves in the Earth and its crust. A seismometer detects and measures the size of earthquakes.

Singularity: A point in space with an infinite density, such as a black hole

Software: A set of instructions that tells a computer what to do

Species: A kind of animal that can mate with others of its own kind to produce living young

Spectrum: The group of colors that a ray of light can be separated into, as in all the colors of the rainbow

Spores: Tiny reproductive cells made by fungi and other nonflowering plants. Instead of seeds, they sprout to form new organisms.

Stamen: The part of a flower that produces pollen

Subatomic: Less than, or smaller than, an atom

Subduction: A process in which one of Earth's plates slides underneath another plate

Supernova: An explosion at the end of a massive star's life cycle, when its core collapses and releases huge amounts of energy. It burns brightly for a while and then fades away.

Sustainability: A way of living that uses and takes care of water, air, and other parts of the environment so that they will be able to support both humans and other organisms now and in the future

Symbiosis: A partnership between organisms of different species that work together to benefit each other. For example, the oxpecker bird rides on the back of a black rhino and eats the bugs on the rhino's skin. The bird gets food, and the rhino gets rid of bugs.

Synthetic: A man-made material created by a chemical process to imitate a natural product

Tissue: The part of a living body that is made of similar cells, such as nerve tissue or the cardiac tissue of the heart

Transistor: A device used to control electronic signals and the flow of electricity in radios, computers, and other electronics

Transpiration: A plant's release of water vapor. Plants pull in water through their roots and release it into the air through the pores of their leaves.

Troposphere: The layer of the atmosphere closest to the Earth

ANDROMEDA GALAXY

Tsunami: A huge, long wave usually caused by an underground earthquake, a volcanic eruption, or a coastal landslide. A tsunami can cause tremendous damage.

Turbine: A fanlike machine that is built to turn a forward flow of air, steam, or water into a spinning motion. The spinning motion generates electricity.

Ultraviolet radiation: Electromagnetic radiation with wavelengths just shorter than those of visible light

Vaccine: A substance that is injected into the body to help prevent a disease

Vacuum: A space where there is no air, and nothing else at all

Venom: A poison made by an animal that is injected into another animal through teeth or a sting

Vertebrate: An animal with a backbone, like a mammal, reptile, bird, amphibian, or fish

Virus: A microbe that must occupy a living cell in order to survive and reproduce

Viscosity: The ability of a liquid or a gas to flow. Highly viscous liquids, like lava, don't flow as easily as less viscous liquids, like water.

Volume: The amount of space a substance takes up

Wavelength: The distance between successive crests of waves, measured in sound waves and electromagnetic waves

X-rays: High beams of energy that can shine through the tiny gaps between atoms in matter

Xylem: The layer of tree bark that carries water from a tree's roots to its leaves

CHAIN SWING CAROUSEL

FIND OUT MORE

WEBSITES

CDC: Body and Mind: cdc.gov/bam
Discovery Kids: discoverykids.com
Ducksters: Physics for Kids: ducksters.com/science/physics
Dynamic Periodic Table: ptable.com
EPA Student's Guide to Global Climate Change: www3.epa.gov/climatechange/kids
ESA Kids: Our Universe: esa.int/esaKIDSen/OurUniverse.html
Explain That Stuff! Computers: explainthatstuff.com/howcomputerswork.html
Explain That Stuff! Electricity: explainthatstuff.com/electricity.html
FCC Kids Zone: How Does a Cell Phone Work?: transition.fcc.gov/cgb/kidszone/faqs_cellphones.html#howdoesacellphonework
Kids Health: How the Body Works: kidshealth.org/kid/htbw
Kids.gov: Plants: kids.usa.gov/science/plants/index.shtml
Life of a Tree: arborday.org/kids/carly/lifeofatree
NASA Climate Kids: climatekids.nasa.gov
NASA Mission Science: Radio Waves: missionscience.nasa.gov/ems/05_radiowaves.html
NASA: Solar System 101: solarsystem.nasa.gov/kids/index.cfm
NASA: What Is a Satellite?: nasa.gov/audience/forstudents/5-8/features/nasa-knows/what-is-a-satellite-58.html
National Earth Science Teachers Association: Windows to the Universe: windows2universe.org
National Geographic Kids: kids.nationalgeographic.com
National Geographic: Science and Space: science.nationalgeographic.com
NOAA Kids: oceanservice.noaa.gov/kids
Oxford University Museum of Natural History: The Learning Zone: The History of Life in a Single Year!: www.oum.ox.ac.uk/thezone/fossils/history/calendar.htm
Physics 4 Kids!: physics4kids.com
San Diego Zoo Kids: kids.sandiegozoo.org/animals
Science Kids: Space for Kids: sciencekids.co.nz/space.html
Science Kids: Technology Facts: sciencekids.co.nz/sciencefacts/technology/typesofrobots.html
Science **Magazine:** news.sciencemag.org
Smithsonian National Zoological Park: Just for Kids: nationalzoo.si.edu/Audiences/Kids/facts.cfm
Space.com: space.com
StarChild: starchild.gsfc.nasa.gov/docs/StarChild/StarChild.html
The Scale of the Universe: htwins.net/scale2
University of California Museum of Paleontology: Understanding Geologic Time: ucmp.berkeley.edu/education/explorations/tours/geotime
USGS: Earthquakes for Kids: earthquake.usgs.gov/learn/kids
USGS: Summary of the Water Cycle: water.usgs.gov/edu/watercyclesummary.html

FILMS/SHOWS

ANIMALS
"Amazing Animals" video series
(kids.nationalgeographic.com/videos/amazing-animals)

EARTH, OCEAN, CLIMATE
The Blue Planet (2008)
Oceans (2010)
Oceans: Exploring the Secrets of Our Undersea World (2008)
Planet Ocean (2012)

HUMAN BODY
Inside the Human Body (2011)
Inside the Living Body (2007)

BOOKS

Aguilar, David. *Space Encyclopedia: A Tour of Our Solar System and Beyond.* National Geographic Kids Books, 2013.

Daniels, Patricia. *My First Pocket Guide: Weather.* National Geographic Kids Books, 1999.

Editors of Time-Life Books. *Physical Science.* Alexandria, VA: Time-Life Books, 2000.

Editors of Time-Life Books. *Planet Earth.* Alexandria, VA: Time-Life Books, 1997.

Furgang, Kathy. *Everything Weather: Facts, Photos, and Fun That Will Blow Your Mind!* National Geographic Kids Books, 2012.

Gundersen, P. Erik. *The Handy Physics Answer Book.* Visible Ink Press, 1999.

Krull, Kathleen. *Lives of the Scientists: Experiments, Explosions (and What the Neighbors Thought).* Boston, MA: HMH Books for Young Readers, 2013.

Lessem, Don. *The Ultimate Dinopedia: The Most Complete Dinosaur Reference Ever.* National Geographic Kids Books, 2010.

Murawski, Darlyne, and Nancy Honovich. *Ultimate Bugopedia: The Most Complete Bug Reference Ever.* National Geographic Kids Books, 2013.

Spelman, Lucy. *Animal Encyclopedia.* National Geographic Kids Books, 2011.

Tomecek, Steve. *Dirtmeister's Nitty Gritty Planet Earth: All About Rocks, Minerals, Fossils, Earthquakes, Volcanoes, & Even Dirt!* National Geographic Kids Books, 2015.

Wilsdon, Christina, Patricia Daniels, and Jen Agresta. *Ultimate Bodypedia: An Amazing Inside-Out Tour of the Human Body.* National Geographic Kids Books, 2014.

INDEX

ENDEAVOUR SPACE SHUTTLE LAUNCH, CAPE CANAVERAL, FLORIDA, U.S.A.

INDEX

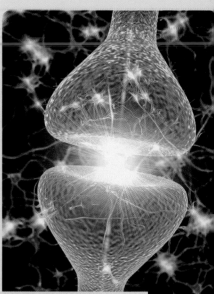

ILLUSTRATION OF NERVE SYNAPSE

AFRICAN LION

YELLOWSTONE HOT SPRING AKA GRAND PRYSMATIC SPRING

ILLUSTRATION OF HUMAN HEART

INDEX

SKYDIVERS

JUPITER'S MOON EUROPA

ACKNOWLEDGMENTS

The publishers would like to thank the following scientists for sharing their time and expertise in their review of the National Geographic *Science Encyclopedia:*

SCIENCE EDUCATION REVIEW

Mark Hannum: Mr. Hannum is a physics instructor and the director of the Neuroscience Lab at the Thomas Jefferson High School for Science and Technology in Alexandria, Virginia. Mr. Hannum is a National Science Foundation Albert Einstein Distinguished Fellow. He is a former science teacher in the Washington, D.C., public school system.

LIFE SCIENCES REVIEW

Edward M. Barrows: Dr. Barrows is a professor of biology in the Department of Biology at Georgetown University in Washington, D.C. His research focuses on arthropod and plant biodiversity and conservation and scientific communication. His teaching includes forest ecology and biology for undergraduates and graduates. He serves as an advisor for biology students and environmental studies minors and is the director of the Georgetown University Center for the Environment.

PHYSICAL SCIENCES REVIEW

Dr. Brian Greene: Dr. Greene is an American theoretical physicist and string theorist. He has been a professor at Columbia University since 1996. In 2008 he co-founded the World Science Festival and serves as its chairman.

Dr. William E. Kastenberg: The Daniel M. Tellep Distinguished Professor of Engineering Emeritus from the University of California, Berkeley, Dr. Kastenberg is a member of the National Academy of Engineering and is a Fellow of the American Association for the Advancement of Science and of the American Nuclear Society.

Apurva Errabelli: A test engineer for Dahl Consulting in Minneapolis, Minnesota, Ms. Errabelli works on-site in the motorcycle group at Polaris Industries. She was co-president of Engineers Without Borders when she graduated from Smith College with a bachelor of science in engineering in 2014.

Richard I. Sayler: Mr. Sayler is working on his Ph.D. in physical chemistry, under the supervision of Dr. R. Dave Britt, at the University of California Davis (projected graduation 2019). He studied chemistry and physics at Uppsala University (Uppsala, Sweden) and the University of Utah and earned a bachelor's degree in chemistry from the University of Oregon in 2012.

68 (up), GI; 68 (lo le), SH/Krivosheev Vitaly; 68 (lo md), SH/MyImages–Micha; 68 (lo rt), SH/Abel Tumik; 69 (up), SH/Izf; 69 (md le), GI North America; 69 (md rt), SH/Doug James; 69 (lo), SH/Georgios Kollidas; 70 (up), SH/Samo Trebizan; 70 (lo le), f/2.8 by ARC–Fotolia; 70 (lo rt), SH/Damiano Poli; 71 (up le), SH/fpdress; 79 (up rt), Corbis; 79 (lo), SH/Germanskydiver; 72 (up), SH/Vitaly Korovin; 72 (md le), APIC/GI; 72 (md rt), SH/general-fmv; 72 (lo le), David Mack/SS; 72 (lo rt), SS; 73 (up), SH/Bangkokhappiness; 73 (lo), Photo Researchers/SS; 74 (up), SH/Albert Pego; 74 (md), SH/supergenijalac; 74 (lo), GI; 75 (up le), SH/Kzenon; 75 (up rt), Pavel Losevsky–Fotolia; 75 (lo), David Ducros/SS; 76 (up), MARK THIESSEN/National Geographic Creative; 76 (lo le), mtsaride–Fotolia; 76 (lo rt), akg-images; 77 (up), GI/Flickr RM; 77 (md le), www.bridgemanimages.com; 77 (md rt), SH/123dartist; 77 (lo), SH/R.M. Nunes; 78 (up le), SH/Olesia Bilkei; 78 (up rt), Alamy Stock Photo; 78 (lo le), SSPL via GI; 78 (lo rt), SH/prudkov; 78 (up le), SH/mffoto; 79 (up rt), SH/Marcin Poziemski; 79 (md), SH/Tania Zbrodko; 79 (lo), Mary Evans/SS; 80 (up), SH/Nomad_Soul; 80 (lo), SH/AZP Worldwide; 81 (up), SH/picture-partners; 81 (md le), SH/Sergej Razvodovskij; 81 (md rt), Duomo/Corbis; 81 (lo), William H. Bond/National Geographic Creative; 82 (up), SH/WDG Photo; 82 (lo), SH/De Visu; 83 (up), SH/Aleksei Andreev; 83 (lo le), Claus Lunau/Bonnier Publications/SS; 83 (lo rt), Ashley Cooper/Corbis; 84 (up), SPL/SS; 84 (md), SH/Ruth Peterkin; 84 (lo), Emory Kristof/National Geographic Creative; 85 (up), SH/Steve Bower; 85 (md), SH/NoPainNoGain; 85 (lo), SH/Tolga Tezcan; 86 (up), SH/Carlos Wunderlin; 86 (lo le), SH/italianphoto; 86 (lo md), Wikimedia Commons; 86 (lo rt), AndreasJ–Fotolia; 87 (up le), GI; 87 (up rt), Gamma-Keystone via GI; 87 (md up), GI; 87 (md lo), GI; 87 (lo le), GI North America; 87 (lo rt), Mark Williamson/SS; 88 (up), SH/Richard Griffin; 88 (lo), GI/iStockphoto; 89 (up le), GI/Dorling Kindersley RF; 89 (up rt), SH/studioVin; 89 (lo le), SH/DeepGreen; 89 (lo md), SH/Boris Toshev; 89 (lo rt), SH/SusaZoom; 90 (up), SH/Milos Stojiljkovic; 90 (lo), dechevm–Fotolia; 91 (up le), SH/bogdanhoda; 91 (up rt), SH/Steve Heap; 91 (md), SH/Carlo Toffolo; 91 (lo), SH/Juanan Barros Moreno; 92 (up), SH/kurhan; 92 (lo), SH/CRM; 93 (up), GI/Stocktrek Images; 93 (md up le), Alamy Stock Photo; 93 (md up rt), Bloomberg News/GI; 93 (md lo le), Ryan Pyle/Corbis; 93 (md lo rt), NASA/Roger Ressmeyer/Corbis; 93 (lo), SH/Dell; 94 (up), GI/AWL Images RM; 94 (lo), SH/sculpies; 95 (up le), SH/Sophie James; 95 (up rt), GI/iStockphoto; 95 (lo), SH/Cyril Hou; **Energy:** 96 (up le), SH/donfiore; 96 (up rt), SH/Runrun2; 96 (lo le), SH/zatvornik; 96 (lo rt), SH/zatvornik; 96 (lo), SH/Kletr; 97, Solar Dynamics Observatory/NASA; 98 (up), SH/Filip Fuxa; 98 (md le), SH/Oleksiy Rezin; 98 (md rt), SH/Doug James; 98 (lo), SH/paintings; 99 (up le), GI; 99 (up rt), SH/Andrey_Popov; 99 (lo le), Rostislav Sedlacek–Fotolia; 99 (lo rt), SH/Gustavo Miguel Fernandes; 100 (up le), GI; 100 (up md), www.bridgemanart.com; 100 (up rt), www.bridgemanimages.com; 100 (lo le), SH/milosk50; 100 (lo rt), SH/milosk50; 100 (up le), www.bridgemanimages.com; 100 (up md), SSPL via GI; 100 (up rt), Print Collector/GI; 101 (lo le), AFP/GI; 101 (lo rt), SH/mj007; 102 (up), SH/Steve Collender; 102 (md), SH/Sergey Mironov; 102 (lo), GI/SS; 103 (up), GI/Cultura RF; 103 (md le), SH/Richard Peterson; 103 (lo md), SH/Kuttelvaserova Stuchelova; 103 (lo rt), SH/[illegible]; 104 (up), SH/Andrey_Popov; 104 (lo), SH/Dziewul; 105 (up le), SH/Levent Konuk; 105 (up rt), NIST/SS; 105 (lo le), SS; 105 (lo rt), SH/Volt Collection; 106 (up), Ted Kinsman/SS; 106 (lo), SH/andrea lehmkuhl; 107 (up), SH/Denis Dryashkin; 107 (md), SH/Josemaria Toscano; 107 (lo), SH/auremar; 108 (up le), SS; 108 (up rt), SSPL via GI; 108 (lo le), SS; 108 (lo rt), Alamy Stock Photo; 109 (up le), The Granger Collection, New York; 109 (up rt), www.bridgemanimages.com; 109 (lo le), Alfredo Dagli Orti/The Art Archive/Corbis; 109 (lo md), Monica Schroeder/SS; 109 (lo rt), SH/carrie-nelson; 110 (up), Claus Lunau/Bonnier Publications/SS; 110 (md), Solar Dynamics Observatory/NASA; 110 (lo), Wikimedia Commons; 111 (up), SH; 111 (lo), Ted Kinsman/SS; 112 (up), SH/Dell; 112 (lo le), SH/Garsya; 112 (lo md), SH/Mega Pixel; 112 (lo rt), SH/Oliver Hoffmann; 113 (up le), Spencer Grant/SS; 113 (up rt), SH/Vitaly Korovin; 113 (md), SH/cyo bo; 113 (lo), Wellcome Images/SS; 114 (up), Science Photo Library; 114 (lo le), Royal Institution of Great Britain/SS; 114 (lo rt), Gideon Mendel/In Pictures/Corbis; 115 (up rt), SS; 115 (md le), SH/Viktorus; 115 (md md), SH/urciser; 115 (md rt), SH/lafoto; 115 (md lo), SH/gyn9037; 115 (lo), SH/xuanhuongho; 116 (up), SH/Peter Gudella; 116 (lo lo), Kino/VWPics/Agefotostock; 116 (lo rt), Bruce Dale/National Geographic Creative, 117 (up), Wikimedia Commons; 117 (md), Aania–Fotolia; 117 (lo), Roger Ressmeyer/Corbis; 118 (up), SH/Dell; 118 (md), AguaSonic Acoustics/SS; 118 (lo le), SH/outc; 118 (lo rt), SH/NCAimages; 119 (up), SH/Peter Gudella; 119 (md), SH/Claudia Paulussen; 119 (lo), SS; 120 (up), SH/Danil Nevsky; 120 (lo), SH/Djomas; 121 (up le), GI/Photo Researchers RM; 121 (up rt), GI/Dorling Kindersley; 121 (lo le), Victor Habbick Visions/SS; 121 (lo rt), SH/katatonia82; 122 (up), SH; 122 (md), SH/Christian Bertrand; 122 (lo), Robert C. Magis/National Geographic Creative; 123 (up), SH/Oleg Znamenskiy; 123 (lo le), ER Degginger/SS; 123 (lo md), SH/Marques; 123 (lo rt), SH/ifong; 124 (up), SH/FreshPaint; 124 (lo le), Erich Schrempp/SS; 124 (lo rt), GI; 125 (up), SH/Shane Myers Photography; 125 (md), Cyril Ruoso/Minden Pictures/National Geographic Creative; 125 (lo), Vera Kuttelvaserova–Fotolia; 126, GI; 127 (up), Mehau Kulyk/SS; 127 (md le), SH/comodigit; 127 (md rt), Claus Lunau/SS; 127 (lo), GI/Photo Researchers RM; 128 (up), SPL/SS; 128 (lo), SH/anweber; 129 (up le), Monkey Business–Fotolia; 129 (up rt), William Morse–Fotolia; 129 (lo le), UIG via GI; 129 (lo rt), SH/Rido; 130 (up), NASA/SS; 130 (lo le), SS; 130 (lo rt), GI/Photo Researchers RM; 131 (up), Marc Ward/SS; 131 (md), SH/06photo; 131 (lo), Patrick Landmann/SS; 132 (up), GIPhotoStock/SS; 132 (lo le), SH/Alex Mit; 132 (lo rt), SH/cristovao; 133 (up), SH/Kodda; 133 (md le), GI/Cultura RF; 133 (md rt), SH/Mariyana; 133 (lo), SS; 134 (up), SH/Alila Medical Media; 134 (lo), SH/Alexilusmedical; 135 (up le), SH/PathDoc; 135 (up rt), SH/lassedesignen; 135 (lo le), SH/Tomatito; 136 (up), SH/Vitaly Korovin; 136 (md le), SH/foaloce; 136 (md rt), SH/wavebreakmedia; 136 (lo le), SH/Matej Kastelic; 136 (lo rt), SH/Best dog photo; 137 (up le), Bjorn Rorslett/SS; 137 (up rt), Ronny Hirschmann–Fotolia; 137 (md le), SH/fenkieandreas; 137 (md rt), SH/Dudarev Mikhail; 137 (lo le), Norbert Wu/Minden Pictures; 137 (lo md), Danté Fenolio/SS; 137 (lo rt), Wellcome Images/SS; 138 (up), SH/Lemonakis Antonis; 138 (md), SH/Valerio Pardi; 138 (lo), SH/Gallinago_media; 139 (up), SH/adike; 139 (lo le), SH/Peter Bernik; 139 (lo rt), SH/Quang Ho; 140 (le), SH/paulista; 140 (rt), John R. Foster/SS; 141 (up le), NASA; 141 (up rt), GI/Universal Images Group; 141 (lo le), SS; 141 (lo rt), SH/Eduard Moldoveanu; 142 (up), SH/Vitaly Korovin; 142 (md le), GI/age fotostock RM; 142 (md md), Cheryl Power/SS; 142 (md rt), SH/Valua Vitaly; 142 (lo), Ted Kinsman/SS; 143 (up), Roger J. Bick & Brian J. Poindexter/UT-Houston Medical School/SS; 143 (md le), University of Victoria, Canada; 143 (md rt), Martin Oeggerli/National Geographic Creative; 143 (lo), SS; **Electronics:** 144 (up le), diffraction–Fotolia; 144 (up rt), GI/iStockphoto; 144 (lo le), SH/TATSIANAMA; 144 (lo rt), SH/Claudio Bravo; 144 (lo), Tyrone Turner/National Geographic Creative; 145, SH/Juergen Faelchle; 146 (up), Clive Streeter/Dorling Kindersley/Marconi Instruments Ltd/SS; 146 (lo), diffraction–Fotolia; 147 (up), SH/Monkey Business Images; 147 (md le), SolisImages–Fotolia; 147 (md rt), SH/mikeledray; 147 (lo le), SS; 147 (lo rt), Joe Gough–Fotolia; 148 (up), GI/Brand X; 148 (lo), ESA/J.Huart; 149 (up le), Coneyl Jay/SS; 149 (up rt), SH/nechaevkon; 149 (lo le), Detlev van Ravenswaay/SS; 149 (lo rt), SH/cunaplus; 150 (up), GI/iStockphoto; 150 (lo le), SH/Claudio Bravo; 150 (lo rt), SH/Hung Chung Chih; 151 (up), SH/Rasstock; 151 (md), Photothek via GI; 151 (lo), GI North America; 152 (up), SH/Vitaly Korovin; 152 (md le), GI/Photo Researchers RM; 152 (md rt), SSPL via GI; 152 (lo), Rue des Archives/PVDE/GI; 153 (up le), Bettmann/Corbis; 153 (up rt), Roger Ressmeyer/Corbis; 153 (md le), SH/SGM; 153 (md rt), WireImage/GI; 153 (lo), Richard Kail/SS; 154 (up), SH/y.maruyama; 154 (md), SH/Chris Hellyar; 154 (lo), SH/Vlad Teodor; 155 (up le), SH/Joseph Sohm; 155 (up rt), Karen Roach–Fotolia; 155 (lo le), SH/Chase Clausen; 155 (lo rt), pixelrobot–Fotolia; 156 (up), AFP/GI; 156 (lo), GI; 157 (up le), GI; 157 (up rt), Max Aguilera-Hellweg/National Geographic Creative; 157 (md), SH/Lightspring; 157 (lo), Mondadori via GI; **PART 2: LIFE SCIENCE:** 158-159, SH/Dmussman; 159 (lo le), Lynette Cook/SS; 159 (up md), SH/Alfredo Maiquez; 159 (up rt), SH/Szabo Magda; **The Universe:** 160 (up le), GI; 160 (up rt), John R. Foster/SS; 160 (lo le), Detlev van Ravenswaay/SS; 160 (lo rt), NASA; 160 (lo), SS; 161, SH/inigocia; 162 (up), Detlev van Ravenswaay/SS; 162 (lo le), GI; 162 (lo rt), Mark Garlick/SS; 163 (up), NASA; 163 (md), Jerry Lodriguss/SS; 163 (lo), NASA/JPL-Caltech; 164 (up), ESO/Martin Kornmesser/SS; 164 (lo), Lynette Cook/SS; 165 (up le), SS; 165 (up rt), Atlas Photo Bank/SS; 165 (md le), SS; 165 (md rt), NASA/JPL-Caltech; 165 (lo), Emilio Segre Visual Archives/American Institute of Physics/SS; 166 (up), NASA; 166 (lo), John R. Foster/SS; 167 (up), Babak Tafreshi/SS; 167 (md rt), NASA/JPL-Caltech; 167 (lo), SS; 168 (up), Mark Garlick/SS; 168 (lo), Science Picture Co/SS; 169 (up), SOHO/NASA; 169 (md le), NASA; 169 (md rt), SH/Elena Elisseeva; 169 (lo), LOC; 170 (lo), Project with vigour/A/Agefotostock; 171 (up), GI; 171 (md le), Jerry Lodriguss/SS; 171 (md rt), Eckhard Slawik/SS; 171 (lo), www.bridgemanimages.com; 171 (up), SS; 172 (lo), Detlev van Ravenswaay/SS; 173 (up le), Atlas Photo Bank/SS; 173 (up rt), NASA; 173 (md), Laurent Laveder/SS; 173 (lo), SS; 174 (up), NASA; 174 (lo le), SS; 174 (lo rt), Alan Dyer, Inc/Visuals Unlimited/Corbis; 175 (up), NASA; 175 (md le), NASA/SS; 175 (md rt), SS; 175 (lo), SS; 176 (up), Mark Garlick/SS; 176 (lo), Mark Garlick/SS; 177 (up), Photo Library International/SS; 177 (md le), SH/dk tazunoki; 177 (md up), Luciano Corbella/Dorling Kindersley/SS; 177 (md lo), David Ducros/SS; 177 (lo), www.bridgemanimages.com; 178 (up), John Sanford/SS; 178 (lo), Dana Berry/National Geographic Stock; 179 (up le), Mark Garlick/SS; 179 (up rt), Paul Wootton/SS; 179 (lo), NASA; 180 (up le), SH/Pecold; 180 (up rt), GI; 180 (lo le), Otis Imboden/National Geographic Creative; 180 (lo md), Sheila Terry/SS; 180 (md rt), SH/MarcelClemens; 180 (lo rt), NASA/JPL; 181 (up le), Pierre Mion/National Geographic Creative; 181 (up rt), AFP/GI; 181 (md le), SH/Yurij Omelchenko; 181 (md up), NASA; 181 (md lo le), NASA/National Geographic Creative; 181 (md lo rt), NASA/SS; 181 (md rt), Roger Ressmeyer/Corbis; 181 (lo le), SS; 181 (lo rt), GI/Stocktrek Images; 182 (up), NASA; 182 (lo), NASA; 140 (up le), Lawrence Sromovsky, University of Wisconsin-Madison/W.W. Keck Observatory; 141 (up rt), NASA/JPL; 183 (md le), Mark Garlick/SS; 183 (md rt), NASA; 183 (lo), Sheila Terry/SS; 184 (up), Detlev van Ravenswaay/SS; 184 (lo), GI/Photo Researchers RM; 185 (up), NASA, ESA; 185 (md le), Victor Habbick Visions/SS; 185 (md rt), John Chumack/SS; 185 (lo), SS; 186 (up), SS; 186 (lo), NASA/JPL-Caltech; 187 (up), Julian Baum/SS; 187 (md le), NASA; 187 (md rt), NASA/JPL/Space Science Institute; 187 (lo), Detlev van Ravenswaay/SS; 188 (up), NASA/JPL/Ted Stryk; 188 (lo), Detlev van Ravenswaay/SS; 189 (up), NASA/ESA/The Hubble Heritage Team; 189 (md le), Science Photo Library; 189 (md rt), Lorne Hofstetter and J.R. Gott; 189 (lo le), Babak Tafreshi/SS; 189 (lo rt), Detlev van Ravenswaay/SS; **Life on Earth:** 190 (up le), SH/Borislav Borisov; 190 (up rt), SPL/SS; 190 (lo le), SH/vitstudio; 190 (lo rt), SH/Triff; 190 (lo), SH/Ralwel; 191, Alamy Stock Photo; 192 (up), GI/iStockphoto; 192 (md), Science Picture Co/SS; 192 (lo), Spencer Sutton/SS; 193 (up le), GI/Minden Pictures RM; 193 (up rt),

SCUBA DIVING IN RED SEA, EGYPT

Since 1888, the National Geographic Society has funded more than 12,000 research, exploration, and preservation projects around the world. The Society receives funds from National Geographic Partners, LLC, funded in part by your purchase. A portion of the proceeds from this book supports this vital work. To learn more, visit www.natgeo.com/info.

NATIONAL GEOGRAPHIC and Yellow Border Design are trademarks of the National Geographic Society, used under license.

For more information, please visit nationalgeographic.com, call 1-800-647-5463, or write to the following address:
National Geographic Partners
1145 17th Street N.W.
Washington, D.C. 20036-4688 U.S.A.

Visit us online at nationalgeographic.com/books

For librarians and teachers: ngchildrensbooks.org

More for kids from National Geographic: natgeokids.com

For information about special discounts for bulk purchases, please contact National Geographic Books Special Sales: specialsales@natgeo.com

For rights or permissions inquiries, please contact National Geographic Books Subsidiary Rights: bookrights@natgeo.com

Produced by Potomac Global Media, LLC. Kevin Mulroy, Publisher; Barbara Brownell Grogan, Editorial Director; Patricia Daniels, Tom Jackson, Christina Wilsdon, Authors; Johnna Beecham, Editor and Contributing Writer; Malcolm Hilgartner, Contributing Editor; Edward Barrows, Mark Hannum, Brian Greene, Consultants; Carol Norton, Art Director; Matt Propert, Picture Editor; Tim Griffin, Indexer

Art Directed for National Geographic by Callie Broaddus

Hardcover ISBN: 978-1-4263-2542-7
Reinforced library edition ISBN: 978-1-4263-2543-4

Printed in the United States of America
17/WOR/3